☆☆Forbes
TRAVEL GUIDE
Formerly Mobil Travel Guide

MID-ATLANTIC
2011

ACKNOWLEDGMENTS

We gratefully acknowledge the help of our representatives for their efficient and perceptive inspections of the lodgings listed. Forbes Travel Guide is also grateful to the talented writers who contributed to this book.

Front Cover image: ©iStockphoto.com
All maps: Mapping Specialists

ISBN: 9781936010868
Manufactured in the USA
10 9 8 7 6 5 4 3 2 1

CONTENTS

CONTENTS

CONTENTS

STAR ATTRACTIONS

If you've been a reader of Mobil Travel Guide, you will have heard that this historic brand partnered in 2009 with another storied media name, Forbes, to create a new entity, Forbes Travel Guide. For more than 50 years, Mobil Travel Guide assisted travelers in making smart decisions about where to stay and dine when traveling. With this new partnership, our mission has not changed: We're committed to the same rigorous inspections of hotels, restaurants and spas—the most comprehensive in the industry with more than 500 standards tested at each property we visit—to help you cut through the clutter and make easy and informed decisions on where to spend your time and travel budget. Our team of anonymous inspectors are constantly on the road, sleeping in hotels, eating in restaurants and making spa appointments, evaluating those exacting standards to determine a property's rating.

What kinds of standards are we looking for when we visit a property? We're looking for more than just high-thread count sheets, pristine spa treatment rooms and white linen-topped tables. We look for service that's attentive, individualized and unforgettable. We note how long it takes to be greeted when you sit down at your table, or to be served when you order room service, or whether the hotel staff can confidently help you when you've forgotten that one essential item that will make or break your trip. Unlike any other travel ratings entity, we visit each place we rate, testing hundreds of attributes to compile our ratings, and our ratings cannot be bought or influenced. The Forbes Five Star rating is the most prestigious achievement in hospitality—while we rate more than 5,000 properties in the U.S., Canada, Hong Kong, Macau and Beijing, for 2011, we have awarded Five Star designations to only 54 hotels, 23 restaurants and 20 spas. When you travel with Forbes, you can travel with confidence, knowing that you'll get the very best experience, no matter who you are.

We understand the importance of making the most of your time. That's why the most trusted name in travel is now Forbes Travel Guide.

STAR RATED HOTELS

Whether you're looking for the ultimate in luxury or the best value for your travel budget, we have a hotel recommendation for you. To help you pinpoint properties that meet your needs, Forbes Travel Guide classifies each lodging by type according to the following characteristics:

★★★★★These exceptional properties provide a memorable experience through virtually flawless service and the finest of amenities. Staff are intuitive, engaging and passionate, and eagerly deliver service above and beyond the guests' expectations. The hotel was designed with the guest's comfort in mind, with particular attention paid to craftsmanship and quality of product. A Five-Star property is a destination unto itself.

★★★★These properties provide a distinctive setting, and a guest will find many interesting and inviting elements to enjoy throughout the property. Attention to detail is prominent throughout the property, from design concept to quality of products provided. Staff are accommodating and take pride in catering to the guest's specific needs throughout their stay.

★★★These well-appointed establishments have enhanced amenities that provide travelers with a strong sense of location, whether for style or function. They may have a distinguishing style and ambience in both the public spaces and guest rooms; or they may be more focused on functionality, providing guests with easy access to local events, meetings or tourism highlights.

Recommended: These hotels are considered clean, comfortable and reliable establishments that have expanded amenities, such as full-service restaurants.

For every property, we also provide pricing information. All prices quoted are accurate at the time of publication; however, prices cannot be guaranteed. Because rates can fluctuate, we list a pricing range rather than specific prices.

STAR RATED RESTAURANTS

Every restaurant in this book has been visited by Forbes Travel Guide's team of experts and comes highly recommended as an outstanding dining experience.

★★★★★Forbes Five-Star restaurants deliver a truly unique and distinctive dining experience. A Five-Star restaurant consistently provides exceptional food, superlative service and elegant décor. An emphasis is placed on originality and personalized, attentive and discreet service. Every detail that surrounds the experience is attended to by a warm and gracious dining room team.

★★★★These are exciting restaurants with often well-known chefs that feature creative and complex foods and emphasize various culinary techniques and a focus on seasonality. A highly-trained dining room staff provides refined personal service and attention.

★★★Three Star restaurants offer skillfully prepared food with a focus on a specific style or cuisine. The dining room staff provides warm and professional service in a comfortable atmosphere. The décor is well-coordinated with quality fixtures and decorative items, and promotes a comfortable ambience.

Recommended: These restaurants serve fresh food in a clean setting with efficient service. Value is considered in this category, as is family friendliness.

Because menu prices can fluctuate, we list a pricing range rather than specific prices. The pricing ranges are per diner, and assume that you order an appetizer or dessert, an entrée and one drink.

STAR RATED SPAS

Forbes Travel Guide's spa ratings are based on objective evaluations of more than 450 attributes. About half of these criteria assess basic expectations, such as staff courtesy, the technical proficiency and skill of the employees and whether the facility is clean and maintained properly. Several standards address issues that impact a guest's physical comfort and convenience, as well as the staff's ability to impart a sense of personalized service. Additional criteria measure the spa's ability to create a completely calming ambience.

★★★★★ Stepping foot in a Five Star Spa will result in an exceptional experience with no detail overlooked. These properties wow their guests with extraordinary design and facilities, and uncompromising service. Expert staff cater to your every whim and pamper you with the most advanced treatments and skin care lines available. These spas often offer exclusive treatments and may emphasize local elements.

★★★★ Four Star spas provide a wonderful experience in an inviting and serene environment. A sense of personalized service is evident from the moment you check in and receive your robe and slippers. The guest's comfort is always of utmost concern to the well-trained staff.

★★★ These spas offer well-appointed facilities with a full complement of staff to ensure that guests' needs are met. The spa facilties include clean and appealing treatment rooms, changing areas and a welcoming reception desk.

YOUR QUESTIONS ANSWERED

IS D.C. REALLY A POWER TOWN?

You bet. In fact, in this power town, a long list of iPhone contacts trumps a fat bank account any day of the week.

Former Secretary of State Henry Kissinger said it best when he told *The New York Times* in 1973 that "power is the ultimate aphrodisiac." It's what drives Washington and the people who run it. From lobbyists to lawyers to journalists to politicos, Washingtonians make a living off of knowing who matters—and who doesn't.

And it's not just the headline makers who are in on the action. For every senator, there are a dozen staffers and interns working hard to make connections behind the scenes. Every bill that passes through Congress represents hundreds of hidden handshakes and off-the-record quid pro quos. It's good old-fashioned networking, and it's how Washington's power-game is played.

You can see it everywhere—from the highway-clearing motorcades that shuttle diplomats around town to the sequestered tables at top restaurants that cater to an elite group of regulars. At happy hour, you're more likely to overhear ladder-climbing twenty-somethings debating international policy than the merits of a college football team. Even playtime nods to power, with popular annual events like the Roll Call Congressional Baseball Game, when Republicans and Democrats duke it out on the diamond.

Visitors can get a taste of the power game if they know where to look. Congressmen like to close lunch deals at Charlie Palmer Steak (*101 Constitution Ave. N.W., National Mall, 202-547-8100; www.charliepalmer.com*), while White House staffers head to The Oval Room (*800 Connecticut Ave. N.W., Downtown, 202-463-8700; www.ovalroom.com*) near Lafayette Park. Journalists woo sources over breakfast at the Hay-Adams, or over after-work drinks at the Palm (*1225 19th St., N.W., Dupont Circle, 202-293-9091; www.thepalm.com*).

Want to spot the commander-in-chief? President Obama's power-lunch habits are harder to predict, but he's dined twice just across the river at Ray's Hell Burger (*1725 Wilson Blvd., Arlington, Va., 703-841-0001*). Keep your eyes peeled for a motorcade as you nosh on the area's tastiest hamburgers.

WHAT'S THE BEST WAY TO BLEND IN LIKE A LOCAL IN D.C.?

Nothing screams tourist like ignoring the local mores. Some tips: When you're on the Metro (*www.wmata.com*), let passengers exit the train before you try to board, and move to the center of the car to make room for other riders. Remember that you'll need to use your fare card at the exit gate, so keep it handy. And only one person can use a fare card at a time—no sharing. When on an escalator, locals observe a simple unwritten rule: Stand to the right, walk to the left. If you stand on the wrong side, you'll likely be asked to move.

Looking for a late night coffee fix? You might be out of luck in this town. D.C.'s an early-to-bed city, and most businesses, including coffee shops, don't stay open past 8 or 9 p.m. Many neighborhoods, such as family-friendly Capitol Hill, can feel like ghost towns after dark. Stick to U Street or Adams Morgan for livelier nightlife options.

When it comes to local vernacular, Washingtonians love acronyms. There are the obvious ones—CIA, FBI—but there's also POTUS (President of the United States), FLOTUS (First Lady of the United States), and SCOTUS (Supreme Court of the United States). Bureaucracies get the same treatment: The Department of State is simply DOS.

TOP HOTELS, RESTAURANTS AND SPAS

HOTELS

★★★★★FIVE STAR
Falling Rock at Nemacolin
Woodlands Resort
(Farmington, Pennsylvania)
Four Seasons Hotel,
Washington, D.C.
(Washington, D.C.)
The Inn at Little Washington
(Washington, Virginia)
The Jefferson Hotel
(Richmond, Virginia)

★★★★FOUR STAR
The Fairfax at Embassy Row
(Washington, D.C.)
Four Seasons Hotel Philadelphia
(Philadelphia, Pennsylvania)
The Greenbrier
*(White Sulphur Springs,
West Virginia)*
The Hay-Adams
(Washington, D.C.)
The Hotel Hershey
(Hershey, Pennsylvania)
The Jefferson *(Washington, D.C.)*
Mandarin Oriental Washington, D.C.
(Washington, D.C.)
Nemacolin Woodlands Resort
(Farmington, Pennsylvania)
The Ritz-Carlton, Georgetown
(Washington, D.C.)
The Ritz-Carlton, Pentagon City
(Arlington, Virginia)
The Ritz-Carlton, Tysons Corner
(McLean, Virginia)
The Ritz-Carlton, Washington, D.C.
(Washington, D.C.)
The St. Regis Washington, D.C.
(Washington, D.C.)
Williamsburg Inn
(Williamsburg, Virginia)

RESTAURANTS

★★★★★FIVE STAR
Fountain Restaurant
(Philadelphia, Pennsylvania)
The Inn at Little Washington
(Washington, Virginia)
Lautrec
(Farmington, Pennsylvania)

★★★★FOUR STAR
Adour *(Washington, D.C.)*
Charleston
(Baltimore, Maryland)
Circular Dining Room
(Hershey, Pennsylvania)
CityZen *(Washington, D.C.)*
The Jockey Club
(Washington, D.C.)
Lacroix at the Rittenhouse
(Philadelphia, Pennsylvania)
Michel Richard Citronelle
(Washington, D.C.)
Palena *(Washington, D.C.)*
Plume *(Washington, D.C.)*

SPAS

★★★★FOUR STAR
The Greenbrier Spa
*(White Sulphur Springs,
West Virginia)*
The Spa at Mandarin Oriental,
Washington, D.C.
(Washington, D.C.)
Woodlands Spa at Nemacolin
Woodlands Resort
(Farmington, Pennsylvania)

WELCOME TO DELAWARE

ONLY 96 MILES LONG AND FROM NINE TO 35 MILES WIDE,

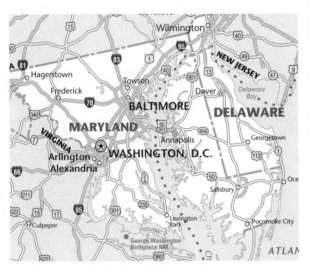

Delaware is a corporate and agricultural superpower. Favorable state policies have persuaded more than 183,000 corporations to base their headquarters in the "corporate capital of the world". For all you shoppers out there, Delaware is where you want to hit the stores. With no sales tax, you'll save much more money than you would anywhere else. You'll find plenty of outlet malls here to add on to the goodness of no sales tax.

Despite Delaware's current riches, the state's history started on a grim note. The first 28 colonists landed in the spring of 1631, and after an argument with a Lenni-Lenape chief, their bones were found mingled with those of cattle and strewn over their burned fields. In 1638, a group of Swedes established the first permanent settlement in the state—and the first permanent settlement of Swedes in North America—at Fort Christina, in what is now Wilmington. Henry Hudson, in Dutch service, first discovered Delaware Bay in 1609. A year later, Thomas Argall reported it to English navigators and named it for his superior, Lord de la Warr, governor of Virginia. Ownership changed rapidly from Swedish to Dutch to English hands. The Maryland-Delaware boundary was set by a British court order in 1750 and surveyed, forming part of the Mason-Dixon Line. Today, the line divides Delmar—a small town said to be over-populated for one state. The "First State" is proud of its history of sturdy independence; however, it is a common misconception that Delaware gets its motto from being the first state discovered. It was actually the first state to adopt the Constitution on December 7, 1787.

HIGHLIGHTS

DELAWARE'S BEST ATTRACTIONS

BEACH TOWNS
Visit the Rehoboth Beach boardwalk and beach for a hefty dose of fun. From arcades to thrill rides to pizza, there is plenty to do for the whole family.

NORTHERN DELAWARE
For the history lesson that Delaware is dying to give you, head to Wilmington. Don't miss Nemours Mansion and Gardens.

DOVER
With a healthy mix of fun and history, Dover has plenty to offer. Don't miss Dover Downs for slots and horseracing.

You just have to walk through the streets to discover the charm that Delaware has to offer. The small towns bring you back to a simpler time; the beaches transport you to paradise. Discover all that the "First State" has to offer, whether it be history or just plain fun.

BEACH TOWNS

People flock from Washington D.C. every summer to relax in these charming seaside towns. Located along Delaware's Atlantic Coast, Bethany Beach, Fenwick Island, Lewes and Rehoboth all have charming centers with plenty to do. Bethany Beach is a popular spot for families, with plenty of houses to rent and a beautiful beach. An old historic totem pole marks the center of the town, which is filled with surf shops and beach fare. To the south is Fenwick Island, just before the Maryland-Delaware border. Once known for its "salt making"—after residents James and Jacob Brasure began extracting salt from the ocean in 1775—the island has become a popular summer resort. To the north of Bethany lies Rehoboth Beach. The largest summer resort in Delaware began as a spot for camp meetings amid sweet-smelling pine groves. Lewes has been home base to Delaware Bay pilots for 300 years. Weather-beaten, cypress-shingled houses still line the streets where pirates plundered and Captain Kidd bargained away his loot. The treacherous sandbars outside the harbor have claimed their share of ships, and stories of sunken treasures have circulated for centuries. The "nation's summer capital" got its nickname because it was a favorite of Washington diplomats and legislators.

WHAT TO SEE

BETHANY BEACH

HOLTS LANDING STATE PARK

Road 346, Millville, 302-227-2800; www.destateparks.com

This 203-acre park located along the Indian River Bay offers fishing, crabbing, clamming, sailing, boating and picnicking, as well as a playground and ball fields. The park contains a beach, fields of grass and forests. There are also picnic areas with tables and grills set up for the public to use.

Daily 8 a.m.-dusk

FENWICK ISLAND

DISCOVERSEA SHIPWRECK MUSEUM

708 Ocean Highway, Fenwick Island, 302-539-9366, 888-743-5524; www.discoversea.com

Opened in 1995, this museum contains changing exhibits of shipwreck artifacts recovered on the Delmarva Peninsula. They have around 10,000 artifacts along with rotating exhibits that have been found after years of research.

June-August, daily 11 a.m.-8 p.m.; September-May, Saturday-Sunday 11 a.m.-4 p.m.

FENWICK ISLAND LIGHTHOUSE

146th Street and Lighthouse Lane, Fenwick Island, 302-539-4115; www.fenwickislandlighthouse.org

Built in 1858, this popular attraction is 89 feet tall and houses a mini-museum in its base. While the tower is closed, you can still explore the grounds and the museum. There's also a gift shop nearby.

May-June, October, Friday-Monday 10 a.m.-2 p.m.; July-September, Thursday-Tuesday 10 a.m.-2 p.m.

LEWES

BURTON-INGRAM HOUSE

110 Shipcarpenter St., Lewes, 302-564-7670; www.historiclewes.org

This Federal-style house is made from hand-hewn timbers and cypress shingles. There is a three-story staircase open through the floors from which you can see the entire house. It is home to beautiful antiques, artifacts and impressive artwork.

May-early June, mid-September-early October, Saturday 11 a.m.-4 p.m.; Mid-June-mid-September, Monday-Saturday 11 a.m.-4 p.m.

CAPE HENLOPEN STATE PARK

42 Cape Henlopen Drive, Lewes, 302-645-8983; www.destateparks.com

The park has more than 3,000 acres at the confluence of Delaware Bay and the Atlantic Ocean with six miles of beach to enjoy. There are two swimming beaches, a bathhouse and a concession area. There's also an 18-hole disc golf course, basketball courts, three-miles of paved trails for hiking, biking and more. The park sits on the site of decommissioned Fort Miles, part of the U.S. coastal defense system during World War II. For amazing vistas, climb up to the top of an old military bunker.

Daily 8 a.m.-dusk.

HIGHLIGHTS

WHAT ARE THE TOP THINGS TO DO IN DELAWARE'S BEACH TOWNS?

DISCOVER DUTCH HERITAGE IN HISTORIC LEWES
Wander through the historic beach town filled with shingled houses. Explore the remains of what was once a Dutch whaling community.

GRAB YOUR PEG LEG AND EYE PATCH TO UNCOVER BOOTY
Venture to DiscoverSea Shipwreck Museum in Fenwick and explore artifacts from shipwrecks off the Delmarva Peninsula.

PACK IN A HISTORY LESSON
Take in the history of Lewes at Zwaanendael Museum. You'll learn the town's connection with Native Americans, Dutch and water.

FOLLOW THE LIGHT
Head to Fenwick's main attraction, the Fenwick Lighthouse, to discover the historic ship navigator.

HIRAM R. BURTON HOUSE
Second and Shipcarpenter streets, Lewes, 302-564-7670; www.historiclewes.org
Named after a prominent Lewes physician and congressman, Hiram Rodney Burton, this house dating back to 1720 features antique furnishings and an 18th-century kitchen. There's also a reading room with materials dedicated to Delaware history and a beautiful garden.
May-early June, mid-September-early October, Saturday 11 a.m.-4 p.m.; Mid-June-mid-September, Monday-Saturday 11 a.m.-4 p.m.

LEWES HISTORICAL SOCIETY COMPLEX
110 Shipcarpenter St., Lewes, 302-564-7670; www.historiclewes.org
Restored buildings were moved to this site to create a feel for Lewes' early days. The Historical Society owns 12 properties, nine of which are part of this complex.
Admission: adults $5, children 12 and under free. May-early June, mid-September-early October, Saturday 11 a.m.-4 p.m.; Mid-June-mid-September, Monday-Saturday 11 a.m.-4 p.m.

RABBIT'S FERRY HOUSE

Third Street, Lewes, 302-564-7670; www.historiclewes.org

This traditional farmhouse was built around 1741 and contains original paneling and period pieces. It provides a good example of how a traditional farmhouse was organized.

May-early June, mid-September-early October, Saturday 11 a.m.-4 p.m.; Mid-June-mid-September, Monday-Saturday 11 a.m.-4 p.m.

THOMPSON COUNTRY STORE

Third Street, Lewes, 302-564-7670; www.historiclewes.org

This country store was moved from its original location in Thompsonville to Lewes. The Thompson family ran it as a store until 1962. It also functioned as a post office for a time.

May-early June, mid-September-early October, Saturday 11 a.m.-4 p.m.; Mid-June-mid-September, Monday-Saturday 11 a.m.-4 p.m.

ZWAANENDAEL MUSEUM

102 Kings Highway, Lewes, 302-645-1148; www.history.delaware.gov

This adaptation of the Hoorn town hall in Holland was built in 1931 as a memorial to the original 1631 Dutch founders of Lewes. It highlights the town's maritime heritage with colonial, Native American and Dutch exhibits.

Admission: Free. Tuesday-Saturday 10 a.m.-4:30 p.m., Sunday 1:30-4:30 p.m.

REHOBOTH BEACH

DELAWARE SEASHORE STATE PARK

850 Inlet Road, Rehoboth Beach, 302-227-2800; www.destateparks.com

This 7-mile strip of land separates the Rehoboth and Indian River bays from the Atlantic. There are two swimming areas, fishing, surfing and boating to keep you occupied. Picnic pavilions, a concession area and a bathhouse equipped with showers and a changing room are also onsite.

Daily 8 a.m.-dusk.

BOARDWALK AND BEACH

Between Surf Ave. and Prospect St., Rehoboth Beach

Filled with attractions such as Funland, restaurants, arcades and shops, the Rehoboth boardwalk is the top hang-out in this beach town. Inevitably, you'll have to go on the boardwalk to get to the beach. Whether lounging on the beach, spinning on the Gravitron at Funland or chowing down on Thrashers fries, the boardwalk and beach has it all. Lifeguard stands 13 and 14 are where you want to stake out your spot in the sun.

WHERE TO STAY

LEWES

★★★HOTEL RODNEY

142 Second St., Lewes, 302-645-6466, 800-824-8754; www.hotelrodneydelaware.com

Built in 1926, this stylish boutique hotel is located in historic downtown Lewes, minutes from Rehoboth Beach as well as shopping and dining options. Rooms are simple and chic with neutral décor. Recently renovated, they have flat-screen TVs, iPod clock radios, hardwood floors and comfortable bedding.

Room service is available from the onsite restaurant, Beseme.

20 rooms. Restaurant. Fitness center. Pets accepted. $151-250

★★★INN AT CANAL SQUARE

122 Market St., Lewes, 302-644-3377, 888-644-1911; ww.theinnatcanalsquare.com

Adjacent to the beautiful historic district, this charming "Nantucket-style" bed and breakfast offers private waterfront porches in many of the rooms, along with mini-refrigerators, coffee makers, robes and flat-screen TVs. A popular vacation headquarters in summer, it's only a mile from Cape Henlopen State Park's beaches. Guests are served a large European-style breakfast each morning.

24 rooms. Complimentary breakfast. Fitness center. $151-250

REHOBOTH BEACH

★★★BOARDWALK PLAZA HOTEL

Olive Avenue and the Boardwalk, Rehoboth Beach, 302-227-7169, 800-332-3224; www.boardwalkplaza.com

This Victorian-style hotel on Rehoboth Beach offers state-of-the-art comfort with high-speed Internet access and whirlpool tubs. Enjoy the scenic ocean views at Victoria's restaurant. Or enjoy tea and sandwiches by the ocean at the afternoon tea.

84 rooms. Restaurant, bar. Business center. Fitness center. Pool. $251-350

WHERE TO EAT

LEWES

★★★THE BUTTERY RESTAURANT AND BAR

102 Second St., Lewes, 302-645-7755; www.butteryrestaurant.com

This charming Victorian restaurant located in the restored Trader Mansion offers a variety of entrées, from Maryland crab cakes to sea scallops and Maine lobster tail. Sunday's brunch features a fruit plate and fresh pastries along with an array of tasty options, including eggs Benedict, Belgian waffles, omelets or crepes. To spice things up, opt for a glass of champagne, a mimosa or a Bloody Mary.

American. Lunch, dinner, Sunday brunch. $36-85

NORTHERN DELAWARE

At the tip of Delaware lies New Castle, Newark and Wilmington. Close to the Delaware River, these three cities make up much of Delaware's industrial area. Established in 1651, New Castle is one of Delaware's first settlements. Earning many accolades, it served as a meeting place for the Colonial assemblies, was the first capital of the state, and became an early center of culture and communication. To the west of New Castle lies Newark, home to the University of Delaware and a storied past. It was established at the crossroads of two well-traveled Native American trails and some of the Revolutionary War was fought here. The story is that Betsy Ross's flag was first raised in battle at Cooch's Bridge on September 3, 1777. Northeast of Newark is Wilmington, the "chemical capital of the world" and the largest city in Delaware. The Swedes settled first, seeking their fortunes and founding the colony of New Sweden. Wilmington has flourished as an industrial port because of its abundant waterpower and proximity to other eastern ports.

HIGHLIGHTS

WHAT ARE THE TOP THINGS TO DO IN NORTHERN DELAWARE?

GO BACK TO YOUR COLLEGE DAYS
Visit the University of Delaware in historic Newark. The campus is attractive and filled with bright young students.

WARM UP YOUR SINGING VOICE
The Grand Opera House in Wilmington is a beautiful Masonic landmark.

VENTURE BACK TO THE 1700S
The Old Dutch House in New Castle is one of the oldest in the state.

HOP ON THE BOAT TO PEA PATCH ISLAND
Fort Delaware State Park in New Castle can only be accessed by ferry—so grab your stuff and don't miss the boat.

WHAT TO SEE

NEW CASTLE
AMSTEL HOUSE MUSEUM
2 E. Fourth St., New Castle, 302-322-2794; www.newcastlehistory.org

This 1730 restored brick mansion was built by Dr. John Finney, a wealthy landowner. The seventh governor of Delaware lived here, and George Washington attended a wedding at the home. It now houses colonial furnishings, art and a complete colonial kitchen. You can also walk the grounds of the beautiful garden.
Admission: adults $4, children 6-12 $1.50. April-December, Wednesday-Saturday 10 a.m.-4 p.m., Sunday noon-4 p.m. Garden: Daily, dawn-dusk.

FORT DELAWARE STATE PARK
Pea Patch Island, 302-834-7941; www.destateparks.com

This grim, gray fort was built as a coastal defense in 1860 on Pea Patch Island, which is only a mile from Delaware City. The fort was used as a prisoner-of-war depot for three years, housing up to 12,500 Confederate prisoners at a time. Its damp, low-lying terrain and poor conditions encouraged epidemics that led to some 2,400 deaths. The fort was modernized in 1896 and remained in commission until 1943. There are overlooks of heronry, picnicking and living-history programs available for visitors. The museum has a scale model of the fort, model Civil War relics and an orientation video. The only way to gain access to the Fort is by taking a ferry (see website for the schedule).

Ferry: adults $11, seniors $10, children 3-12 $6, children under 2 free.

THE GREEN
Delaware and Third streets, New Castle

Laid out under the direction of Peter Stuyvesant in 1651, this public square is surrounded by dozens of historically important buildings.

OLD DUTCH HOUSE
32 E. Third St., New Castle, 302-322-2794; www.newcastlehistory.org

The Old Dutch House was thought to be Delaware's oldest dwelling in its original late 17th-century form. It's filled with Dutch colonial furnishings, artifacts and decorative arts.

Admission: adults $4, children 6-12 $1.50. April-December, Wednesday-Saturday 10 a.m.-4 p.m., Sunday noon-4 p.m.

OLD NEW CASTLE COURT HOUSE MUSEUM
211 Delaware St., New Castle, 302-323-4453; www.history.delaware.gov

This is the original 1732 colonial capital and oldest surviving courthouse in the state. There are furnishings and exhibits on display. The cupola is the center of a 12-mile circle that delineates the Delaware-Pennsylvania border.

Admission: Free. Tuesday-Saturday 10 a.m.-3:30 p.m., Sunday 1:30-4:30 p.m.

NEWARK

UNIVERSITY OF DELAWARE
196 S. College Ave., Newark, 302-831-2792; www.udel.edu

Now with a student population of almost 16,000 undergraduates, the University of Delaware was founded as a small private academy in 1743. The central campus sits amidst stately elm trees, finely manicured lawns and Georgian-style brick buildings.

Tours: Monday-Friday, 10 a.m., noon, 2 p.m., Saturday 10 a.m., noon.

WILMINGTON

BRANDYWINE CREEK STATE PARK
Routes 92 and 100, Wilmington, 302-577-3534; www.destateparks.com

Brandywine features 933 acres of what used to be a dairy farm in the late 1800s. Today, there are miles of nature and hiking trails to enjoy, fishing, canoeing, tubing, cross-country skiing and disc golf.

Daily 8 a.m.-dusk.

BRANDYWINE ZOO AND PARK
1001 N. Park Drive, Wilmington, 302-571-7788; www.destateparks.com

Designed by Frederick Law Olmsted, the park includes the Josephine Garden with a fountain, roses and stands of Japanese cherry trees. The zoo, along North Park Drive, features animals from both North and South America. There are picnicking areas and playgrounds to enjoy.

Admission: October-May, adults $4, children 3-11 and seniors $2, children under 3 free; June-September, adults $5, children 3-11 $3, seniors $4, children under 3 free. Daily 10 a.m.-4 p.m.

DELAWARE ART MUSEUM
2301 Kentmere Parkway, Wilmington, 302-571-9590; www.delart.org

This museum features the Howard Pyle Collection of American Illustrations, with works by Pyle, N.C. Wyeth and Maxfield Parrish; an American painting collection with works by West, Homer, Church, Glackens and Hopper; the Bancroft Collection of English Pre-Raphaelite art including works by Rossetti and Burne-Jones; and the Phelps Collection of Andrew Wyeth works. There are also changing exhibits and a children's participatory gallery.

Admission: adults $12, seniors $10, students and children 7-18 $6, children 6 and under free. Free Sunday. Wednesday-Saturday 10 a.m.-4 p.m., Sunday noon-4 p.m.

DELAWARE HISTORY MUSEUM
504 Market St., Wilmington, 302-656-0637; www.hsd.org

This museum is located in an old Woolworth store that has since been remodeled. There are three different galleries which feature changing exhibits on the history of Delaware such as costumes, paintings and decorative arts.

Admission: adults $4, seniors, students and military personnel $3, children 3-18 $2, children under 3 free. Wednesday-Friday 11 a.m.-4 p.m., Saturday 10 a.m.-4 p.m.

DELAWARE MUSEUM OF NATURAL HISTORY
4840 Kennett Pike, Wilmington, 302-658-9111; www.delmnh.org

This museum features exhibits of shells, dinosaurs, birds and mammals. Also on display are the largest bird egg and a 500-pound clam. There are hands-on activities for young children to enjoy along with a butterfly garden and a nature trail.

Admission: adults $6, children $5, seniors $4, children under 3 free. Monday-Saturday 9:30 a.m.-4:30 p.m., Sunday noon-4:30 p.m.

GRAND OPERA HOUSE
818 Market St., Mall, Wilmington, 302-658-7898; www.grandopera.org

This historic 1871 Victorian landmark was built by Masons. Since then, it has been restored and now serves as Delaware's Center for the Performing Arts, home of Opera Delaware, the First State Ballet Theatre and the Delaware Symphony. The façade is a fine example of Second Empire style interpreted in cast iron.

Box Office: Monday-Friday 10 a.m.-7 p.m., Saturday-Sunday noon-5 p.m.

NEMOURS MANSION AND GARDENS
1600 Rockland Road, Wilmington, 302-651-6912, 800-651-6912; www.nemours.org

This is the country estate of Alfred I. DuPont. The mansion, built in 1910, is in modified Louis XVI style by Carre and Hastings, with 102 rooms of rare antique furniture, Asian rugs, tapestries and paintings dating from the 12th-century. There are formal French gardens with terraces, statuaries and pools. It is also the site of the Alfred I. DuPont Hospital for Children.

Admission: $15. Tours: May-December, Tuesday-Saturday 9 a.m., 11 a.m., 1 p.m., 3 p.m., Sunday 11 a.m., 1 p.m., 3 p.m.

WILMINGTON & WESTERN RAILROAD
Greenbank Station, 2201 Newport Gap Pike, Wilmington, 302-998-1930; www.wwrr.com

This railroad line transported passengers through numerous communities in 1867. Now, its serves as a tourist railroad offering round-trip steam-train rides

to and from Mount Cuba picnic grove.
Schedules and prices vary; see website for information.

WHERE TO STAY

NEWARK
★★★HILTON WILMINGTON/CHRISTIANA
100 Continental Drive, Newark, 302-454-1500, 800-445-8667; www.hilton.com

This family- and business-friendly hotel is situated on a sprawling country estate. For an afternoon respite, take advantage of the hotel's high tea. Enjoy a meal in one of two restaurants—the casual Hunt Club Lounge and the more upscale Brasserie Grille—or explore shopping and dining nearby.

266 rooms. Restaurant, bar. Business center. Fitness center. Pool. Pets accepted. $151-250

WILMINGTON
★★★HOTEL DUPONT
11th and Market streets, Wilmington, 302-594-3100, 800-441-9019; www.hoteldupont.com

The Hotel du Pont has been a Delaware institution since 1913. Constructed to rival the grand hotels of Europe with ornate plasterwork and gleaming brass, this palatial hotel enjoys proximity to the city's attractions while remaining in the heart of the scenic Brandywine Valley. The guest rooms are classically decorated with mahogany furnishings, cream tones and imported linens. Patrons can dine on French cuisine at the onsite restaurant, Green Room.

217 rooms. Restaurant, bar. Business center. Fitness center. $251-350

★★★SHERATON SUITES WILMINGTON
422 Delaware Ave., Wilmington, 302-654-8300, 800-325-3535; www.sheraton.com

Located in the heart of downtown Wilmington, this all-suite hotel offers spacious rooms and conference facilities just a short drive from a number of museums, within walking distance from headquarters of several Fortune 500 companies and a few miles from major shopping malls. The contemporary guest rooms are decorated in navy and taupe and feature comfortable Sweet Sleeper mattresses.

223 rooms. Restaurant, bar. Fitness center. Pool. Pets accepted. $151-250

WHERE TO EAT

WILMINGTON
★★★GREEN ROOM
Hotel du Pont, 11th and Market streets, Wilmington, 302-594-3155, 800-441-9019; www.hoteldupont.com

Located inside the historic Hotel du Pont, this restaurant's sophisticated décor is perfect for a romantic night out or special celebration. In season, feast on a meal of crispy soft shell crabs with crab, caper rouille, heirloom tomato, chorizo quinoa, baby arugula and chorizo dust. Live music enhances the dining experience nightly.

French. Breakfast, lunch, dinner (Monday-Saturday). Sunday brunch. Bar. $36-85

★★★HARRY'S SAVOY GRILL
2020 Naaman's Road, Wilmington, 302-475-3000; www.harrys-savoy.com

A Brandywine Valley staple since 1988, Harry's Savoy Grill serves up the classics in an upscale English pub atmosphere. The bar and grill is known for its prime rib, its wine list and its "famous eight-shake martinis."

American. Lunch (Monday-Friday), dinner, late night, Sunday brunch. Bar. Outdoor seating. $36-85.

DOVER

Dover, Delaware's capital since 1777, was designed around the city's lovely green by William Penn, who founded Dover in 1683. Lovely 18th- and 19th-century houses still line State Street. Because of Delaware's favorable corporation laws, more than 60,000 U.S. firms pay taxes in Dover. At Dover Air Force Base, the Military Airlift Command operates one of the biggest air cargo terminals in the world. The city is also home to Delaware State College, Wesley College and the Terry campus of Delaware Technical and Community College.

WHAT TO SEE

AIR MOBILITY COMMAND MUSEUM
1301 Heritage Road, Dover, 302-677-5938; www.amcmuseum.org

Located in a historic hangar on Dover Air Force Base, the museum houses a collection of more than two-dozen aircraft and historical artifacts dating back to World War II. There are flight simulators and a junior pilot's plane for kids to check out. There's also a museum store to purchase souvenirs.

Admission: Free. Tuesday-Sunday 9 a.m.-4 p.m.

DOVER DOWNS HOTEL, CASINO & INTERNATIONAL SPEEDWAY
1131 N. DuPont Highway, Dover, 302-674-4600, 800-711-5882; www.doverdowns.com

This hotel, casino and speedway is a great way to get your gambling fix. Head to the casino, which is open 24 hours a day and features almost 3,200 slot machines. The Colonnade offers restaurants and shopping. Dover Downs also provides plenty of entertainment in the Rollins Center, which has 1,600 seats and hosts acts such as Wayne Newton, Bill Cosby, Kenny Rogers, Tom Jones, Gladys Knight and others. If that's not enough, Dover Downs also has live harness horse racing at the Dover International Speedway where you can also catch racing events including NASCAR Winston Cup auto racing.

Casino: Daily 24 hours. Horse Racing: Late-October-mid-August. Auto Racing: June, September.

FIRST STATE HERITAGE PARK
152 S. State St., Dover, 302-739-9194; www.destateparks.com

This park actually connects historical and cultural sites, including the Briggs Museum of American Art, the Delaware Public Archives, Legislative Hall, Museum Square, the State House Museum, Delaware Visitor Center and Woodburn House. You can take a guided walking tour of this park. Every first Saturday of the month, each site hosts special programs designed for the specific

HIGHLIGHTS

WHAT ARE THE TOP THINGS TO DO IN DOVER?

DISCOVER THE GEMS OF SMALL TOWN LIFE
Dover's Museum of Small Town Life allows visitors to discover the way of life in a small Delaware town.

STEP INSIDE THE FIRST STATE'S COURTHOUSE
The state seat since 1791, the Old Court House is a functioning historic building.

month as well as tours of Legislative Hall.
Monday-Saturday 9 a.m.-3 p.m., Sunday 1:30-3 p.m. First Saturday of the month: 9 a.m.-5 p.m.

JOHN DICKINSON PLANTATION
340 Kitts Hummrock Road, Dover, 302-739-3277; www.history.delaware.gov
This is the restored 1740 boyhood residence of John Dickinson, the "penman of the Revolution." Here, you can learn about Dickinson's life and background on his plantation. Take a tour led by historic interpreters dressed in period costumes, depicting characters from the early 1700s and 1800s.
Admission: Free. March-December, Tuesday-Saturday 10 a.m.-3:30 p.m., Sunday 1:30-4:30 p.m.

JOHNSON VICTROLA MUSEUM
Museum Square, 375 S. New St., Dover, 302-739-4266; www.dovermuseums.org
This museum was created as a tribute to Eldridge Reeves Johnson, founder of the Victor Talking Machine Company. Johnson retired in 1827 and the company was sold to RCA in 1930. (You might recognize the image of a terrier looking into a phonograph, the logo for Victor.) Johnson received a Grammy Award posthumously in 1985, which is on display here. The museum holds a collection of talking machines, Victrolas, early recordings and equipment.
Admission: Free. Tuesday-Saturday 9 a.m.-4:30 p.m., Sunday 1:30-4:30 p.m.

MUSEUM OF SMALL TOWN LIFE
316 S. Governors Ave., Dover, 302-739-3261;www.dovermuseums.org
Housed in a building of the Old Presbyterian Church of Dover, this museum recreates life in the late 19th century. Exhibits showcase a turn-of-the-century drugstore, printing press, pharmacy, carpenter shop, general store, post office, shoemaker's shop and printer's shop. There are also changing exhibits, which take a look at life in the small towns of Delaware. The building has beautiful stained glass windows that were designed in the late 19th century.
Admission: Free. Tuesday-Saturday 9 a.m.-4:30 p.m., Sunday 1:30-4:30 p.m.

THE OLD STATE HOUSE

The Green, 406 Federal St., Dover, 302-739-4266; www.history.delaware.gov

Delaware's seat of government since 1791, the State House, restored in 1976, contains a courtroom, ceremonial governor's office, legislative chambers and county offices. A portrait of George Washington in the Senate Chamber was commissioned in 1802 by the legislature as a memorial to the nation's first president. Although Delaware's General Assembly moved to nearby Legislative Hall in 1933, the 1792 State House remains the state's symbolic capital.

Admission: Free. Tuesday-Saturday 9 a.m.-4:30 p.m., Sunday 1:30-4:30 p.m.

WHERE TO STAY

★★★SHERATON DOVER HOTEL

1570 N. DuPont Highway, Dover, 302-678-8500, 888-625-5144; www.sheratondover.com

This hotel is conveniently located just a few minutes from shopping and local attractions in historic Dover. Guest rooms are spacious and subdued with neutral colors and traditional furniture. Bring your dog along and it will be treated to the Sheraton Sweet Sleeper pet bed. After a day of relaxing in the heated pool, head to Chops Grille for an intimate dinner in a romantic setting.

152 rooms. Business center. Fitness center. Pool. Pets accepted. $151-250

WELCOME TO MARYLAND

IN MARYLAND, THE ORIOLE IS MORE THAN JUST THE STATE
bird, turtles are sports heroes and crabs are regular fixtures at the dinner table. The seventh state owns a celebrated sports history, producing superstars such as Babe Ruth and Cal Ripken, Jr., and building the Orioles' Camden Yards, lauded for its classic design. Several noteworthy colleges and universities call Maryland home, including Johns Hopkins University and the University of

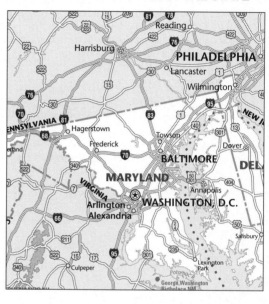

Maryland, home of the Terrapins. And Maryland's Chesapeake Bay keeps restaurants across the nation well stocked with crabs, producing more than 50 percent of the United States' harvest of hard-shell crabs.

Maryland prides itself on its varied terrain and diverse economy. Metropolitan areas around Baltimore and Washington, D.C. contrast with life in the rural areas in central and southern Maryland, and on the Eastern Shore, across the Chesapeake Bay. Green mountains in the western counties offset the east's white Atlantic beaches.

Named in honor of Henrietta Maria, wife of Charles I, King of England, Maryland was established in 1634 by Leonard Calvert, Lord Baltimore's brother. Calvert and 222 passengers aboard his ships purchased a Native American village and named it "Saint Maries Citty" (now St. Mary's City). The land was cleared, tobacco was planted, and over the years, profits built elegant mansions, many of which still stand.

Maryland has played a pivotal role in every war waged on U.S. soil. In 1755, British General Edward Braddock, assisted by Lieutenant Colonel George Washington, trained his army at Cumberland for the fight against the French and Indians. In the War of 1812, Baltimore's Fort McHenry

BEST ATTRACTIONS

MARYLAND'S BEST ATTRACTIONS

BALTIMORE
Explore everything this port city has to offer. Catch an Orioles or Ravens Game at the stadiums just minutes from the water.

CAPITAL REGION
Venture into the small town of Bethesda, where you'll find arts, shopping, restaurants and plenty of history.

CENTRAL REGION
Explore Maryland's capital, Annapolis, by water. Hop aboard one of the various boat tours offered.

EASTERN SHORE
Run with the horses on Assateague Island. This state park is the most unique in the region.

ST. MARY'S CITY
Explore Historic St. Mary's City with a guide dressed in period attire.

WESTERN MARYLAND
Discover the geological phenomenon that is The Narrows.

withstood attacks by land and sea. The action was later immortalized in the national anthem by Francis Scott Key, a Frederick lawyer. And in the Civil War, Maryland was a major battleground at Antietam.

BALTIMORE

Baltimore is a city of neighborhoods built on strong ethnic foundations. Baseball fans flock to red brick Camden Yards, while football fans come out in force to support the Baltimore Ravens at M&T Bank Stadium. Residents and visitors alike crowd Baltimore's Inner Harbor to enjoy its museums, restaurants and nightlife. Lying midway between the North and South—and enjoying a rich cultural mixture of both—Baltimore is one of the nation's oldest cities. When British troops threatened Philadelphia during the Revolutionary War, the Continental Congress fled to Baltimore, which served as the nation's capital for a little more than two months. In October 1814, a British fleet attacked the city by land and sea. The defenders of Fort McHenry withstood the naval bombardment for 25 hours until the British gave up. Francis Scott Key saw the huge American flag still flying above the fort and was inspired to pen "The Star-Spangled Banner." In the 1950s and early 1960s, Baltimore was a victim of the apathy and general urban decay that struck the industrial Northeast. But the city fought back, replacing hundreds of acres of slums, rotting wharves and warehouses with gleaming new office plazas, parks and public buildings. The Inner Harbor was transformed into a huge public area with shops, museums, restaurants and frequent concerts and festivals.

WHAT TO SEE

ANTIQUE ROW

North Howard and West Read streets, Baltimore; www.shopantiquerow.com

Antique Row, a Baltimore fixture for more than a century, hosts more than 20 dealers and shops, along with restoration services. Shops specialize in items such as European furniture, Tiffany lamps, china and rare books.

BABE RUTH BIRTHPLACE AND MUSEUM

301 W. Camden St., Baltimore, 410-727-1539; www.baberuthmuseum.com

Although Babe Ruth played for the New York Yankees, Baltimore calls him one of its native sons. The house where this legend was born has been transformed into a museum that showcases his life and career. Visitors can see rare family photographs as well as a complete record of his home runs. The museum also features exhibits about the Baltimore Colts and Orioles. Every February 6th, the museum commemorates Babe Ruth's birthday by offering free admission to all visitors.

Daily 10 a.m.-5 p.m., 10 a.m.-7 p.m. on baseball game days

BALTIMORE & OHIO RAILROAD MUSEUM

901 W. Pratt St., Baltimore, 410-752-2490; www.borail.org

This museum, affiliated with the Smithsonian, celebrates the birthplace of railroading in America and depicts the industry's economic and cultural influences. Encompassing 40 acres, the museum's collection of locomotives is the oldest and most comprehensive in the country. In the Roundhouse, visitors can board and explore more than a dozen of the iron horses, which include a rail post office car and the Tom Thumb train. The second floor of the Annex building has an impressive display of working miniature-scale trains. The Mount Clair Station, exhibiting the story of the B&O Railroad, was built in 1851 to replace the 1829 original, which was the first rail depot in the country.

HIGHLIGHT

WHAT ARE THE TOP THINGS TO DO IN BALTIMORE?

DISCOVER BALTIMORE NIGHTLIFE
Dance, eat and drink at one of the various restaurants, clubs and pubs in Fells Point.

GO WHERE CULTURE AND FOOD MEET
Venture inside Lexington Market to get the real view of the city's culture.

HEAD TO THE AQUARIUM
Explore marine life at one of the most fascinating aquariums in the area.

Outside, the museum features more trains, such as the "Chessie," the largest steam locomotive. On certain days, visitors can take a train ride.

Admission: adults $14, seniors $12, children 2-12 $8. Monday-Saturday 10 a.m.-4 p.m., Sunday 11 a.m.-4 p.m.

BALTIMORE MARITIME MUSEUM
301 E. Pratt St., Baltimore, 410-396-3453; www.baltomaritimemuseum.org

This museum's featured ships include the *USS Torsk*, a World War II submarine, the Coast Guard cutter *Taney* and the lightship *Chesapeake*. All the ships have been designated National Historic Landmarks. Also here is the Seven Foot Knoll Lighthouse that was built in 1855.

Admission: adults $11, seniors $9, children 6-14 $5, military personnel and children 5 and under free. March-October, daily 10 a.m.-5:30 p.m.; November-February, daily 10 a.m.-4:30 p.m.

BALTIMORE MUSEUM OF ART
10 Art Museum Drive, Baltimore, 410-573-1700; www.artbma.org

Located near Johns Hopkins University, this museum opened in 1923 and was designed by John Russell Pope, the architect of the National Gallery in Washington, D.C. The museum has eight permanent exhibits featuring works from the periods of Impressionism to modern art. It boasts the second largest collection of works by Andy Warhol. However, its jewel is the Cone collection, which includes more than 3,000 pieces by artists such as Picasso, Van Gogh, Renoir, Cézanne and Matisse. The Matisse collection is the largest in the Western Hemisphere. Visitors will also want to see the three-acre sculpture

garden, which contains art by Alexander Calder and Henry Moore.
Admission: Free. Wednesday-Friday 11 a.m.-5 p.m., Saturday-Sunday 11 a.m.-6 p.m.

BALTIMORE ORIOLES

Oriole Park at Camden Yards, 333 W. Camden St., Baltimore, 410-685-9800, 888-848-2479;
www.orioles.mlb.com

The Orioles are Baltimore's professional baseball team in the American League.
Fans call them the Birds or the O's. They were actually moved to New York in
1903 to become the New York Yankees. Babe Ruth began his career playing
with the Orioles for just five months.

BALTIMORE RAVENS

M&T Bank Stadium, 1101 Russell St., Baltimore, 410-261-7283; www.baltimoreravens.com

Moving from Cleveland in 1996, the former Browns changed their name to
the Ravens after the story by Edgar Allan Poe. In just four short years, the
Ravens made a name for themselves by winning Super Bowl XXXV against the
New York Giants. Fans from all over Maryland support this Baltimore team.
Originally owned by Art Modell, the team was bought by part owner Steve
Bisciotti in 2004. Bisciotti hired the new coach, John Harbaugh, in 2008. The
Ravens fans are some of the rowdiest in the league, especially against longtime
rival Pittsburgh Steelers. With purple body paint and purple beer, the fans
cheer on their beloved Ravens every game, rain or shine.

BALTIMORE STREETCAR MUSEUM

1901 Falls Road, Baltimore, 410-547-0264; www.baltimorestreetcar.org

This museum holds eleven electric streetcars and two horse cars used in the
city between 1859 and 1963. The admission price includes unlimited rides on
the original streetcars.
*Admission: adults $7, seniors and children 4-11 $5, children under 4 free. November-May,
Sunday noon-5 p.m.; June-October, Saturday-Sunday noon-5 p.m.*

THE BATTLE MONUMENT

Calvert and Fayette streets, Baltimore

This 1815 Memorial is dedicated to those who fell defending the city in the
War of 1812. Climb the 228 steps to the top of the monument for a breathtaking view of the city.

CYLBURN ARBORETUM

4915 Greenspring Ave., Baltimore, 410-367-2217; www.cylburnassociation.org

This arboretum is located at Cylburn Mansion. You'll find marked nature trails
among the 207 acres of the park filled with maples, conifers, oaks and other
trees and landscaped gardens.
Daily 8 a.m.-8 p.m.

EDGAR ALLAN POE HOUSE AND MUSEUM

203 N. Amity St., Baltimore, 410-396-7932; www.ci.baltimore.md.us

The famed author and father of the macabre lived in this house from 1832 to
1835. Haunted or not, the house and museum have scared up many Poe artifacts
such as period furniture, a desk and telescope owned by Poe, and Gustave Dore's
illustrations of "The Raven". Around January 19, the museum hosts a birthday

celebration that includes readings and theatrical performances of Poe's work.
April-early December, Wednesday-Saturday noon-3:45 p.m.

FEDERAL HILL
Charles and Cross streets, Baltimore

Bordered by Hughes Street, Key Highway, Hanover Street and Cross Street Inner Harbor area, Federal Hill offers views of the city harbor and skyline. Named after a celebration that occurred here in 1788 to mark Maryland's ratification of the Constitution, Federal Hill is filled with shops, restaurants and pubs on tree-lined streets.

FELL'S POINT
Visitors Center, 812 S. Ann St., Baltimore, 410-675-6750; www.fellspoint.us

A shipbuilding and maritime center, this neighborhood that dates back to 1730 has approximately 350 original residential structures. Working tugboats and tankers can be observed from the docks. Its cobblestone streets are lined with plenty of shops, restaurants, clubs and pubs. Locals flock here for the vibrant nightlife.

FLAG HOUSE & STAR-SPANGLED BANNER MUSEUM
844 E. Pratt St., Baltimore, 410-837-1793; www.flaghouse.org

Open to the public for more than 75 years, this museum was the home of Mary Pickersgill, who sewed the flag that Francis Scott Key memorialized in America's national anthem. Although the flag now hangs in the Smithsonian's National Museum of American History, visitors can tour the house to learn about its origins and Pickersgill's life. The house has an adjoining War of 1812 museum, which exhibits military and domestic artifacts and presents an award-winning video.
Admission: adults $7, seniors, students and military personnel $5, children under 6 free. Tuesday-Saturday 10 a.m.-4 p.m. Tours: 10:30 a.m.-2:30 p.m. (every half hour), 3:15 p.m.

FORT MCHENRY NATIONAL MONUMENT AND HISTORIC SHRINE
End of East Fort Avenue, Baltimore, 410-962-4290; www.nps.gov

Fort McHenry boasts a stunning view of the harbor, authentic re-created structures and a wealth of living history. Not only was it the site of the battle that inspired Francis Scott Key to pen the national anthem in 1814, but the fort was also a defensive position during the Revolutionary War, a POW camp for Confederate prisoners during the Civil War and an army hospital during World War I. Summer weekends feature precision drills and music performed by volunteers in Revolutionary War uniforms.
Grounds: September-May, daily 8 a.m.-5 p.m.; June-August, daily 8 a.m.-8 p.m. Fort: September-May, daily 8 a.m.-4:45 p.m.; June-August, daily 8 a.m.-6:30 p.m.

HARBORPLACE
200 E. Pratt St., Baltimore, 410-332-4191; www.harborplace.com

This shopping mecca boasts more than 130 stores and restaurants. Visitors who want to take a break can go outside and walk on the brick-paved promenade that runs along the water's edge. Harborplace also has a small outdoor amphitheater, where in good weather, guests are treated to free performances.
Monday-Saturday 10 a.m.-9 p.m., Sunday noon-6 p.m.

HOLOCAUST MEMORIAL AND SCULPTURE
Water, Gay and Lombard streets, Baltimore

Located in the Inner Harbor, this large marble slab memorializes the victims of the Holocaust. There is also the Joseph Sheppard Holocaust sculpture that symbolizes the horror of the Holocaust with bodies entwined in flames. The center plaza forms a triangle similar to the badges holocaust victims wore.

JOHNS HOPKINS UNIVERSITY
3400 N. Charles St., Baltimore, 410-516-8000; www.jhu.edu

Founded in 1876 and located in northern Baltimore, Johns Hopkins enrolls 18,000 students and is renowned for the Bloomberg School of Public Health, the Peabody Institute (a music conservatory) and its Applied Physics Laboratory located 30 minutes outside of Baltimore. Its affiliated hospital, which has its own separate campus in eastern Baltimore, is consistently ranked as one of the top medical facilities in the country.

JOSEPH MEYERHOFF SYMPHONY HALL
1212 Cathedral St., Baltimore, 410-783-8000, 877-276-1444; www.baltimoresymphony.org

This is the permanent residence of the Baltimore Symphony Orchestra. The striking modern circular facade was constructed of glass, brick and wood.

Box Office: Monday-Friday 10 a.m.-6 p.m., Saturday-Sunday noon-5 p.m. (also open 60 minutes before performances and during intermission).

LACROSSE HALL OF FAME MUSEUM
113 W. University Parkway, Baltimore, 410-235-6882; www.lacrosse.org

This museum is completely dedicated to lacrosse. This sport is a big part of life in Maryland and much of the East Coast. Discover the Hall of Fame located on the edge of Johns Hopkins University campus. The Lacrosse Hall of Fame Museum showcases the history of America's oldest sport. Displaying equipment from Native American origins to modern times, this museum is a popular spot for those diehard laxers. Find your favorite player's name in the Hall of Fame Gallery and study their finest moments.

Admission: adults $3, children 5-15 $2, children under 5 free. February-May, Tuesday-Saturday 10 a.m.-3 p.m.; June-January, Monday-Friday 10 a.m.-3 p.m.

LEXINGTON MARKET
400 W. Lexington St., Baltimore, 410-685-6169; www.lexingtonmarket.com

This roofed market is more than two centuries old. Covering two blocks, it has more than 130 stalls offering fresh vegetables, seafood, meats, baked goods and prepared foods. Vendors outside the market sell clothing, jewelry, T-shirts and other items. Throughout the year, the market hosts several events, such as the Chocolate Festival in October, which boasts free samples and a chocolate-eating contest. But the most anticipated event at the market is Lunch with the Elephants. Every March, Ringling Bros. and Barnum & Bailey Circus elephants parade up Eutaw Street accompanied by fanfare, live music and clowns. When they finally reach the market, they are served lunch, consisting of 1,100 oranges, 1,000 apples, 500 heads of lettuce, 700 bananas, 400 pears and 500 carrots.

Monday-Saturday 8:30 a.m.-6 p.m.

MARYLAND HISTORICAL SOCIETY

201 W. Monument St., Baltimore, 410-685-3750; www.mdhs.org

The state's oldest cultural institution includes a library, a museum and even a small press that promotes scholarship about Maryland's history and material culture. The library has more than 5.4 million works and is a valuable resource for genealogists. The society's collection of historical artifacts includes the original draft of "The Star Spangled Banner".

Admission: Museum, adults $4, seniors, students and children 13-17 $3, children under 13 free; Library, $6. First Thursday of the month free. Museum: Wednesday-Sunday 10 a.m.-5 p.m. Library: Wednesday-Saturday 10 a.m.-4:30 p.m.

MARYLAND SCIENCE CENTER & DAVIS PLANETARIUM

601 Light St., Baltimore, 410-685-5225; www.mdsci.org

Located in the Inner Harbor, the three-story building contains hundreds of exhibits guaranteed to spark young (and old) minds. In the Chesapeake Bay exhibit, you can learn about the bay's delicate ecosystem, or you can explore the mysteries of the human body in BodyLink. The Kids Room, for guests eight and younger, gives children the chance to operate a fish camera or dress up like turtles. Don't miss the Hubble Space Telescope National Visitor Center, a 4,000-square-foot interactive space gallery with 120 high-resolution images that allow guests to see space through the Hubble's eye.

April-mid-June, Monday-Friday 10 a.m.-5 p.m., Saturday 10 a.m.-6 p.m., Sunday 11 a.m.-5 p.m.; Mid-June-August, Sunday-Thursday 10 a.m.-6 p.m., Friday-Saturday 10 a.m.-8 p.m. Kid's Room: Late-March-mid-June, Monday-Friday 10 a.m.-4 p.m., Saturday 10 a.m.-5 p.m., Sunday 11 a.m.-4 p.m.

MARYLAND ZOO

Druid Hill Park Lake Drive, Baltimore, 410-366-5466; www.marylandzoo.org

Located in Druid Hill Park, the third-oldest zoo in the United States covers 180 acres and features more than 2,250 animals. Children can visit the giraffes and elephants in the African Safari exhibit, as well as ride the carousel or try out the climbing wall. The zoo also hosts special events during some holidays.

Admission: Monday-Friday, adults $11, seniors $10, children $9; Saturday-Sunday, adults $15, seniors $12, children $11. Daily 10 a.m.-4 p.m. Closed mid-December-mid-March.

MOUNT CLARE MUSEUM HOUSE

1500 Washington Blvd., Baltimore, 410-837-3262; www.mountclare.org

A National Historic Landmark, Mount Clare is the oldest mansion in Baltimore, dating back to 1760. It is the former home of barrister and senator Charles Carroll, who was a relative of Charles Carroll of Carrollton who signed the Declaration of Independence. The interior has 18th- and 19th-century furnishings. Guided tours take place on the hour.

Admission: adults $6, seniors $5, students 18 and under $4. Tuesday-Saturday 10 a.m.-4 p.m.

NATIONAL AQUARIUM BALTIMORE

501 E. Pratt St., Baltimore, 410-576-3800; www.aqua.org

The National Aquarium introduces guests to stingrays, sharks, puffins, seals and a giant Pacific octopus. Visitors can explore the danger and mystery of a South American tropical rainforest complete with poisonous frogs, exotic birds,

HIGHLIGHT

WHAT ARE BALTIMORE'S CAN'T MISS FIRST VISIT ATTRACTIONS?

A rich history, revamped harbor and delicious blue crab make a trip to Baltimore a definite must. Whether you're into sports or want to see great art, there's something for everyone. Get ready to say good morning, Baltimore.

Sports fans will want to catch an Orioles game at the beautiful **Oriole Park at Camden Yards** (*333 W. Camden St., 888-848-2473; www.orioles.mlb.com*), overlooking the Inner Harbor and just two blocks from the birthplace of baseball great Babe Ruth. Be sure to pick up some beef, which is sold by the pound and comes with buns and BBQ sauce, at Boog's Barbecue, a popular concession stand owned by ex-Oriole Boog Powell.

If it's not baseball season, head next door to watch the Ravens play at **M&T Bank Stadium** (*1101 Russell St., 410-261-7283; www.baltimoreravens.com*). The high-definition video boards allow you to see close-ups of what's happening on the field. And where else can you watch an NFL team named after a poem ("The Raven", by Edgar Allan Poe, who lived in Baltimore for some time and died here in 1849).

For a bit of history, check out the **Inner Harbor**. The center of Baltimore was once a working commercial port. Hop aboard the *U.S.S. Constellation* (*Pier 1, 301 E. Pratt St., 410-539-1797; www.historicships.org*) to learn about the naval history of this 18th-century monument.

Next, it's time to partake in Maryland's single greatest contribution to mankind: crab. Sit yourself down at one of the pine tables on the outdoor deck at **Waterman's Crab House** (*21055 Sharp St., 410-639-2261, www.waterman-scrabhouse.com*), where you can grab a beer from the bucket and get messy with a pile of blue crabs.

If you're traveling with kids, you'll want to make a stop at **The National Aquarium** (*501 E. Pratt St., 410-576-3800; www.aqua.org*), home to more than 16,500 animals and a 4-D Immersion Theater.

Of course, you'll want to visit **Fort McHenry** (*2400 E. Fort Ave., 410-962-4290; www.nps.gov/fomc*), where Francis Scott Key was inspired to write a poem, "The Star-Spangled Banner", after seeing the flag still flying there after the bombardment by the British during the War of 1812.

To see the great art that this city has to offer, pay a visit to **The Baltimore Museum of Art** (*10 Art Museum Drive, 443-573-1700; www.artbma.org*), which houses a fabulous collection of 19th-century, modern and contemporary art.

For a bit of shopping, hit up **Harborplace & The Gallery** (*200 E. Pratt St., 410-332-4191; www.harborplace.com*). You'll find stores selling local products as well as national retailers, plus a slew of restaurants. Grab a bite at **Phillips Seafood** (*301 Light St., 410-685-6600; www.phillipsseafood.com*) in the Light Street Pavilion. The Chesapeake crab cakes here are unrivaled.

After hours, head to **Power Plant Live!** (*34 Market Place, 410-757-5483; www.powerplantlive.com*) for a collection of bars, live music and more restaurants. At this point, you're probably more than ready to say goodnight to Baltimore.

piranha and swinging tamarin monkeys, or delight in the underwater beauty of the replicated Atlantic coral reef. The Children's Cove, a touch pool, provides an interactive experience for kids. Feeding schedules are posted in the lobby. The Marine Mammal Pavilion features a 1,300-seat amphitheater surrounding a 1.2-million-gallon pool that houses Atlantic bottlenose dolphins and underwater viewing areas that enable visitors to observe the mammals from below the surface. There is also a dolphin show and 4-D Immersion Theater.

Admission: adults $24.95, seniors $23.95, children 3-11 $19.95. Daily, hours vary.

PORT DISCOVERY

35 Market Place, Baltimore, 410-727-8120; www.portdiscovery.org

Opened in 1998 in collaboration with Walt Disney Imagineering, Port Discovery is widely considered one of the best children's museums in the country. Kids will have a blast exploring the three-story urban tree house. In MPT Studioworks, they can become producers of their own television broadcasts. The museum also operates the HiFlyer, a giant helium balloon anchored 450 feet above the Inner Harbor. The enclosed gondola holds 20 to 25 passengers and offers a spectacular view of the city.

Admission: $11.75, children under 2 free. September-May, Tuesday-Friday 9:30 a.m.-4:30 p.m., Saturday 10 a.m.-5 p.m., Sunday noon-5 p.m.; June-August, Monday-Saturday 10 a.m.-5 p.m., Sunday noon-5 p.m.

POWER PLANT LIVE

601 E. Pratt St., Baltimore, 410-752-5444; www.powerplantlive.com

This commercial complex was once a power plant owned by Baltimore Gas & Electric. The renovated plant now houses a two-story Barnes & Noble bookstore, a Hard Rock Café and the original ESPN Zone, a 35,000-square-foot sports-themed restaurant and arcade. There are also other restaurants and bars located here. From May through October, there are concerts on the Plaza stage outside featuring both regional and national acts.

SENATOR THEATRE

5904 York Road, North Baltimore, 410-435-8338; www.senator.com

Movie buffs will appreciate the charm and history of the Senator. Showing first-run, independent and classic films, the theater seats 900 and has a 40-foot-wide screen. Listed on the National Register of Historic Places, its architecture is elegant Art Deco. The theater recently added its own mini Walk of Fame outside the entrance.

TOP OF THE WORLD

World Trade Center, 401 E. Pratt St., Baltimore, 410-837-8439; www.viewbaltimore.org

This is the observation deck and museum on the 27th floor of the World Trade Center Baltimore, which was designed by I.M. Pei. Exhibits illustrate the city's history, famous residents and the activities of the port.

Admission: adults $5, seniors and military personnel $4, children 3-12 $3, children under 3 free. September-May, Wednesday-Sunday 10 a.m.-6 p.m.; June-August, Monday-Friday, Sunday, 10 a.m.-6 p.m., Saturday 10 a.m.-8 p.m.

U.S.S. CONSTELLATION
301 E. Pratt St., Pier 1, Baltimore, 410-539-1797; www.constellation.org

This retired sloop, anchored at Pier 1 in the Inner Harbor, has a proud naval history that spans from the Civil War to World War II. Visitors can board the ship for a self-guided audio tour. Kids can participate in the Powder Monkey program, in which they learn what it was like to serve in President Lincoln's navy.

Admission: adults $10, seniors $8, children 6-14 $5, children under 6 and military personnel free. November-February, Monday-Thursday 10 a.m.-4:30 p.m., Friday-Sunday 10 a.m.-4:30 p.m.; March-October, Monday-Thursday 10 a.m.-5 p.m., Friday-Sunday 10 a.m.-5 p.m.

VAGABOND PLAYERS
806 S. Broadway, Baltimore, 410-563-9135; www.vagabondplayers.org

The Vagabond Players are the oldest continuously operating "little theater" in the United States, having started in 1916. The players perform recent Broadway shows, revivals and original scripts as well.

Tickets: $15; $20 musicals. Friday-Sunday.

WALTERS ART MUSEUM
600 N. Charles St., Baltimore, 410-547-9000; www.thewalters.org

This museum's collection traces the history of the world from ancient times to the present day. Father and son William and Henry Walters gave the museum and its numerous holdings to Baltimore, though the New York Metropolitan Museum of Art also coveted it. With more than 30,000 pieces of art, the collection is renowned for its French paintings and Renaissance and Asian art. The museum also exhibits Imperial Fabergé eggs, paintings by Raphael and El Greco, and an impressive assortment of ivories and Art Deco jewelry. Visitors will also want to check out the unique Roman sarcophagus.

Admission: Free. Wednesday-Sunday 10 a.m.-5 p.m.

GEORGE WASHINGTON MONUMENT AND MUSEUM
699 N. Charles St., Baltimore, 410-396-1049; www.baltimoremuseums.org

This was the first major monument to honor George Washington. There's a museum in the base and you can view the city from the top. Other monuments nearby honor Lafayette, Chief Justice Roger Brooke Taney, philanthropist George Peabody, lawyer Severn Teackle Wallis and Revolutionary War hero John Eager Howard.

Admission: $1. Wednesday-Friday 10 a.m.-4 p.m. Saturday-Sunday 10 a.m.-5 p.m.

WHERE TO STAY

★★★HYATT REGENCY BALTIMORE ON THE INNER HARBOR
300 Light St., Baltimore, 410-528-1234, 800-233-1234; www.baltimore.hyatt.com

Conveniently located across the street from Baltimore's Inner Harbor, this hotel is linked by a skywalk to the convention center and shopping at Harborplace. It is also situated within minutes of the National Aquarium, Maryland Science Center and Oriole Park. Guest rooms are decorated with wall coverings resembling white leather, white bedding with gold accents and marble bathrooms. In addition to a rooftop pool and a huge fitness center, amenities include a basketball half-court, putting green and jogging track, along with 29,000 square feet of meeting space.

488 rooms. Restaurant, bar. Business center. Fitness center. Pool. $251-350

★★★INTERCONTINENTAL HARBOR COURT BALTIMORE

550 Light St., Baltimore, 410-234-0550, 800-496-7621; www.intercontinental.com

The InterContinental Harbor Court Hotel, located across the street from the Inner Harbor and Harborplace, recreates the spirit of a grand English manor home. Guest rooms offer views of the harbor or the garden on the courtside. The professional staff tends to your every need, even offering hot, buttery popcorn for guests enjoying in-room movies. The hotel has a fitness center and yoga studio for athletic-minded guests.

195 rooms. Restaurant, bar. Business center. Fitness center. Pool. Spa. $61-150

★★★MARRIOTT BALTIMORE WATERFRONT

700 Aliceanna St., Baltimore, 410-385-3000, 800-228-9290; www.marriott.com

From its large rooms offering stunning views of the harbor to its amenities, this hotel puts you in the center of everything at Baltimore's Inner Harbor. Walk (or take a water taxi) to some of the city's premier tourist destinations: Little Italy, Pier 6 Concert Pavilion or Harborplace.

754 rooms. Restaurant, bar. Business center. Fitness center. Pool. $251-350

★★★MARRIOTT BALTIMORE WASHINGTON INTERNATIONAL AIRPORT

1743 W. Nursery Road, Linthicum, 410-859-8300, 800-228-9290; www.marriott.com

This Marriott is perfect if you need to stay close to the airport. Rooms are bright and cheery with upgraded bedding, Internet access and more. Dining options onsite include Champions Sports Bar, serving American fare, and Monikers Grille, which serves continental cuisine. Enjoy the fitness center and indoor pool when you're not exploring the sites.

309 rooms. Restaurant, bar. Business center. Fitness center. Pool. $151-250

★★★RENAISSANCE BALTIMORE HARBORPLACE HOTEL

202 E. Pratt St., Baltimore, 410-547-1200, 800-535-1201; www.renaissancehotels.com

This hotel adjoins the upscale Gallery mall, with four floors of shopping and dining. Nearby attractions include the National Aquarium, the Baltimore Convention Center and Ride the Ducks of Baltimore. Many guest rooms offer views of the harbor.

622 rooms. Restaurant, bar. Business center. Fitness center. Pool. $251-350

★★★SHERATON BALTIMORE NORTH

903 Dulaney Valley Road, Baltimore, 410-321-7400, 800-325-3535;www.sheraton.com

Located near the Towson business district, Baltimore's Inner Harbor, Camden Yard and the Timonium Fairgrounds, this hotel couldn't be more convenient. Lodgings are roomy and the heated indoor pool provides a built-in playground for the family. It's also connected by a skywalk to the Towson Town Center for all your shopping needs.

283 rooms. Restaurant, bar. Business center. Fitness center. Pool. Pets accepted. $151-250

WHERE TO EAT

★★★BLACK OLIVE

814 S. Bond St., Baltimore, 410-276-7141; www.theblackolive.com

This Mediterranean restaurant, formerly Fells Point's General Store, has retained the building's original hardwood floors and brick archways. The restaurant serves its organic fare al fresco under a grape arbor. Fresh fish are displayed in front of the open kitchen and filleted tableside. The carrot cake is a perfect finale.

Mediterranean, seafood. Lunch, dinner, brunch. Reservations recommended. Outdoor seating. Bar. $36-85

★★★★CHARLESTON

1000 Lancaster St., Baltimore, 410-332-7373; www.charlestonrestaurant.com

Chef/owner Cindy Wolf's regional restaurant serves up dishes such as sautéed heads-on Gulf shrimp with andouille sausage and Tasso ham with creamy stone-milled grits. The restaurant also has an impressive wine program that includes several dozen sparkling wines and a selection of about 600 well-chosen whites and reds from the New World (Australia, South Africa, New Zealand and Chile) and the Old (France, Italy and Spain). Charleston offers more than a dozen microbrews and imported beers.

American, French. Dinner. Closed Sunday. Reservations recommended. Outdoor seating. Bar. $36-85

★★★DELLA NOTTE

801 Eastern Ave., Baltimore, 410-837-5500; www.dellanotte.com

A popular spot, Della Notte's interior is replete with faux-white brick walls covered with murals and busts of Roman emperors. The menu offers a selection of antipasti, fish, meats and daily specials, along with a vast wine list of more than 1,400 selections. After dinner, settle into the Emperor's Lounge with an after-dinner drink and enjoy the live entertainment offered daily.

Italian. Lunch, dinner. Reservations recommended. Bar. $36-85

★★★LINWOOD'S

25 Crossroads Drive, Owings Mills, 410-356-3030; www.linwoods.com

This sophisticated restaurant is one of Baltimore's most popular and for good reason. The dining room is formal but not stuffy and the menu is inventive and enticing. Dishes have included crab cakes with corn pudding and fried tomatoes and grilled veal porterhouse with sautéed spinach, grilled onions and fingerling potatoes. They also have wood-burning oven pizzas and comfort foods like hamburgers and mac and cheese.

American. Lunch, dinner. Bar. Reservations recommended. Outdoor seating. Bar. $36-85

WHICH BALTIMORE RESTAURANT HAS THE BEST FRENCH CUISINE?

Charleston:
This Baltimore restaurant serves up superb French-influenced American food and has an excellent wine list to match.

★★★THE MILTON INN

14833 York Road, Sparks, 410-771-4366; www.miltoninn.com

This old stone house has been restored for use as a country inn that serves exceptional food in an authentic colonial atmosphere. The cozy spot serves tasty dishes including roast Hudson Valley duck and cinnamon-crusted Atlantic salmon.

American. Lunch (Monday-Friday), dinner, Sunday brunch. Reservations recommended. Outdoor seating. Bar. $36-85

★★★THE OCEANAIRE SEAFOOD ROOM

801 Aliceanna St., Baltimore, 443-872-0000; www.theoceanaire.com

The restaurant's upscale décor features hardwood floors, rich cherry wood accents, wood blinds and leather. The menu changes daily, since seafood is the specialty and the restaurant has it flown and trucked in every morning. Diners choose their fish preparation—grilled, broiled, sautéed, steamed or fried.

Seafood. Dinner. Reservations recommended. Bar. $36-85

★★★PAZO

1425 Aliceanna, Baltimore, 410-534-7296; www.pazorestaurant.com

Pazo gives diners a taste of Spain without having to travel overseas. The tapas dishes here are delicious and feature Mediterranean cuisine (vegetarian dishes are also available). Group dining is popular, with diners ordering multiple tapas entrées and sharing with their dining companions. The restaurant is also a popular romantic spot, with soft lighting, wood tables, soaring ceilings, and wrought-iron accents. After dinner, guests can stroll on the famed Inner Harbor where they'll find shops, activities and attractions.

Mediterranean. Dinner. Reservations recommended. Bar. $36-85

★★★THE PRIME RIB

1101 N. Calvert St., Baltimore, 410-539-1804; www.theprimerib.com

The Prime Rib has been serving consistently good steaks, chops and seafood since 1965. With black walls, candlelit tables and tuxedoed waiters, it's known as "the civilized steakhouse." They also have an extensive wine list so you can be sure to find something to complement your meal.

American. Dinner. Bar. Reservations recommended. $36-85

CAPITAL REGION

Suburbs of the nation's capital make up this region of Maryland. Filled with commuters, history and fun, these towns are worth a visit. A suburb of Washington, D.C., Bethesda is home to the National Institutes of Health, the National Library of Medicine and the Bethesda National Naval Hospital. Another affluent suburb of Washington is Chevy Chase, a quiet town with plenty of tree-lined streets and amazing shopping just outside Washington, D.C. Just off the Capital Beltway is College Park. It is the location of the University of Maryland flagship campus as well as the College Park Aviation Museum. Next to College Park lies the planned community of Greenbelt, which was modeled after 19th-century English garden cities and is surrounded by forests. At the northern edge of D.C., Rockville is the second-largest city in Maryland. Rockville offers a busy downtown area with plenty of shops and restaurants to explore and art and culture abounds.

HIGHLIGHTS

WHAT ARE THE TOP THINGS TO DO IN THE CAPITAL REGION?

3, 2, 1 BLAST OFF
Visit the NASA/ Goddard Space Center and see what the latest and greatest space equipment.

DISCOVER WHAT A TERRAPIN IS
Explore the flagship campus of University of Maryland.

WHAT TO SEE

BETHESDA

BETHESDA THEATRE
7719 Wisconsin Ave., Bethesda, 301-657-7827; www.bethesdatheatre.com
This 650-seat Art Deco theatre hosts off-Broadway plays and musicals. On the National Register of Historic Places, the Bethesda Theatre opened in 1938.

NATIONAL LIBRARY OF MEDICINE
8600 Rockville Pike, Bethesda, 301-594-5983, 888-346-3656; www.nlm.nih.gov
This is the world's largest biomedical library filled with rare books, manuscripts, prints and medical art displays.
Reading Room: Monday-Friday 8:30 a.m.-5 p.m., Saturday 8:30 a.m.-2 p.m. Tours: Monday-Friday 1:30 p.m.

COLLEGE PARK

COLLEGE PARK AVIATION MUSEUM
1985 Corporal Frank Scott Drive, College Park, 301-864-6029;
www.collegeparkaviationmuseum.com
This museum is located on the site of the world's oldest operating airport, started by Wilbur Wright in 1909 to train two military officers in the operation of aircraft. The first airplane machine gun and radio navigational aids were tested here as well as the first airmail and controlled helicopter flights. There is a museum with a gallery of historic aircrafts as well as changing exhibits.
Admission: adults $4, seniors $3, students and children under 2 free. Daily 10 a.m.-5 p.m.

UNIVERSITY OF MARYLAND
Highway 1, College Park, 301-405-1000; www.umd.edu
Home to more than 35,000 students, University of Maryland attracts students of all kinds. From top ACC sports to Greek life, this university has it all. Catch

a football game at Byrd Stadium, where you'll find students covered head to toe in red cheering on the terps. If you're lucky, enjoy a basketball game at the almost always sold out Comcast Center. The campus is beautiful considering its location and size. Outfitted with a barn for its agriculture school, columns decorating each brick building and several large sports complexes, University of Maryland is worth a visit even if you've already graduated from college. Make sure to see Testudo, the terrapin statue, guarding McKeldin Library.

GREENBELT

NASA/GODDARD SPACE FLIGHT CENTER & VISITOR CENTER

Greenbelt, 301-286-3978; www.gsfc.nasa.gov

The Goddard Space Flight Center's Visitor Center showcases satellites, rockets, capsules and exhibits in all phases of space research.

Admission: Free. September-May, Tuesday-Friday 10 a.m.-3 p.m., Saturday-Sunday noon-4 p.m.; June-August, Tuesday-Friday 10 a.m.-5 p.m., Saturday noon-4 p.m.

ROCKVILLE

BEALL-DAWSON HOUSE

103 W. Montgomery Ave., Rockville, 301-762-1492; www.montgomeryhistory.org

The Beall-Dawson House is an example of Federal architecture with an interior that has rooms with period furnishings, changing exhibits, a library, museum shop and a 19th-century doctor's office. Tours guided by docents cover the culture of the Bealls, an upper-class family and their African American slaves who worked in the house.

Admission: adults $3, seniors and children $2. Tuesday-Sunday noon-4 p.m.

CABIN JOHN REGIONAL PARK

7700 Tuckerman Lane, Rockville, 301-299-0024; www.mcparkandplanning.org

Spend the day at this 551-acre park which has plenty to keep you busy, including playgrounds, a miniature train ride, a nature center offering educational programs, walks, films and more. Concerts are offered during the summer at the outdoor amphitheater. Indoor tennis courts, game fields, an ice skating rink, nature trails, a campground and picnicking areas are also onsite.

Daily dawn-dusk.

F. SCOTT FITZGERALD THEATRE

603 Edmonston Drive, Rockville, 240-314-8690; www.rockvillemd.gov

Rockville's theater features performances of classics such as Eugene O'Neil's *A Long Day's Journey Into Night.* The Victorian Lyric Opera Company, Rockville Civic Ballet and others also perform here.

Box Office: Tuesday-Saturday 2-7 p.m.

WHERE TO STAY

BETHESDA

★★★HYATT REGENCY BETHESDA

1 Bethesda Metro Center, Bethesda, 301-657-1234; www.bethesda.hyatt.com

Located at Metro Center and within steps to restaurants, theaters and shopping, this hotel is perfect for both the business and leisure traveler. The rooms offer

Hyatt Grand beds, iPod docking stations and deluxe bathrooms with Portico products. The onsite restaurant, Morton's, The Steakhouse, provides delicious steaks and seafood and great cocktails.

390 rooms. Restaurant, bar. Business center. Fitness center. Pool. $61-150

GREENBELT
★★★MARRIOTT GREENBELT
6400 Ivy Lane, Greenbelt, 301-441-3700, 800-228-9290; www.marriott.com

The close proximity to BWI airport and downtown Washington, D.C., along with laptop plug-in connections to flat-screen HDTVs, makes this hotel ideal for business travelers. And the pillow-top beds guarantee that you'll be well rested for your morning meeting. Enjoy the fitness center, the indoor and outdoor pools and an outdoor whirlpool.

288 rooms. Restaurant, bar. Business center. Fitness center. Pool. Tennis. $151-250

WHERE TO EAT

BETHESDA
★★★CESCO TRATTORIA
4871 Cordell Ave., Bethesda, 301-654-8333

This intimate Italian restaurant features breads that are baked fresh daily in a wood-burning oven, which is visible to diners. You can't go wrong choosing any of the pasta dishes.

Italian. Lunch (Tuesday-Friday), dinner. Outdoor seating. Bar. $36-85

★★★LE VIEUX LOGIS
7925 Old Georgetown Road, 301-652-6816; www.levieuxlogisrestaurant.com

Mixing American and Scandinavian techniques with their classic French menu, Le Vieux Logis creates dishes that are innovative and delicious. The menu includes dishes like pan-seared tilapia with tomatoes, garlic and saffron, as well as rack of grilled lamb chops with tarragon sauce. The exterior of the restaurant is painted with murals of a town in the French countryside; on the interior, the ambience is romantic with dim lighting and warm tones.

French. Dinner. Closed Sunday-Monday. Outdoor seating. $36-85

★★★RUTH'S CHRIS STEAK HOUSE
7315 Wisconsin Ave., Bethesda, 301-652-7877; www.ruthschris.com

Thick, juicy USDA Prime steaks slathered with butter, as well as market fresh seafood, are the hallmarks of Ruth's Chris, and the Bethesda outpost is no exception. Found on the ground floor of the Air Rights building, the dining room features a relaxed, informal atmosphere with dark wood accents, a large lobster tank, and a cigar lounge. In addition to hearty cuts of meat like the filet, rib eye, and T-bone, and seafood items such as fresh lobster and seared ahi tuna, Ruth's Chris offers a number of tasty sides.

American, steak. Dinner. Bar. $36-85

★★★TRAGARA
4935 Cordell Ave., Bethesda, 301-951-4935; www.tragara.com

Tragara is one of Bethesda's most elegant and romantic restaurants, offering delightful Italian cuisine and impeccable service. Bathed in soft light, with fresh roses on every linen-topped table, Tragara is serene and relaxing—a lovely place to dine and then linger. Tables fill up quickly at lunch and dinner with smartly dressed business executives and stylish quartets of 30-something couples. The impressive Italian kitchen draws them all in with a tempting menu of pastas, fish, meat, and antipasti, but be sure to save room to indulge in the house-made gelato before saying, "Ciao."

Italian. Lunch (Monday-Friday), dinner. Reservations recommended. Bar. $36-85

CHEVY CHASE

★★★LA FERME
7101 Brookville Road, Chevy Chase, 301-986-5255; www.lafermerestaurant.com

In a French country-house setting, La Ferme serves entrées such as hickory-smoked and grilled double-cut pork chops with potato gratin, grilled vegetables and Meaux mustard sauce. In warmer weather, the outdoor terrace is the perfect spot to grab a quick lunch or romantic dinner. Desserts might include chocolate and Grand Marnier mousse cake or warm brioche pudding with rum-raisin ice cream and caramel sauce.

French. Lunch (Monday-Friday), dinner, Sunday brunch. Reservations recommended. Outdoor seating. Bar. $16-35

ROCKVILLE

★★★NORMANDIE FARM
10710 Falls Road, Potomac, 301-983-8838; www.popovers.com

Normandie Farm is reminiscent of a country home, serving entrées such as fresh sea scallops with bacon, scallions, pine nuts and citrus beurre blanc or beef medallions with truffle sauce and béarnaise-filled artichoke bottoms. The atmosphere is relaxed and welcoming. Friday and Saturday nights, guests spill into Margery's Lounge next to the restaurant's lobby, for drinks by the fireplace and live entertainment. The outdoor Café Normandie is open all day, offering a lighter menu and complimentary Internet access.

French, seafood. Lunch, dinner, Sunday brunch. Closed Monday. Reservations recommended. Outdoor seating. Children's menu. Bar. $16-35

★★★OLD ANGLER'S INN
10801 MacArthur Blvd., Potomac, 301-299-9097; www.oldanglersinn.com

Located in a Tudor-style house built in 1860, the rustic dining room is a perfect spot for a cozy evening. In winter, get a table near the fireplace for a romantic meal. In summer, the terrace provides a lovely setting beneath the trees. New Point oysters are always on the menu and the wild Chesapeake rockfish with corn salad is delicious. They also have an extensive wine list to choose from along with delectable desserts such as the warm Braeburn apple tart with cinnamon ice cream.

Seafood. Lunch, dinner. Closed Monday. Reservations recommended. Outdoor seating. Children's menu. Bar. $16-35

CENTRAL MARYLAND

Filled with charm and history, Central Maryland is an area popular among tourists and residents alike. Annapolis, the capital of Maryland is 350-years old and proud of its colonial heritage. It is where the Puritans settled, the Treaty of Paris ending the Revolutionary War was ratified and the United States Naval Academy was founded in 1885. Beautiful colonial homes line the compact streets, many of which bear plaques revealing a bit of their history. To the northwest of Annapolis lies Ellicott City, a quaint town with plenty of history. Originally named Ellicott Mills, this town was founded by three Quaker brothers as the site of their gristmill and eventually became the site of ironworks, rolling mills and the first railroad terminus in the United States.

WHAT TO SEE

ANNAPOLIS
BOAT TRIPS
980 Awald Road at City Dock, 410-268-7600; www.watermarkcruises.com
Take one of a few different sightseeing cruises and learn about the culture of Annapolis. Choose between a 40-minute narrated tour of Annapolis Harbor and the U.S. Naval Academy aboard the Harbor Queen or tour the Old Annapolis neighborhood and Spa Creek and the U.S. Naval Academy aboard *Miss Anne*. There's a 90-minute cruise to the Severn River, the Annapolis Harbor, the U.S. Naval Academy, the Chesapeake Bay Bridge or the Thomas Point Lighthouse. There are other cruises to choose from including the Pirate Cruise on Chesapeake Bay, which includes a theatre performance.
Schedule and prices vary; see website for information.

CHESAPEAKE BAY BRIDGE
357 Pier 1 Road, Annapolis
One of the most beautiful bridges around, the Chesapeake Bay Bridge is a 4¾-mile link of Highway 50 across the Bay to Baltimore, Annapolis and Washington D.C. Opened in 1952, the Bay Bridge, as it is known by locals, created an alternate, and albeit much shorter, path from Maryland's Eastern Shore to Annapolis. This is also the route many use to the Atlantic coast beaches. There is one toll, which is charged eastbound only.

GOVERNOR'S MANSION
State Circle, Annapolis, 410-260-3930; www.mdarchives.state.md.us
This 1868 Victorian structure was remodeled in 1935 into a Georgian country house with furnishings that reflect Maryland's history and culture. It is the home of the governor of Maryland, Governor Martin O'Malley, and is located across the street from the Maryland State House. It has been the residence of every governor since 1870. Tours are available by appointment only.
Tours: Monday, Wednesday, Friday 10:30 a.m.-2:30 p.m.

HAMMOND-HARWOOD HOUSE
19 Maryland Ave., Annapolis, 410-263-4683; www.hammondharwoodhouse.org
Located on historic Maryland Avenue, the Hammond-Harwood House

HIGHLIGHTS

WHAT ARE THE TOP THINGS TO DO IN CENTRAL MARYLAND?

TOUR THE NAVAL ACADEMY
The beautiful United States Naval Academy is located right on the water in Annapolis.

SET SAIL ON THE CHESAPEAKE BAY
Aboard *The Woodwind*, you'll discover the town of Annapolis in a whole new way. Relax and watch the sunset with a glass of champagne on this cruise.

ALL ABOARD
Explore the historic B&O Railroad beyond the Monopoly board. This Ellicott City museum is housed in the oldest standing station in America.

GO BACK IN TIME
Stroll through the streets of Annapolis with a colonial guide good enough to make you think you're stepping back in time.

showcases colonial Annapolis at its finest. William Buckland designed this 1774 Georgian house. It is filled with antique furnishings and has a beautiful garden. Matthias Hammond, a Revolutionary patriot, was its first owner. After a few transactions, it was acquired by Judge Jeremiah Townley Chase, passing it down through the family. Judge Chase's granddaughter married William Harwood, the grandson of the original architect, William Buckland. Thus, it became known as the Hammond-Harwood House. It is now a National Historic Landmark.

Admission: adults $6, students $5.50, children $3. April-October, Tuesday-Sunday noon-5 p.m.

HISTORIC ANNAPOLIS FOUNDATION WELCOME CENTER AND MUSEUM STORE
77 Main St., Annapolis, 410-268-5576, 800-639-9153; www.annapolis.org

This 1815 building stands on the site of a storehouse for Revolutionary War troops that burned in 1790. Self-guided digital access audio walking tours can be purchased here. The store features products reflecting Annapolis history including books, jewelry, gifts and more. This foundation offers self-guided digital audio walking tours along with guided walking and carriage tours. Depending on what you want to see, certain tours include the Historic District,

State House, Old Treasury, U.S. Naval Academy and William Paca House.
Monday-Thursday 10 a.m.-5 p.m., Friday-Saturday 10 a.m.-6 p.m., Sunday 11 a.m.-5 p.m.

SAILING TOURS

80 Compromise St., Annapolis, 410-263-7837; www.schooner-woodwind.com

If you want to set sail in Chesapeake Bay, these two-hour narrated trips aboard the 74-foot sailing yacht *Woodwind* are the way to go. While on board, you can actually help raise the sails or steer the boat. There are certain cruises that include a themed dinner or wine tastings. It departs from Pusser's Landing Restaurant at the Annapolis Marriott Waterfront Hotel.

Admission: Monday-Friday, adults $34, seniors $32, children under 13 $22; Sunset Sails and Saturday-Sunday, adults $37, seniors $35, children under 13 $22. May-September: Tuesday-Sunday four trips daily, Monday sunset sail only; schedule varies rest of year.

ST. JOHN'S COLLEGE

60 College Ave., Annapolis, 410-263-2371, 800-727-9238; www.sjca.edu

This nonsectarian liberal arts college has a campus in Annapolis as well as in Santa Fe, New Mexico; each has only 475 students. The 36-acre campus is one of the oldest in the country and is a National Historic Landmark. The college succeeded King William's School, founded in 1696. George Washington's two nephews and step-grandson studied here; and Francis Scott Key was an alumnus.

STATE HOUSE

350 Rowe Blvd., State Circle, Annapolis, 410-974-3400, 800-235-4045; www.msa.md.gov

As the oldest state house in continuous legislative use in United States, this was the first peacetime capitol of the nation. Here in 1784, a few weeks after receiving George Washington's resignation as commander-in-chief, Congress ratified the Treaty of Paris, which officially ended the Revolutionary War.

Monday-Friday 9 a.m.-5 p.m., Saturday-Sunday 10 a.m.-4 p.m.

UNITED STATES NAVAL ACADEMY

121 Blake Road, Annapolis, 410-263-6933; www.usna.edu

Opened in 1845, the U.S. Naval Academy sits at the edge of the Chesapeake Bay and Severn River, occupying 338 acres. Tours of the campus are available through the academy's Armel-Leftwich visitor center. You will see the tomb of John Paul Jones, the chapel, the midshipmen's living quarters and the naval museum. The center also exhibits the original wooden figurehead of Tecumseh from the *USS Delaware* and displays the Freedom 7 space capsule. If you time your visit right, you can witness the Noon Formation, during which all present midshipmen line up and march in for the noon meal with military precision. Access to the Academy grounds is limited, so check the current security restrictions before planning a visit.

Daily 9 a.m.-5 p.m.

WATERMARK TOURS

26 West St., Annapolis, 410-268-7601, 800-569-9622; www.annapolis-tours.com

These are walking tours of the U.S. Naval Academy and Historic District conducted by guides in colonial attire. The tour includes the historic Maryland

HIGHLIGHT

WHAT'S THE BEST WAY TO SEE ANNAPOLIS IN A DAY?

Locals have lived here for generations, and the city's hometown atmosphere welcomes you as soon as you drive in. But it's not all about the past here. This community on the Chesapeake Bay is also the self-proclaimed sailing capital of the world. Locals are mad for sailing, even burning their socks in a springtime ritual that welcomes sailing season. To really experience the Annapolitan life, you have to get out on the water. Hop aboard the *Woodwind* (*80 Compromise St., 410-263-7837; www.schoonerwoodwind.com*), a two-hour public cruise, or arrange for a private charter on the *Woodwind II*. You may recognize the identical sister ships from the popular movie *Wedding Crashers*. If you're short on time, the *Harbor Queen* (*410-268-7601; www.watermarkcruises.com*) offers a 40-minute narrated cruise that departs every hour, on the hour, from Annapolis City Dock. If you can't see her, you'll hear her.

After sailing, it's time to eat some crabs. Head to a locals' spot for Chesapeake Bay blue crabs. At **Cantler's Riverside Inn** (*458 Forest Beach Road, 410-757-1311; www.cantlers.com*) you'll overlook a creek off the Magothy River while eating the best crabs in the world. Locals will tell you the best way to eat crabs is with a vinegar and Old Bay seasoning—which locals will put on just about anything—and a beer in hand.

After washing up, navigate back to downtown Annapolis for a dose of history. To get the low down from a real history buff, take a stroll with **Annapolis Tours** (*410-268-7601; www.annapolis-tours.com*). The guides are dressed in fully authentic colonial garb and usually speak with a British accent as they did in the early days of the city. The Four Centuries walking tour includes a visit to the Old Senate Chamber where in 1783 George Washington resigned as Commander-in-Chief. You'll also be taken on a tour of the United States Naval Academy.

Annapolis is small (population 36,900) and you can easily get around on foot. A walk up and down Main Street will take you past several shops where you can pick up something to remember this quaint town. Stores like **A.L. Goodie's General Store** (*112 Main St., 410-269-0071*) and **Pepper's** (*133 Main St., 410-267-8722*) offer plenty of t-shirts and other knick-knacks. For more stylish clothing, stop in **Horse Boutique** (*158 Main St., 410-626-9726; www.horseboutique.com*), **Madison** (*181 Main St., 410-295-7878; www.shopmadison-boutique.com*), or **Paradigm** (*179 Main St., 410-626-6030; www.shopparadigm.com*). Forgot your foul weather gear? Sail into **Helly Hansen** (*132 Main St., 410-990-4359; www.hellyhansen.com*) for fantastic sport gear.

Next, drift over to the newly renovated West Street, the "uptown" of Annapolis, for more shops and restaurants. You'll find contemporary clothing shops, including **Mi'Chek Boutique** (*162A West St., 410-267-1202; www.michekboutique.com*), and home stores, such as **The Annapolis Furniture Company** (*238 West St., 410-295-7463; www.annapolisfurniture.com*).

After a full day, head to **McGarvey's** (*8 Market Space, 410-263-5700; www.mcgarveys.net*) for some oysters on the half shell—only in the months with an 'r' in them—and an Aviator (beer from their microbrewery). If you're still hungry, order one of the juicy charbroiled burgers.

HIGHLIGHT *continued*

If you're not an oyster fan, try them anyway. But seriously, there are other things to eat besides crab and oysters. If you're a sushi lover, go to **Joss Café & Sushi Bar** (*195 Main St., 410-263-4688; www.josscafe-sushibar.com*), the best in town. You won't find many tourists here because the locals try to keep this secret for themselves. Order up a Softshell Crab Roll for a neighborhood delicacy (okay, so you can't totally get away from crab but why would you want to?) or try the Chesapeake Roll (a blend of shrimp tempura and crabmeat with avocado, cucumber and roe) for something different. Sit at the sushi bar to watch the chefs hand-making roll after roll.

The next morning, meander down **Main Street to Chick & Ruth's Delly** (*165 Main St., 410-269-6737; www.chickandruths.com*) for the best breakfast in town. Run by locals, serving locals, they may not be the nicest staff, but it's worth it. Check out the photos covering the walls, you may recognize a few famous faces. Order up eggs any way you like them or pancakes the size of your head. Don't forget the milkshake or delly potatoes (delicious fried hashbrown potatoes)—they are a must have. If it is a weekend, there will be a line out the door. Make sure you have cash, no credit cards are accepted at this local joint.

State House, St. John's College, Naval Academy Chapel, the crypt of John Paul Jones, Bancroft Hall dormitory and Armel-Leftwich visitor center. Tours depart from the visitor center or the information booth (located at 1 Dock Street).
Late-March-October, daily 10:30 a.m.; November-March, Saturday 1:30 p.m.

WILLIAM PACA HOUSE AND GARDEN
186 Prince George St., Annapolis, 410-990-4538, 800-603-4020; www.annapolis.org
William Paca, a signer of the Declaration of Independence and one of Maryland's governors during the Revolutionary War, built this five-part Georgian mansion in 1765. It's filled with furnishings from the period along with antiques from the Paca family. Surrounding the home is the beautifully restored two-acre pleasure garden that was originally developed in 1765 by Paca himself. The property includes waterways, formal parterres and a garden wilderness.
House: adult $8, senior $7, children 6-17 $5, children under 6 free. Tours: Monday-Saturday 10 a.m.-5p.m., Sunday noon-5 p.m. Garden: Admission: $6, daily.

ELLICOTT CITY
ELLICOTT CITY B&O RAILROAD STATION MUSEUM
2711 Maryland Ave., Ellicott City, 410-461-1945; www.ecborail.org
Completed by the Baltimore and Ohio Railroad in 1830, the Ellicott City Station is the oldest standing railroad station in America and the site of the first 13 miles of commercial track constructed in the United States. In the 1970s the station was restored as a museum, and a second restoration in 1999 returned the building to its 1857 appearance. Today, the site interprets the story of transportation and travel in early America through seasonal exhibits, education programs and living history programs.
Admission: adults $5, seniors $4, children 2-12 $3. Wednesday-Sunday 11 a.m.-4 p.m.

PATAPSCO VALLEY STATE PARK

8020 Baltimore National Pike, Ellicott City, 410-461-5005, 888-432-2267; www.dnr.state.md.us

Spread across three counties, this great nature and recreational area runs along a 32-mile stretch of the scenic Patapsco River, spans 14,000 acres and contains five sites. Visitors can hike, bike, horseback ride, fish, camp, canoe, tube or picnic. The park also includes the world's largest multiple-arched stone railroad bridge, a 300-foot suspension bridge and a paved hiking trail for the disabled.

Park: Daily dawn-dusk. Information desk: Daily 8 a.m.-4:30 p.m.

WHERE TO STAY

ANNAPOLIS
★★★LOEWS ANNAPOLIS HOTEL

126 W. St., Annapolis, 410-263-7777, 800-235-6397; www.loewshotels.com

The Loews Annapolis Hotel is located in the heart of downtown Annapolis within walking distance of the city's historic sites. It offers newly renovated rooms—18 of which are suites—with onsite laundry service, a fitness center and a day spa. With plenty of meeting rooms, the hotel is a great spot for business or special events.

217 rooms. Restaurant, bar. Fitness center. Spa. $151-250

★★★MARRIOTT ANNAPOLIS WATERFRONT

80 Compromise St., Annapolis, 410-268-7555, 888-773-0786; www.annapolismarriott.com

True to its name, many of the rooms in the Marriott Annapolis Waterfront offer views of the Chesapeake Bay and Annapolis Harbor. Guest rooms are decorated in a nautical theme with sea blue tones and comfortable furnishings. Convenience is a top priority, and rooms have Internet access, terry cloth robes and come with complimentary newspaper delivery each morning. You can rent bicycles to check out the town.

150 rooms. Restaurant, bar. Business center. Fitness center. $251-350

★★★SHERATON ANNAPOLIS HOTEL

173 Jennifer Road, Annapolis, 410-266-3131, 800-325-3535; www.sheraton.com

This warm, contemporary and newly renovated Sheraton hotel is located just outside the downtown area of Annapolis. Guest rooms feature comfortable bedding and bathrobes. Guests can take advantage of the hotel's transportation to go downtown.

196 rooms. Restaurant, bar. Business center. Fitness center. Pool. Pets accepted. $61-150

RECOMMENDED

THE WESTIN ANNAPOLIS

100 Westgate Circle, Annapolis, 410-972-4300; www.westinannapolis.com

Opened in 2007, this Westin hotel boosted the popularity to the uptown region of Annapolis. It is located within the development, Park Place, which has residences, shops, restaurants and salons. This is a great location, within walking distance from downtown. Sleep on one of the signature Heavenly Beds and enjoy the modern surroundings of this hotel.

225 rooms. Restaurant, bar. Fitness center. Pool. Pets accepted. $151-250

ELLICOTT CITY
TURF VALLEY RESORT AND CONFERENCE CENTER
2700 Turf Valley Road, Ellicott City, 410-465-1500, 888-833-8873; www.turfvalley.com

This full-service resort (formerly a thoroughbred farm and country club) is convenient to Baltimore and offers well-appointed guest rooms. The resort also features a full-service European spa, two golf courses, tennis courts and a nightly hors d'oeuvres and cocktail reception.

234 rooms. Restaurant, bar. Business center. Fitness center. Pool. Spa. Golf. Tennis. $151-250

WHERE TO EAT

ANNAPOLIS
★★★CAFÉ BRETTON
849 Baltimore-Annapolis Blvd., Severna Park, 410-647-8222

Whether or not you like French cooking, the amicable servers, appealing atmosphere and classically prepared dishes will win you over. If the Chilean sea bass is on the menu, order it. Also be sure to try a glass of wine from the extensive wine list.

French. Dinner. Closed Monday. Reservations recommended. Bar. $36-85

RECOMMENDED

CANTLER'S RIVERSIDE INN
458 Forest Beach Road, Annapolis, 410-757-1311; www.cantlers.com

This local crab house offers some of the best crabs in the world, Chesapeake Bay Blue Crabs. Sit at the long picnic tables on the patio overlooking Mill Creek. Order up a dozen of "number one jimmies," and a beer and get ready to get messy. The crabs are steamed up with Old Bay, a spice that locals swear by. If you've never picked a crab, the staff will be happy to show you how. You don't want to miss this gem. They serve crabs year round, but the best time to go is during the summer season when the crabs are really running in the bay.

Seafood. Lunch, dinner. Outdoor seating. $16-35

CHICK AND RUTH'S DELLY
165 Main St., Annapolis, 410-269-6737; www.chickandruths.com

Every morning, the whole restaurant gets on their feet and recites the Pledge of Allegiance. This is just one of the things that makes Chick and Ruth's Delly unique. This spot is best for breakfast, which is served all day. Locals and tourists flock here on Saturday and Sunday morning. No reservations are taken at this local joint—so beware, the wait can be very long. The owner, Ted Levitt, is quite the entertainer; add a very diverse staff and you get a fun, family friendly meal. This Jewish delicatessen offers a variety of sandwiches named for locals such as the "Governor of Maryland, Martin O'Malley," or the "St. Johnnies." If you're lucky, Ted will let you sit in the governor's booth, usually roped off and reserved.

American. Breakfast, lunch, dinner. $15 and under

JOSS CAFÉ & SUSHI BAR
195 Main St., Annapolis, 410-263-4688; www.josscafe-sushibar.com

This is the best sushi this town has to offer. Order up a Soft shell Crab Roll for a neighborhood delicacy, or try the Chesapeake Roll for a nice treat. Sit at the sushi bar for the best view of the chefs hand-making roll after roll. Joss doesn't take reservations and tends to fill up quickly on the weekends. The wait can be up to an hour, but once you pop that first roll in your mouth, it will all be worth it.

Japanese. Lunch, dinner. $16-35

LEWNES' STEAKHOUSE

401 Fourth St., Eastport, 410-263-1617; www.lewnessteakhouse.com

The Lewnes family opened up their steakhouse in 1921 and business has been booming ever since. One of the local gems of the city, Lewnes' has a very intimate atmosphere. Although steak is the focus here, the seafood is local and fresh, being that the restaurant is one block from the water. The wine list is extensive.

Steak. Dinner. $36-85

MCGARVEY'S OYSTER BAR & SALOON

8 Market Space, Annapolis, 410-263-5700; www.mcgarveys.net

This saloon is a legend among Annapolitans. Whether you get oyster shooters or a signature burger, you won't be disappointed. The dimly lit restaurant is a go-to spot for locals and tourists alike. The crab dip is one of the best in the city. Add in the house Aviator beer, and your meal will be complete. This dimly lit restaurant turns into a bar at night and quickly fills up with Navy midshipmen, college students and local twenty-somethings. McGarvey's offers a great location, great food, and a great atmosphere.

American, Seafood. Lunch, dinner, Sunday brunch, late-night. Outdoor seating. $16-35

MIDDLETON TAVERN

2 Market Space, Annapolis, 410-263-3323; www.middletontavern.com

Located just steps away from the harbor, Middleton's is the perfect spot for an outdoor meal. Watch midshipmen wander down the street as you throw back some oyster shooters. Order up the infamous Caesar salad prepared tableside. Inside, the walls are covered with history, including old Naval Academy uniforms and Civil War muskets. Middleton's is one of the oldest continuously operating taverns in the country. The building itself is more than 250 years old.

American. Lunch, dinner. Bar. Children's menu. Outdoor seating. $16-35

SEVERN INN

1993 Baltimore Annapolis Blvd., Annapolis, 410-349-4000; www.severninn.com

Located right next to the Naval Academy Bridge, this building had a long history of failures. That is, until Severn Inn moved in and made this waterfront property a success. Offering amazing views of the Naval Academy and the Severn River, this restaurant has excellent food to match. Seafood dominates the menu, with dishes like the jumbo lump crab cake sandwich or the grilled fish taco. On a warm day, opt for a spot on the patio to watch the boats fly up and down the river.

American, Seafood. Lunch, dinner, Sunday brunch. Outdoor seating. $36-85

ELLICOTT CITY
TERSIGUEL'S
8293 Main St., Ellicott City, 410-465-4004; www.tersiguels.com

Located in historic downtown, Tersiguel's brings spectacular French cuisine to Ellicott City. Chef/owner Michel Tersiguel has dazzled plenty of palettes with his divine cooking. The restaurant is housed in a 19th-century home in the heart of the city. Fernand and Odette Tersiguel founded the restaurant, sharing family recipes with their son, Michel. Often, you'll find Fernand hosting groups and playing maître d' at this place he calls home. You'll be safe with almost everything on the menu. Try one of the classics like the escargots de Bourgogne, or filet mignon drizzled with truffle sauce.

French. Lunch, dinner. Reservations recommended. Bar. $36-85

EASTERN SHORE

Crossing over the Chesapeake Bay Bridge onto Maryland's Eastern Shore transports you to a simpler time. The farms, the quaint towns and the easygoing life attract people from all over to buy farmland or bay houses. The majestic twin spans of the Bay Bridge carry visitors to the patchwork of small picturesque towns, lighthouses and fishing villages tucked away from the city. Scenic rivers and bays, wildlife, gardens and wildflowers fill the countryside. The main attractions of any visit, however, are the many fine inns and the restaurants specializing in local seafood. A little over an hour past the bridge is the adorable town of Cambridge, the home of Annie Oakley, Harriet Tubman, and *Golden Girls'* Bea Arthur. Easton might be small, but it offers quite a lot. It's easy to escape from the city here and enjoy sailing and canoeing on the Chesapeake Bay or at the charming shops and restaurants you will find here. Ocean City is a hot spot for beachgoers on the Maryland coast. The white-sand beach, three-mile boardwalk, amusements, golf courses and boating draw thousands of visitors every summer. The "Central City of the Eastern Shore" and of the Delmarva Peninsula, Salisbury is home to Salisbury University. On the Chesapeake Bay side of the Eastern Shore is St. Michaels, a quaint port city. Chartered in 1804, St. Michaels now offers visitors an abundance of shops, marinas, restaurants, bed and breakfasts and country inns, as well as many Federal- and Victorian-period buildings.

WHAT TO SEE

CAMBRIDGE
J.M. CLAYTON COMPANY
108 Commerce St., Cambridge, 410-228-1661; www.jmclayton.com

This seafood company has been supplying the country with crabs and seafood since 1890. J.M. Clayton Company has remained in the family for more than four generations. This is a dirty job, but someone has to do it. J.M. Clayton Company picks the crabs and shucks the oysters by hand. Take a tour of the plant to see this longstanding tradition for yourself.

Admission: $5. By appointment only.

HIGHLIGHT

WHAT ARE THE TOP THINGS TO DO
IN EASTERN MARYLAND?

GET A QUICK HISTORY LESSON
Visit the Historical Society of Talbot County for a history lesson on the other side of the bay.

SOAK UP THE SUN
Take a stroll down the Ocean City Boardwalk where you'll discover arcades, shops, restaurants and the beach.

HEAD TO THE WATERFRONT
The lighthouse at the Chesapeake Maritime Museum is as important to this port town's history as oystering is to its people.

HARRIET TUBMAN MUSEUM & EDUCATION CENTER
424 Race St., Cambridge, 410-228-0401; www.harriettubman.com

Cambridge native, Harriet Tubman was born a slave only to become a famous conductor of the Underground Railroad. This museum highlights the many achievements of Harriet Tubman. There is a Harriet Tubman reenactor here to provide you with details about her life.

Tuesday-Friday 10 a.m.-3 p.m., Saturday noon-4 p.m.

RICHARDSON MARITIME MUSEUM
401 High St., Cambridge, 410-221-1871; www.richardsonmuseum.org

From model boats to tools, this museum is all about the town's most important aspect, the water. Explore more than 50 Chesapeake Bay wooden model boats, boatbuilding tools, and waterman's gear at this maritime museum.

Wednesday, Sunday 1-4 p.m., Saturday 10 a.m.-4 p.m.

RUARK BOATWORKS
103 Hayward St., Cambridge, 410-221-1871; www.richardsonmuseum.org

Part of the Richardson Maritime Museum, Ruark Boatworks is located on Cambridge Creek. Named after native boat designer and modeler, Harold Ruark, this museum is run by the James B. Richardson Foundation. The foundation is working to restore and preserve the 100-year-old Boatworks Building. With the mission to teach traditional wooden boatbuilding techniques, Ruark Boatworks is a great place to visit to get a taste of the Cambridge culture.

Monday, Wednesday, Friday 9 a.m.-2 p.m.

CHESAPEAKE BAY BRIDGE AREA
WYE OAK STATE PARK
Highway 662, Wye Mills, 410-820-1668; www.dnr.state.md.us

On the Eastern Shore in Talbot County, the park is approximately one mile from the junction of Routes 50 and 404. The official state tree of Maryland is in this 29-acre park; it is the largest white oak in the United States (108 feet high, 28 feet around) and is believed to be more than 460 years old. A new tree has even been started from one of its acorns. A restored 18th-century one-room schoolhouse and the Old Wye Mill (used since the late 1600s) are nearby.

EASTON
ACADEMY ART MUSEUM
106 South St., Easton, 410-822-2787; www.art-academy.org

Housed in a renovated 1820s schoolhouse, the Academy exhibits works by local and national artists in its permanent collection. It also hosts more than 250 visual and performing arts programs annually.

Admission: Free. Monday, Friday 10 a.m.-4 p.m., Tuesday-Thursday 10 a.m.-7 p.m., Saturday 10 a.m.-3 p.m.

HISTORICAL SOCIETY OF TALBOT COUNTY
25 S. Washington St., Easton, 410-822-0773; www.hstc.org

This Historical Society includes a three-gallery museum in a renovated early commercial building with changing exhibits and a museum shop. Also onsite are three historic houses including an 1810 Federal town house, a 1700s Quaker cabinetmaker's cottage, Forman's Studio as well as period gardens.

Admission: Free. Monday-Saturday 10 a.m.-4 p.m.

OCEAN CITY
ASSATEAGUE ISLAND NATIONAL SEASHORE
7206 National Seashore Lane, Berlin, 410-641-1441, 800-365-2267; www.nps.gov

Visitors interested in sandy beaches and wildlife should visit Assateague Island, which is about a four-hour drive from Baltimore. Straddling Maryland and Virginia, it contains a state park and wildlife refuge with swimming, hiking, canoeing, sea kayaking, biking and camping on the beach, as well as some of the best surf-fishing on the Atlantic Coast. The visitor center offers more information about the horses as well as the seashore's many activities.

Daily dawn-dusk.

BAHIA MARINA
2107 Herring Way, Ocean City, 410-289-7438; www.bahiamarina.com

The Bahia Marina is the place to go for boating rentals and tackle and bait. Charter fishing fleets leave from here to go offshore to fish for bluefish, marlin and tuna or to spot sharks and dolphins. You can take scenic cruises if you're not into fishing. There's also a restaurant here, Fish Tales, on the bay.

OCEAN CITY BEACH & BOARDWALK
S. Second St.-27 St., Ocean City

Ten miles of beach bring mobs of people out during warm weather to swim, surf, fish, boogie board, sunbathe, play on the beach and just enjoy the ocean.

The nearly three-mile boardwalk and pier is filled with shops, restaurants and amusements. Try to stay at the boardwalk long enough to see the sunset.
Daily.

SALISBURY
POPLAR HILL MANSION
117 Elizabeth St., Salisbury, 410-749-1776; www.poplarhillmansion.org

The Poplar Hill Mansion is an example of Georgian- and Federal-style architecture with Palladian and bull's-eye windows, large brass box locks on the doors and mantels and fireplaces. The interior is decorated with period furniture, and there is a country garden to peruse.
Admission: $3 (Tuesday-Saturday). Free Sunday.

ST. MICHAELS
CHESAPEAKE BAY MARITIME MUSEUM
Mill Street and Navy Point, St. Michaels, 410-745-2916; www.cbmm.org

This non-profit museum sits on the edge of the water at Navy Point in historic St. Michaels. This 18-acre museum campus includes a lighthouse, working boatyard, lookout tower and a few buildings with various exhibits inside. Learn about oystering on the Chesapeake onboard a skipjack. The Hooper Strait Lighthouse is one of the best parts of the museum. Built in 1879, the lighthouse once navigated boats through the tricky waters of the Hooper Strait. Discover all that the Chesapeake Bay has to offer at this one of a kind maritime museum.
Admission: adults $13, seniors $10, children 6-17 $6, children under 6 free. April-May, September-October, daily 10 a.m.-5 p.m.; June-August, daily 10 a.m.-6 p.m.; November-March, daily 10 a.m.-4 p.m.

THE FOOTBRIDGE
109 S. Talbot St., St. Michaels; www.stmichaelsmd.org

This footbridge joins Navy Point to Cherry Street and is the only bridge remaining of three. It is often called other names such as the "Sweetheart" or "Lovers'" bridge.

PATRIOT CRUISES
Chesapeake Bay Museum Dock, St. Michaels, 410-745-3100; www.patriotcruises.com

Take a one-hour narrated cruise aboard the *Patriot* on Miles River, which is part of the Chesapeake Bay Estuary.
Admission: adults $24.50, seniors $21, children 12-17 $12.50, children 3-11 $5. April-October, daily 11 a.m., 12:30 p.m., 2:30 p.m., 4 p.m.; March, November, Friday-Sunday 11 a.m., 12:30 p.m., 2:30 p.m., 4 p.m.

ST. MARY'S SQUARE
This public square was laid out in 1770 by Englishman James Braddock. Several buildings date to the early 1800s, including the Cannonball House and Dr. Miller's Farmhouse. The Ship's Carpenter Bell was cast in 1842; across from the bell stand two cannons, one dating from the Revolution, the other from the War of 1812.

WHERE TO STAY

CHESAPEAKE BAY BRIDGE AREA

★★★KENT MANOR INN

500 Kent Manor Drive, Stevensville, 410-643-7716, 800-820-4511; www.kentmanor.com

This historic 1820 inn sits among 220 wooded acres on picturesque Thompson Creek, a tributary to the Chesapeake Bay. Its location just 12 miles from Annapolis makes it a convenient spot for both business and leisure travelers. The luxurious and romantic guest rooms are beautifully decorated in Victorian style and feature four poster beds, Italian marble fireplaces, and stunning views of the grounds. Several rooms also have window seats and porches. There are many outdoor activities for guests to enjoy: a walk through the flower garden, an outdoor pool, and bike and paddleboat rentals. The Restaurant at Kent Manor is the perfect choice for a quiet, intimate fine-dining meal.

24 rooms. Restaurant. Complimentary breakfast. Pool. $61-150

OXFORD

★★★ROBERT MORRIS INN

314 N. Morris St., Oxford, 410-226-5111, 888-823-4012; www.robertmorrisinn.com

Rooms at the Robert Morris Inn include private porches with views of the Chesapeake Bay. Relax in an Adirondack chair on the inn's property, which stretches down to the water's edge. You can visit the nearby marine museum, go for a bike ride or scout for antiques in Oxford.

34 rooms. Complimentary breakfast. Closed December-March. No children under 10. Restaurant. $151-250

ST. MICHAELS

★★★THE INN AT PERRY CABIN

308 Watkins Lane, St. Michaels, 410-745-2200, 866-278-9601; www.perrycabin.com

Built just after the War of 1812, the Inn at Perry Cabin looks and feels like a manor house, with mahogany sleigh beds, antiques and views of the Miles River. Cycling, golfing and sailing are popular pastimes. The inn offers high tea and scones with Devonshire cream and shortbread served at evening turndown.

78 rooms. Restaurant, bar. Fitness center. Pool. Spa. $251-350

★★★ST. MICHAELS HARBOUR INN, MARINA & SPA

101 N. Harbor Road, St. Michaels, 410-745-9001, 800-955-9001; www.harbourinn.com

From this waterfront resort, visitors can take a short stroll down the main road to shops, museums and historical sites. Rooms are spacious and many have Jacuzzi tubs, panoramic views of the harbor and private balconies. The onsite Spa at Harbour Inn offers relaxing treatments after a day of activity around the bay.

46 rooms. Restaurant, bar. Pool. Spa. $251-350

RECOMMENDED

CAMBRIDGE

HYATT REGENCY CHESAPEAKE BAY GOLF RESORT, SPA AND MARINA

100 Heron Blvd., Cambridge, 410-901-1234; www.chesapeakebay.hyatt.com

Set right on the water, this hotel feels as if it's a world away. The beautiful grounds compliment the spectacular white castle on the river. Whether there with the family or significant other, the Hyatt Regency is bound to satisfy every need. Hit the spa for a bit of relaxation, or head to the water slide to awaken your inner child. Enjoy a nice meal at one of the three restaurants or eat poolside if that strikes your fancy. In the fall, roast s'mores by the fire pit and enjoy the sunset on the river.

400 rooms. Business Center. Restaurant, Bar. Pool. Golf. Spa. Tennis. Fitness Center. Pets accepted. $151-250

WHERE TO EAT

CHESAPEAKE BAY BRIDGE AREA
★★★NARROWS
3023 Kent Narrows Way South, Grasonville, 410-827-8113; www.thenarrowsrestaurant.com

This restaurant offers waterfront dining with a spectacular view of the Kent Narrows. The crab cakes are their signature; in fact, they have become so popular that the restaurant now ships them anywhere in the country.

American. Lunch, dinner, brunch. Children's menu. Bar. $36-85

EASTON
★★★RESTAURANT LOCAL
Tidewater Inn, 101 E. Dover St., Easton, 410-822-1300; www.tidewaterinn.com

Opened in 2006 as part of the Historic Tidewater Inn's renovations, Restaurant Local serves contemporary American cuisine in a modern but casual setting. Entrées include a local rockfish filet with shrimp and basil risotto, mushrooms and saffron butter, and filet mignon with roasted garlic potatoes, grilled asparagus and wild mushroom bordelaise.

American. Breakfast, lunch, dinner, Sunday brunch. Outdoor seating. Bar. $36-85

OCEAN CITY
★★★FAGER'S ISLAND
201 60th St., Ocean City, 410-524-5500, 888-371-5400; www.fagers.com

At Fager's Island, the outdoor deck overlooking the bay is the perfect spot to take in a glorious summer sunset. The menu excels at creative seafood preparations as well as classics like prime rib. Choose from a wine list that features over 500 bottles to accompany your meal. The Sunday brunch offers inventive and delicious dishes.

Pacific-Rim/Pan-Asian, seafood. Lunch, dinner, Sunday brunch. Reservations recommended. Outdoor seating. Children's menu. Bar. $16-35

★★★HOBBIT
101 81st St., Ocean City, 410-524-8100; www.thehobbitrestaurant.com

This restaurant serves many of your old favorites, as well as creative new items. The crab cakes are outstanding. For dessert, try the decadent Chambord cake, a yellow bundt cake with raspberry Chambord liqueur poured over it and doused in whipped cream.

American, seafood. Lunch, dinner. Reservations recommended. Bar. $16-35

ST. MICHAELS

★★★208 TALBOT

208 N. Talbot St., St. Michaels, 410-745-3838; www.208talbot.com

Chef Brendan Keegan puts a sophisticated, soulful twist on local ingredients, serving entrées including cornflake-crusted fried mahi mahi with basil potato salad, sweet corn cream and grape tomato relish; and braised pork shoulder with peach chutney, corn tamale and salsa roja. The atmosphere is as upscale and sophisticated as the cuisine, with rich décor and a knowledgeable waitstaff.

American. Dinner. Closed Sunday-Tuesday. Bar. $36-85

★★★SHERWOOD'S LANDING

308 Watkin Lane, St. Michaels, 410-745-2200, 866-278-9601; www.perrycabin.com

Located in the Inn at Perry Cabin, Sherwood Landing serves continental selections made with regional ingredients such as crab spring rolls with pink grapefruit, avocado and toasted almonds; and honey- and tarragon-glazed lamb shank with sun-dried tomato sauce.

American. Breakfast, lunch, dinner. Outdoor seating. Bar. $36-85

RECOMMENDED

CAMBRIDGE

BISTRO POPLAR

535 Poplar St., Cambridge, 410-228-4884; www.bistropoplar.com

Housed in the historic Hopkins Building, which dates back to 1895, Bistro Poplar has made quite a name for itself. This adorable French bistro keeps the historic tie between Dorchester County and France alive. Whether the onion soup gratinée or the farm raised quail, the taste of France is vibrant.

French. Lunch (Thursday-Monday), dinner, Sunday brunch. $36-85

CHESAPEAKE BAY BRIDGE AREA

HARRIS CRAB HOUSE

Kent Narrows Way North, Grasonville, 410-827-9500; www.harriscrabhouse.com

Just over the Bay Bridge lies this little slice of heaven. Harris Crab House offers spectacular views and fresh seafood year round. Grab a table outside on the patio, order a dozen or so crabs and watch the boats go by on the picturesque Chesapeake Bay. In the fall, opt for the rockfish sandwich—there is a good chance it was caught in the water surrounding you.

Seafood. Lunch, dinner. Children's menu. Outdoor Seating.

ST. MICHAELS

THE CRAB CLAW

304 Mill St., St. Michaels, 410-745-2900; www.thecrabclaw.com

This clam shucking and crabbing business turned into one of the best crab houses in 1965. Overlooking the water in historic St. Michaels, The Crab Claw yields fresh steamed Maryland crabs, a fully stocked raw bar and even Delmarva fried chicken. Get ready to get messy—this no frill crab joint is filled with tables covered with the crab feast signature brown paper. Of course, nothing goes better with crabs than an ice-cold beer and some Old Bay seasoning.

Seafood. March-November, Lunch, dinner. $16-35

WESTERN MARYLAND

Western Maryland is filled with mountains, valleys and plenty of history. Home of McDaniel College, Westminster is one of the historic towns in Western Maryland. Located in the heart of Western Maryland and the Great Appalachian Valley, Hagerstown exhibits the hometown feel for which Western Maryland is known. South Prospect Street is one of the city's oldest neighborhoods, listed on the National Register of Historic Places. Home of fearless Barbara Frietchie, who reportedly spoke her mind to Stonewall Jackson and his "rebel hordes," Frederick is a town filled with history. During the Civil War, Frederick was a focal point for strategic operations by both sides. It's also quite a charming town that is only an hour from Baltimore, perfect for a day trip. Cumberland is nestled between Pennsylvania and West Virginia in Western Maryland. George Washington, who once defended the town, thought the nation's primary east-west route would eventually pass through Cumberland. In 1833, the National Road made the town a supply terminus for overland commerce.

WHAT TO SEE

CUMBERLAND
FORT CUMBERLAND TRAIL
Cumberland

This walking trail covers several city blocks downtown around the site of Fort Cumberland. Boundary markers with narrative plaques lead you through sites such as Riverside Park, the Narrows, Allegany County Library, Folck's Mill and others.

THE NARROWS
Route 40, Cumberland

This picturesque 1,000-foot gap through the Alleghenies was used by pioneers on their way West. This is a great spot to photograph the surrounding beauty. There's also an old stone bridge that goes across Wills Creek.

ROCKY GAP STATE PARK
12500 Pleasant Valley Road N.E., Cumberland, 301-722-1480, 888-432-2267; www.dnr.state.md.us

Rocky Gap State Park covers 3,000 acres of mountain scenery around a 243-acre lake with three swimming beaches. Tourists and locals come here for the swimming, fishing, boating, nature and hiking trails. There's also picnicking, camping and lodging onsite. Activities include an 18-hole Jack Nicklaus golf course, playground, tennis and volleyball courts.

WESTERN MARYLAND SCENIC RAILROAD
13 Canal St., Cumberland, 301-759-4400, 800-872-4650; www.wmsr.com

This excursion train makes a scenic trip 17 miles through the Allegheny Mountains to Frostburg where you stop for lunch then take a trip through the Thrasher Carriage Museum and back. A narrator provides information about the history of the area. Passengers sit in restored coaches that have large picture

HIGHLIGHTS

WHAT ARE THE TOP THINGS TO DO IN WESTERN MARYLAND?

SAY CHEESE
Stop at The Narrows for a once in a lifetime photo opportunity. See the path the pioneers took to the West.

STROLL DOWNTOWN CUMBERLAND
The Fort Cumberland Trail winds through downtown, surrounding the site of Fort Cumberland.

SEE HISTORIC FREDERICK
Discover the sights and stories that downtown Frederick has to offer. Start at the Historical Society of Frederick County Museum.

windows, a snack car and gift shop. Tickets are available on the second floor of the Western Maryland Station.

Admission: adults $29, seniors $27, children $15. May-October, Thursday-Sunday, 11:30 a.m.; November-mid-December, Friday-Sunday, 11:30 a.m.

FREDERICK
BARBARA FRITCHIE HOUSE AND MUSEUM
154 W. Patrick St., 301-698-8992, Frederick; www.fredericktourism.org

This is the old home of Barbara Frietchie, who was the heroine in John Greenleaf Whittier's poem about the Civil War and a friend of Francis Scott Key. The house has been reconstructed and the exterior is available to view. For a look at the interior, call for an appointment.

HISTORICAL SOCIETY OF FREDERICK COUNTY MUSEUM
24 E. Church St., Frederick, 301-663-1188; www.hsfcinfo.org

This house, built in the early 1800s, shows both Georgian and Federal-style details in the center of downtown Frederick. Inside the house, portraits of early Frederick residents and tall case clocks are on display. The Heritage Garden features flower gardens, brick paths, trellises and grassy areas.

Admission: adults $3. Monday-Saturday 10 a.m.-4 p.m., Sunday 1-4 p.m. Closed first two weeks in January.

MONOCACY NATIONAL BATTLEFIELD
4801 Urbana Pike, Frederick, 301-662-3515; www.nps.gov

On July 9, 1864, Union General Lew Wallace and 5,000 men delayed General

Jubal Early and his 23,000 Confederate soldiers for 24 hours, during which Grant was able to reinforce and save Washington, D.C., New Jersey, Vermont and Pennsylvania. Confederate monuments mark the area.

Daily 8:30 a.m.-5 p.m.

MOUNT OLIVET CEMETERY

515 S. Market St., Frederick, 301-662-1164, 888-662-1164; www.mountolivetcemeteryinc.com

This beautiful cemetery houses the marked graves of Francis Scott Key and Barbara Frietchie, along with Governor Thomas Johnson, who was the first governor of Maryland. A flag flies over Key's grave.

HAGERSTOWN

HAGERSTOWN ROUNDHOUSE MUSEUM

300 S. Burhans Blvd., Hagerstown, 301-739-4665; www.roundhouse.org

The museum houses photograph exhibits of the seven railroads of Hagerstown, as well as historic railroad memorabilia, tools and equipment, archives of maps, books, papers and related items. There is also a gift shop.

Friday-Sunday 1-5 p.m.

JONATHAN HAGER HOUSE AND MUSEUM

Hagerstown City Park, 110 Key St., Hagerstown, 301-739-8393; www.fortedwards.org

This stone house located in Hagerstown City Park is the old home of Jonathan Hager, who was the co-founder of Hagerstown. Inside are authentic 18th-century furnishings as well as artifacts from the 18th and 19th century.

Admission: adults $3, seniors $2, children 6-12 $1. April-December, Tuesday-Saturday 10 a.m.-4 p.m., Sunday 2-5 p.m. Closed January-March.

MILLER HOUSE

135 W. Washington St., Hagerstown, 301-797-8782; www.msa.md.gov

This is the site of the Washington County Historical Society headquarters. This federal townhouse circa 1820 has a three-story spiral staircase, period furnishings and Bell pottery collections. There are also Chesapeake and Ohio Canal and Civil War exhibits and a 19th-century country store display.

Admission: adults $5, seniors $3, children 16 and under free. April-December, Wednesday-Saturday 1-4 p.m.

WASHINGTON COUNTY MUSEUM OF FINE ARTS

91 Key St., Hagerstown, 301-739-5727; www.wcmfa.org

Founded in 1929, this fine arts museum displays paintings, sculptures and changing exhibits. They also offer films, classes, concerts and lectures.

Tuesday-Friday 9 a.m.-5 p.m., Saturday 9 a.m.-4 p.m., Sunday 1-5 p.m.

WHERE TO EAT

CUMBERLAND

★★★AU PETIT PARIS

86 E. Main St., Frostburg, 301-689-8946;
www.aupetitparis.com

The atmosphere at this cozy French bistro is intimate and relaxed. The à la carte menu will satisfy even the most discriminating gourmet with dishes like duck a l'orange and le coq au vin. The wine cellar boasts the most extensive collection in western Maryland.

French. Dinner. Closed Sunday-Monday. Children's menu. Bar. $36-85

WESTMINSTER

★★★ANTRIM 1844

30 Trevanion Road, Taneytown, 410-756-6812, 800-858-1844; www.antrim1844.com

The Paris-trained chef at Antrim 1844 serves a unique menu each night, with entrées such as filet mignon with bacon and walnut, braised lamb volcano or porcupine shrimp. On a nice night, there isn't a better seat than on the spacious verandah overlooking the formal gardens.

American, French. Breakfast, dinner. Reservations recommended. Outdoor seating. Bar. $86 and up.

WELCOME TO NEW JERSEY

FROM INDUSTRIAL CITIES TO LUSH TREE-SHADED,

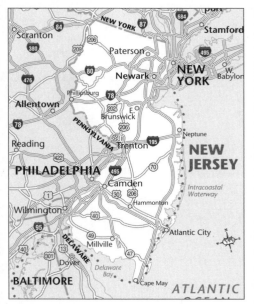

18th-century towns to small seaside communities, New Jersey is a state of contrasts. Hard-working areas such as Newark and Elizabeth might lead the unacquainted visitor to believe that the Garden State is a misnomer, but traveling deeper into New Jersey—out of the cities and off the highways—will reveal the flourishing greenery that earned the state its nickname.

The swampy meadows west of the New Jersey Turnpike have been reclaimed and transformed into commercial and industrial areas. The Meadowlands, a multimillion-dollar sports complex, offers horse racing, the New York Giants and the New York Jets NFL football teams and the New Jersey Devils NHL hockey team. But commercial and industrial interests have reached only so far into the state's natural resources. More than 800 lakes and ponds, 100 rivers and streams and 1,400 miles of freshly stocked trout streams are scattered throughout the state's wooded, scenic northwest corner. The coastline, stretching 127 miles from Sandy Hook to Cape May, is a summer vacation destination for many.

New Jersey is also rich in history. George Washington spent a quarter of his time as commander-in-chief of the Revolutionary Army here. On Christmas night in 1776, he crossed the Delaware and surprised the Hessians at Trenton. A few days later, he marched to Princeton and defeated three British regiments. He then spent the winter in Morristown, where the memories of his campaign are preserved in a national historical park.

BEST ATTRACTIONS

NEW JERSEY'S BEST ATTRACTIONS

PRINCETON
Check out New Jersey's Ivy League college, Princeton. The charming campus and town is a lovely place to stroll through.

LIBERTY STATE PARK
Visit Liberty State Park to get a great view of Lady Liberty. The picturesque skyline of Manhattan is just across the bay.

THE JERSEY SHORE
Head to the beach for some sun and good old-fashioned fun. Many of the popular beaches have large boardwalks.

ATLANTIC CITY
Casinos dazzle the waterfront at night and umbrellas dot the beach during the day. While the boardwalk retains its zaniness, Atlantic City has been undergoing a transformation in recent years.

VERNON
Hit the slopes in Vernon for some winter fun. Summertime? Vernon also boasts a water park.

DELAWARE RIVER REGION

This area along the Delaware River border is rich in history and charming towns. Camden's growth as the leading industrial, marketing and transportation center of southern New Jersey dates from post-Civil War days. Its location across the Delaware River from Philadelphia prompted large companies such as Campbell's Soup (national headquarters) to establish plants here. Visitors will want to stop in Camden to see the aquarium.

Haddonfield is named for Elizabeth Haddon, a 20-year-old Quaker girl whose father sent her here from England in 1701 to develop 400 acres of land. This assertive young woman built a house, started a colony and proposed to a Quaker missionary who promptly married her.

Its lush campus and small-town charm have made Princeton a popular backdrop for numerous films and TV shows over the years. But don't expect to find any Hollywood glitz here. This town is all about quiet elegance, rich history and deep intellect. History buffs will relish the breadth of notable sites it contains, from the homes of Albert Einstein and Woodrow Wilson to an American Revolution battleground. And for those who prefer to leave history in the past, there's still plenty to enjoy in this highly walkable small city: cozy eateries, inviting shops, hiking trails and plenty of culture.

The capital of New Jersey since 1790, Trenton is one of the fastest-growing business and industrial areas in the country and has been a leading rubber-manu-facturing center since colonial times.

WHAT TO SEE

CAMDEN
CAMDEN COUNTY HISTORICAL SOCIETY-POMONA HALL
1900 Park Blvd., Camden, 856-964-3333; www.cchsnj.com

The Historical Society is located in this brick Georgian house that belonged to descendants of William Cooper, an early Camden settler. The exhibits focus on regional history and include antique glass, lamps, toys, early hand tools, fire-fighting equipment and Victor Talking Machines. The library has more than 20,000 books, as well as maps from the 17th century to the present, newspapers from the 18th to the 20th century and more.

Mansion/Museum Tours: Tuesday-Thursday, Sunday, noon-3:30 p.m.

NEW JERSEY STATE AQUARIUM
1 Riverside Drive, Camden, 856-365-0352; www.adventureaquarium.com

This home to more than 4,000 total fish of some 500 species is just minutes across the Ben Franklin Bridge in Camden, on the Delaware River waterfront. Curious kids can find out how fish sleep and which fish can change from male to female and back again. You will also find exhibits of seals, penguins, sharks, turtles and tropical fish, as well as elaborate rain forest, water filtration and conservation awareness displays.

Admission: adults $21.95, children 2-12 $17.95. Daily 9:30 a.m.-5 p.m.

TOMB OF WALT WHITMAN
Harleigh Cemetery, 1640 Haddon Ave., Camden, 856-963-0122; www.harleighcemetery.org

This is the final resting place of Walt Whitman. The vault of the "good gray poet," designed by the poet himself, is of rough-cut stone with a grillwork door.

Monday-Saturday 8:30 a.m.-4:30 p.m.

U.S.S. NEW JERSEY
62 Battleship Place, Camden, 856-966-1652, 866-877-6262; www.battleshipnewjersey.org

The United States Navy permanently berthed the *USS New Jersey* (or "Big J"), one of the nation's largest and most decorated battleships, at the Camden Waterfront in 2000 and transformed it into a floating museum. First launched in 1942, the ship was commissioned for operations during World War II at Iwo Jima and Okinawa. The ship conducted its last mission, providing fire support to Marines in embattled Beirut, Lebanon, in 1983. Military history

HIGHLIGHT

WHAT ARE THE TOP THINGS TO DO IN THE DELAWARE RIVER REGION?

VISIT PRINCETON
Stroll through this stunning, 500-acre Ivy League campus that has a long list of prominent alumni including Michelle Obama and F. Scott Fitzgerald.

GO FISH
Gaze at the exhibits at the New Jersey State Aquarium that feature 4,000 total fish of some 500 species at this aquarium that is just minutes across the Ben Franklin Bridge in Camden, on the Delaware River waterfront.

GET AT TASTE OF COLONIAL AMERICA
Visit Trenton's oldest building, the William Trent House, built in 1719. It was the home of chief Justice William Trent, for whom the city was named.

buffs will be awed by the guided two-hour tour through this 887-foot, 11-story, 212,000-horsepower, Iowa-class ship. Big J is available for special events, retreats and overnight encampments.

Tour: adults $18.50, seniors, veterans and children 6-11 $14, children under 6 and military personnel free.

WALT WHITMAN ARTS CENTER
Second and Cooper streets, Camden, 856-964-8300; www.waltwhitmancenter.org

Providing art programs to Camden, this art center features poetry readings, concerts, performances, a children's theater and gallery exhibits.

Hours and schedules vary; see website for information.

WALT WHITMAN HOUSE STATE HISTORIC SITE
328 Mickle Blvd., Camden, 856-964-5383; www.waltwhitman.org

The last residence of the poet and the only house he ever owned; he lived here from 1884 until his death on March 26, 1892. It contains original furnishings, including the bed in which Whitman died, as well as books and photographs, Whitman's death notice and mementos.

Admission: adults $5, seniors and students $4, children under 6 free. Mid-June-August, Monday-Friday 11 a.m.-4 p.m., Saturday-Sunday 11 a.m.-5 p.m.; September-mid-June, Wednesday-Friday 1-4 p.m., Saturday-Sunday 11 a.m.-4 p.m.

HADDONFIELD

GREENFIELD HALL

343 Kings Highway E. (Route 41), Haddonfield, 856-429-7375;
www.historicalsocietyofhaddonfield.org

Haddonfield's Historical Society headquarters is situated in the old Gill House and contains personal items of Elizabeth Haddon including furniture, costumes and a doll collection. There is also the Boxwood garden and a library on local history here. Also on the grounds is a house once owned by Elizabeth Haddon. *Library: Tuesday, Thursday 9:30-11:30 a.m., first Sunday of each month 1-3 p.m. Museum: Wednesday-Friday 1-4 p.m., first Sunday of the month 1-3 p.m. Closed August.*

INDIAN KING TAVERN MUSEUM STATE HISTORIC SITE

233 Kings Highway E., Haddonfield, 856-429-6792

Built as an inn, state legislatures met here frequently, including when they passed a bill in 1777 substituting "State" for "Colony" in all state papers. The museum has colonial furnishings.
Wednesday-Friday, Saturday 10 a.m.-noon, 1-4 p.m. Sunday 1-4 p.m.

THE SITE OF THE ELIZABETH HADDON HOUSE

Wood Lane and Merion Avenue, Haddonfield

Isaac Wood built this house in 1842, on the foundation of Elizabeth Haddon's 1713 brick mansion, immediately after it was destroyed by fire. The original brew house Haddon built and the English yew trees she brought over from England in 1712 are in the yard. This is a private residence and is not open to the public.

PRINCETON

BAINBRIDGE HOUSE

158 Nassau St., Princeton, 609-921-6748; www.princetonhistory.org

Built by a prosperous tanner in 1766 and fully restored in 1992, the Bainbridge House now serves as headquarters for the Historical Society of Princeton. Both inside and out, much of the original structure remains—from the wall paneling right down to the flooring. It also houses exhibitions, a library and a museum shop, and is the point of departure for guided walking tours of the historic district (Sundays at 2 p.m., weather permitting).
Tuesday-Sunday noon-4 p.m.

MCCARTER THEATRE

91 University Place, Princeton, 609-258-2787; www.mccarter.org

This leading regional theatre stages more than 200 performances each year, including drama, dance and music, as well as special events and programs. Its offerings are so impressive that the McCarter earned a Tony award in 1994 for Outstanding Regional Theatre.
See website for schedule and ticket information.

MORVEN MUSEUM & GARDEN

55 Stockton St., Princeton, 609-924-8144; www.historicmorven.org

In the past, this National Historic Landmark housed Richard Stockton (a signer of the Declaration of Independence) and more recently, New Jersey governors. These days, it's home to galleries that display New Jersey-themed artwork; a historic garden with majestic trees, heirloom annuals from the 18th and 19th centuries, and a re-creation of Morven's Colonial-Revival-style garden; and a museum shop with pottery, books, stationery and garden-related items.

Admission: adults $5, seniors and students $4. April-October, Wednesday-Friday 11 a.m.-3 p.m., Saturday-Sunday noon-4 p.m. Tours: Wednesday-Friday 11:15 a.m., 12:15, 1:15, 2:15 p.m., Saturday-Sunday 12:15, 1:15, 2:15, 3:15 p.m.

NASSAU HALL
Princeton University, Princeton, 609-258-3000; www.princeton.edu

The first thing you'll notice about Princeton University's Nassau Hall are the two big, bronze tigers (the school's mascot) that flank its entrance. Nassau Hall has been the epicenter of the university's campus from the time it was built in 1756. During the Revolution, it served as a barracks and hospital, and in 1776, New Jersey's first legislature met there. These days, it houses the university's administrative offices, including that of the president.

PRINCETON BATTLE MONUMENT
Monument Drive and Stockton streets, Princeton, 609-921-0074; www.state.nj.us

Take a drive through Princeton and you can't miss it: The work of Beaux Arts sculptor Frederick W. MacMonnies (who had help from architect Thomas Hastings), this massive limestone monument commemorates the famous 1777 Battle of Princeton, in which George Washington's troops defeated the British. The sculpture depicts Washington leading his troops into battle, along with the death of General Hugh Mercer.

PRINCETON CEMETERY
Nassau Presbyterian Church, Witherspoon and Wiggens streets, Princeton, 609-924-1369; www.princetonol.com/groups/cemetery

This cemetery houses some of Princeton's most beloved and well-known figures from throughout history. It includes a Presidents' Plot of former university presidents (among them Aaron Burr Sr., Jonathan Edwards and John Witherspoon), a monument to Grover Cleveland and the grave of Paul Tulane, for whom Tulane University was named.

PRINCETON UNIVERSITY
Princeton, 609-258-3000; www.princeton.edu

Stroll through this stunning, 500-acre campus, and you may run into a future president, senator or Pulitzer Prize-winning author. Founded in 1746, this Ivy League institution is the fourth-oldest college in the U.S. Its long list of prominent alumni includes Michelle Obama, F. Scott Fitzgerald, George F. Kennan, John Nash, Ralph Nader and Jonathan Safran Foer. The sprawling campus contains 180 buildings, and serves about 5,000 undergraduate and 2,500 graduate students.

PRINCETON UNIVERSITY ART MUSEUM
Princeton University, Princeton, 609-258-3788; www.princetonartmuseum.org

Like a typical Princeton University overachiever, this art museum is one of the most ambitious around. Its collections include some 72,000 works, ranging from antiquities to contemporary, and including Manet, Monet and Warhol. The museum presents about a dozen special exhibitions every year, and also offers lectures, artist talks, scholarly symposia, concerts, film screenings and family programs.

Admission: free. Tuesday-Wednesday, Friday-Saturday 10 a.m.-5 p.m., Thursday 10 a.m.-10 p.m., Sunday 1-5 p.m.

THE PUTNAM COLLECTION OF SCULPTURE

Princeton University, Princeton; www.princeton.edu

Embark on your own artwork treasure hunt by tracking down all 20 works in this leading collection of outdoor 20th-century sculpture. Scattered throughout the university's 500-acre campus, the collection includes Picasso's *Head of a Woman*, Calder's *Five Disks: One Empty* and Moore's *Oval with Points*. The collection serves as a memorial for Princeton alumnus John Putnam, Jr., who died in World War II.

WOODROW WILSON SCHOOL OF PUBLIC AND INTERNATIONAL AFFAIRS

Princeton University, Robertson Hall, Princeton, 609-258-2943; www.princeton.edu

The striking Robertson Hall, with tapered columns and gray glass windows, was designed by Minoru Yamasaki, the architect of the World Trade Center. The building is meant to invoke a modern Greek temple, right down to its marble floors. Outside, there's Scudder Plaza, home to the popular penny depository/reflecting pool/sculpture Fountain of Freedom by James Fitzgerald.

TRENTON
COLLEGE OF NEW JERSEY

Trenton, 609-771-1855; www.tcnj.edu

Founded in 1855, this 289-acre wooded campus has 5,900 students and is located within a suburban community. The highly selective liberal arts college offers seven different schools in which students can study and has gained national recognition.

JOHNSON FERRY HOUSE STATE HISTORIC SITE

Washington Crossing State Park, 355 Washington Crossing, Titusville, 609-737-2515; www.state.nj.us

Located in Washington Crossing State Park, this building sheltered General Washington and some of his men on December 25, 1776 after they had crossed the Delaware from Pennsylvania. It is believed that the strategy for the attack on Trenton was discussed here.

Monday-Sunday 9 a.m.-4 p.m.

NEW JERSEY STATE MUSEUM

205 W. State St., Trenton, 609-292-6464; www.newjerseystatemuseum.org

Adjacent to the Capitol, this museum is like having four museums in one as it covers archaeology and ethnology; cultural history, fine art; and natural history. Check out the Planetarium with cutting-edge technology used in their Full Dome Video that feels like you're looking at the entire solar system.

Admission: Free. Tuesday-Sunday, Saturday 9 a.m.-5 p.m., Sunday noon-5 p.m.

OLD BARRACKS MUSEUM

Barrack St., Trenton, 609-396-1776; www.barracks.org

One of the finest examples of colonial barracks in the United States. Built between 1758 and 1759, it housed British, Hessian and Continental troops during the Revolutionary War. The museum contains restored soldiers' squad room, antique furniture, ceramics, firearms and dioramas. Tour guides in period costumes take you around and give you an overview of everything.

Admission: adults $8, seniors and children 6-18 $6, children under 6 free. Daily 10 a.m.-5 p.m.

SESAME PLACE

100 Sesame Road, Langhorne, 215-752-7070; www.sesameplace.com

If your children love Oscar, Elmo and Big Bird, this family play park featuring characters from *Sesame Street* is the perfect place to take them. This park has everything kids will love: a water park, shows and parades, *Sesame Street* characters, rides and other attractions.

Admission: adults and children 2-18 $50.95, seniors $45.95, children under 2 free. Hours vary; see website for information.

WASHINGTON CROSSING STATE PARK

355 Washington Crossing-Pennington Road, Titusville, 609-737-0623; www.state.nj.us

This 3,126-acre park commemorates the famous crossing on Christmas night, 1776, by the Continental Army under the command of General George Washington. There are nature trails, picnicking areas, campsites, a playground, a visitor center and a nature center. There's also an open-air summer theater. The Johnson Ferry House is also located here.

Admission: $5 per vehicle. Visitor center and Museum: Monday-Sunday 9 a.m.-4 p.m.

WILLIAM TRENT HOUSE

15 Market St., Trenton, 609-989-3027; www.williamtrenthouse.org

Trenton's oldest building, the William Trent House, built in 1719, is an example of Georgian architecture. It was the home of chief Justice William Trent, for whom the city was named. Also here is a colonial garden filled with vegetables, and programs are offered to learn about gardening methods of the 18th century.

Admission: Free. Daily 12:30-4 p.m.

WHERE TO STAY

HADDONFIELD

★★★HADDONFIELD INN

44 West End Ave., Haddonfield, 856-428-2195, 800-269-0014; www.haddonfieldinn.com

Located in a Victorian home, the Haddonfield Inn offers well-appointed rooms and suites with varying styles and themes, including the Dolley Madison Room, with an antique desk, Franklin stove and pewter light fixtures, and the Dublynn Room, with antiques and a lace-canopied, four-poster King bed. All rooms feature fireplaces and high-speed Internet access. Each morning, a gourmet breakfast is served in the dining room or on the wraparound porch and complimentary beverages, coffee, tea and snacks are available throughout the day.

9 rooms. Complimentary breakfast. Pets accepted. $151-250

PRINCETON

★★★HYATT REGENCY PRINCETON
102 Carnegie Center, Princeton, 609-987-1234; princeton.hyatt.com

Nestled on 16 acres of landscaped property, this hotel is close to Princeton's business center, train station, university—just about anywhere you'd want to be. It's not exactly a walkable area, but a complimentary shuttle will take you anywhere within a five-mile radius of the property.

347 rooms. Restaurant, bar. Business center. Fitness center. Pool. Tennis. $251-350

★★★PRINCETON MARRIOTT HOTEL & CONFERENCE CENTER AT FORRESTAL
100 College Road East, Princeton, 609-452-7800, 800-943-6709; www.marriott.com

Located on 25 wooded acres, this newly renovated hotel offers a full-service spa, along with a health club, pool and jogging and recreational facilities. Spacious guest rooms are bright and cheery and feature a work desk, refrigerator and wireless Internet access. Enjoy a burger and a cold beer at Barley's Pub, or opt for a heartier meal at the Fireside Grill, a casual steakhouse.

300 rooms. Restaurant, bar. Business center. Fitness center. Pool. Spa. $251-350

TRENTON

★★★TRENTON MARRIOTT AT LAFAYETTE YARD
1 W. Lafayette St., Trenton, 609-421-4000, 888-796-4662; www.marriott.com

New Jersey's capital city is home to this downtown hotel, located near a number of historical sites, family activities and sports facilities. Like all Marriott hotels, the Lafayette Yard is created with comfort in mind; guest rooms offer luxurious linens, fluffy comforters and pillows, and a host of amenities like in-room coffee and tea and high-speed Internet access. Archives Restaurant offers a casual and comfortable setting along with an appetizing American menu for breakfast, lunch and dinner, while the Archives Bar and Lounge features lighter fare.

197 rooms. Restaurant, bar. Business center. Fitness center. $151-250

RECOMMENDED

PRINCETON

THE NASSAU INN
10 Palmer Square East, Princeton, 609-921-7500, 800-862-7728; www.nassauinn.com

This historic hotel has deep roots. Dating back to its days as the College Inn in 1769, it has provided shelter for Paul Revere, Robert Morris and Thomas Paine, along with signers of the Declaration of Independence, who stopped by in 1776 on their way to Philadelphia. Its rooms offer "18th-century elegance and 21st-century comfort"—after all, Revere wouldn't have had an in-room wet bar or iPod docking station at his disposal. Downstairs, there's the Yankee Doodle Tap room—a popular local restaurant that serves up contemporary American fare.

203 rooms. Restaurant, bar. Business center. Fitness center. $251-350

WHERE TO EAT

CAMDEN
★★★BRADDOCK'S TAVERN
39 S. Main St., Medford Village, 609-654-1604; www.braddocks.com

This casual restaurant features traditional American cuisine with European influences. Don't miss the cooking classes held throughout the year and other fun events like wine tastings.

American. Lunch, dinner, Sunday brunch. Bar. $16-35

PRINCETON
★★★TRE PIANI
120 Rockingham Row, Princeton, 609-452-1515; www.trepiani.com

In its dining room, bistro and banquet space, Tre Piani (meaning three floors in Italian) serves up tempting entrées like grilled smoked rib-eye steak with creamy local polenta, mushroom and green onion sauce; Osso Buco with saffron-scented risotto; and roasted chicken breast with whipped potatoes, lemon-tarragon jus and fresh asparagus.

Italian, Mediterranean. Lunch (Monday-Friday), dinner. Closed Sunday. Outdoor seating. Bar. $35-86

RECOMMENDED

PRINCETON
BLUE POINT GRILL
258 Nassau St., Princeton, 609-921-1211; bluepoint.jmgroupprinceton.com

Wishing you'd opted for the beach instead of the suburbs? This restaurant will transport you straight to the sea, with an ever-changing menu that features fresh seafood and shellfish, along with staples like crab cakes, a raw bar and New England clam chowder.

Seafood. Dinner. Outdoor seating. $35-86

MEDITERRA
29 Hulfish St., Princeton, 609-252-9680; www. mediterrarestaurant.com

Overlooking Princeton's charming Palmer Square, Mediterra offers casual cuisine from the 21 countries that surround the Mediterranean Sea, with an emphasis on Italy and Spain. Ingredients are locally sourced when possible. Entrées include dishes like classic paella; Moroccan scallops with chickpea polenta, Swiss chard and spiced carrots; and grass-fed New York strip steak with red bliss potatoes, ceci beans and greens.

Italian, Spanish, Mediterranean. Lunch, dinner. Outdoor seating. Bar. $35-86

WHERE TO SHOP

PRINCETON
JAZAMS
25 Palmer Square East, Princeton, 609-924-8697; www.jazams.com

Whether you need a gift for the little one in your life or just want to indulge your Peter Pan Syndrome, a visit to this toy store will transport you back to

childhood lickety split. Jazams specializes in unique toys, books and music for children of all ages that you're unlikely to see in big-box or chain stores—that includes organic stuffed animals and bacon versus tofu action figures.
Monday-Saturday 10 a.m.-9 p.m., Sunday 11 a.m.-5 p.m.

NEARLY NEW SHOP
234 Nassau St., Princeton, 609-924-5720

Housed above a liquor store and accessed via alleyway, you might think Nearly New required a secret knock for entry. Consignment shops are key players on the Princeton shopping scene, and this is one is a favorite among locals. Enhance your wardrobe with styles from Polo, Lilly Pulitzer, Tommy Hilfiger and more.
Monday-Saturday 10 a.m.-4 p.m.

PRINCETON CONSIGNMENT BOUTIQUE
1378 U.S. 206, Skillman, 609-924-2288

We weren't kidding about the plethora of consignment shops in town. You'll find plenty of upscale, heavy-hitting designers in this store—think Louis Vuitton, Jimmy Choo, Kate Spade, Prada, Gucci—and plenty of couture, too. Locals swear by it as their go-to shop for anything from jeans to eveningwear.
Monday-Wednesday, Friday 10 a.m.-6 p.m., Thursday 10 a.m.-7 p.m., Saturday 10:30 a.m.-5 p.m.

PRINCETON RECORD EXCHANGE
20 South Tulane St., Princeton, 609-921-0881; www.prex.com

Established in 1980, back when vinyl still reigned supreme, the Record Exchange carries plenty of LPs—along with a more modern assortment of CDs and DVDs. Come with an armful of your old music, and you'll receive cash or store credit. Browse through the 140,000 new and used CDs, records and movies, and you're likely to leave with a new armful to add to your own collection. Don't miss the hidden gems in the "Cheap CD" section, where more than 20,000 discs are priced at $4.99 or less.
Monday-Saturday 10 a.m.-9 p.m., Sunday 11 a.m.-6 p.m.

THE GATEWAY

The Gateway is made up of towns considered suburbs of New York City. Many commuters live the quiet life here when they're able to escape from the busy city life. It was in the small town of Edison that Thomas Edison invented the phonograph and perfected the first practical incandescent light. Located on the Hudson River, due west of the southern end of Manhattan Island, Jersey City is now the second-largest city in New Jersey. On the south bank of the Raritan River, New Brunswick is both a college town and a diversified commercial and retail city.

Once a strict Puritan settlement, Newark has grown to become the largest city in the state and one of the country's leading manufacturing cities. Located directly north of Newark is the city of Paterson. Named after Governor William Paterson, this city owes its present and historic eminence as an industrial city to Alexander Hamilton. He was the first to realize the possibility of harnessing the Great Falls of the Passaic River for industrial purposes.

Only eight miles from New York City, Rutherford is popular for commuters to and from the city. It's home to the Meadowlands, home of the New York Jets and

HIGHLIGHTS

WHAT ARE THE TOP THINGS TO DO IN THE GATEWAY?

SEE LADY LIBERTY
At Liberty State Park, you're less than 2,000 feet from The Statue of Liberty. Be sure to pack a camera for the breathtaking vistas.

CATCH A JETS OR GIANTS GAME
Head to the Meadowlands for a football game. Both the New York Jets and the New York Giants call the Meadowlands home.

BE ONE WITH NATURE
Venture to the Great Falls Historic District Cultural Center for relaxing picnic areas with the 77-foot falls in the background.

ENROLL IN A TOUR
Tour Rutgers University for a look at college life in New Jersey.

New York Giants and Meadowlands Racetrack. West Orange is only 17 miles from New York City, making it a convenient commuter suburb.

WHAT TO SEE

EDISON
EDISON MEMORIAL TOWER AND MENLO PARK MUSEUM
37 Christie St., Edison, 732-248-7298; www.menloparkmuseum.com
A 131-foot tower topped by a 13 ½-foot-high electric light bulb stands at the birthplace of recorded sound. Edison's other inventions are also here.
Thursday-Saturday 10 a.m.-4 p.m.

JERSEY CITY
LIBERTY SCIENCE CENTER
Liberty State Park, 222 Jersey City Blvd, Jersey City, 201-200-1000; www.lsc.org
This four-story structure encompasses environment, health and invention areas that feature more than 250 hands-on exhibits. A geodesic dome houses an IMAX theater with a six-story screen featuring fascinating animal and nature films.
Admission: adults $15.75, children 2-12 and seniors $11.50, children under 2 free. September-June, Monday-Friday 9 a.m.-4 p.m., Saturday-Sunday 9 a.m.-5 p.m.; July-August, Monday-Friday 9 a.m.-5 p.m., Saturday-Sunday 9 a.m.-6 p.m.

LIBERTY STATE PARK
Morris Pesin Drive, Jersey City, 201-915-3400; www.libertystatepark.org

Liberty State Park is located just off the New Jersey Turnpike, on the New York Harbor, less than 2,000 feet from the Statue of Liberty. It offers breathtaking views of the New York City skyline; a flag display includes state, historic and U.S. flags; a boat launch; a fitness course, and a picnic area. The historic railroad terminal has been partially restored. The Interpretive Center houses an exhibit area; adjacent to the Center is a 60-acre natural area consisting mostly of salt marsh. Nature trails and observation points complement this wildlife habitat. Boat tours and ferries to Ellis Island and Statue of Liberty are available.

Daily 6 a.m.-10 p.m.

NEW BRUNSWICK

BUCCLEUCH MANSION AND PARK
George Street and Easton Avenue, New Brunswick, 732-745-5094

This mansion was built in 1739 by Anthony White, the son-in-law of Lewis Morris, a colonial governor of New Jersey. It features rooms with period furnishings. The park offers athletic fields, a fitness trail, a playground, gardens and a picnic area.

June-October, Sunday 2-4 p.m.

GEORGE STREET PLAYHOUSE
9 Livingston Ave., New Brunswick, 732-246-7717; www.georgestplayhouse.org

This nationally recognized regional theater offers a six-show season of plays and musicals, such as *The Seafarer*, as well as touring Outreach program for students.

Tuesday-Sunday.

JANE VOORHEES ZIMMERLI ART MUSEUM
Rutgers University, George and Hamilton streets, New Brunswick, 732-932-7237;
www.zimmerlimuseum.rutgers.edu

This museum holds paintings from early 16th century through the present with changing exhibits.

Admission: $3, children under 18 free. Tuesday-Friday 10 a.m.-4:30 p.m., Saturday-Sunday noon-5 p.m.

RUTGERS-THE STATE UNIVERSITY OF NEW JERSEY
126 College Ave., New Brunswick, 732-932-1766; www.rutgers.edu

Founded in 1766, Rutgers consists of three campuses in Newark, Camden and New Brunswick, including 27 schools and colleges serving more than 50,000 students at all levels through postdoctoral studies; the main campus is on College Avenue.

THE RUTGERS GARDENS
Rutgers University, 112 Ryder's Lane (Route 1), New Brunswick, 732-932-8451;
www.rutgersgardens.rutgers.edu

Here, you'll find extensive gardens including the largest display of American hollies, shrub collections, rhododendrons, azaleas, evergreens and more.

Tour Admission: adults $10, seniors $8, children $5; Saturday, adults $12, seniors $10, children $5. Monday-Saturday.

NEWARK

NEW JERSEY HISTORICAL SOCIETY

52 Park Place, Newark, 973-596-8500; www.jerseyhistory.org

This museum has collections of paintings, prints, furniture and decorative arts. There is also a reference and research library of state and local history including manuscripts, documents and maps.

Admission: $4 (suggested donation). Society: Tuesday-Saturday 10 a.m.-5 p.m. Library: Wednesday-Thursday, Saturday noon-5 p.m.

NEW JERSEY NETS (NBA)

Prudential Center, 165 Mulberry St., Newark, www.njnets.com

New Jersey's professional basketball team, the New Jersey Nets, hasn't been good in years. But the 2010-2011 season is looking up for them, as they have just acquired Brian Zoubek of Duke and Jordan Farmar of the Lakers, both recent champions. Rumor has it that the New Jersey Nets will be moving back to New York in 2012 to play at new Barclays Center. In the meantime, the Nets will be playing at the Prudential Center in Newark.

NEW JERSEY PERFORMING ARTS CENTER

1 Center St., Newark, 973-297-5857, 888-466-5722, 973-642-8989; www.njpac.org

This is the home to New Jersey Symphony Orchestra.

See website for schedule and ticket information.

NEWARK MUSEUM

49 Washington St., Newark, 973-596-6550; www.newarkmuseum.org

This museum of art and science features changing exhibitions including American paintings and sculpture; American and European decorative arts; classical art; and more. Also here are the Junior Museum, Mini Zoo, Dreyfuss Planetarium and the Newark Fire Museum. There are special programs, lectures, concerts and a café serving lunch.

Admission: adults $10, children, seniors and students $6. Planetariaum: adults $3, children under 12, seniors and students $2. Wednesday-Friday noon-5 p.m.; October-June, Saturday-Sunday 10 a.m.-5 p.m.; July-September, Saturday-Sunday noon-5 p.m.

SYMPHONY HALL

1020 Broad St., Newark, 973-643-4550; www.newarksymphonyhall.org

In 1925 this 2,811-seat auditorium was built by the Shriner's Salaam Temple, it is now home to the New Jersey State Opera, the New Jersey Ballet Company and the Theatre of Universal Images. Also here is the famous Terrace Ballroom, which is a large meeting space used for dance classes, weddings and more.

See website for schedules and ticket information.

PATERSON

GREAT FALLS HISTORIC DISTRICT CULTURAL CENTER

155 Market St., Paterson, 973-321-9587; www.patersonnj.gov

The Great Falls district includes 77-foot-high falls, a park and picnic area, a renovated raceway system and restored 19th-century buildings.

Monday-Friday 8:30 a.m.-4.30 p.m.

LAMBERT CASTLE

Garret Mountain Reservation, 3 Valley Road, Paterson, 973-247-0085;
www.lambertcastle.com

Built by an English immigrant who rose to wealth as a silk manufacturer, the 1893 castle of brownstone and granite houses a local history museum, restored period rooms, an art history gallery and a library.

Grounds: Daily dawn-dusk.

RIFLE CAMP PARK

Rifle Camp Road, West Paterson, 973-881-4832

This 158-acre park is 584 feet above sea level. It includes nature and geology trails, nature center with astronomical observatory, walking paths, a fitness course and picnic areas.

Daily.

RUTHERFORD

MEADOWLANDS RACETRACK

50 State Route 120, East Rutherford, 201-843-2446; www.thebigm.com

The suburban leafy Meadowlands complex offers fine thoroughbred racing from September through mid-December and harness racing for the remainder of the year.

Wednesday-Sunday.

NEW YORK GIANTS (NFL)

New Meadowlands Stadium, 50 Highway 120, East Rutherford, 201-935-8111; www.giants.com

The New York Giants call East Rutherford "home". Playing in their fair share of Super Bowls and NFC championships, the Giants most recently won the title in 2007. An off-and-on again team, the Giants' roster has included stars such as Tiki Barber, Eli Manning and Plaxico Burress. Beginning the 2010 season in the new $1.6 billion New Meadowlands Stadium, the New York Giants have plenty to work toward. The stadium includes its own rail stop, for easy access to the games.

NEW YORK JETS (NFL)

New Meadowlands Stadium, 50 Highway 120, East Rutherford, 201-583-7000, 800-469-5387; www.newyorkjets.com

New York's other professional football team, the Jets, will share the brand new stadium with the Giants. The Jets have struggled over the years in the AFC. With players such as Mark Sanchez and Leon Washington, it's hard to believe they aren't a better team. Hopefully the New Meadowlands Stadium will help; with all its amenities, maybe it will help the Jets.

WEST ORANGE

EAGLE ROCK RESERVATION

Prospect and Eagle Rock avenues, West Orange, 973-268-3500; www.essex-countynj.org

This reservation covers 408 acres with a 644-foot elevation in the Orange Mountains with streams, hills and valleys. It stretches from the Passaic River Valley east to New York City. Visitors can hike along the many trails, picnic and ride along bridle paths. There is also a September 11, 2001 commemorative memorial here.

Daily.

RICHARD J. CODEY ARENA AT SOUTH MOUNTAIN
560 Northfield Ave., West Orange, 973-731-3828; www.essexcountynj.org

This indoor ice rink hosts hockey games, special events and is open to the public for ice skating. It is the official practicing and training home of the New Jersey Devils.

Admission: adults $6, children and seniors $4. Skate rental: $4. Call for public skating schedule.

THOMAS EDISON NATIONAL HISTORICAL PARK & EDISON LABORATORY
Main St. and Lakeside Ave., West Orange, 973-324-9973; www.nps.gov

This park is the site of Edison's home and laboratory. Built by Thomas A. Edison in 1887, this was his laboratory for 44 years. During that time, he was granted more than half of his 1,093 patents (an all-time record). Here he perfected the phonograph, motion picture camera and electric storage battery. There is a one-hour lab tour that includes the chemistry lab and library and demonstrations of early phonographs. The visitor center has exhibits and films.

Admission: $3. Estate Tour: Friday-Sunday noon-4 p.m. (on the hour). Grounds: Friday-Sunday 11:30 a.m.-5 p.m.

WHERE TO STAY

EDISON
★★★SHERATON EDISON HOTEL RARITAN CENTER
125 Raritan Center Parkway, Edison, 732-225-8300, 800-325-3535; www.sheraton.com

Just a half-hour from New York City, the Sheraton Edison Hotel Raritan Center offers a convenient location along with elegant accommodations. Fluffy robes and Sheraton's signature Sweet Sleeper Beds with thick duvets and down pillows are just some of the amenities guests will find in their rooms. A large indoor pool, a well-equipped fitness facility and a sauna offer onsite recreation, while Lily's Restaurant is the hotel's casual bistro-style dining facility.

276 rooms. Restaurant, bar. Business center. Fitness center. Pool. Pets accepted. $151-250

★★★SOMERSET HILLS HOTEL
200 Liberty Corner Road, Warren, 908-647-6700, 800-688-0700; www.shh.com

Visitors will find that this hotel, located in the Watchung Mountains, combines the service of a country inn with the facilities, entertainment and accommodations expected from a full-service hotel.

111 rooms. Restaurant, bar. Fitness center. Pool. Pets accepted. $151-250

NEW BRUNSWICK
★★★CROWNE PLAZA HOTEL SOMERSET-BRIDGEWATER
110 Davidson Ave., Somerset, 732-560-0500, 877-227-6963; www.crowneplaza.com

Sleep comfortably on this hotel's 300 thread-count sheets. If you can pull the kids away from the hotel's connecting indoor/outdoor pool, you can visit nearby attractions, including Six Flags Great Adventure, golf courses and Rutgers University. The Garden State Exhibit Center and Ukrainian Cultural Center are adjacent to the hotel.

440 rooms. Restaurant, bar. Business center. Fitness center. Pool. Pets accepted. Tennis. $151-250

★★★HILTON EAST BRUNSWICK

3 Tower Center Blvd., East Brunswick, 732-828-2000, 800-445-8667; www.hilton.com

The Hilton East Brunswick offers spacious guest rooms with Hilton's Serenity Collection bedding, which features pillow-top mattresses and luxurious bed linens. Nearby attractions include Princeton University and Six Flags Great Adventure Theme Park.

405 rooms. Restaurant, bar. Business center. Fitness center. Pool. Pets accepted. $151-250

★★★HYATT REGENCY NEW BRUNSWICK

2 Albany St., New Brunswick, 732-873-1234, 800-233-1234; www.hyatt.com

This property is located downtown on a six-acre lot, midway between New York and Philadelphia. The central location offers easy access to shopping, restaurants and nearby attractions. Spacious guest rooms offer luxurious bedding, pillow-top mattresses, Internet access, an iPod dock, and a complimentary newspaper delivered in the morning.

288 rooms. Restaurant, bar. Business center. Fitness center. Pool. $151-250

NEWARK

★★★NEWARK LIBERTY INTERNATIONAL AIRPORT MARRIOTT

Newark International Airport, Newark, 973-623-0006, 800-882-1037; www.marriott.com

Located on the premises of Newark Airport, this Marriott features a connecting indoor/outdoor pool, complimentary coffee in the lobby, laundry, dry cleaning and babysitting services. Guest rooms offer convenience and comfort with high-quality, 300 thread-count linens, fluffy down duvets and high-speed Internet access. The hotel's three restaurants—Mangiare di Casa, JW Prime Steakhouse and Chatfields English Pub—cater to all tastes. Area attractions include Ellis Island and the Statue of Liberty, the Jersey Gardens Outlet Mall and Six Flags Great Adventure.

591 rooms. Restaurant, bar. Business center. Fitness center. Pool. $151-250

PATERSON

★★★THE INN AT MILLRACE POND

313 Johnsonberg Road, Route 519 N., Hope, 908-459-4884, 800-746-6467; www.innatmillracepond.com

This colonial-style bed and breakfast features guest rooms in three historic buildings: the Grist Mill, built in 1769 by Moravian settlers; the Miracle House, built in the early 19th century and the Stone Cottage, the home of the mill's caretaker. Some accommodations feature fireplaces, televisions and whirlpool tubs. The onsite restaurant offers a freshly prepared, contemporary American menu for dinner, while the Colonial Tavern features casual pub fare in 18th-century surroundings.

17 rooms. Complimentary breakfast. Restaurant, bar. $151-250

★★★SHERATON MAHWAH HOTEL

1 International Blvd., Mahwah, 201-529-1660, 800-325-3535; www.sheraton.com

Located nearly 35 miles from Newark International Airport and not far from New York City, this hotel offers spacious rooms with a garden or a fountain view as well as an indoor heated pool, tennis courts, two restaurants and two lounges. Rooms have the Sheraton Sweet Sleeper Bed, oversized desks, Internet access, and microwaves. Golfers will enjoy the nearby courses, Central

Valley Golf Club and Darlington County Course.

225 rooms. Restaurant, bar. Fitness center. Pool. Tennis. Pets accepted. $151-250

RUTHERFORD

★★★SHERATON MEADOWLANDS HOTEL AND CONFERENCE CENTER

2 Meadowlands Plaza, East Rutherford, 201-896-0500, 800-325-3535; www.sheraton.com

Located just across the river, this newly renovated hotel is only minutes from Manhattan. Many guest rooms offer views of the city's sparkling skyline. Grab a cup of coffee from the full-service Starbucks onsite before heading out to shop at the nearby outlets, or hunker down in the Chairman's Grill for a hearty bite before the Giants game.

427 rooms. Restaurant, bar. Business center. Fitness center. Pool. Pets accepted. $61-150

WHERE TO EAT

NEW BRUNSWICK

★★★THE FROG AND THE PEACH

29 Dennis St., New Brunswick, 732-846-3216; www.frogandpeach.com

Housed in a converted factory, this restaurant has been in business since 1983 and features painted brick walls and exposed ductwork. Entrées include summer mushroom and local chard strudel with goat cheese and Jersey tomato emulsion; and Moroccan-spiced lamb sirloin with corn and garlic flan, popcorn shoots and pine nut yogurt sauce.

American. Lunch (Monday-Friday), dinner. Reservations recommended. Outdoor seating. Children's menu. Bar. $36-85

★★★STAGE LEFT RESTAURANT

5 Livingston Ave., New Brunswick, 732-828-4444; www.stageleft.com

Since 1992, Stage Left has been serving up creative American cuisine in a warm setting. Selections from an extensive wine list can be paired with menu options such as pistachio-studded organic free-range chicken breast, pan-roasted cod and apple cider-braised pork belly. Wine-tasting dinners with guest speakers and festive brunches are among the special events offered.

American. Lunch (Friday), dinner. Reservations recommended. Outdoor seating. Bar. $36-85

WEST ORANGE

★★★HIGHLAWN PAVILION

Eagle Rock Reservation, West Orange, 973-731-3463; www.highlawn.com

This restaurant offers a picturesque view of the Manhattan skyline. The 1909 building was restored and opened as a restaurant in 1986. A French rotisserie and Italian brick wood-burning oven bring out the flavors of the delightful American cuisine.

American. Lunch (Monday-Friday), dinner. Reservations recommended. Outdoor seating. Bar. $36-85

★★★THE MANOR

111 Prospect Ave., West Orange, 973-731-2360; www.themanorrestaurant.com

One of the most well-known (and most formal) restaurants in New Jersey, the Manor offers dishes such as Maine lobster braised in sweet butter with wild mushrooms, and English pea risotto; and filet mignon with truffled mashed potatoes, green beans, baby carrots, mushrooms and perigourdine sauce. You'll also find foie gras, oysters and caviar on the menu.

American. Lunch (Wednesday), dinner, Sunday brunch. Closed Monday. Reservations recommended. Bar. $36-85

JERSEY SHORE

The Jersey Shore is made up of unique towns along the Atlantic Ocean. Many of them are filled with the private homes and quaint downtown areas. Honeymooners, conventioneers, the Miss America Pageant (until it moved to Las Vegas) and some 37 million annual visitors have made Atlantic City the best-known New Jersey beach resort. At the southernmost tip of the shore lies Cape May, the nation's oldest seashore resort. Popular with Philadelphia and New York society since 1766, the entire town has been proclaimed a National Historic Landmark because it has more than 600 Victorian homes and buildings, many of which have been restored. Four miles of beaches and a 1 ¼-mile paved promenade offer vacationers varied entertainment. Atlantic City has everything from restaurants, shops, casinos, carnival rides and resorts to peruse. Get some famous saltwater taffy from James' at the Tropicana, where you can see the taffy being pulled and chocolate being made. Head to the beach to sunbathe, swim, have some cocktails and enjoy the shore. If you want to surf, head to Crystal Beach, Delaware Avenue Beach or the Downtown Beach.

WHAT TO SEE

ATLANTIC CITY
ABSECON LIGHTHOUSE
31 S. Rhode Island Ave., Atlantic City, 609-449-1360; www.abseconlighthouse.org

Climb the 228 steps to the top of this 1857 lighthouse, designed by Civil War general George Gordon Meade. This is the tallest lighthouse in New Jersey, and the third tallest in the United States.

Admission: adults $7, seniors $5, children 4-12 $4, children 3 and under and military personnel free. July-August, daily 10 a.m.-5 p.m.; September-June, Thursday-Monday 11 a.m.-4 p.m.

ATLANTIC CITY BOARDWALK HALL
2301 Boardwalk, Atlantic City, 609-348-7000, 800-736-1420; www.boardwalkhall.com

This National Historic Landmark seats 13,800 people for special events, concerts, boxing, ice shows and sports events. It's also the former site of the Miss America Pageant, which now takes place in Las Vegas.

Box office: Monday-Saturday 11 a.m.-5 p.m.

FISHING & DIVING
Go surf and deep-sea fishing on a chartered boat. A license may be required, depending on the company. Kammerman's Atlantic City Marina features Atlantic Star Charters (*447 Carson Ave., Atlantic City, 609-348-8418; www.atlanticstarcharters.com*) offering fishing charters, party cruises and a kayaking cruise, depending on your interests. Atlantic City Fishing and Dive Center

HIGHLIGHT

WHAT ARE THE TOP THINGS TO DO ON THE JERSEY SHORE?

BRING YOUR LUCK TO ATLANTIC CITY
This resort town has plenty of casino action, plus great dining and entertainment.

STROLL THE BOARDWALKS
Most of the beach towns have boardwalks. Each is unique in its own way, but they all are filled with hoagie stands and pizza joints.

SAIL OFFSHORE
Charter boats are available for deep sea fishing trips. Diving is also offered, but you won't see much in the murky Atlantic Ocean.

(455 N. Maryland Ave., Atlantic City, 609-926-5353; www.missac.com) offers fishing and diving charters.
Daily.

GARDEN PIER
Boardwalk and New Jersey Ave., Atlantic City, 609-347-5837; www.acmuseum.org

Garden Pier features Spanish Renaissance architecture with landscaped gardens. Opened in 1913, it held the B.F. Keith's Theater and a large ballroom. The restored pier is also the home to the Atlantic City Art Center and Atlantic City Historical Museum.
Admission: Free. Daily 10 a.m.-4 p.m.

HISTORIC GARDNER'S BASIN
800 N. New Hampshire Ave., Atlantic City, 609-348-2880;
www.gardnersbasin.com

An eight-acre, sea-oriented park featuring working lobstermen. The Ocean Life Center contains eight tanks totaling 29,800 gallons of aquariums, exhibiting more than 100 varieties of fish and marine animals. There are also 10 exhibits featuring themes on the marine and maritime environment.
Admission: adults $8, seniors $6, children 4-12 $5, children 3 and under free. Daily 10 a.m.-5 p.m.

CAPE MAY
CAPE MAY MID-ATLANTIC CENTER FOR THE ARTS
Trolley tours, 202 Ocean St., Cape May, 809-884-5404; www.capemaymac.org

These trolley tours feature many options depending upon what you're interested in. Curious about ghosts? Take the Ghosts of Cape May tour, which takes you through the streets documenting the paranormal activity. If you're a nature lover, take the Cape Island Nature Tour, which will take you through wildlife habitats.

EMLEN PHYSICK ESTATE

1048 Washington St., Cape May, 609-884-5404; www.capemaymac.org

This authentically restored 18-room Victorian mansion, built in 1879, was designed by Frank Furness. It's said that this estate is haunted by Dr. Physick's Aunt Emilie along with a few of Physick's dogs and other ghosts. The mansion is also the headquarters for the Mid-Atlantic Center for the Arts.

Daily.

HISTORIC COLD SPRING VILLAGE

720 Route 9, Cape May, 609-898-2300; www.hcsv.org

The village subsists of a restored early 1800s South Jersey farm village, including 25 restored historic buildings on 22 acres. Craft shops, spinning, blacksmithing, weaving, pottery, broom making, ship modeling demonstrations, folk art are displayed throughout the village.

June, daily 10 a.m.-4:30 p.m.; July-August, Tuesday-Sunday 10 a.m.-4:30 p.m.

WHERE TO STAY

ATLANTIC CITY

★★★BALLY'S PARK PLACE CASINO RESORT

Park Place and Boardwalk, Atlantic City, 609-340-2000, 800-225-5977; www.ballysac.com

A geometric glass chandelier twinkles overhead at the entrance to this large, classic Boardwalk casino. There are several dining options to choose from, including some that fit into the Wild West theme of the hotel's annex casino.

1,246 rooms. Restaurant, bar. Business center. Fitness center. Pool. Spa. Casino. Golf. $151-250

★★★BORGATA CASINO HOTEL AND SPA

1 Borgata Way, Atlantic City, 609-317-1000, 866-638-6748; www.theborgata.com

The Borgata Hotel Casino and Spa is a stylish resort, where the rooms and suites are luxurious havens with cool earth tones, contemporary furnishings and advanced in-room technology. The hotel's five restaurants include Wolfgang Puck's American Grille and Bobby Flay Steak. Those who are not successful at the blackjack tables may want to ensconce themselves in the confines of Spa Toccare, where a wide variety of relaxing treatments melt tension away, or in one of the hotel's several high-end boutiques.

2,000 rooms. Restaurant, bar. Business center. Fitness center. Pool. Spa. Casino. $251-350

★★★CAESARS ATLANTIC CITY HOTEL CASINO

2100 Pacific Ave., Atlantic City, 609-348-4411, 800-223-7277; www.caesarsac.com

This oceanfront hotel, dubbed "Rome on the Jersey shore", houses 26,000 square feet of meeting space and a nicely appointed business center. Choose from the hotel's many dining establishments, including Chinese, Japanese and American restaurants, Roman-themed eateries, casual restaurants and lounges. Head to the Pier Shops at Caesars for some shopping and then to Qua Baths and Spa for some pampering.

1,144 rooms. Restaurant, bar. Fitness center. Pool. Spa. Beach. Casino. Golf. $151-250

★★★DOLCE SEAVIEW RESORT AND SPA
401 S. New York Road, Galloway, 609-652-1800, 800-983-6523; www.seaviewgolf.com

A golfer's dream, this hotel is located on 670 secluded acres near Reeds Bay and offers two 18-hole championship golf courses. It is also only 15 minutes from the bright lights of Atlantic City. The hotel's lobby has a traditional 1912 elegance and features black-and-white antique golf pictures, mahogany furniture and bar, overstuffed brown leather chairs and large windows with views of the grounds. Guests can enjoy volleyball and basketball courts, a kids' playground and the Seaview Golf Academy.

297 rooms. Restaurant, bar. Business center. Fitness center. $251-350

★★★HILTON CASINO RESORT
Boston Ave. and Boardwalk, Atlantic City, 609-340-7235, 800-257-8677; www.hiltonac.com

The Hilton Casino Resort offers convenient access to everything in the area. Onsite offerings include a 9,000-square-foot pool, full-service health spa, 60,000-square-foot casino with poker room and Asian gaming room, an assortment of fine dining restaurants and an entertainment venue.

800 rooms. Restaurant, bar. Fitness center. Pool. Spa. Beach. Casino. Reservations recommended. $151-250

★★★RESORTS ATLANTIC CITY
1133 Boardwalk, Atlantic City, 609-344-6000, 800-336-6378; www.resortsac.com

Opened in 1978, Resorts Atlantic City offered the first casino in the area. The hotel's charmingly, beachy 480-room Ocean Tower offers views of and convenient access to the boardwalk, and the newly renovated Rendezvous Tower boasts the largest guest rooms in Atlantic City.

538 rooms. Restaurant, bar. Fitness center. Pool. Spa. Casino. $151-250

★★★SHERATON ATLANTIC CITY CONVENTION CENTER HOTEL
2 Miss America Way, Atlantic City, 609-344-3535, 800-325-3535; www.sheraton.com

This tower hotel with Art Deco accents is near Atlantic City's boardwalk as well as designer outlet shops. Guests will appreciate the Sheraton's signature "Sweet Sleeper Bed" (also available for man's best friend) and in-room movies and games, while business travelers will be able to work in comfort with oversized desks, ergonomic chairs and an in-room fax/copier/printer. During the summer, in-room and poolside massages are available.

502 rooms. Restaurant, bar. Business center. Fitness center. Pool. Pets accepted. $151-250

★★★TRUMP PLAZA HOTEL & CASINO
Boardwalk and Mississippi Ave., Atlantic City, 609-441-6000, 800-677-7378;
www.trumpplaza.com

If you're looking for a little relaxation along with some Atlantic City excitement, the Trump Plaza Hotel and Casino is for you. Whether you're willing to gamble with $5 or $5,000, the casino offers games for every skill level and interest, from slots to blackjack, roulette and Caribbean stud poker. When you've had enough casino excitement and want to unwind, head to the hotel's health spa, where you can relax in the sauna or Jacuzzi, indulge in a massage, body scrub or wrap, or take in a workout in the well-equipped fitness center.

906 rooms. Restaurant, bar. Fitness center. Pool. Spa. Beach. Casino. $151-250

★★★TRUMP TAJ MAHAL CASINO HOTEL

1000 Boardwalk, Atlantic City, 609-449-1000, 800-825-8888; www.trumptaj.com

To say that the Trump Taj Mahal Casino Resort is opulent is an understatement. After all, where else can you find a 4,500-square-foot suite named for Alexander the Great that features its own steam room, sauna, weight room, lounge and pantry? Covering 17 acres, this resort offers comforts you wish you had at home. Rooms are spacious and feature beautiful decor, marble bathrooms and spectacular views of the city. Treat yourself to a day in the health spa, where therapists will pamper you with luxurious treatments like reflexology and Swedish massages. Hotel dining options range from upscale to casual, while the casino can keep you going all night with 4,000 slot machines, 210 gaming tables and a baccarat pit.

1,250 rooms. Restaurant, bar. Fitness center. Pool. Spa. Casino. $151-250

★★★THE WATER CLUB AT BORGATA

1 Renaissance Way, Atlantic City, 800-800-8817; www.thewaterclubhotel.com

Soaring 43 stories above Atlantic City, Borgata's upscale sister property is large without feeling impersonal. The contemporary vibe carries from the verdant sunroom off the lobby to the nature-inspired guest rooms, each with a stunning water view. Flat-screen TVs, iPod docking stations and 400-thread-count Egyptian sheets are just some of the pleasures awaiting boardwalk-weary guests. The five indoor and outdoor pools, state-of-the-art fitness center and top-notch Immersion Spa give little reason to leave the hotel. A view may not be the first thing that comes to mind when you think spa, but the 360-degree floor-to-ceiling water views at Immersion are hard not to notice. Located on the 32nd and 33rd floors of the hotel, the spa is all about relaxation and rejuvenation with spacious "experience" rooms, a 25-yard infinity lap pool and delicious spa cuisine.

800 rooms. Fitness center. Pool. Spa. Business center. $151-250

CAPE MAY

★★★CONGRESS HALL

251 Beach Ave., Cape May, 609-884-8421, 888-944-1816; www.congresshall.com

Guests feel like royalty when they step beneath the 32-foot tall colonnade and into Congress Hall's beautiful lobby, complete with the hotel's original black-and-white marble floor, 12-foot tall doors and black wicker furniture. The guest rooms feature views of the Atlantic, antiques, custom furnishings and large bathrooms with 1920s-style tubs and pedestal sinks. The Blue Pig Tavern is a great place to stop for a bite to eat or to meet up with friends, and the Grand Ballroom is not to be missed.

108 rooms. Closed mid-week January and February. Restaurant, bar. Fitness center. Pool. Beach. $151-250

★★★MAINSTAY INN

635 Columbia Ave., Cape May, 609-884-8690; www.mainstayinn.com

Guests at this beautiful Victorian-style inn near the water will find their stay in Cape May to be serene and somewhat luxurious. Rooms are spacious and decorated with oriental carpets and silk-screened wallpaper, and each morning, guests can enjoy a large family-style breakfast by the fireplace or on the private porch. Guests are provided with beach towels and beach chairs with umbrellas, and there's a shower and changing room to use as well.

6 rooms. Complimentary breakfast. Beach. $151-250

★★★THE SOUTHERN MANSION

720 Washington St., Cape May, 609-884-7171, 800-381-3888; www.southernmansion.com

Originally built as a country estate in 1863 by Philadelphia industrialist George Allen, the Victorian décor of this painstakingly restored home has graced the covers of several magazines. Each room is meticulously decorated with antiques and vibrant colors, and features private bathrooms. The hotel's location is within walking distance of beaches, shops and restaurants.

24 rooms. Complimentary breakfast. No children under 10. Beach. $151-250

★★★VIRGINIA HOTEL

25 Jackson St., Cape May, 609-884-5700, 800-732-4236; www.virginiahotel.com

This elegant hotel, built in 1879, has been remodeled and no detail was over-looked. Bright and airy rooms feature flat-screen televisions, Italian duvet covers, Belgian linens and Bulgari bath products.

24 rooms. Restaurant, bar. Complimentary breakfast. No children under 12. Beach. $151-250

WHERE TO EAT

ATLANTIC CITY
★★★RAM'S HEAD INN

9 W. White Horse Pike, Galloway, 609-652-1700; www.ramsheadinn.com

Only eight miles from Atlantic City, this continental restaurant is also a busy banquet facility that can accommodate up to 350 people. Dine in a glass-enclosed veranda, ballroom or brick courtyard.

American. Lunch, dinner. Closed Monday. Children's menu. Reservations recommended. Outdoor seating. Bar. $36-85

★★★SEABLUE BY MICHAEL MINA

1 Borgata Way, Atlantic City, 609-317-1000, 866-692-6742; www.theborgata.com

Guests can enjoy an eclectic dining experience at Seablue, located in the upscale Borgata Casino Hotel & Spa. The ultramodern décor features blue deco-type lighting, terra cotta and gold colors, and lavender suede-covered chairs (in the bar area). The restaurant features the creations of well-known executive chef Michael Mina, with many of the fresh fish options being grilled over mesquite wood in a tandoori oven. The eight-page menu includes a page for guests to design their own salad—crayons are placed on the table for filling in the blanks—and dessert consists of three different items, one always being ice cream or sherbet.

Seafood. Dinner. Closed Tuesday-Wednesday. Reservations recommended. Bar. $36-85

CAPE MAY
★★★EBBITT ROOM

The Virginia Hotel, 25 Jackson St., Cape May, 609-884-5700, 800-732-4236; www.virginiahotel.com

Nestled in a circa-1870s Victorian in the charming Virginia Hotel, the equally inviting Ebbitt Room reflects the quaint Cape May atmosphere. Crystal

HIGHLIGHT

WHAT ARE THE BEST BEACHES ON THE JERSEY SHORE?

Every summer, Jerseyens flock to the shore. You won't find many hotels on this strip of land—the area is mostly filled with houses that families rent during the summer season—but day trips are sufficient enough to see many of the beaches. The only trick: some of the beaches require a permit to be on the beach. Call ahead to make sure you're in the clear.

If you are looking for a quiet spot to take the family, head to the oyster shell driveway-lined streets of **Stone Harbor. Stop at Bradley's** (*10725 Third Ave., Stone Harbor, 609-368-2039; www.bradleyssteaks.com*) for an authentic Jersey Shore hoagie, which is essentially a fantastic cheese steak.

The next town over, Avalon, is just as quiet and family oriented. With beautiful white-sand beaches, oyster shell driveways and families strolling the sidewalks, Avalon is the perfect place for a quick family getaway. To get a taste of the history of the Jersey Shore, visit **Avalon Free Library History Center** (*215 39th St., Avalon, 609-967-0090; www.avalonhistorycenter.com*), where you'll find photographs, postcards and even surfboards depicting Avalon's past.

For more amusement, head to Ocean City and enjoy the eight miles of beaches and more than two miles of boardwalk. The area caters to both families and singles. Catch a concert at **The Ocean City Music Pier** (*Boardwalk at Moorlyn Terrace, Ocean City; www.oceancitychamber.com*), built in 1928 and extending 300 feet over the Atlantic Ocean. Between Sixth and 14th streets, you'll find amusement parks offering rides, mini-golf and arcades.

Kids and adults will love **Morey's Piers** (*3501 Boardwalk, Wildwood, 609-522-3900; www.moreyspiers.com*) in Wildwood. Comprised of five attractions, these piers offer fun for everyone. The crowd is unique, but it comes with the territory. Walk along the boardwalk after exhausting yourself on all the rides.

For that small town feel, visit Long Beach Island. Separated by two bays from the mainland, this island is home to many wealthy families' summer residences. No wider than three blocks, Long Beach Island boasts an array of activities. Catch a show at **Surflight Theatre** (*Beach and Engleside avenues, Beach Haven, 609-492-9477; www.surflight.org*). Visit the historic **Barnegat Lighthouse State Park** (*Barnegat Light, 609-494-2016; www.state.nj.usl*), featuring Barnegat Lighthouse, a 167-foot red and white tower, engineered by General George G. Meade and completed in 1858. Its 217-step spiral staircase leading to the lookout offers a spectacular view.

The town of Ocean Grove is an adorable historical town. Stay at **Albatross Hotel** (*34 Ocean Pathway, Ocean Grove, 732-775-2085; www.albatrosshotel.net*), for a European style lodge with all the charm this borough has to offer.

At the tip of the Jersey Shore is Cape May, known for its history and its charm. The nation's oldest seashore has been claimed a National Historic Landmark in its entirety. Laying eyes on the more than 600 Victorian houses, you'll see why. Book a room at **Congress Hall** (*251 Beach Ave., Cape May, 609-884-8421, 888-944-1816; www.congresshall.com*) and feel like royalty as you step upon the beautiful black-and-white marble floor that dominates the lobby.

chandeliers, floral arrangements, and soft colors set an elegant and romantic mood, perfectly complementing the unique plates of contemporary cuisine.

American fare. American. Dinner. Reservations recommended. Outdoor seating. Bar. $36-85

★★★WASHINGTON INN

801 Washington St., Cape May, 609-884-5697; www.washingtoninn.com

The Washington Inn is located in a former plantation house in the heart of the Cape May Historic District. An impressive wine list beautifully complements the seasonal American menu, which may include appetizers such as a warm goat cheese tart and entrées like pan-seared filet mignon and rack of lamb.

American. Dinner. Reservations recommended. Outdoor seating. Bar. $36-85

SPA

ATLANTIC CITY

★★★SPA TOCCARE

Borgata Hotel, Casino and Spa, 1 Borgata Way, Atlantic City, 609-317-7555, 866-692-6742; www.theborgata.com

Spa Toccare looks to nature for much of its inspiration, and its treatment menu highlights the healing properties of many botanicals. Facials employ bilberry for sensitive skin and rainforest propolis for supreme hydration. Pamper the body with a healing mud or green tea body treatment, or let the oil of Kamani restore firmness. Hot stone, deep tissue, Swedish, and reflexology massage are among the tension tamers, or retreat to the bath to soak your troubles away. One step inside Spa Toccare and your gambling losses will quickly disappear. Its contemporary Mediterranean style makes modern sophisticates feel instantly at home. From coifs at the Salon to circuit training at the Pump Room and cabanas at the Pool & Gardens, this spa offers a complete approach to perfecting and pampering.

WELCOME TO PENNSYLVANIA

FROM ITS EASTERN MOST TIP NEAR BORDENTOWN, NEW Jersey, to its straight western boundary with Ohio and West Virginia, Pennsylvania's 300-mile stride across the country covers a mountain-and-farm, river-and-stream, mine-and-mill topography. Its cities, people and resources are just as diverse. In the eastern part of the state, Philadelphia is a treasure chest of tradition and historical shrines; in the west, Pittsburgh is a mighty museum of our nation's industrial heritage. Pennsylvania miners dig nearly all the anthracite coal in the United States and still work some of the oldest iron mines in the country.

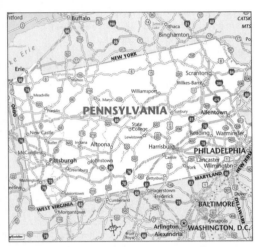

Pennsylvania has also been a keystone of culture. The first serious music in the colonies was heard in Bethlehem; today, both Pittsburgh and Philadelphia have well-known symphonies. Celebrated art galleries, museums and more than 140 institutions of higher learning (including the oldest medical school in the United States at the University of Pennsylvania) are based here.

Swedes made the first settlement on this fertile land in 1643 at Tinicum Island in the Delaware River. The territory became Dutch in 1655 and British in 1664. After Charles II granted William Penn a charter that made him proprietor of "Pennsilvania," the Quaker statesman landed here in 1682 and invested the land with his money and leadership. Commercial, agricultural and industrial growth came quickly. Of course, The Declaration of Independence was signed in Pennsylvania, and the Constitution was drafted here.

BEST ATTRACTIONS

PENNSYLVANIA'S BEST ATTRACTIONS

DELAWARE VALLEY
Explore where the West was born at Daniel Boone's birthplace. At this Reading estate, you'll find a blacksmith, sawmill and 579 acres.

LAUREL HIGHLANDS
Hike to the highest point in Pennsylvania for views of the surrounding park and even Maryland.

LEHIGH VALLEY
Check out the natural phenomenon that is known as the Delaware Water Gap. The river cuts through the mountains at nearly a quarter-mile above sea level.

PHILADELPHIA
This city has a lot more to offer than history. If you can, try to catch a sports game. It doesn't matter if it's the Phillies, 76ers, the Flyers or the Eagles, the city loves them all and it's a great way to get a real flavor the city today.

PITTSBURGH
Check out a Steelers game, but don't dress in the opponent's colors.

THE POCONOS
Head to the mountains for beautiful summer views and plenty of winter adventure.

THE ALLEGHENIES

Often considered the countryside of Pittsburgh, The Alleghenies is filled with beautiful vistas and a hearty helping of history. Altoona, located among the Allegheny Mountains, has grown up around railroads. It expanded rapidly after 1852, when the difficult task of spanning the Alleghenies with track to link Philadelphia and Pittsburgh was completed. The small town of Bedford, just

HIGHLIGHT

WHAT ARE THE TOP THINGS TO DO IN THE ALLEGHENIES?

SEE FRANK LLOYD WRIGHT'S ALLEGHENY MASTERPIECE

Fallingwater, built in 1936, is considered to be one of the most influential architectural structures of the twentieth century.

ENTER THE NITTANY LIONS' DEN

State College revolves around the campus of Pennsylvania State University. Catch a football game in the fall or a lacrosse game in the spring.

VENTURE TO THE LAND OF LOG CABINS

Old Bedford Village is full of log cabins built in the 18th and 19th centuries.

over 100 miles from Harrisburg, is a town full of history. Fort Bedford was a major frontier outpost in pre-Revolutionary War days. After the war, it became an important stopover along the route of western migration. Connellsville is a small suburb of Pittsburgh along the Youghiongheny River, founded in 1793 by Zachariah Connell. You'll find Frank Lloyd Wright's Fallingwater here. Often called "Happy Valley", State College is the home of Pennsylvania State University.

WHAT TO SEE

ALTOONA

BAKER MANSION MUSEUM

3500 Oak Lane, Altoona, 814-942-3916; www.blairhistory.org

This stone Greek Revival house of an early ironmaster was built from 1844 to 1848. Blair County Historical Society now occupies it. The home is furnished with hand-carved Belgian furniture of the period and displays transportation exhibits, gun collection, clothing and house wares.

Admission: adults $6, students and seniors $4.50, children 5-12 $3. June-September, Tuesday-Friday 11 a.m.-3 p.m., Saturday-Sunday 12:30-2:15 p.m.; September-May, by appointment only.

CANOE CREEK STATE PARK

Altoona, 814-695-6807; www.dcnr.state.pa.us

This 950-acre park features a 155-acre lake where visitors can hit the beach, go hiking, have a picnic, or in winter, enjoy cross-country skiing, sledding, ice boating and ice skating.

DELGROSSOS PARK

Altoona, 814-684-3538; www.delgrossos.com

Kids can enjoy a day of fun at this theme park with more than 30 rides and attractions, including an antique carousel, miniature golf and pony rides. There are also arcade games, picnic pavilions and restaurants. You'll find the Tipton Waterworks and Tipton Rapids water parks here.

Admission: $12.95 (all-day rides), $15.95 (all-day rides, waterworks and rapids). May-September, hours vary.

FORT ROBERDEAU

Altoona, 814-946-0048; www.fortroberdeau.org

This reconstructed Revolutionary War fort built with horizontal logs contains a blacksmith shop, barracks, a storehouse and a powder magazine. Costumed guides perform historical skits and demonstrations. There are areas for picnicking and nature trails.

Admission: Free. May-October, Tuesday-Saturday 11 a.m.-5 p.m., Sunday-Monday 1-5 p.m.

LAKEMONT PARK

700 Park Ave., Altoona, 800-434-8006; www.lakemontparkfun.com

This amusement park has more than 30 rides and attractions and is home of the nation's oldest wooden roller coaster. Families can also enjoy a water park, miniature golf and other entertainment.

Admission: all day pass $9.95. May-September, closed Monday-Tuesday.

RAILROADER'S MEMORIAL MUSEUM

1300 Ninth Ave., Altoona, 814-946-0834, 888-428-6662; www.railroadcity.com

This museum features exhibits displaying railroad artifacts and railroad rolling stock, steam and electric locomotive collections.

Admission: adults $9, seniors $7, children 4-12 $5, children 3 and under free. May-November, Monday-Saturday 10 a.m.-5 p.m., Sunday 11 a.m.-5 p.m.; November-December, Friday-Saturday, Monday 10 a.m.-5 p.m., Sunday 11 a.m.-5 p.m.

BEDFORD

OLD BEDFORD VILLAGE

220 Sawblade Road, Bedford, 814-623-1156, 800-238-4347; www.oldbedfordvillage.com

This village consists of more than 40 authentic log and frame structures built between 1750 and 1851. There are crafts demonstrations and an operating pioneer farm, plus many special events throughout the year.

Admission: adults $10, students $5, children 5 and under free. June-August, Thursday-Tuesday 9 a.m.-5 p.m.; September-October, Thursday-Sunday 9 a.m.-5 p.m.

CONNELLSVILLE

FALLINGWATER (KAUFMANN CONSERVATION ON BEAR RUN)

Highway 381 S., Mill Run, Connellsville, 724-329-8501; www.fallingwater.org

One of the most famous structures of the 20th century, Fallingwater, designed by Frank Lloyd Wright in 1936, is cantilevered on three levels over a waterfall. The interior features Wright-designed furniture, textiles and lighting, as well as sculpture by modern masters; extensive grounds are heavily wooded and planted with rhododendron, which bloom in early July. The visitor center has a self-guided orientation program, concessions and a gift shop.

Admission (tours): adults $18, children 6-12 $12. Admission (grounds): $8. Daily. Closed Wednesday mid-March-late November; January-February. No children under age 6 (for regular tour). Reservations required.

STATE COLLEGE
MOUNT NITTANY VINEYARD & WINERY
350 Houser Road, State College, 814-466-6373; www.mtnittanywinery.com

Opened in 1990, the winery is located within a stone-faced, chalet-style building nestled on the southern slopes of Mount Nittany. The tasting room offers a variety of wines and a lovely view of a large pond, the vineyard and the mountains in the background. Tastings are free.

Tuesday-Friday 1:30-5 p.m., Saturday 10 a.m.-5 p.m., Sunday 12:30-4 p.m. Closed January.

PENNSYLVANIA STATE UNIVERSITY
College and Atherton streets, State College, 814-865-4700; www.psu.edu

Founded in 1855, today this university is home to more than 43,000 students. There are approximately 760 major buildings on this 15,984-acre campus, which is the land grant institution of Pennsylvania. The first college to be established here was the College of Agricultural Studies, which is a showplace for the state's dairy industry and includes their dairy center, the largest university creamery in the country. It has five herds of cows and automatic milking equipment. The creamery (in the Food Science Building) has a retail salesroom for cheeses, milk, cream and ice cream.

Creamery: Monday-Thursday 7 a.m.-10 p.m., Friday 7 a.m.-11 p.m., Saturday 8 a.m.-11 p.m., Sunday 9 a.m.-10 p.m.

WHERE TO STAY

BEDFORD
★★★MERCERSBURG INN
405 S. Main St., Mercersburg, 717-328-5231;
www.mercersburginn.com

Located between the civil war battlefield and other historic sites, the Mercersburg Inn is a 17-room turn-of-the-century Georgian mansion. Golf courses, tennis facilities, skiing, fly-fishing, mountain biking and hiking trails are all located within a short distance.

17 rooms. Restaurant, bar. Complimentary breakfast. $61-150

STATE COLLEGE
★★★ATHERTON HOTEL
125 S. Atherton St., State College, 814-231-2100, 800-832-0132; www.athertonhotel.net

This inn is located half a mile from Penn State. The Anthropology Museum, Historic Boalsburg Village and Palmer Museum of Art are also nearby. Guest lodgings are roomy with large picture windows and work desks.

150 rooms. Restaurant, bar. Fitness center. $61-150

★★★CARNEGIE HOUSE
100 Cricklewood Drive, State College, 814-234-2424, 800-229-5033;
www.carnegiehouse.com

When you've conquered the links, stow your golf gear in your cozy guest room, relax in a deep library chair and have a celebratory drink. Carnegie House offers packages for golf and Penn State football weekends. Guest rooms have dormer windows and floral bedspreads.

22 rooms. Restaurant, bar. Complimentary breakfast. $61-150

★★★THE NITTANY LION INN
200 W. Park Ave., State College, 800-233-7505; www.pshs.psu.edu

Managed by the surrounding University, this hotel offers standard rooms with free high-speed Internet access, king-sized beds and coffee makers. It's located on the Penn State campus.

223 rooms. Restaurant, bar. Fitness center. Pool. $61-150

★★★TOFTREES GOLF RESORT AND CONFERENCE CENTER
1 Country Club Lane, State College, 814-234-8000, 800-252-3551; www.toftrees.com

This "home among the trees" sits in 1,500 wooded acres and offers private patios and balconies from which guests can enjoy the view. Enjoy the 18-hole golf course, volleyball court, tennis courts and outdoor heated pool.

113 rooms. Restaurant, bar. Business center. Fitness center. Pool. Golf. Tennis. $61-150

WHERE TO EAT

BEDFORD
★★★MERCERSBURG INN
405 S. Main St., Mercersburg, 717-328-5231; www.mercersburginn.com

Built in 1909, this Georgian-style mansion resides in a charming, 230-year-old village. With both a prix fixe and an à la carte menu, the inn's restaurant serves entrées such as sautéed skate à la meuniere with capers, preserved lemon and caramelized onion risotto, or rosemary lemon Cornish hen with roasted fingerling potatoes.

French. Dinner. Closed Monday-Wednesday. Bar. $36-85

DELAWARE VALLEY

The region along the Delaware River borders New Jersey and is often referred to as the countryside of Philadelphia. On the border of New Jersey is the quaint town of New Hope. This river village was originally the largest part of a 1,000-acre land grant from William Penn to Thomas Woolrich of Shalford, England. Norristown is just six miles outside of Philadelphia's city limits. A city of railroads and industry famous for its superb pretzels, Reading was the second community in the United States to vote a Socialist government into office; however, the city has not had such a government for many years. Valley Forge is one of the most famous places in the Delaware Valley. Two thousand soldiers died here from hunger, disease and cold, but General George Washington and his beleaguered army ultimately triumphed over the British in 1778. Today, Valley Forge has come to symbolize American perseverance and sacrifice on a lush, hilly, 3,600-acre expanse with rich historical significance and beautiful scenery. Keeping with the Revolutionary War theme is West Chester. In the heart of three Pennsylvania Revolutionary War historic sites, West Chester today is a university and residential community with fine examples of Greek Revival and Victorian architecture.

HIGHLIGHT

WHAT ARE THE TOP THINGS TO DO IN THE DELAWARE VALLEY?

PADDLE DOWN THE RIVER
Hop aboard Coryell's Ferry for an old-time ride on the Mississippi-style riverboat.

VISIT WASHINGTON'S HEADQUARTERS
Located within Valley Forge, this was once the site of George Washington's home and the headquarters for the Continental Army.

TAKE A PEEK AT THE TOWN OF HOPEWELL
Built around the furnaces in the late 1700s, Hopewell now acts as a national historic site dedicated to the iron industry of the early days.

SEE WHERE THE WEST WAS BORN
Explore Daniel Boone's birthplace, where you'll find a blacksmith, sawmill and 579 acres.

WHAT TO SEE

NEW HOPE
BOWMAN'S HILL WILDFLOWER PRESERVE
New Hope, 215-862-2924; www.bhwp.org

Pennsylvania's native plants come into focus at this 134-acre preserve located 40 miles northeast of Philadelphia. Hike or walk along woodland, a meadow, a creek or an arboretum. Botanic enthusiasts will discover 1,000 species of trees, shrubs, ferns, vines and herbaceous wildflowers. There are many contemplative places for meditation and study, scenic picnic spots and several historic sites within hiking distance. Head five miles south to Washington Crossing Historic Park (1112 River Road, Washington Crossing; 215-493-4076), where George Washington crossed the Delaware River in 1776. Bowman's Hill Tower, a lookout commemorating the American Revolution, offers a view of the Delaware River and rolling countryside one mile on foot or by car.

Admission: adults $5, seniors $3 and students $3, children 4-14 $2, children 3 and under free.
Visitor center: Daily 9 a.m.-5 p.m. Grounds: Daily 8:30 a.m.-dusk.

PARRY MANSION MUSEUM AND BARN
South Main and Ferry streets, New Hope, 215-862-5652; www.newhopehistoricalsociety.org

This restored stone house was built in 1784 by Benjamin Parry, a prosperous merchant and mill owner. There are eleven rooms on view, all of which have been restored and furnished to depict period styles from the late 18th to early 20th centuries.

Admission: adults $6, seniors and children 12-18 $5, children 11 and under $2. May-October, Saturday-Sunday 1:30 p.m., 3 p.m.

NORRISTOWN
ELMWOOD PARK ZOO
1661 Harding Blvd., Norristown, 610-277-3825; www.elmwoodparkzoo.org

This zoo features an extensive North American waterfowl area as well as other animals including cougars, bobcats, bison and elk. There is an outdoor aviary, a children's zoo barn and a museum with an exhibit on animal senses. There are also different habitats to visit including farmland, grasslands, bayou, wetlands and more.

Admission: adults $10.75, seniors $7.75, children 2-12 $7.75, children 1 and under and military personnel free. Daily 10 a.m.-5 p.m.

READING
BERKS COUNTY HERITAGE CENTER
2201 Tulpehocken Road, Reading, 610-374-8839; www.countyofberks.com

Here are the Gruber Wagon Works, where finely crafted wagons were produced for farm and industry; Wertz's Red Bridge, the longest single-span covered bridge in the state; Deppen Cemetery, with the graves of Irish workers who died of "swamp fever" while building the Union Canal; and the C. Howard Hiester Canal-Center, with its collection of canal artifacts. There are tours of the wagon works and canal center as well as an orientation slide program.

May-October, Tuesday-Saturday 10 a.m.-4 p.m., Sunday noon-5 p.m.

DANIEL BOONE HOMESTEAD
400 Daniel Boone Road, Reading, 610-582-4900; www.danielboonehomestead.org

This was the birthplace of Daniel Boone in 1734. The homestead covers approximately 579 acres and includes Boone House, barn, blacksmith shop and sawmill. There are picnicking areas, nature trails and a visitor center.

Admission: adults $6, seniors $5.50, students $4. Tuesday-Saturday 9 a.m.-4:30 p.m., Sunday noon-4:30 p.m.

THE READING PUBLIC MUSEUM AND ART GALLERY
500 Museum Road, Reading, 610-371-5850; www.readingpublicmuseum.org

This 25-acre museum has exhibits on art and science. There are also galleries with art collections covering Asia, Ancient Civilizations, Africa and more. Check out the planetarium located within the museum.

Admission: adults $7, seniors, students and children 4-18 $5, children 3 and under free. Tuesday-Thursday, Saturday 11 a.m.-5 p.m., Friday 11 a.m.-8 p.m., Sunday noon-5 p.m.

HOPEWELL FURNACE NATIONAL HISTORIC SITE
2 Mark Bird Lane, Elverson, 610-582-8773; www.nps.gov

Hopewell, an early industrial community, was built around a charcoal-burning cold-blast furnace, which made pig iron and many other iron products from 1771 to 1883. Nearby mines and forests supplied ore and charcoal for the furnace. The National Park Service has restored the buildings, and interpretive programs emphasize the community's role in the history of American industry. Hopewell is surrounded by French Creek State Park. The visitor center has a museum and audiovisual program on iron-making and community life. A self-guided tour includes a charcoal house, blacksmith shop, office store and more. Stove molding and casting demonstrations are given from late June-early September. *Daily.*

VALLEY FORGE NATIONAL HISTORICAL PARK
NATIONAL MEMORIAL ARCH
Valley Forge National Historical Park, 610-783-1099; www.nps.gov/vafo

Built in 1917 to commemorate General George Washington's army, this memorial stands in remembrance of the arrival of the army into Valley Forge. Inscribed in the arch is a quote from General Washington: "Naked and starving as they are, we cannot enough admire the incomparable patience and fidelity of the soldiery."

WASHINGTON HEADQUARTERS
Valley Forge National Historical Park, 610-783-1099; www.nps.gov/vafo

Park staff will provide information about the house where Washington lived for six months and which served as military headquarters for the Continental Army during that time.
Daily 9 a.m.-5 p.m.

WASHINGTON MEMORIAL CHAPEL
Highway 23, Valley Forge, 610-783-0120; www.washingtonmemorialchapel.org

This is a private property within park boundaries. Stained-glass windows depict the story of the New World, its discovery and development. There are hand-carved oak choir stalls, Pews of the Patriots and the Roof of the Republic bearing the State Seal of all the states. Also part of the chapel is the 58 cast-bells Washington Memorial National Carillon, with bells honoring states and territories. You can tour the chapel or attend one of the church services.
Monday-Saturday 10 a.m.-5 p.m., Saturday 1-5 p.m. Services: Saturday 5 p.m., Sunday 8 a.m., 10 a.m.

WHERE TO STAY

NEW HOPE
★★★HOTEL DU VILLAGE
2535 N. River Road, New Hope, 215-862-9911; www.hotelduvillage.com

Simple and intimate, Hotel du Village offers 20 cozy guest rooms, two tennis courts, a pool and a restaurant specializing in French country cuisine. Situated just north of New Hope, the inn is only a short distance to shops, art galleries and entertainment options.
20 rooms. Restaurant, bar. Complimentary breakfast. Tennis. $61-150

★★★THE INN AT BOWMAN'S HILL
518 Lurgan Road, New Hope, 215-862-8090; www.theinnatbowmanshill.com

The Inn at Bowman's Hill consists of stone and stucco buildings sitting on five acres of well-manicured grounds. An 80-foot stream runs out front, and the property adjoins the Bowman's Hill Wildflower Preserve. The décor and furnishings are rustic yet sophisticated, with lots of natural wood. Guest rooms are intimate, with gas fireplaces and large whirlpool tubs. Guests can enjoy a three-course gourmet breakfast in the breakfast room or in their own rooms, and afternoon snacks are offered from 3 to 7 p.m.

5 rooms. Restaurant, bar. Complimentary breakfast. Pool. $251-350

★★★THE MANSION INN

9 S. Main St., New Hope, 215-862-1231; www.themansioninn.com

This grand 1865 Baroque Victorian mansion is located along a tranquil canal in the center of downtown New Hope, within walking distance to numerous shops and restaurants as well as the Michener Art Museum. The stately building welcomes guests with its garden, gazebo, refreshing outdoor pool and beautifully decorated Empire/French Victorian rooms.

7 rooms. Restaurant, bar. Complimentary breakfast. Pool. No children under 14. $151-250

NORRISTOWN
★★★SHERATON BUCKS COUNTY HOTEL

400 Oxford Valley Road, Langhorne, 215-547-4100, 800-325-3535; www.sheratonbuckscounty.com

Only 25 miles from Philadelphia in the foothills of Bucks County, this full-service hotel features well-appointed rooms, as well as complimentary fitness classes and certified personal trainers in its fitness center.

186 rooms. Restaurant, bar. Business center. Fitness center. Pool. Pets accepted. Tennis. $151-250

★★★WILLIAM PENN INN

US 202 & Sumneytown Pike, Gwynedd, 215-699-9272; www.williampenninn.com

Since 1714, this inn has offered guests a luxurious stay with period furnishings and a large, delicious breakfast in the morning. The restaurant, claiming more than 300 years of service and experience, is a picturesque dining spot and a popular choice for weddings and other celebratory events. The menu leans heavily on seafood with such signature dishes as snapper soup and baked Maryland crab imperial. The Sunday brunch is a hit with locals.

4 rooms. Restaurant, bar. Complimentary breakfast. $61-150

WEST CHESTER
★★★DULING-KURTZ HOUSE & COUNTRY INN

146 S. Whitford Road, Exton, 610-524-1830; www.dulingkurtz.com

Rich in history and comfort, this small inn offers a homey, elegant atmosphere for relaxation. The Duling-Kurtz House was built in 1783 and is located within walking distance of shopping, the train station and more. Rooms are small but comfortable and cozy.

13 rooms. Complimentary breakfast. Restaurant, bar. $61-150

WHERE TO EAT

NEW HOPE
★★★THE MANSION INN

The Mansion Inn, 9 S. Main St., New Hope, 215-862-1231; www.themansioninn.com

Situated in the Mansion Inn, this casual yet stately restaurant offers continental cuisine in candlelit dining rooms. The restaurant serves entrées including pan-seared sea scallops with lobster ravioli, porcini mushrooms, cream sauce and sautéed organic spinach or a slow-braised lamb shank with sweet potato risotto, wilted leek fondue and minted demi-glace.

Continental. Lunch, dinner, Sunday brunch. Reservations recommended. Outdoor seating. Bar. $36-85

NORRISTOWN
★★★THE JEFFERSON HOUSE
2519 DeKalb Pike, Norristown, 610-275-3407; www.jefferson-house.com

Since 1926, this casual lakefront dining spot has been pleasing locals with a craving for fresh seafood and friendly service. Try the shrimp scampi or the cheeseburger with a side of perfectly browned fries.

American. Lunch, dinner, Sunday brunch. Children's menu. Bar. $36-85

READING
★★★GREEN HILLS INN
2444 Morgantown Road, Reading, 610-777-9611

The owner of this small-town spot has a big-city pedigree: He was a student of Georges Perrier, owner of Philadelphia's renowned La Bec-Fin. It should come as no surprise that the kitchen churns out impeccable French fare including grilled moulard duck breast and chateaubriand.

French, American. Dinner. Closed Sunday. $36-85

DUTCH COUNTRY

The Pennsylvania Dutch Country is one of the most charming areas in the country. Home to many Quakers and Amish, this area takes you back to a simpler time. The mid-state metropolis of Harrisburg holds what many consider the finest capitol building in the nation. One of America's most fascinating success stories, the planned community of Hershey takes its name from founder M.S. Hershey, who established his world-famous chocolate factory here in 1903. The site of a critical turning point in American history, Gettysburg offers a variety of things to see and do. Lahaska is located within Bucks County's countryside and is known for its many antique shops and Peddler's Village. The small town of Ephrata holds on to Pennsylvania's Dutch and Amish cultures and offers a diverse setting with plenty to see and do. To fully appreciate the city of Lancaster, visitors should leave the main highways and travel on country roads, which Amish buggies share with automobiles. York claims to be the first capital of the United States. The Continental Congress met here in 1777 and adopted the Articles of Confederation, using the phrase "United States of America" for the first time.

WHAT TO SEE

EPHRATA
EPHRATA CLOISTER
632 W. Main St., Ephrata, 717-733-6600; www.ephratacloister.org

These buildings stand as a monument to an unusual religious experiment. In

WHAT ARE THE TOP THINGS TO DO IN DUTCH COUNTRY?

DISCOVER THE RELIGIOUS COMMUNITY OF EPHRATA
Established in 1732, Ephrata was home to a Brotherhood, Sisterhood and a group of married "householders". Members lived in solitary order until 1934.

GET IN TOUCH WITH GETTYSBURG HISTORY
Embark on Ghosts of Gettysburg Candlelight Walking Tour, which will take you through the streets of the historic area. One of the bloodiest battles of the time, there are said to be plenty of soldiers still haunting their graves.

STEP INSIDE THE PENNSYLVANIA CAPITOL
Dominating the vista is the Capitol in Harrisburg. The building is one of the most beautiful capitols in the nation.

SATISFY YOUR SWEET TOOTH
Head to HersheyPark for all kinds of fun. Between touring the chocolate factory and riding the thrill rides, you are guaranteed a good time.

1732 Conrad Beissel, a German Seventh-Day Baptist, began to lead a hermit's life here. Within a few years he established a religious community of recluses, with a Brotherhood, a Sisterhood and a group of married "householders". The members of the solitary order dressed in concealing white habits; the buildings were without adornment, the halls were narrow, the doorways were low and board benches served as beds with wooden blocks as pillows. Their religious zeal and charity, however, proved to be their undoing. After the Battle of Brandywine, the cloistered community nursed the revolutionary sick and wounded but contracted typhus, which decimated their numbers. Celibacy also contributed to the decline of the community, but the Society was not formally dissolved until 1934.

Admission: adults $9, seniors $8, children 3-11 $6, children under 3 free. Monday-Saturday 9 a.m.-5 p.m., Sunday noon-5 p.m. Closed January-February, Monday-Tuesday.

GETTYSBURG
A VISIT WITH MR. LINCOLN
571 Steinwehr Ave., Gettysburg, 717-334-6049; www.jimgetty.com
Go back in time to discover Abraham Lincoln as a young boy through his

presidency. This theatrical live portrayal of the 16th president is by well-known actor and Lincoln historian, Jim Getty. The audience is presented with a first-hand look at Honest Abe's life as if it were yesterday. From tales of his youth to his love for Gettysburg, Getty enthralls his audience just like the former president. A "press conference" follows this remarkable Lincoln portrayal.
Call for information. Booked for groups only.

BOYDS BEAR COUNTRY
75 Cunningham Road, Gettysburg, 717-630-2600, 866-367-8338; www.boydsbearcountry.com

Step inside the three-story atrium of this spectacular stuffed animal lovers' dream come true. "The World's Most Humongous Teddy Bear Store" features four floors of bears (plus rabbits, moose and other furry friends) in a giant barn. At the Boyd's Teddy Bear Nursery, kids can adopt their very own baby bear. Create your very own teddy bear at the Super Duper Bear Factory. Located just five miles south of Gettysburg, Boyds offers a unique experience for the whole family. Cuddle up with your new bear and some good ole country grub in front of the stone fireplace. Live entertainment every weekend adds to the fun.
Daily 10 a.m.-6 p.m.

EISENHOWER NATIONAL HISTORIC SITE
97 Taneytown Road, Gettysburg, 717-338-9114; www.nps.gov

Dwight D. Eisenhower fell in love with the quaint town of Gettysburg when he was sent there to conduct a training camp for his troops. After being elected as president, Eisenhower bought a hunk of land in this beloved town to build his home away from home. Adjacent to Gettysburg Battlefield, is the farm and former home of the 34th President of the United States and his wife, Mamie. It served as a weekend retreat for Ike during World War I, his presidency and years later. Take a guided 90-minute tour of the grounds and home or explore the farm and skeet range by yourself. This site can only be accessed by shuttle from the National Park Service Visitor Center.
Admission: adults $6.50, children 6-12 $4. Daily 9 a.m.-4 p.m.

GENERAL LEE'S HEADQUARTERS
401 Buford Ave., Gettysburg, 717-334-3141; www.civilwarheadquarters.com

Once occupied by the town widow, the infamous confederate general set up camp here in July 1863. Widow Thompson was not pleased about having to share her humble abode with a "Rebel". Robert E. Lee planned Confederate strategy for the Gettysburg battle in this house, which now contains a collection of historical items from the battle. The house was opened to the public in 1922. Today, it remains one of the oldest continually operating museums in Gettysburg.
Mid-March-November, daily 9 a.m.-5 p.m.

GETTYSBURG COLLEGE
300 N. Washington St., Gettysburg, 717-337-6300; www.gettysburg.edu

Take a stroll through this gorgeous campus, located in the center of historic Gettysburg. The small liberal arts college only has 2,600 students. Founded in 1832, it is the oldest Lutheran-affiliated college in the U.S. The beautiful brick buildings of Gettysburg College are just part of the draw. Besides being the site of Lincoln's "Gettysburg Address," this selective liberal arts school has an impressive history. Take a look inside Pennsylvania Hall, the oldest building on campus, which was used as a Civil War hospital. President Eisenhower served on the Board of Trustees and eventually wrote his memoires in the admissions office, now called the Eisenhower House.

GETTYSBURG NATIONAL MILITARY PARK

97 Taneytown Road, Gettysburg, 717-334-1124; www.nps.gov

The site of one of the Civil War's most decisive battles and immortalized by Lincoln's Gettysburg Address is preserved by the National Park Service. Nearly one hundred and fifty years ago on July 1-3, 1863, General Robert E. Lee led his Confederate Army in its greatest invasion of the North. The defending Northerners, under Union General George Meade, repulsed the Southern assault after three days of fierce fighting. There are more than 35 miles of roads through 5,900 acres of the battlefield area, not to mention more than 1,300 monuments, markers and tablets of granite and bronze, and 400 cannons here. Choose to take a tour guided by a battlefield guide or explore the historical site on your own.

Admission: adults $7.50, seniors and military personnel $6.50, children 5-18 $5.50, children 5 and under free. Visitor center and Museum: April-May, September-October, daily 8 a.m.-6 p.m.; June-August, daily 8 a.m.-7 p.m.; November-March, daily 8 a.m.-5 p.m.

GHOSTS OF GETTYSBURG CANDLELIGHT WALKING TOURS

271 Baltimore St., Gettysburg, 717-337-0445; www.ghostsofgettysburg.com

Armed with tales from Mark Nesbitt's "Ghosts of Gettysburg" books, knowledgeable guides lead tours through sections of town that were bloody battlefields 130 years ago. March up Baltimore Street to the County Court House, previously a Civil War hospital or down Carlisle Street and around the college campus. The tours begin at the headquarters.

March and November, Saturday-Sunday; April-October, daily.

HARRISBURG

CAPITOL

Third and State streets, Harrisburg, 717-787-6810; www.pacapitol.com

The Capitol of Pennsylvania is an Italian Renaissance building, which was dedicated in 1906 and covers two acres. The spectacular building has an impressive 651 rooms, and a 26,000-ton, 272-foot dome, imitating that of St. Peter's in Rome, which dominates the city skyline. It includes murals by Philadelphia painter Edwin Austin Abbey and Violet Okley, the first woman artist to be commissioned to work on a capitol building.

Tours: Monday-Friday 8:30 a.m.-4 p.m. (every half hour); Saturday-Sunday 9 a.m.-3 p.m. (every two hours)

FORT HUNTER MANSION & PARK

5300 N. Front St., Harrisburg, 717-599-5751; www.forthunter.org

This historic 37-acre property is the site of a British-built fort erected in 1754 to combat mounting threats prior to the French and Indian War. In 1787, the land was purchased and became a farm that eventually grew into a self-sufficient village. The Pennsylvania Canal runs through the park. The Federal-style stone mansion was built in three sections: the front stone portions were built in 1786 and 1814; the rear wooden portion was built in 1870. The spacious mansion displays period furnishings, clothing, toys and other artifacts.

Admission: adults $5, seniors $4, students $3. Tours: May-December, Tuesday-Saturday 10:30 a.m.-4:30 p.m., Sunday noon-4:40 p.m.

THE STATE MUSEUM OF PENNSYLVANIA
300 N. St., Harrisburg, 717-787-4980; www.statemuseumpa.org

This six-story circular building houses four stories of galleries, an authentic early country store, a Native American life exhibit, technological and industrial exhibits, a collection of antique autos and period carriages, a planetarium, natural history and geology exhibits and one of the world's largest framed paintings, Rothermel's *The Battle of Gettysburg*. The planetarium has public shows on Saturday and Sunday.

Admission: adults $5, seniors and children1-12 $4, children under 1 free. Free every third Saturday of the month. Mid-June-July, Tuesday-Saturday 9 a.m.-5 p.m., Sunday noon-5 p.m.; July-rest of year, Thursday-Saturday 9 a.m.-5 p.m., Sunday noon-5 p.m.

HERSHEY
HERSHEY GARDENS
170 Hotel Road, Hershey, 717-534-3492; www.hersheygardens.org

From mid-June to first frost, 8,000 rose plants bloom on 23 acres. There is a tulip garden (mid-April-mid-May), chrysanthemums and annuals, a butterfly house featuring 500 butterflies and six theme gardens including the Children's Garden.

Admission: adults $10, seniors $9, children 3-12 $6, children under 3 free. March, November-December, daily 10 a.m.-4 p.m.; April-late-May, mid-September-October, daily 9 a.m.-5 p.m.; June-early-September, daily 9 a.m.-8 p.m.; January-February, Saturday-Sunday 10 a.m.-4 p.m.

HERSHEYPARK
100 W. Hershey Park Drive, Hershey, 800-437-7439; www.800hershey.com

This 110-acre theme park includes the water park Boardwalk at Hersheypark with nine water rides, Pioneer Frontier, Midway America, Music Boz Way, Minetown and Founder's Circle. There's also plenty of entertainment, more than 60 rides (including 11 roller coasters), live family shows and plenty of food and beverage vendors. ZooAmerica is also located at Hersheypark.

Admission (one day): adults and children 9-18 $51.95, seniors (ages 55-69) $30.95, seniors plus (ages 70 and over) $20.95, children 3-8 $30.95, children under 3 free. Mid-May-August, daily; hours vary.

HERSHEYPARK STADIUM AND THE STAR PAVILION
100 W. Hersheypark Drive, Hershey, 717-534-3911; www.hersheyparkstadium.com

The stadium hosts professional hockey games, basketball games, ice skating, variety shows and concerts including the Dave Matthews Band and U2. The Star Pavilion puts on summer concerts and includes a lawn seating area.

HERSHEY'S CHOCOLATE WORLD
251 Park Blvd., Hershey, 717-534-4900; www.hersheys.com

Chocolate lovers can have their day learning lots of interesting things about chocolate and how it is made. Tours are conducted using an automated conveyance, during which the steps of making chocolate are stimulated. Enjoy Hershey's really big 3-D Show featuring Hershey's products' characters. There are also tropical gardens, a shopping village, restaurants and marketplace shops so that you can bring home plenty of the good stuff.

May-December; hours vary.

ZOO AMERICA
100 W. Hershey Park Drive, Hershey, 717-534-3900; www.zooamerica.com

While you're at Hershey, you can see this 11-acre environmental zoo, which features five climatic regions of North America. The zoo is home to more than 200 animals and 75 different species. If you're also visiting Hershey Park, you can visit Zoo America for free with a combined admission fee.

Admission: adults and children 9-18 $9, seniors $7.50, children 3-8 $7.50, children under 3 free. November-March, daily 10 a.m.-4:30 p.m.; April-October, daily; hours vary.

LAHASKA
PEDDLER'S VILLAGE
Highways 202 and 263, Lahaska, 215-794-4000; www.peddlersvillage.com

This 18th-century-style country village with 42 acres of landscaped gardens and winding brick paths makes a great day trip from Philadelphia. Browse through a selection of more than 70 specialty shops for handicrafts, toys, accessories, leather goods, collectibles and gourmet foods. Take the kids for a ride on an antique carousel, or take advantage of the many free family events and seasonal festivals.

Daily.

LANCASTER
AMISH FARM AND HOUSE
2395 Lincoln Highway, East Lancaster, 717-394-6185; www.amishfarmandhouse.com

See what Amish life is like by paying a visit to this farm. Listen to a lecture on the Amish and tour the early 19th-century stone buildings furnished and decorated as an old-order Amish household. The grounds include waterwheels, a windmill, a hand-dug well, carriages, a spring wagon and sleighs.

Admission: adults $7.95, seniors $7.25, children 5-11 $5.25, children 4 and under free. January-March, November-December, daily 8:30 a.m.-4 p.m.; April-May, September-October, daily 8:30 a.m.-5 p.m.; June-August, daily 8:30 a.m.-6 p.m.

DUTCH WONDERLAND
2249 Lincoln Highway, East Lancaster, 866-386-2839; www.dutchwonderland.com

This family fun park has 30 rides, botanical gardens, diving shows, shops and a monorail.

Admission: adults and children 3-18 $31.95, seniors $26.95, seniors 70 and over $19.95, children 2 and under free. June-August, daily 10 a.m.-8:30 p.m.; May, September-October; hours vary.

FULTON OPERA HOUSE
12 N. Prince St., Lancaster, 717-394-7133; www.thefulton.org

First opened in 1852, this is one of the oldest American theaters. Many legendary people have performed here, including members of the Barrymore family and W.C. Fields. It is believed that more than one ghost haunts the theater's Victorian interior. Haunted or not, today the opera house is home to professional regional and community theaters, and opera and symphony organizations.

See website for schedule and ticket information.

HISTORIC LANCASTER WALKING TOUR

100 S. Queen St., Lancaster, 717-392-1776; www.padutchcountry.com

For a great overview of Lancaster, take this 90-minute tour during which costumed guides take you through the historic downtown area pointing out architectural or historic features of the town.

Tours: April-October, Sunday-Monday, Wednesday-Thursday 1 p.m., Tuesday, Friday-Saturday 10 a.m., 1 p.m.

HISTORIC ROCKFORD

881 Rockford Road, Lancaster, 717-392-7223; www.rockfordplantation.org

See the preserved 1794 home of General Edward Hand, Revolutionary War commander and member of Continental Congress.

Admission: adults $6, seniors $5, children 6-12 $4. April-October, Wednesday-Sunday 11 a.m.-3 p.m. (last tour at 3 p.m.).

JAMES BUCHANAN'S WHEATLAND

1120 Marietta Ave., Lancaster, 717-392-8721; www.wheatland.org

Built in 1828, this building served as the residence of President James Buchanan from 1848 to 1868. Today, the restored Federal mansion with period rooms containing American Empire and Victorian furniture and decorative arts are available to tour.

Admission: adults $8, seniors $7, students $6, children 6-11 $3, children 5 and under free. April-October, Tuesday-Saturday 10 a.m.-4:30 p.m. Christmas candlelight tours early December.

LANDIS VALLEY MUSEUM

2451 Kissel Hill Road, Lancaster, 717-569-0401; www.landisvalleymuseum.org

The Landis Valley Museum interprets Pennsylvania German rural life with the largest collection of Pennsylvania-German objects in the U.S. You'll also find craft and living history demonstrations, and a country store.

Admission: adults $12, seniors $10, children 3-11 $8, children 2 and under free. Monday-Saturday noon-5 p.m.

YORK

CENTRAL MARKET HOUSE

34 W. Philadelphia St., York, 717-848-2243

Opened in March 1888, this street market features more than 70 vendors who offer fresh produce, homemade baked goods, regional handcrafts and specialty items.

Tuesday, Thursday, Saturday.

COLONIAL COMPLEX GENERAL GATES HOUSE AND GOLDEN PLOUGH TAVERN

157 W. Market St., York, 717-845-2951; www.yorkheritage.org

There is plenty to see at this complex, including General Horatio Gates' House, where Marquis de Lafayette gave a toast to Washington, marking the end of a movement to replace him. Also here is Golden Plough Tavern, one of the earliest buildings in York, which reflects the Germanic background of many of the settlers in its furnishings and half-timber architecture, as well as the Bobb Log House, furnished with painted and grained furniture. The York County Colonial Court House is a replica of the 1754 original. Exhibits include a multimedia presentation the Continental Congress's adoption of the Articles of Confederation, audiovisual story of 1777-1778 historic events, an original printer's copy of the Articles of Confederation, and other historic documents and artifacts.

Admission: adults $10, students $7, children 8-18 $5. Tuesday-Saturday 10 a.m.-4 p.m.

FIRE MUSEUM OF YORK COUNTY

757 W. Market St., York, 717-846-6452; www.yorkheritage.org

This turn-of-the-century firehouse preserves two centuries of firefighting history, from leather bucket brigades to hand-drawn hose carts and pumps, and horse-drawn equipment. You can also see what the first motorized equipment looked like, as well as a recreated fire chief's office and firefighter's sleeping quarters, complete with brass slide pole.

Admission: adults $10, children 8-18 $5, students $7. Mid-April-mid-December, Saturday 10 a.m.-4 p.m.

WHERE TO STAY

GETTYSBURG

★★★THE INN AT HERR RIDGE

900 Chambersburg Road, Gettysburg, 717-334-4332, 800-362-9849; www.innatherrridge.com

Built in 1815, The Inn at Herr Ridge has a long history, having served as the first confederate hospital during the Battle of Gettysburg. Guest rooms have been modernized with a light touch that has not marred their quaint, historic charm. Each room is unique with its own décor. Whether you are in town for the history or romance, The Inn at Herr Ridge offers the perfect getaway.

16 rooms. Restaurant, bar. Complimentary breakfast. No children under 12. $61-150

HARRISBURG

★★★CROWNE PLAZA HOTEL HARRISBURG-HERSHEY

23 S. Second St., Harrisburg, 717-234-5021, 800-496-7621; www.crowneplaza.com

A smart choice for families, this full-service hotel is near all the attractions of Harrisburg. HersheyPark is minutes away, as are Chocolate World, the Carlisle Fairgrounds, the National Civil War Museum and the Capitol Complex. Restaurant Row, a collection of more than 30 restaurants, clubs, pubs and shops, is literally outside the front door and should not be missed.

261 rooms. Restaurant, bar. Business center. Fitness center. Pool. Pets accepted. $61-150

★★★HILTON HARRISBURG

1 N. Second St., Harrisburg, 717-233-6000, 800-445-8667; www.harrisburg.hilton.com

This elegant, family-friendly hotel is located in the heart of historic Harrisburg and is connected to the Whitaker Center by an enclosed walkway. Although the standard guest rooms are well appointed, guests who choose to upgrade to Tower Level rooms will enjoy upgraded amenities including access to a private lounge that serves complimentary continental breakfast and evening hors d'oeuvres. The hotel also features three restaurants, including a seasonal restaurant.

341 rooms. Restaurant, bar. Business center. Fitness center. Pool. Pets accepted. $151-250

★★★SHERATON HARRISBURG HERSHEY HOTEL

4650 Lindle Road, Harrisburg, 717-564-5511, 800-325-3535; www.sheraton.com

Minutes from downtown Harrisburg and the airport, this full-service hotel is also near many attractions such as HersheyPark, Hershey Chocolate World, historic Gettysburg, the Pennsylvania Dutch Country and the State Museum of Pennsylvania. The traditional-style guest rooms are spacious and include large work desks. The Dog and Pony Restaurant serves breakfast, lunch and dinner in a casually elegant setting, and the Dog and Pony Pub is a nice place for a nightcap.

348 rooms. Restaurant, bar. Business center. Fitness center. Pool. Pets accepted. $61-150

HERSHEY

★★★HERSHEY LODGE AND CONVENTION CENTER

West Chocolate Avenue and University Drive, Hershey, 717-533-3311, 800-437-7439; www.hersheylodge.com

The Hershey Lodge stays true to its name, with chocolate-themed décor in every guest room and special Hersheypark privileges including discounted tickets and early access to certain rides. Kids can even check themselves in at their own check-in desk and greet the friendly Hershey's product characters that might make an appearance in the lobby.

665 rooms. Restaurant, bar. Complimentary breakfast. Business center. Fitness center. Pool. $151-250

★★★★THE HOTEL HERSHEY

100 Hotel Road, Hershey, 717-533-2171, 800-437-7439; www.thehotelhershey.com

Perched atop a hill overlooking town, The Hotel Hershey sits on 300 acres of formal gardens, fountains and reflecting pools. Instead of mints, you'll find chocolate kisses on your pillow at evening turndown. With a multi-million dollar renovation completed in 2009, the grounds include a new recreation campus with 72 holes of golf, six miles of nature trails, basketball, volleyball, bocce ball and tennis courts, pools, a fitness center and an ice skating rink. You'll also find 10 new luxurious cottages with multiple rooms and the new Shops at Hotel Hershey, which feature seven boutiques. Rest your sweet tooth with a meal at the Fountain Café, or at the Circular Dining Room, Hotel Hershey's spot for fine dining. Or head to the brand new Harvest restaurant serving American cuisine in a casual environment. The Spa at Hotel Hershey is a wonderfully sinful place, with whipped cocoa baths and chocolate fondue wraps.

278 rooms. Restaurant, bar. Business center. Fitness center. Pool. Spa. Golf. Tennis. $251-350

LAHASKA

★★★GOLDEN PLOUGH INN

41 Peddler's Village, Lahaska, 215-794-4004; www.peddlersvillage.com

Scattered throughout Peddler's Village on 42 acres, this inn charms guests in every season. Many of the beautifully appointed rooms have gas-lit fireplaces and whirlpools. Guests are greeted with a snack basket upon arrival.

71 rooms. Restaurant, bar. Complimentary breakfast. Fitness center. Pool. $61-150

WHERE TO EAT

GETTYSBURG

★★★THE HERR TAVERN & PUBLICK HOUSE

The Inn At Herr Ridge, 900 Chambersburg Road, Gettysburg, 717-334-4332, 800-362-9849;
www.herrtavern.com

This restaurant is housed in the historic inn of the same name, which served
as the first Confederate hospital during the Battle of Gettysburg. Thomas
Sweeney built this tavern in 1815, selling it 15 years later to Frederick Herr.
Guests here are treated to friendly, pleasant service and an appetizing menu
of American-inspired fare that includes some Mediterranean influences.
Because most ingredients are obtained from local farmers, the menu frequently
changes. Past dishes have included shrimp and scallops in a red pepper fondue
with baby spinach and fettuccine, and Black Angus filet mignon with port wine
demi-glace and a stuffed potato.

*American. Lunch (Wednesday-Saturday). Dinner. Sunday Brunch. Reservations required on
weekends.*

HARRISBURG

★★★ALFRED'S VICTORIAN RESTAURANT

38 N. Union St., Middletown, 717-944-5373; www.alfredsvictorian.com

Housed in a picturesque, 1888-Victorian brownstone, this 30-year-old restaurant offers five intimate dining rooms, each with authentically restored design
elements and period décor. The menu has a Northern Italian influence and
offers nearly 30 different entrées, such as lobster tail and filet mignon.

*American, Italian. Lunch (Tuesday-Friday), dinner. Closed Monday. Reservations recom-
mended. Outdoor seating. Bar. $36-85*

HERSHEY

★★★★CIRCULAR DINING ROOM

1 Hotel Road, Hershey, 717-534-8800, 800-437-7439; www.hersheypa.com

This elegant dining destination is tucked away in the Hotel Hershey. Its circular
design—the idea of founder Milton S. Hershey—affords all guests, no matter
where they are seated, unobstructed views of the exquisite formal gardens
and reflecting pools from the room's soaring windows. The contemporary-
American menu is as refined as the restaurant's surroundings, and changes
seasonally to ensure only the freshest and most flavorful ingredients are used.
Past menus have included cocoa-braised beef short ribs, pulled pork shoulder
with housemade sauerkraut, and grilled beef filet with truffled dauphinoise
potatoes. Decadent desserts feature many choices for chocolate lovers, such
as warm chocolate soufflé and the Chocolate Evolution, a tasting of chocolate.

*American. Breakfast, lunch (Saturday), dinner (Thursday-Saturday). Sunday brunch.
Children's menu. Reservations recommended. $36-85*

LANCASTER

★★★HAYDN ZUG'S

1987 State St., East Petersburg, 717-569-5746; www.haydnzugs.com

Open since 1969, Haydn Zug's restaurant has a piece of history in East
Petersburg. The building actually was built in 1852 as a general store. Today,

HIGHLIGHT

WHAT ARE THE TOP THINGS TO DO IN THE LAUREL HIGHLANDS?

STAND ATOP MOUNT DAVIS
The highest point in Pennsylvania stands at the end of High Point Trail. On clear days, you can see Maryland from this scenic spot.

EXPLORE THE CAVES OF PENNSYLVANIA
The largest cave in Pennsylvania, Laurel Caverns offers various adventures.

GRAB YOUR PADDLE
See a different side of Pennsylvania while white water rafting. Quests of all levels are available.

owner/chef Terry Lee hails from Petersburg and offers an award-winning wine list and exceptional cuisine. For dinner, start with sea scallops wrapped in bacon, then for an entrée, try the beef tenderloin medallions with crabmeat and lobster sauce or the charred boneless breast of duck with Grand Marnier sauce. *American. Lunch, dinner. Closed Sunday. Bar. $36-85*

YORK
★★★ACCOMAC INN
6330 S. River Drive, York, 717-252-1521; www.accomac.com
This elegant country restaurant comes complete with white tablecloths and tableside preparation and serves delicious French fare, including beef tenderloin medallions with a mushroom Madeira sauce and brandy flambéed tableside with potatoes and roasted Cornish game hen served with cous cous, slow-roasted tomato and sweet corn salsa. Enjoy your meal in the lovely screened-in porch.
French, American. Dinner, Sunday brunch. Bar. $36-85

SPA

HERSHEY
★★★THE SPA AT THE HOTEL HERSHEY
100 Hotel Road, Hershey, 717-533-2171, 800-437-7439; www.chocolatespa.com
The Spa at Hotel Hershey doesn't skimp on using its signature luscious ingredient. Chocolate reigns at this three-story spa, from the chocolate bean polish and whipped cocoa bath to the chocolate fondue wrap and the chocolate

scrub. Or enjoy a Cuban-influenced mojito sugar scrub or body wrap, inspired by Milton Hershey's love of Cuba, where he owned many sugar plantations. The 30,000-square-foot facility includes an inhalation room, a quiet room for meditation, soaking tubs, steam rooms, saunas and signature showers for hydrotherapy treatments. There's also an indoor swimming pool and fitness center for guests to use along with fitness classes offered daily.

LAUREL HIGHLANDS

Pennsylvania's Laurel Highlands is part of the beautiful countryside near Pittsburgh. Located in the southwestern part of the state, there is everything from Pennsylvania's highest mountains and breathtaking caverns to lavish spas and exquisite restaurants. Farmington is a small town located in Pennsylvania's Laurel Highlands where nature is at your fingertips. The center stage for the Whiskey Rebellion of 1794, Somerset was described in James Whitcomb Riley's poem "Mongst the Hills of Somerset". Coal and its byproducts made Uniontown prosperous, but with the decline in coal mining, the city has developed a more diverse economic base. The Friendship Hill National Historic Site is located here where you can view the home of Albert Gallatin and explore the natural surroundings.

WHAT TO SEE

FARMINGTON
BRADDOCK'S GRAVE AT FORT NECESSITY NATIONAL BATTLEFIELD
1 Washington Parkway, Farmington, 724-329-5512; www.nps.gov
A granite monument marks the burial place of British General Edward Braddock, who was wounded in battle with French and Native American forces on July 9, 1755, and died four days later.
Fort Necessity Education Center: Daily 9 a.m.-5 p.m.

LAUREL CAVERNS
200 Caverns Park Road, Farmington, 724-438-2070, 800-515-4150; www.laurelcaverns.com
This 435-acre geological park holds the largest cave found in Pennsylvania with colored lighting and unusual formations. There are group tours of the caves available; see website for information. There is also an eighteen-hole indoor miniature golf course along with repelling courses and exploring trips.
May-October, daily 9 a.m.-5 p.m.; April and November, Saturday-Sunday 9 a.m.-5 p.m. Closed December-March.

MOUNT DAVIS
Forbes State Forest, Somerset, 724-238-1200; www.dcnr.state.pa.us
Mount Davis is the highest point in the state at 3,213 feet. Take the High Point Trail to the top, and on a clear day you can even see parts of Maryland.

UNIONTOWN
FRIENDSHIP HILL NATIONAL HISTORIC SITE
1 Washington Parkway, Uniontown, 724-329-5512; www.nps.gov
This historic site preserves the restored home of Albert Gallatin, a Swiss

immigrant who served his adopted country in public and private life for nearly seven decades. Gallatin made significant contributions to the young republic in the fields of finance, politics, diplomacy and scholarship. He is best known as the treasury secretary under Jefferson and Madison. The home includes exhibits, audiovisual programs and an audio tour. There are ten miles of wooded trails to explore here.

Park: Daily dawn-dusk. Visitor center: April-October, daily 9 a.m.-5 p.m.

WHITE WATER ADVENTURERS

6 Negley St., Ohiopyle, 800-992-7238; www.wwaraft.com

If you're interested in white water rafting, the Youghiogheny River has some of the wildest and most scenic water in the eastern United States. Decide on a trip based on experience and what level of rapids you want to navigate. Plenty of different trips are offered for thrill-seekers and families alike. This outfitter also offers bike and raft rentals.

Call or check website for information.

WILDERNESS VOYAGEURS

103 Garrett St., Ohiopyle, 800-272-4141; www.wilderness-voyageurs.com

These trips run on the lower, upper and middle Youghiogheny River. Rent bicycles or sign up for a kayaking or canoe lesson. The company offers instruction for mountain biking, climbing, fly fishing and more.

Call or see website for more information.

WHERE TO STAY

FARMINGTON

★★★★★FALLING ROCK AT NEMACOLIN WOODLANDS RESORT

150 Falling Rock Blvd., Farmington, 724-329-8555; www.nemacolin.com

Inspired by the architecture of Frank Lloyd Wright, Falling Rock extends almost organically from the Pennsylvania countryside with its natural stone exterior, fountains and seasonally open, heated outdoor infinity pool. All of the streamlined, luxurious rooms include 24-hour butler service and 1,200-thread-count sheets. But perhaps its most indulgent quality, at least for duffers, is its location—at the 18th hole of the Mystic Rock Golf Course, within the Nemacolin Woodlands Resort, and the accompanying 50,000-square-foot clubhouse.

42 rooms. Restaurant, bar. Business center. Fitness center. Pool. Golf. Tennis. Beach. Closed December-April. $251-350

★★★★NEMACOLIN WOODLANDS RESORT & SPA

1001 Lafayette Drive, Farmington, 724-329-8555, 866-344-6957; www.nemacolin.com

Tucked away in Pennsylvania's scenic Laurel Highlands, this comprehensive resort offers a multitude of recreational opportunities, from the Hummer driving club, equestrian center and shooting academy to the adventure and activities centers, culinary classes and art museums. Two golf courses and a renowned golf academy delight players, while special activities entertain children and teenagers. Grand European style defines the guest accommodations at Chateau LaFayette, while the Lodge maintains a rustic charm. Families enjoy the spacious accommodations in the townhouses, and the luxury homes add a touch of class to group travel.

293 rooms. Restaurant, bar. Business center. Fitness center. Pool. Spa. Golf. Tennis. Beach. $251-350

★★★SUMMIT INN RESORT

101 Skyline Drive, Farmington, 724-438-8594, 800-433-8594; www.summitinnresort.com

Located at the peak of Mount Summit, the Summit Inn Resort offers sparkling panoramic views of the surrounding counties. The 1907 inn is an architecture lover's dream: It's located near Frank Lloyd Wright's Fallingwater and has its own spot on the National Register of Historic Places.

94 rooms. Restaurant, bar. Pool. Closed early November-mid-April. $61-150

SOMERSET
★★★INN AT GEORGIAN PLACE

800 Georgian Place Drive, Somerset, 814-443-1043; www.theinnatgeorgianplace.com

This bed and breakfast overlooks Lake Somerset and is packed with antiques. The restaurant offers classic dishes wish seasonal ingredients such as salmon filet with a maple mustard sauce served with asparagus and wild rice pilaf.

11 rooms. Restaurant, bar. Complimentary breakfast. $61-150

WHERE TO EAT

FARMINGTON
★★★AQUEOUS

Falling Rock Hotel, 150 Falling Rock Blvd., Farmington, 724-329-8555; www.nemacolin.com

Plunge into a true farm-to-table experience with local meats and produce at this upscale American steakhouse overlooking the Mystic Rock Golf Course. Porterhouse, bone-in rib-eye, filet mignon and New York strip are available with a choice of delectable sauces, such as classic béarnaise and roasted red pepper. Country-style sides "big enough for two" include creamed spinach, creamed corn, onion rings and plenty of potatoes. Don't forget the surf and turf with king crab, jumbo shrimp and Maine lobster tail.

American. Breakfast, lunch, dinner. $36-85

WHICH LAUREL HIGHLANDS HOTELS HAVE THE MOST UNIQUE LOCATION?

Nemacolin Woodlands Resort & Spa:
Located in the Pennsylvania countryside, Nemacolin Woodlands Resort feels like a world away. The natural environment creates a tranquil aura.

Falling Rock at Nemacolin:
Situated within Nemacolin Woodlands Resort, Falling Rock at Nemacolin is an oasis in the woods. It's restaurant, Lautrec, is also one of the finest in the country.

★★★★★LAUTREC

Chateau LaFayette, 1001 LaFayette Drive, Farmington, 724-329-8555; www.nemacolin.com

Savor a bit of fine French cuisine—the restaurant wasn't named after French artist Henri de Toulouse-Lautrec for nothing—in Pennsylvania's Laurel Highlands. Chef Kristin Butterworth's frequently changing menu featuring the freshest ingredients is a delight. Spend an entire evening focusing on the complexities of a four-course meal plus dessert, or go all out with the Grand Tasting Menu that includes over a dozen selections. Wine pairings are offered by a polished, affable staff, and are carefully chosen to make the French cuisine sing.

French. Dinner. Reservations recommended. Bar. $36-85

SOMERSET

★★★HELEN'S

Seven Springs Mountain Resort, 777 Waterwheel Drive, Seven Springs, 814-352-7777; www.7springs.com

The formal service, complete with tableside carving and preparations, comes as a surprise considering the rural setting. Though the menu changes with the seasons, it leans towards classics with dishes such as pork osso bucco with cheese risotto and grilled trout with baby beans and watercress.

American. Dinner. Closed Monday-Thursday. Reservations recommended. Bar. $36-85

UNIONTOWN

★★★CHEZ GERARD AUTHENTIC FRENCH RESTAURANT

1187 National Pike, Highway 40 E., Hopwood, 724-437-9001; www.chezgerard.net

Chez Gerard is located in the historic Hopwood House, which dates to 1790. The all-French staff prides itself on providing the most authentic French experience, serving entrées such as grilled and smoked duck breasts with a plum and ginger reduction, grilled marinated zucchini and potato au gratin.

French. Lunch, dinner, Sunday brunch. Closed Tuesday. Reservations recommended. Bar. $36-85

SPA

FARMINGTON

★★★★WOODLANDS SPA AT NEMACOLIN RESORT

1001 LaFayette Drive, Farmington, 724-329-8555, 800-422-2736; www.nemacolin.com

Famed interior designer Clodagh created the look of this spa using natural materials and the guiding properties of feng shui, the ancient Chinese philosophy of balancing the forces of nature. Achieving inner tranquility is the mission here, and the treatments embrace this guiding principle. An extensive massage menu includes favorites such as Swedish, sports, aromatherapy, shiatsu and deep tissue, as well as Eastern methods such as reflexology and reiki. From Japanese citrus and Balinese hibiscus to German chamomile and Greek mint, the body scrubs embody international personalities. Fitness and nutrition consultations help you gain insight into your body and its needs. The onsite spa restaurant makes healthy eating easier.

LEHIGH VALLEY

Much of the Lehigh Valley region falls into Pennsylvania Dutch Country. This beautiful region of picturesque south-central Pennsylvania combines history and nature. Situated in the heart of it is Allentown, greatly influenced by the Pennsylvania Germans who settled the surrounding countryside. Practically next door to Allentown lies Bethlehem, "America's Christmas City." Bethlehem Steel products have put this city on the map, but Bethlehem is also known for its Bach Festival and historic district. Moravians, members of a very old Protestant denomination, assembled here on Christmas Evening 1741. Singing a hymn that praised Bethlehem, they found a name for their village.

WHAT TO SEE

ALLENTOWN

DORNEY PARK AND WILDWATER KINGDOM
3830 Dorney Park Road, Allentown, 610-395-3724; www.dorneypark.com

This amusement and water park is one of the country's oldest. The 200-acre park is home to nearly 100 rides, 11 water slides and four roller coasters. Little ones can discover turtle fountains and squirt guns. Bigger kids can climb and play on a submarine. Older kids may want to torpedo through an enclosed tube or float slowly down a 1,600-foot winding river. Just an hour from Philadelphia, the park also features song and dance revues and 40 food locations.

Admission: adults $39.99, children and seniors $19.99. Daily; hours vary. Closed November-April.

LIBERTY BELL SHRINE
622 Hamilton St., Allentown, 610-435-4232; www.libertybellmuseum.org

This reconstructed Zion's church has a shrine in basement area where the Liberty Bell was hidden in 1777. It contains a full-size replica of the original bell along with other historical exhibits and an art collection.

Admission: Free. Mid-January-March Wednesday-Saturday noon-4 p.m.; April-November, Monday-Saturday noon-4 p.m.

BETHLEHEM

CENTRAL MORAVIAN CHURCH
73 W. Church St., Bethlehem, 610-866-5661; www.centralmoravianchurch.org

This federal-style church built in 1806 features hand-carved detail and is considered the foremost Moravian church in the U.S. It has been noted for its music, including a trombone choir in existence since 1754.

MORAVIAN MUSEUM (GEMEINHAUS)
66 W. Church St., Bethlehem, 610-867-0173; www.historicbethlehem.org

This five-story log building was built in 1741 and is the oldest structure in the city. Docents interpret the history and culture of early Bethlehem and the Moravians.

Admission: free. Thursday-Sunday noon-4 p.m.

HIGHLIGHT

DELAWARE WATER GAP RECREATIONAL AREA

It is difficult to believe that the quiet Delaware River could carve a path through the Kittatinny Mountains, which are nearly a quarter of a mile high at this point. Conflicting geological theories account for this natural phenomenon. The prevailing theory is that the mountains were formed after the advent of the river, rising up from the earth so slowly that the course of the Delaware was never altered.

Despite the speculation about its origin, there is no doubt about the area's recreational value. The relatively unspoiled area along the river boundary between Pennsylvania and New Jersey stretches approximately 35 miles from Matamoras to an area just south of I-80.

Trails and overlooks offer scenic views. Visitors can go canoeing and swimming and picnicking are available at Smithfield and Milford beaches. Dingmans Falls and Silver Thread Falls, two of the highest waterfalls in the Poconos, are near here. Several 19th-century buildings are also in the area, including Millbrook Village (several buildings open May-October) and Peters Valley. The visitor center is located off I-80 in New Jersey, at Kittatinny Point.

WHERE TO STAY

ALLENTOWN
★★★THE GLASBERN INN
2141 Pack House Road, Fogelsville, 610-285-4723; www.glasbern.com

Stay in rustic luxury, amidst both antique furnishings and all of the contemporary comforts. Built in the late 1800s on 100 acres near Allentown, the inn is housed in an old farm and includes a renovated farmhouse, barn, gatehouse and carriage house.

38 rooms. Complimentary breakfast. Business center. Fitness center. Pool. Spa. Pets accepted. $61-150

WHERE TO EAT

BETHLEHEM
★★★MAIN STREET DEPOT
61 W. Lehigh St., Bethlehem, 610-868-7123; www.mainstreetdepotrestaurant.com

On the National Registry of Historic Buildings, the location out of which the Main Street Depot now operates was built in 1873 and served as a station for the Jersey Central railroad. Grab a depot burger at the bar, or sit down for dinner and enjoy an entrée like butter rum chicken with cashews, coconut and fresh pineapple over rice or filet mignon wrapped in bacon and served with asparagus and béarnaise sauce.

American. Lunch, dinner. Closed Sunday. Bar. $36-85

HIGHLIGHT

WHAT ARE THE TOP THINGS TO DO IN THE LEHIGH VALLEY?

UNCOVER THE LIBERTY BELL'S HIDING PLACE
In 1777, the famous bell was hidden in the basement of Zion's Church. Now containing a full-size replica, the secret spot acts as a museum.

EXPLORE THE OLDEST HOUSE IN THE CITY
Trout Hall was built in 1770 by James Allen, the son of Allentown's founder. The once summer estate is the oldest surviving home in the city.

VISIT THE DELAWARE WATER GAP
Between New Jersey and Pennsylvania lies the Delaware Water Gap. Over the years, the river has carved a path through the Kittatinny Mountains.

PENNSYLVANIA WILDS

Covering most of northern Pennsylvania, the Pennsylvania Wilds region is just as the name suggests: natural. When oil was discovered in Bradford in the late 1800s, the price of land jumped from about six cents to $1,000 an acre, and wells appeared on front lawns, in backyards and even in a cemetery. The third-largest city in Pennsylvania, Erie is the state's only port on the Great Lakes and boasts a wealth of natural beauty and fascinating historical tales. The lake and city take their name from the Erie tribe, who were killed by the Seneca around 1654. At the junction of the Allegheny and Conewango rivers, Warren is the headquarters and gateway of the famous Allegheny National Forest. The town was once the point where great flotillas of logs were formed for the journey to Pittsburgh or Cincinnati.

WHAT TO SEE

ERIE
BICENTENNIAL TOWER
7 Dobbins Landing, Erie, 814-455-6055

Commemorating Erie's 200th birthday, this 187-foot tower features two observation decks with an aerial view of the city, bay and Lake Erie.

Admission: adults $3, children 7-12 $2, children 6 and under free. May, daily 10 a.m.-8 p.m.; June-August, daily 9:30 a.m.-10 p.m.; September-October 10 a.m.-6 p.m.; November-March, Saturday-Sunday noon-4 p.m.; April 10 a.m.-6 p.m. Free Sunday.

HIGHLIGHT

WHAT ARE THE TOP THINGS TO DO IN THE PENNSYLVANIA WILDS?

TAKE IN BICENTENNIAL VIEWS
The Bicentennial Tower features two observation decks, creating spectacular vistas of the city, bay and Lake Erie.

EXPLORE PREQUE ISLE STATE PARK
You'll find Waldameer Amusement Park and Water World Water Park here. There are rides, an arcade, roller coasters, a kiddieland, water rides, and much more.

WILDLIFE IN PENNSYLVANIA WILDS
All kinds of animals roam the 510,000 acres of the Allegheny National Forest. From black bears to wild turkeys, there is sure to be some wildlife combing the grounds.

ERIE ART MUSEUM
411 State St., Erie, 814-459-5477; www.erieartmuseum.org

Temporary art exhibits in a variety of media are on display here, including regional artwork and lectures in the restored Greek Revival Old Customs House. Art classes, concerts, lectures and workshops are also offered.

Admission: adults $4, seniors and students $3, children under 13 free. Tuesday-Saturday 11 a.m.-5 p.m., Sunday 1-5 p.m. Free Wednesday.

ERIE LAND LIGHTHOUSE
2 Lighthouse St., Erie, 814-870-1452; www.nps.gov

The first lighthouse on the Great Lakes was constructed on this site in 1818. *Daily.*

ERIE ZOO
423 W. 38th St., Erie, 814-864-4091; www.eriezoo.org

The Erie Zoo houses more than 300 animals, including gorillas, polar bears and giraffes on 15 acres. There is also a children's zoo and a one-mile tour of grounds on Safariland Express Train. There is an indoor ice rink open during the fall and winter months. Be sure to check out the some of the baby animals, including a tiger cub, otter pup and baby orangutan.

Admission: March-November, adults $7, seniors $6, children 2-11 $4, children 1 and under free. Monday-Saturday 10 a.m.-5 p.m., Sunday 10 a.m.-6 p.m. Free Sunday 3-5 p.m.

FIREFIGHTERS HISTORICAL MUSEUM

428 Chestnut St., Erie, 814-456-5969; www.firefightershistoricalmuseum.com

More than 1,300 items of firefighting memorabilia are displayed in the old Number 4 Firehouse. Exhibits include fire apparatus dating from 1823, alarm systems, uniforms, badges, ribbons, helmets, nozzles, fire marks and fire extinguishers; fire safety films are shown in the Hay Loft Theater.

Admission: adults $4, seniors and firefighters $2.50, children 6-12 $1. May-August, Saturday 10 a.m.-5 p.m., Sunday 1-5 p.m.; September-October, Saturday-Sunday 1-5 p.m.

PRESQUE ISLE STATE PARK

1 Peninsula Drive, Erie, 814-833-7424; www.presqueisle.org

This peninsula stretches seven miles into Lake Erie and curves back toward the city. There are approximately 3,200 acres of recreation and conservation areas, in which visitors can go swimming, fishing, boating, hiking, birding, cross-country skiing, ice skating, ice fishing, ice boating and picnicking. There are also concessions available here. The Tom Ridge Environmental Center offers environmental education and interpretive programs along with exhibits, a theater, nature shop and gallery, cafe and visitor's center. Also here in Misery Bay, where you'll find the Perry monument, named after Perry's naval squadron that defeated the British; the fleet suffered the cold and privations of a bitter winter. The Presque Isle Lighthouse is located here; it's the second lighthouse built on Lake Erie.

Environmental center: Daily 10 a.m.-8 p.m.

WALDAMEER PARK & WATER WORLD

220 Peninsula Drive, Erie, 814-838-3591; www.waldameer.com

At the entrance to Presque Isle State Park, you'll find Waldameer Amusement Park and Water World Water Park. There are rides, an arcade, roller coasters, a kiddieland, water rides, a picnic area, food stands, and a dance pavilion.

Admission to the park is free but you must purchase passes for individual parks to enjoy the rides. Admission: Free. Admission to Water World: over 48 inches tall $15.45, under 48 inches tall $10.95. Waldameer: over 48 inches $20.45, under 48 inches $12.95. Combo (both parks): over 48 inches tall $22.95, under 48 inches tall $16.95. June-August, Tuesday-Sunday.

WARREN

ALLEGHENY NATIONAL FOREST

222 Liberty St., Warren, 814-723-5150; www.fs.fed.us

This national forest is more than 510,000 acres south and east on Highways 6 and 62, located in Warren, Forest, McKean and Elk counties. You'll find black bears, whitetail deer, wild turkey, a diversity of small birds and mammals and streams and reservoirs with trout, walleye, muskellunge, northern pike and bass. There are rugged hills, quiet valleys, open meadows, and dense forest. These lures, plus swimming, boating, hiking, camping and picnicking facilities, draw more than 2 million visitors a year.

KINZUA DAM AND ALLEGHENY RESERVOIR

1205 Kinzua Road, Warren, 814-726-0661

The Kinzua Dam, at 179 feet high and 1,877 feet long has a 24-mile-long lake where visitors can enjoy swimming, fishing, boating, picnicking, and vistas from overlooks. This is a popular destination in the summertime. There are also campsites here.

Visitor center: June-August, daily; September-October, Saturday-Sunday.

WHERE TO STAY

BRADFORD
★★★GLENDORN
1000 Glendorn Drive, Bradford, 814-362-6511, 800-843-8568; www.glendorn.com
Set on 1,280 acres, this one-time private estate offers a sophisticated twist on the traditional wooded retreat. A long, private drive welcomes visitors to this hideaway, where guests enjoy walks in the woods, canoe and fishing trips, hiking and biking adventures, and a host of other outdoor pursuits. The accommodations in the Big House reflect a warm, country house spirit, while the cabin suites have a rugged charm. Fine dining is a hallmark of this country lodge, with hearty country breakfasts, delicious lunches and four-course prix fixe dinners.

17 rooms. Restaurant, bar. Pool. Pets accepted. No children under 8. Tennis. $351 and up.

PHILADELPHIA

In the mid-18th century, Philadelphia was the second largest city in the English-speaking world. Today, Philadelphia is the second largest city on the East Coast and the fifth largest in the country. Here, in William Penn's "City of Brotherly Love," the Declaration of Independence was written and adopted, the Constitution was molded and signed, the Liberty Bell was rung, Betsy Ross was said to have sewn her flag and Washington served most of his years as president. The first Quakers, who came here in 1681, lived in caves dug into the banks of the Delaware River. During the first year, 80 houses were raised; by the following year, William Penn's "greene countrie towne" was a city of 600 buildings. The Quakers prospered in trade and commerce, and Philadelphia became the leading port in the colonies. Both Continental Congresses convened here, and Philadelphia became the headquarters of the Revolution. After the Declaration of Independence was composed and accepted by Congress, the city gave its men, factories and shipyards to the cause. Philadelphia continued as the seat of government until 1800, except for a short period when New York City held the honor. Since those historic days, Philadelphia has figured prominently in the country's politics, economy and culture.

WHAT TO SEE

ACADEMY OF MUSIC
Broad and Locust streets, Philadelphia, 215-893-1999; www.academyofmusic.org
The city's opera house and concert hall, this academy was built in 1857 and is home of the Philadelphia Orchestra, Opera Company of Philadelphia and Pennsylvania Ballet.

See website for schedule and ticket information.

HIGHLIGHT

WHAT ARE THE TOP THINGS TO DO IN PHILADELPHIA?

VISIT THE HALL WHERE OUR NATION WAS BORN
The Declaration of Independence was read publicly for the first time at Independence Hall. Book a tour to see the inside of this historic place.

TOUR THE SEAT OF PHILADELPHIA'S GOVERNMENT
City Hall stands a whopping 548-feet-tall, with a 37-foot statue of William Penn gazing down from the roof. Originally the tallest building in the city, it is now the second tallest masonry building in the world.

GET A TASTE OF THE PHILADELPHIA ITALIANS
Head to Ninth Street Italian Market for a taste of culture. The Italian cuisine overwhelms the senses with goodness.

ACADEMY OF NATURAL SCIENCES MUSEUM
1900 Ben Franklin Parkway, Philadelphia, 215-299-1000; www.acnatsci.org
This museum displays dinosaurs, Egyptian mummies, animal displays in natural habitats and live animal programs. There is also a hands-on children's museum.
Admission: adults $12, seniors $10, students and military personnel $10, children 3-12 $10, children 2 and under free. Monday-Friday 10 a.m.-4:30 p.m., Saturday-Sunday 10 a.m.-5 p.m.

AFRICAN-AMERICAN MUSEUM OF PHILADELPHIA
701 Arch St., Philadelphia, 215-574-0380; www.aampmuseum.org
Built to house and interpret African-American culture, this museum has changing exhibits and lectures, workshops, films and concerts.
Admission: adults $10, seniors, students and children 4-12 $8. Tuesday-Saturday 10 a.m.-5 p.m., Sunday noon-5 p.m.

ANTIQUE ROW
Ninth to 17th streets along Pine Street, Philadelphia; www.antique-row.org
Dozens of antique, craft and curio shops as well as restaurants, bars and cafes line this popular row.

ATHENAEUM OF PHILADELPHIA
219 S. Sixth St., Philadelphia, 215-925-2688; www.athenaonline.org
This landmark is an example of Italian Renaissance architecture. The restored building has American neoclassical-style decorative arts, paintings, sculpture; a research library; furniture and art from the collection of Joseph Bonaparte,

King of Spain and older brother of Napoleon; changing exhibits of architectural drawings, photos and rare books.

Tours by appointment. Monday-Friday 9 a.m.-5 p.m., first Saturday of the month 10 a.m.-2 p.m.

ATWATER KENT MUSEUM OF PHILADELPHIA

15 S. Seventh St., Philadelphia, 215-685-4830; www.philadelphiahistory.org

Hundreds of fascinating artifacts, toys and miniatures, maps, prints, paintings and photographs reflect the city's social and cultural history.

Monday-Friday 9 a.m.-5 p.m.

BETSY ROSS HOUSE

239 Arch St., Philadelphia, 215-686-1252; www.betsyrosshouse.org

This house is where the famous seamstress is said to have made the first American flag. You can see the upholsterer's shop and memorabilia. Flag Day ceremonies take place June 14.

Admission: adults and seniors $3, students and children 12 and under $2. Audio tour: $5 (includes admission). April-October, daily 10 a.m.-5 p.m.; November-March, Tuesday-Sunday 10 a.m-5 p.m.

BLUE CROSS RIVER RINK

Festival Pier at Penn's Landing, Columbus Boulevard and Spring Garden Street, Philadelphia, 215-925-7465; www.riverrink.com

Few outdoor ice-skating rinks are as well located as this one along the Delaware River. Visitors have a great vantage point from which to view the Benjamin Franklin Bridge and the Philadelphia skyline. This Olympic-size rink, at 200 feet by 85 feet, can accommodate 500 skaters. After skating, warm up in the heated pavilion, which features a video game area and concessions.

Late November-February, daily.

CITY HALL

Broad and Market streets, Philadelphia, 215-686-2840; www.phila.gov

A granite statue of William Penn stands 548 feet high above the heart of the city on top of this municipal building, which is larger than the Capitol. It's known as Penn Square and was designated by Penn as the location for a building of public concerns. It also functions as Philadelphia's City Hall and is one of the finest examples of French Second-Empire architectural style. Boasting the tallest statue (37 feet) on a building in the world on its top, this building took 30 years to construct. Penn's famous hat is more than seven feet in diameter, and the brim creates a two-foot-wide track. There are more than 250 sculptures around this marble, granite and limestone structure, 20 elevators, and a four-faced, 50-ton clock. Tours start at the Tour Information Center.

Tours: Monday-Friday 12:30 p.m.

CLIVEDEN

6401 Germantown Ave., Philadelphia, 215-848-1777; www.cliveden.org

This two-story stone Georgian house built in 1767 served as the summer home for Benjamin Chew, Chief Justice of colonial Pennsylvania. On October 4, 1777, British soldiers used the house as a fortress to repulse Washington's attempt to recapture Philadelphia. Used as the Chew family residence for 200 years; it features many original furnishings. This is a National Trust for Historic

Preservation property.

Admission: adults $10, students $8. April-December, Thursday-Sunday noon-4 p.m.

CONGRESS HALL

Independence Park, Sixth and Chestnut streets, Philadelphia, 215-965-2305; www.nps.gov

Located in Independence Park, this hall is where congress met during the last decade of the 18th century. The inaugurations of George Washington and John Adams also took place here. The House of Representatives and Senate chambers are restored.

Admission: Free. Daily 9 a.m.-5 p.m.

DECLARATION HOUSE

701 Market St., Philadelphia, 215-965-2305; www.nps.gov

This reconstructed house is located on the site of the writing of the Declaration of Independence by Thomas Jefferson. The two rooms that Jefferson rented have been reproduced. There is a short orientation and movie about Jefferson, his philosophy on the common man, and the history of the house.

Daily, hours vary.

ELECTRIC FACTORY

421 N. Seventh St., Philadelphia, 215-627-1332; www.electricfactory.info

This all ages live-music venue offers accessibility to lesser-known bands, although well-known national artists play here as well including Lady Gaga, Sonic Youth and others. Arrive early to get a bar table in the upstairs balcony overlooking the stage.

See website for schedule and ticket information.

ELFRETH'S ALLEY

126 Elfreth's Alley, Philadelphia, 215-574-0560; www.elfrethsalley.org

Philadelphians still live in these Georgian- and Federal-style homes along cobblestoned Elfreth's Alley, the nation's oldest continued-use residential street. A few homes have been converted into museums, offering guided tours, a quaint gift shop and handcrafted memorabilia.

Tours: adults $5, children 6-18 $1, children 5 and under free. Tuesday-Saturday 10 a.m.-5 p.m., Sunday noon-5 p.m.

FAIRMOUNT PARK

4231 N. Concourse Drive, Philadelphia, 215-683-0200; www.fairmountpark.org

This is one of America's loveliest parks. With more than 9,200 acres, Fairmount Park is one of the largest. The park is home to more than 215 miles of beautifully landscaped paths for walking and horseback riding. People from all over the city fill the park to enjoy the outdoors. Cyclists love to bike along the Pennypack and Wissahickon trails. Walkers stroll or hike in Valley Green alongside the ducks. In-line skaters and rowing and sculling enthusiasts meet at Boathouse Row to enjoy the sights along the Schuykill River on Kelly Drive. There are more than a hundred tennis courts and numerous picnic spots. The park is also home to the Philadelphia Zoo, the Shofuso Japanese House, the Philadelphia Museum of Art, the Philadelphia Orchestra's summer amphitheater (Mann Music Center) and Memorial Hall, the only building remaining from the 1876 Centennial Exhibition. What really set this park apart is that it contains America's largest collection of authentic colonial homes. These handsome 18th-century dwellings in varying architectural styles are authentically preserved and furnished. Stop in the Philadelphia Museum of Art for details on touring them.

Hours and admission vary; see website for information.

FIREMAN'S HALL MUSEUM
147 N. Second St., Philadelphia, 215-923-1438; www.firemanshall.org

This museum features a collection of antique firefighting equipment along with displays and exhibits of fire department history since it began in 1736.

Admission: Free. Tuesday-Saturday 10 a.m.-4:30 p.m. First Friday of every month 10 a.m-9 p.m.

FIRST BANK OF THE UNITED STATES
Third and Walnut streets, Philadelphia

The first bank was organized by Alexander Hamilton and is the country's oldest bank building. The exterior has been restored and although the building is closed to the public, you can still view the façade.

FORT MIFFLIN
Fort Mifflin and Hog Island roads, Philadelphia, 215-685-4167; www.fortmifflin.us

Fort Mifflin, a Revolutionary War fort strategically located in the Delaware River at the mouth of the Schuylkill, is a complex of 11 restored buildings. Climb into a bombproof enclosure used to shelter troops; witness the uniform and weapons demonstrations that take place throughout the year; explore the soldiers' barracks, officers' quarters and blacksmith's shop; or simply enjoy the spectacular view of Philadelphia and the Delaware from the Northeast Bastion.

Wednesday-Sunday 10 a.m.-4 p.m.

FRANKLIN COURT
Independence Park, 316-322 Market St., Philadelphia, 215-965-2305; www.nps.gov/inde

The site of Benjamin Franklin's house has been developed as a tribute to him and just a steel structure stands outlining where his house once stood (literally just a steel structure; his house was torn down around 1810). The area includes a working printing office and bindery, an underground museum with multimedia exhibits, an archaeological exhibit and the B. Free Franklin Post office.

Printing office: Daily 10 a.m.-5 p.m. Post office: Monday-Saturday 9 a.m.-5 p.m.

THE FRANKLIN INSTITUTE
222 N. 20th St., Philadelphia, 215-448-1200; www2.fi.edu

This 300,000-square-foot science museum complex and memorial hall brings biology, earth science, physics, mechanics, aviation, astronomy, communications and technology to life with a variety of highly interactive exhibits honoring Philadelphia's mechanical inventor Ben Franklin. A 30-foot marble statue of Franklin sits in a Roman Pantheon-inspired chamber known as the Benjamin Franklin National Memorial. Stargazers can witness the birth of the universe or see galaxies form under the Fels Planetarium dome.

Admission: adults $14.75, seniors, students and military personnel $13.75, children under 18 $12. Daily 9:30 a.m.-5 p.m.

THE HISTORICAL SOCIETY OF PENNSYLVANIA

1300 Locust St., Philadelphia, 215-732-6200; www.hsp.org

The Historical Society features a first draft of the U.S. Constitution, 500 artifacts and manuscripts, plus video tours of turn-of-the-century urban and suburban neighborhoods. A research library houses historical and genealogical collections.
Library Admission: adults $6, students $3. Library: Tuesday, Thursday 12:30-5:30 p.m., Wednesday 12:30-8:30 p.m., Friday 10 a.m.-5:30 p.m.

INDEPENDENCE HALL

Fifth and Chestnut streets, Philadelphia, 215-965-2305; www.nps.gov

No first visit to Philadelphia is complete with a stop in Independence Hall. Built in the mid-1700s, Independence Hall is the site of the first public reading of the Declaration of Independence. It also played host to large political rallies during the country's founding years and is considered a fine example of Georgian architecture. Visitors often find the Hall a good first stop for their tour of Independence National Historic Park, which includes the Liberty Bell, Congress Hall, Old City Hall and Carpenters' Hall. The building is open for tours only and you must get a timed ticket.
Daily 9 a.m.-5 p.m.

INDEPENDENCE NATIONAL HISTORICAL PARK

Third and Chestnut streets, Philadelphia, 215-965-2305; www.nps.gov

The park has been called America's most historic square mile. The Independence Visitor Center at Sixth and Market streets has a tour map, and information on all park activities and attractions. Check out the 30-minute film "Independence" for a great overview. Unless otherwise indicated, all historic sites and museums in the park are free and open daily.
Admission: Free. Independence Visitor Center: Daily 8:30 a.m.-7 p.m.

INDEPENDENCE SEAPORT MUSEUM

211 S. Columbus Blvd., Philadelphia, 215-413-8655; www.phillyseaport.org

Maritime enthusiasts of all ages will appreciate the creative interactive exhibits about the science, history and art of boat building along the region's waterways at the Independence Seaport Museum. Oral histories of the men and women who have lived and worked here take visitors through immigration, commerce, defense, industry and the recreational aspects of boats.
Admission: adults $12, seniors $10, students, military personnel and children 2-18 $7. Daily 10 a.m.-5 p.m.

JEWELER'S ROW

Seventh and Sansom streets, Philadelphia

This is the largest jewelry district in the country other than New York City. More than 300 shops, including wholesalers and diamond cutters can be found here.

LIBERTY BELL

Liberty Bell Center, Market and Sixth streets, Philadelphia, 215-597-8974

An international icon and one of the most venerated stops in Independence Park, this mostly copper symbol of religious freedom, justice and independence is believed to hang from its original yoke.
Daily.

MANAYUNK

111 Grape St., Philadelphia, 215-482-9565; www.manayunk.com

This historic district, just seven miles from Center City, makes a great destination point or place to hang out. Old rail lines, canal locks and textile mills dot this quaint northwest neighborhood. Joggers, walkers, hikers and off-road cyclists will enjoy traveling the towpath that edges the town while their shopaholic counterparts check out the more than 70 boutiques and galleries, with 35 of them being furniture shops. You'll feel like you're in a small town in Europe.

MASONIC TEMPLE

1 N. Broad St., Philadelphia, 215-988-1900; www.pagrandlodge.org

Philadelphia's Masonic Temple was designed for the Fraternal Order of Freemasons, of which Benjamin Franklin and George Washington were members. The interior houses seven different halls, including the Gothic Hall, Oriental Hall and the better-known Egyptian Hall. Treasures of freemasonry, including a book written by Franklin and Washington's Masonic apron, are kept here.

Admission: adults $8, students $6, children 12 and under and seniors $5, military personnel and children 5 and under free. Tours: Tuesday-Friday 10 a.m., 11 a.m., 1 p.m., 2 p.m., 3 p.m., Saturday 10 a.m., 11 a.m., noon.

MORRIS ARBORETUM OF THE UNIVERSITY OF PENNSYLVANIA

100 E. Northwestern Ave., Philadelphia, 215-247-5777; www.upenn.edu

Established in 1887, this public garden features more than 13,000 accessioned plants on 92 acres; special garden areas such as Swan Pond, Rose Garden and Japanese gardens are onsite.

Admission: adults $14, seniors $12, students and children 3-17 $7, children 2 and under free. April-October, Monday-Friday 10 a.m.-4 p.m., Saturday-Sunday 10 a.m.-5 p.m.; June-August, Monday-Wednesday, Friday 10 a.m.-4 p.m., Saturday-Sunday 10 a.m.-5 p.m., Thursday 10 a.m.-8:30 p.m.; November-March, daily 10 a.m.-4 p.m.

NINTH STREET ITALIAN MARKET

Ninth Street, between Wharton and Fitzwater, Philadelphia, 215-923-5637; www.9thstreetitalianmarket.com

Head to the Italian Market to sip Italian gourmet coffee, sample imported cheeses and eat cannoli. With more than 100 merchants selling their wares, this is the largest working outdoor market in the United States. Dining choices range from fine Italian dining to lunch counters to an outdoor snack tent.

Tuesday-Sunday, hours vary.

PENNSYLVANIA ACADEMY OF FINE ARTS

118 N. Broad St., Philadelphia, 215-972-7600; www.pafa.org

The nation's oldest art museum and school of fine arts houses paintings, works on paper and sculptures by American artists ranging from colonial masters to contemporary artists within its beautiful Gothic-Victorian structure. Many of the nation's finest artists, including Charles Willson Peale, Mary Cassatt, William Merritt Chase and Maxfield Parrish, were founders, teachers or students here.

Admission: adults $10, seniors and students $8, children 5-18 $6. Tuesday-Saturday 10 a.m.-5 p.m., Sunday 11 a.m.-5 p.m.

PENNSYLVANIA BALLET
1819 JFK Blvd., Philadelphia, 215-551-7000; www.paballet.org

This company with a George Balanchine influence includes a varied reper-toire of ballets ranging from classics like *The Nutcracker* to original works. Performances are held at the Academy of Music and the Merriam Theatre.
See website for schedule and ticket information.

PHILADELPHIA 76ERS (NBA)
Wachovia Complex, 3601 S. Broad St, 215-336-3600, Philadelphia; www.nba.com

Philadelphia's professional basketball team plays at the Wachovia Complex, which was built and opened in 1996. The Sixers have had quite the history, with players such as Allen Iverson, Charles Barkley and Wilt Chamberlain. Philly is very proud of their sports teams and the 76ers fans prove that. The team moved from Syracuse, NY in 1963, marking the beginning of an era. The team won its last conference title in 2001.

PHILADELPHIA EAGLES (NFL)
Lincoln Financial Field, 11th Street and Pattison Avenue, Philadelphia, 215-463-2500;
www.philadelphiaeagles.com

Philadelphia's professional football team, the Eagles, play at Lincoln Financial Stadium. The team traded their beloved quarterback, Donovan McNabb during the 2010 draft to the Washington Redskins. The Eagles tend to be a strong team with a strong fan base. Donned in green and black, the Philadelphia Eagles' roster has included Sonny Jurgensen, Mike Ditka and Michael Vick.

PHILADELPHIA PHILLIES (MLB)
Citizens Bank Park, One Citizens Bank Way, Philadelphia, 215-463-5000;
www.philadelphiaphillies.com

Philadelphia's professional baseball team, the Phillies, is the oldest continuous one-name, one-city franchise in all of American professional sports. Decked out in their red, white and blue uniforms, the Phillies have won two World Series titles, the most recent in 2008. One of the best rivalries in baseball is between the Phillies and the New York Mets, as the teams often battle for play-off position. The Phillies have had their fair share of Hall of Famers, including Sparky Anderson, Bucky Harris and Ed Delahanty.

PHILADELPHIA MUSEUM OF ART
26th Street and the Benjamin Franklin Parkway, Philadelphia, 215-763-8100;
www.philamuseum.org

Modeled after a Greco-Roman temple, this massive museum amplifies the beauty of more than 300,000 works of art, and offers spectacular natural views. From the top of the steps outside (made famous by Sylvester Stallone in *Rocky*), visitors discover a breathtaking view of the Ben Franklin Parkway toward City Hall. Inside, the collections span 2,000 years and many more miles. There's a lavish collection of period rooms, a Japanese teahouse and a Chinese palace hall. Art lovers will also find Indian and Himalayan pieces, European decora-tive arts, medieval sculptures, Impressionist and Post-Impressionist paintings, and contemporary works in many media.
Admission: adults $14, seniors $12, students $10, children 13-18 $10, children 12 and under free. Tuesday-Thursday, Saturday-Sunday 10 a.m-5 p.m., Friday 10 a.m.-8:45 p.m.

THE PHILADELPHIA ORCHESTRA

260 S. Broad St. No. 1600, Philadelphia, 215-893-1900; www.philorch.org

The internationally renowned Philadelphia Orchestra has distinguished itself through a century of acclaimed performances, historic international tours and best-selling recordings. Performances are held at the Kimmel Center for the Performing Arts at Broad and Spruce streets; the Academy of Music at Broad and Locust streets; the Mann Center for the Performing Arts, 52nd Street and Parkside Avenue; Saratoga Performing Arts Center in upstate New York; and annually at New York's Carnegie Hall.

See website for schedule and ticket information.

PHILADELPHIA ZOO

3400 W. Girard Ave., Philadelphia, 215-243-1100; www.philadelphiazoo.org

The Philadelphia Zoo may have been America's first zoo (it was home to the nation's first white lions and witnessed its first successful chimpanzee birth), but you'll see no signs of old age here. Over the last century, the zoo has transformed itself into a preservation spot for rare and endangered animals and as a garden and wildlife destination point. The zoo is home to 1,300 animals, from red pandas to Rodrigues fruit bats. Take a pony, camel or elephant ride; feed nectar to a parrot in a walk-through aviary; or engage with a playful wallaby. Pedal a boat around Bird Lake. Or take a soaring balloon 400 feet up on the country's first passenger-carrying Zooballoon.

Admission: March-October, adults $18, children 2-11 $15; November-February, adults $12.95, children 2-11 $12.95. March-November, daily 9:30 a.m.-5 p.m.; December-February, daily 9:30 a.m.-4 p.m.

PLEASE TOUCH MUSEUM FOR CHILDREN

210 N. 21st St., Philadelphia, 215-581-3181;
www.pleasetouchmuseum.org

A group of artists, educators and parents conceived of this award-winning, interactive exploratory learning center for children of ages one to seven in 1976. The safe, hands-on learning laboratory has since become a model for children's museums nationwide. Story lovers will enjoy having tea with the Mad Hatter or hanging out with Max in the forest where the wild things are. Children who don't want to sit still can board the life-size bus or shop at the miniature supermarket. The ones who like to get their hands dirty can engage in science experiments. Creature lovers can interact with fuzzy human-made barnyard animals. And the entertainment-minded can see themselves on television or audition for a news anchor position.

Admission: adults and children $15, children 1 and under free. Monday-Saturday 9 a.m.-5 p.m., Sunday 11 a.m.-5 p.m.

READING TERMINAL MARKET

12th and Arch streets, Philadelphia, 215-922-2317; www.readingterminalmarket.org

The nation's oldest continuously operating farmers market is alive—and thriving—in downtown Philadelphia. An indoor banquet for the senses, the market offers an exhilarating array of baked goods, meats, poultry, seafood, produce, flowers and Asian, Middle Eastern and Pennsylvania Dutch foods. Head to Fisher's where you'll find Philadelphia soft pretzels. These famous soft

pretzels are hand-rolled, freshly baked, coarsely salted, buttery, golden-brown comfort food served in a paper bag.
Monday-Saturday 8 a.m.-6 p.m., Sunday 9 a.m.-5 p.m.

RITTENHOUSE SQUARE
1800 Walnut St., Philadelphia; www.rittenhouserow.org
In the blocks that surround this genteel urban square in Philadelphia's most fashionable section of town are exclusive shops, restaurants and chic boutiques. Stores include Cole Haan, Club Monaco, Kenneth Cole and Talbots. Restaurants and bars include Fado Irish Pub, Le Bec-Fin, Lacroix at the Rittenhouse and many others. The square also features many hotels such as the Four Seasons Hotel Philadelphia, The Ritz-Carlton, Philadelphia and Rittenhouse Hotel.

RODIN MUSEUM
22nd Street and Franklin Parkway, Philadelphia, 215-568-6026;
www.rodinmuseum.org
This museum, built in the Beaux Arts style, houses more than 200 sculptures created by Auguste Rodin and is considered the largest collection of his works outside his native France. *The Thinker*, Rodin's most famous piece, greets visitors outside at the gateway to the museum.
Admission: $5. Tuesday-Sunday 10 a.m.-5 p.m.

SOCIETY HILL AREA
Seventh and Lombard streets, Philadelphia; www.societyhillcivic.com
Secret parks, cobblestone walkways and diminutive alleys among beauti-fully restored brick colonial townhouses make this historic area a treasure for visitors. A popular, daily 30-minute walking tour will inspire history fans as well as architecture lovers. Highlights along the way include a courtyard designed by I.M. Pei; gardens planted by the Daughters of the American Revolution; a sculpture of Robert Morris, one of the signers of the Declaration of Independence; Greek Revival-style architecture now home to the National Portrait Gallery; and the burial ground of Revolutionary War soldiers. In the summer months, the area hosts outdoor arts festivals in Headhouse Square. It's also home to some of Philadelphia's finest restaurants.

SOUTH STREET DISTRICT
South St., Philadelphia, 215-413-3713; www.south-street.com
On South Street, the young and hip will enjoy the search for thrift store finds and people watching of the pierced and tattooed variety. The rest can rifle through dusty rare books or cruise the art galleries. These blocks at the southern boundary of the city—as well as the numbered streets just off of it—are chock full of offbeat shops, cafés, street musicians and water ice stands, all within walking distance of Penn's Landing and Society Hill. For a Philadelphia signature treat, don't miss the cheesesteaks at Jim's Steaks (*www.jimssteaks.com*).

STENTON HOUSE
4601 N. 18th St., Philadelphia, 215-329-7312; www.stenton.org
This mansion was built between 1723 and 1730 by James Logan, secretary to William Penn, and is an excellent example of Pennsylvania colonial architecture,

furnished with 18th- and 19th-century antiques. General George Washington spent August 23, 1777 here and General Sir William Howe headquartered here for the Battle of Germantown. There is a colonial barn, gardens and kitchen.

March-December, Tuesday-Saturday 1-4 p.m.; also by appointment.

TROCADERO THEATRE

1003 Arch St., Philadelphia, 215-922-5483; www.thetroc.com

This former 1870s opera house hosted vaudeville, burlesque and Chinese movies before it became the beautiful, contemporary live music venue that it is today. The theater now hosts many well-known rock and pop artists. On Movie Mondays, the theater holds almost free ($3 for admission which goes toward a snack of your choice) screenings (on its original screen) of such classic and cult movies such as *Apocalypse Now* and *Donnie Darko*.

Box office: Monday-Friday 11:30 a.m.-6 p.m., Saturday 11:30 a.m.-5 p.m.

UNIVERSITY OF PENNSYLVANIA

32nd and Walnut streets, Philadelphia, 215-898-5000; www.upenn.edu

Founded by Benjamin Franklin, this Ivy League university has more than 24,000 students enrolled. Here, you'll find the prestigious Wharton School for business, the Annenberg School for Communication, the School of Medicine, Law School and other top ranking schools. The Museum of Archaeology (*3260 South St., Philadelphia, 215-898-4000; www.museum.upenn.edu*) features world-famous archaeological and ethnographic collections developed from the museum's own expeditions, gifts and purchases.

Museum admission: adults $10, seniors $7, children 6-17 and students $6, children 5 and under free. Tuesday-Saturday 10 a.m.-4:30 p.m., Sunday 1-5 p.m.

THE U.S. MINT

151 N. Independence Mall East, Philadelphia, 215-408-0110; www.usmint.gov

View a collection of historic coins and see how they are actually made. The U.S. Mint produces coins of all denominations. Visitors also get a behind-the-scenes look at medal-making. Audiovisual, self-guided tours.

Tours: Free. Monday-Friday 9 a.m.-3 p.m.

WALNUT STREET THEATRE

825 Walnut St., Philadelphia, 215-574-3550; www.wstonline.org

America's oldest theater, the Walnut Mainstage offers musicals, classical and contemporary plays. Two studio theaters provide a forum for new and avant-garde works.

See website for schedules and ticket information.

WASHINGTON SQUARE

Walnut and Sixth streets, Philadelphia

Visit the site where hundreds of Revolutionary War soldiers and victims of the yellow fever epidemic are buried. The life-size statue of Washington has a tomb of Revolutionary War's Unknown Soldier at its feet.

WHERE TO STAY

★★★★FOUR SEASONS HOTEL PHILADELPHIA

One Logan Square, Philadelphia, 215-963-1500, 866-516-1100; www.fourseasons.com

Located on historic Logan Square, this hotel puts the city's museums, shops and businesses within easy reach. The eight-story Four Seasons is itself a Philadelphia institution, from its dramatic Swann Fountain to its highly rated Fountain Restaurant, considered one of the best dining establishments in town. The rooms and suites are a celebration of Federalist décor, and some accommodations incorporate deep soaking tubs. City views of the Academy of Natural Science, Logan Square and the tree-lined Ben Franklin Parkway provide a sense of place for some guests, while other rooms offer tranquil views over the inner courtyard and gardens. The Four Seasons Spa focuses on nourishing treatments, while the indoor pool resembles a tropical oasis with breezy palm trees and large skylights.

364 rooms. Restaurant, bar. Business center. Fitness center. Pool. Spa. $251-350

★★★THE HILTON INN AT PENN

3600 Sansom St., Philadelphia, 215-222-0200, 800-774-1500; www.theinnatpenn.com

Experience a distinctly collegiate environment at this hotel, located in the middle of the University of Pennsylvania's campus, not far from the city's central business district. Travelers find the Inn at Penn easily accessible from Interstate 76, Amtrak's 30th Street Station and the Philadelphia International Airport. The Penne Restaurant and Wine Bar features regional Italian cuisine with fresh pasta made daily, while the University Club at Penn serves up breakfast and brunch favorites daily.

238 rooms. Restaurant, bar. Business center. Fitness center. $151-250

★★★HYATT REGENCY PHILADELPHIA AT PENN'S LANDING

201 S. Columbus Blvd., Philadelphia, 215-928-1234, 800-233-1234; www.hyatt.com

Located in the Penn's Landing area of Philadelphia, this Hyatt property offers unobstructed views of the Delaware River. Major historic attractions and many shops and restaurants are within walking distance. Travelers can take advantage of the indoor pool and fitness center after a busy day of work or play; or head to the restaurant for a relaxing dinner.

350 rooms. Restaurant, bar. Business center. Fitness center. Pool. $251-350

★★★THE LATHAM HOTEL

135 S. 17th St., Philadelphia, 215-563-7474, 877-528-4261; www.lathamhotel.com

This charming boutique hotel is a favorite of guests looking for an intimate setting in downtown Philly. Guest rooms are decorated in a Victorian style and feature robes and complimentary wireless Internet access. The hotel is near Rittenhouse Square and Walnut Street, Philadelphia's main shopping area.

139 rooms. $61-150

★★★LOEWS PHILADELPHIA HOTEL

1200 Market St., Philadelphia, 215-627-1200, 800-235-6397; www.loewshotels.com

This 1930s National Historic Landmark building (formerly the Pennsylvania Savings Fund Society) is situated across from the Market East train station and the convention center. The modern, Art Deco guest rooms feel spacious with their 10-foot ceilings. Upscale amenities include 300-thread-count linens, Lather toiletries, flat-screen televisions and large work areas with ergonomic chairs. There are three floors of Concierge-level rooms, which include entry to the private library and lounge. Guests can keep up with their workouts in the nicely equipped Breathe Spa Fitness Salon—a 15,000-square-foot-space, including a full-service spa, fitness room and indoor lap pool.

581 rooms. Restaurant, bar. Business center. Fitness center. Pool. Spa. Pets accepted. Golf. $251-350

★★★OMNI HOTEL AT INDEPENDENCE PARK

401 Chestnut St., Philadelphia, 215-925-0000, 888-444-6664; www.omnihotels.com

Situated in the downtown area, only 10 minutes from Philadelphia International Airport and just a stone's throw from historic sights like the Liberty Bell and Independence Hall, the Omni offers an ideal location for both business and leisure trips to Philadelphia. Each well-appointed guest room combines old-world elegance with modern day luxury. Feather pillows, comfortable bathrobes and executive desks are found in all rooms, while the ultra-plush penthouse suite features marble baths, Jacuzzi tubs and a parlor room with 20-foot cathedral ceilings, multiple sitting areas and a dining table. Kids are welcomed with the Omni Sensational Kids program.

150 rooms. Restaurant, bar. Fitness center. Spa. $251-350

★★★PARK HYATT PHILADELPHIA AT THE BELLEVUE

200 S. Broad and Walnut streets, Philadelphia, 215-893-1234, 800-464-9288;
www.park.philadelphia.hyatt.com

This elegant hotel was built in 1904 and is listed on the National Historic Register. Beautiful, early 20th-century architecture reflects the building's history, yet guests are pampered with a number of modern amenities and comforts. Goose-down duvets are found in each guest room along with luxurious linens, large televisions, DVD players, minibars and plush bathrobes.

172 rooms. Restaurant, bar. Business center. Spa. $251-350

★★★PENN'S VIEW HOTEL

Front and Market streets, Philadelphia, 215-922-7600, 800-331-7634; www.pennsviewhotel.com

Located in historic Old City Philadelphia, near Penn's Landing and the Delaware River, Penn's View Hotel is on the National Historic Register. The décor here is European, but guest rooms have a slightly more modern feel. Guests looking for a smaller hotel with more personal touches will find this property especially appealing.

51 rooms. Restaurant, bar. Complimentary breakfast. $151-250

★★★PHILADELPHIA MARRIOTT DOWNTOWN

1201 Market St., Philadelphia, 215-625-2900, 800-320-5744; www.philadelphiamarriott.com

Guests are assured a comfortable and relaxing stay at the Marriott Philadelphia Downtown. When not outdoors exploring nearby attractions like the Liberty Bell, Independence Park, the Franklin Institute and the waterfront area, guests can work out in the hotel's fitness center or take advantage of the indoor pool, whirlpool and sauna. There are also a number of dining options, from steakhouse to sushi.

1,408 rooms. Restaurant, bar. Fitness center. Pool. Spa. $151-250

★★★THE RADISSON PLAZA WARWICK HOTEL PHILADELPHIA

1701 Locust St., Philadelphia, 215-735-6000, 800-395-7046; www.radisson.com

Just one block from Rittenhouse Park, this property is close to shops, restaurants, performing arts and museums. It is also convenient to the universities. Listed on the National Register of Historic Places, the 1926 hotel has an English Renaissance theme, with guest rooms providing a more contemporary feel.

301 rooms. Restaurant, bar. Business center. Fitness center. Pets accepted. $151-250

★★★THE RITTENHOUSE HOTEL AND CONDOMINIUM RESIDENCES

210 W. Rittenhouse Square, Philadelphia, 215-546-9000, 800-635-1042;
www.rittenhousehotel.com

This intimate hotel occupies a particularly enviable address across from the leafy Rittenhouse Square and is among the prestigious townhouses of this exclusive area. The accommodations are among the most spacious in the city and are decorated with a sophisticated flair. Guests at the Rittenhouse are treated to the highest levels of personalized service. From the mood-lifting décor of the gracious Mary Cassatt Tea Room and Garden and the striking contemporary style of Lacroix, to upscale Bar 210 at Lacroix and the traditional steakhouse feel of Smith & Wollensky, the Rittenhouse Hotel also provides memorable dining experiences to match every taste.

98 rooms. Restaurant, bar. Fitness center. Pool. Spa. Pets accepted. $351 and up.

★★★THE RITZ-CARLTON, PHILADELPHIA

10 Avenue of the Arts, Philadelphia, 215-523-8000, 800-241-3333; www.ritzcarlton.com

Once occupied by both Girard Bank and Mellon Bank at some point, this building was designed in the 1900s by the architectural firm of McKim, Mead and White, and was inspired by Rome's Pantheon. Marrying historic significance with trademark Ritz-Carlton style, this Philadelphia showpiece boasts handsome decor. Impressive marble columns dominate the lobby. The rooms and suites are luxurious, while Club level accommodations offer private lounges filled with five food and beverage selections daily. Dedicated to exceeding visitors' expectations, the Ritz-Carlton even offers a pillow menu, a bath butler and other unique services. Dine at well-known chef Eric Ripert's 10 Arts Bistro.

300 rooms. Restaurant, bar. Spa. Pets accepted. $251-350

★★★SHERATON SOCIETY HILL HOTEL

1 Dock St., Philadelphia, 215-238-6000, 800-325-3535; www.sheraton.com

The Sheraton Society Hill offers affordable comfort in downtown Philadelphia, just steps from Independence Hall, Society Hill, the Liberty Bell, the Philadelphia Zoo and the Pennsylvania Convention Center. Guest rooms are basic but some offer nice views of the city. Enjoy a meal and watch a game at the Wooden Nickel Restaurant, a sports bar. Or retreat to the casual Hadley's Bistro, which also features a lovely outdoor courtyard to enjoy light fare. There's a Starbucks onsite to get you started in the morning.

365 rooms. Restaurant, bar. Business center. Fitness center. Pool. Pets accepted. $151-250

★★★SHERATON UNIVERSITY CITY

36th and Chestnut streets, Philadelphia, 215-387-8000, 800-596-0369;
www.philadelphiasheraton.com

Perfect for visitors to the University of Pennsylvania, this Sheraton is located

WHAT ARE PHILADELPHIA'S MOST LUXURIOUS HOTELS?

Four Seasons Hotel Philadelphia:
The hotel is itself a Philadelphia institution. The rooms and suites have Federalist décor, and some accommodations incorporate deep soaking tubs.

The Ritz-Carlton, Philadelphia:
Marrying historic significance with trademark Ritz-Carlton style, this Philadelphia showpiece boasts handsome décor, luxurious rooms and suites, and top chef Eric Ripert's 10 Arts Bistro.

in the midst of an eclectic university environment. The hotel's early American décor and lobby fireplace give it a cozy feel, and the friendly staff makes a stay here even more pleasant. A "pet suitcase," which includes a bed, bowls, mat, brush, toys and treat, is available for cats and dogs.

316 rooms. Restaurant, bar. Business center. Fitness center. Pool. Pets accepted. $151-250

★★★SOFITEL PHILADELPHIA

120 S. 17th St., Philadelphia, 215-569-8300, 800-763-4835; www.sofitel.com

Modern French style permeates the Sofitel Philadelphia. This elegant hotel sits on the former site of the Philadelphia Stock Exchange, and its downtown Center City location makes it ideal for both business and leisure travelers. Warm and inviting, the accommodations welcome with a variety of thoughtful touches, such as fresh flowers and plush towels. Comfortable chic defines the lobby bar, La Bourse, while the bistro fare and unique setting of Chez Colette recall the romance of 1920s Paris.

306 rooms. Restaurant, bar. Fitness center. Pool. Pets accepted. $251-350

RECOMMENDED

RITTENHOUSE 1715 A BOUTIQUE HOTEL

1715 Rittenhouse Square, Philadelphia, 215-546-6500, 877-791-6500; www.rittenhouse1715.com

Formerly Rittenhouse Square Bed and Breakfast, this renovated 1900s carriage house affords guests a choice of 10 deluxe rooms in an ideal setting just off Rittenhouse Square, one of the city's most fashionable locations. Rooms feature marble bathrooms, plush bathrobes, Molton Brown bath amenities, iPod docking stations and workstations with Internet access. Some rooms also feature a fireplace and walk-in showers with waterfall showerheads. Guests are made comfortable with 24-hour concierge service, nightly turndown service, a nightly complimentary wine and snack reception, and continental breakfast served in the café.

23 rooms. Complimentary breakfast. $151-250

WHERE TO EAT

★★★AZALEA

Omni Hotel at Independence Park, 401 Chestnut St., Philadelphia, 215-925-0000; www.omnihotels.com

Just a block from historic Independence Hall and the

Liberty Bell, this restaurant at the Omni Hotel at Independence Park is a restful spot to enjoy a meal. The décor is stylishly eclectic, and the menus are rooted in classic French technique, featuring contemporary touches and international accents. Dishes range from comfortingly rich (house-made herb spaetzle baked with Gruyère and Emmental cheeses and assorted summer vegetables) to heart-healthy (mustard-glazed salmon over golden whipped potatoes with a sauce verjus and baby bok choy). Sunday brunch is popular here, where live piano, harp or guitar music sets an elegant tone.

Continental. Breakfast, lunch, dinner, Sunday brunch. Closed Monday. Children's menu. Reservations recommended. Bar. $36-85

★★★BISTRO ROMANO

120 Lombard St., Philadelphia, 215-925-8880; www.bistroromano.com

When you walk into this cozy Italian restaurant located in the Society Hill area, one of the first things you see is the majestic oak bar from the *City of Detroit III*, a 1912 side-wheel passenger steamer. There is also a beautiful painting from the ship of a sea nymph in the stairwell that leads downstairs to the romantic dining room. Besides the décor, Bistro Romano is well known for its tableside Caesar salad, homemade ravioli and award-winning tiramisu.

Italian. Dinner. Children's menu. Reservations recommended. Bar. $16-35

★★★BUDDAKAN

325 Chestnut St., Philadelphia, 215-574-9440; www.buddakan.com

Slick, sexy and spectacular, Buddakan is one of Philadelphia's hottest spots for dining, drinking and lounging. Whether you're seated in the shadow of the restaurant's 10-foot gilded Buddha at the elevated communal table or at one of the other more intimate tables for two in chairs backed with black-and-white photo portraits, you will never guess that this den of fabulousness was once a post office. The Asian fusion fare, including lobster fried rice with Thai basil and saffron or crisp pizza topped with seared tuna and wasabi, are consistent crowd-pleasers. Good thing they're meant for sharing.

Asian. Lunch (Monday-Friday), dinner. Reservations recommended. Bar. $36-85

★★★CHEZ COLETTE

Sofitel Philadelphia, 120 S. 17th St., Philadelphia, 215-569-8300; www.sofitel.com

Black-and-white photos decorate the walls in this brasserie, jazz plays in the background, and both the staff and menus are bilingual—French and English. All the pastries, breads and desserts are made on premise. For breakfast, try the fruit sushi.

French. Breakfast, lunch, dinner, Sunday brunch. Bar. $36-85

★★★★★FOUNTAIN RESTAURANT

Four Seasons Hotel Philadelphia, 1 Logan Square, Philadelphia, 215-963-1500; www.fourseasons.com

The Fountain is the stunning flagship restaurant of the Four Seasons Hotel Philadelphia. The wine list, which covers all of France as well as Germany, Italy, the United States, Australia, New Zealand and South America, is just one of the highlights of dining here. The kitchen often uses ingredients from local producers and and farms. Choose from the a la carte menu or from a four-, five- or six-course tasting menu. You'll find entrées such as butter-poached Maine lobster with truffle-butter ravioli, late harvest corn succotash and tarragon jus. As you'll see here, the best ingredients really do make a difference. Vegetarian items are available on request. Be sure to request a window table as it affords beautiful views of the neighboring Swann Memorial Fountain.

American, French. Breakfast, lunch (Monday-Saturday), dinner, Sunday brunch. Children's menu. Reservations recommended. Bar. $36-85

★★★JAKE'S RESTAURANT

4365 Main St., Manayunk, 215-483-0444; www.jakesrestaurant.com

Located in Manayunk, Philadelphia's funky, high-energy, artsy neighborhood, Jake's Restaurant is a lively spot to meet friends for drinks and stay for dinner. Chef/owner Bruce Cooper's chic regulars make a habit of staying all night, savoring his unique brand of stylish, regional American food. While at the bar, go for one of Jake's wild house cocktails or take a chance on a unique microbrew. The kitchen is in sync with its customers' desire for both fun and flavor in their food.

American. Lunch (Monday-Saturday), dinner, Sunday brunch. Reservations recommended. Outdoor seating. Bar. $36-85

★★★JOSEPH AMBLER INN

1005 Horsham Road, Montgomeryville, 215-362-7500; www.josephamblerinn.com

Complex combinations of local fare and international cuisine make up the innovative menu at this rustic country inn. Executive Chef Pedro Luga and his team offer entrées such as pan roasted Chilean sea bass with lump crab and English pea risotto; grilled rack of lamb with Dauphinoise potato, cauliflower puree and red wine demi-glace; and pan roasted chicken breast with potato pancake, fontina tuille, baby asparagus and rosemary pan jus.

International. Lunch (Monday-Friday), dinner. Outdoor seating. Bar. $36-85

★★★★LACROIX AT THE RITTENHOUSE

210 W. Rittenhouse Square, Philadelphia, 215-790-2533; www.rittenhousehotel.com

Set in the stately Rittenhouse Hotel, Lacroix is a restaurant of understated elegance. The kitchen plays up fresh local ingredients with a delicate French hand, while guests dine in posh, sophisticated luxury and enjoy views of charming Rittenhouse Square. While acclaimed chef Jean-Marie Lacroix has retired, the kitchen is still in able hands under the direction of chef Jon Cichon. The tasting menu is the best option here, where diners can choose five or eight small-plate tastings. The Sunday brunch is a Philadelphia favorite.

French. Breakfast, lunch (Monday-Saturday), dinner, Sunday brunch. Reservations recommended. Bar. $36-85

★★★LE BAR LYONNAIS

1523 Walnut St., Philadelphia, 215-567-1000; www.lebecfin.com

Since Georges Perrier added Le Bar Lyonnais to his internationally renowned Le Bec-Fin restaurant in 1990, the bar has achieved status as one of Philadelphia's best French bistros, winning kudos for its comfortable setting and accessible menu. The decor is subdued and casual, with dark wallpaper, dark woods, soft lighting and marble-topped tables. The bistro has featured dishes such as a cassolette of snails in champagne and hazelnut butter sauce, grilled Dover sole with basmati rice and veal medallions with hazelnut mashed potatoes. This lower-level bar is a great choice for diners who want to sample some of Le Bec-Fin's signature dishes without paying for a prix fixe menu.

French. Lunch (Friday-Saturday), dinner. Closed Sunday. Reservations recommended. Bar. $36-85

★★★LE CASTAGNE RISTORANTE

1920 Chestnut St., Philadelphia, 215-751-9913; www.lecastagne.com

This contemporary Italian restaurant offers a menu that concentrates on northern Italian dishes, and in season, a pre-theater menu is offered. Everything is made in-house, including breads, pastas, sauces and desserts. Some dessert and fish selections are prepared tableside.

Italian. Lunch (Monday-Friday), dinner. Closed Sunday. Reservations recommended. Outdoor seating. Bar. $36-85

★★★MOONSTRUCK

7955 Oxford Ave., Philadelphia, 215-725-6000; www.moonstruckrestaurant.com

This elegantly casual northern Italian gem has been doing business for more than 20 years. Menus let customers choose among a wide range of antipasti, primi piatti (pasta appetizers), secondi piatti (second courses) and piatti tradizionale (traditional dishes). The latter menu section features one special dish per night, ranging from caciucco, a bouillabaisse of seafood and fish, to osso buco.

Italian. Dinner. Reservations recommended. Bar. $36-85

★★★MORIMOTO

723 Chestnut St., Philadelphia, 215-413-9070; www.morimotorestaurant.com

Japanese fusion cuisine from Iron Chef Masaharu Morimoto pulsates with life and creativity. His Philadelphia outpost, stunningly shaped by local restaurant impresario Stephen Starr, is Morimoto's first restaurant in the United States. Ceilings undulate, booths change color and the sushi bar at the back never stops bustling. The best way to challenge your taste buds is to select one of Morimoto's omakase menus.

Japanese. Lunch (Monday-Friday), dinner. Reservations recommended. Bar. $36-85

★★★MOSHULU RESTAURANT

401 S. Columbus Blvd., Philadelphia, 215-923-2500; www.moshulu.com

Moshulu is a stunning South Seas-inspired restaurant housed in a 100-year-old, 394-foot, four-mast sailing ship. Its several dining rooms are elegantly decorated with rattan chairs, cane furniture, dark mahogany and Polynesian artwork. The kitchen, headed by executive chef Ralph Fernandez, churns out creative, delicious dishes that will keep you coming back for more.

American. Lunch, dinner, Sunday brunch. Reservations recommended. Outdoor seating. Bar. $36-85

★★★RISTORANTE PANORAMA

Penn's View Hotel, Front and Market streets, Philadelphia, 215-922-7800; www.pennsviewhotel.com

Panorama is part of the boutique-style Penn's View Hotel. The beautiful dining room features marble floors, a wall of windows and murals throughout. The cuisine is gutsy, old-world Italian, featuring dishes such as paillard of beef rolled in garlic, cheese, egg and herbs, slow-cooked in tomato sauce and served with house-made gnocchi. But this place is known for its wine: Daily wine lists offer 22 to 26 different flights (five wines per flight), plus dozens of by-the-glass options. The quality, made possible by the restaurant's cruvinet preservation and dispensing system, is exceptional, earning Panorama numerous awards.

Italian. Lunch (Monday-Friday), dinner. Reservations recommended. Bar. $36-85

★★★THE SALOON

750 S. Seventh St., Philadelphia, 215-627-1811; www.saloonrestaurant.net

Richard Santore has been operating this venerable establishment in Philadelphia's Bellavista neighborhood, bordering Center City and South Philly, for nearly 40 years. The food is classic Italian fare, served for lunch and dinner. Appetizers include poached pear and gorgonzola salad with roasted walnuts, baby greens and red onion with pear vinaigrette. Fettuccini lobster amatriciana is a toss of house-made fettuccini with lobster, bacon, onion, fresh tomato and pecorino cheese in tomato sauce. Dinner specials range from beef carpaccio drizzled with truffle essence and fava beans to a double veal chop marinated in white wine, pan seared and served with Yukon gold potatoes.

Italian. Lunch, dinner. Closed Sunday. Bar. $36-85

★★★SWANN CAFÉ

Four Seasons Hotel Philadelphia, 1 Logan Square, Philadelphia, 215-963-1500,
866-516-1100; www.fourseasons.com

Named for the spectacular Logan Square fountain in front of the Four Seasons Hotel Philadelphia, Swann Café is the more accessible of the hotel's exceptional restaurants. Menus range from light and lovely dishes, such as an appetizer ragout of forest mushrooms and asparagus tips, to a zesty sandwich of pulled osso buco with aged provolone and spicy pepper and onion relish on a stirato roll.

American. Lunch (Monday-Saturday), dinner, Sunday brunch. Children's menu. Reservations recommended. Bar. $36-85

★★★TANGERINE

232 Market St., Philadelphia, 215-627-5116; www.tangerinerestaurant.com

This Middle Eastern-themed restaurant in the heart of Old City Philadelphia features a menu that blends flavors from the Mediterranean, France, Spain, Italy and Africa. The appetizer of harissa-spiced barbecue lamb with rosemary socca bread and smoky vegetable salad is an inspired choice. For an entrée, try the delicious seared suck with creamy polenta, currant jus and grilled radicchio.

Mediterranean. Dinner. Reservations recommended. Bar. $36-85

★★★VETRI

1312 Spruce St., Philadelphia, 215-732-3478; www.vetriristorante.com

Chef Mark Vetri learned to prepare rustic Italian cuisine (think: rabbit loin and sweetbreads wrapped in pancetta with morels or baby goat poached in milk and then oven roasted to crispness) from Italy's best chefs and then brought his skills home to Philly. Ensconced in the tiny, 35-seat space once occupied by other pinnacle establishments (Le Bec-Fin, Chanterelle), Vetri is intent on creating likewise legendary meals. The wine list has been nationally lauded, and the service is seamless. On Saturdays, indulge in Vetri's five- or seven-course prix fixe menus (not available during the summer).

Italian. Dinner. Closed Sunday. Reservations recommended. $86 and up.

★★★XIX

Park Hyatt Philadelphia, 200 S. Broad St., Philadelphia, 215-790-1919; www.nineteenrestaurant.com

XIX (pronounced "nineteen") sits on the top 19th floor of the historic Bellevue Building (now the Park Hyatt), and exudes a level of opulence from a bygone era with two 36-foot-high grand rotundas, mosaic marble and a 19-foot-tall pearl chandelier. The fine dining experience is further enhanced by spectacular views of the city through floor-to-ceiling arched picture windows. The raw bar features a choice of 12 varieties of fresh oysters and a separate café offers its own menu and afternoon tea.

American, French. Breakfast, lunch, dinner, Sunday brunch, late-night. $36-85

RECOMMENDED

LE BEC-FIN

1523 Walnut St., Philadelphia, 215-567-1000; www.lebecfin.com

Georges Perrier's Le Bec-Fin, which opened in 1970, remains a shining star for French cuisine, although the restaurant took a more casual turn in 2009. Perrier's talented team brings out the brilliance in classic dishes, while offering several new creations destined to be classics. Perrier's signature crab cake with French green beans and whole grain mustard sauce is divine and joins an exciting menu that leans on seasonal availability.

French. Lunch (Monday-Saturday), dinner. Closed Sunday. Reservations recommended. Bar. $86 and up.

WHERE TO SHOP

SHOPS AT THE BELLEVUE

200 S. Broad St., Philadelphia, 215-875-8350; www.bellevuephiladelphia.com

Beaux Arts architecture of the former Bellevue Stratford Hotel has been preserved and transformed; it now contains offices, a hotel and a four-level shopping area centered on an atrium court. Shops include Tiffany & Co., Nicole Miller, Williams-Sonoma, Polo Ralph Lauren and others.

Monday-Saturday 10 a.m.-6 p.m., Wednesday 10 a.m.-8 p.m., Sunday, hours varies.

PITTSBURGH

Pittsburgh has become one of the most spectacular civic redevelopments in America, with modern buildings, clean parks and community pride. The new Pittsburgh is a result of a rare combination of capital-labor cooperation, public and private support, enlightened political leadership and imaginative, venturesome community planning. Its $1 billion international airport was designed to be the most user-friendly in the country. After massive war production, Pittsburgh labored to eliminate the 1930s image of an unsophisticated mill town. During the 1950s and 1960s, Renaissance I began, a $500-million program to clean the city's air and develop new structures, such as Gateway Center, the Civic Arena and Point State Park. The late 1970s and early 1980s ushered in Renaissance II, a $3 billion expansion program deflecting the movement away from industry and toward high technology. Today, Pittsburgh has completed this dramatic economic shift and has become an interesting place to visit.

WHAT TO SEE

ALCOA BUILDING/REGIONAL ENTERPRISE TOWER
425 Sixth Ave., Pittsburgh, 412-391-5590; www.spcregion.org

This building was a pioneer in aluminum for skyscraper construction, as the exterior work was done from inside and no scaffolding was required. Draped in aluminum waffle, at 30 stories high it's considered to be one of the country's most daring experiments in skyscraper design. It was built in 1953 for Alcoa; it's now known as the Regional Enterprise Tower.

ALLEGHENY COUNTY COURTHOUSE
436 Grant St., Pittsburgh; www.alleghenycounty.us

One of the country's outstanding Romanesque buildings, the two-square city block structure was designed by Henry Hobson Richardson in 1884.

ANDY WARHOL MUSEUM
117 Sandusky St., Pittsburgh, 412-237-8300; www.warhol.org

Andy Warhol fans will want to make a stop at his hometown museum, which houses more than 500 works by the artist, making it the most comprehensive single-artist museum in the world. Special exhibits have recently featured "Andy Warhol: The College Years", a look at his beginning work and "Marilyn Monroe: Life as a Legend", which showcased art focusing on Monroe from multiple artists, including Warhol.

Admission: adults $15, seniors $9, students and children 3-18 $8. Tuesday-Thursday, Saturday 10 a.m.-5 p.m., Friday 10 a.m.-10 p.m. Half-price admission Friday 5-10 p.m.

BENEDUM CENTER FOR THE PERFORMING ARTS
719 Liberty Ave., Pittsburgh, 412-456-6666; www.pgharts.org

Gilded plasterwork, a 500,000-piece crystal chandelier and a nine-story addition to the backstage area make this an exceptional auditorium with one of the largest stages in the country. The center is home to Pittsburgh Ballet Theatre, the Pittsburgh Dance Council, the Pittsburgh Opera and Civic Light Opera.

See website for schedules and ticket information.

CARNEGIE MELLON UNIVERSITY
5000 Forbes Ave., Pittsburgh, 412-268-2000; www.cmu.edu

Founded by Andrew Carnegie in 1900, this university is composed of seven colleges and is home to more than 1,000 students. While on campus, visit the Carnegie Museum of Art (*412-622-3131; www.cmoa.org*), which is possibly America's first modern art museum. Also, on campus is the Carnegie Museum of Natural History (*412-622-3131; www.carnegiemnh.org*), which houses one

HIGHLIGHT

WHAT ARE THE TOP THINGS TO DO IN PITTSBURGH?

ADMIRE WARHOL IN HIS HOMETOWN
Visit the Andy Warhol Museum, which honors the pop art icon. It is the most complete collection in the world dedicated to a single artist.

HOP ABOARD THE CABLE CAR
From the observation deck at the Duquesne Incline, you can see Pittsburgh like you've never seen it before.

of the most complete collections of dinosaur fossils. For some music, head to Carnegie Music Hall (*412-622-1906; www.carnegiemuseums.org*), which is home to Mendelssohn Choir, Pittsburgh Chamber Music Society and River City Brass Band.

Museums: Admission: adults $15, seniors $12, students and children 3-18 $11, children 2 and under free. Tuesday-Wednesday, Friday-Saturday 10 a.m.-5 p.m., Thursday 10 a.m.-8 p.m., Sunday noon-5 p.m.

CARNEGIE SCIENCE CENTER
1 Allegheny Ave., Pittsburgh, 412-237-3400; www.carnegiesciencecenter.org
This learning and entertainment complex has more than 40,000 square feet of exhibit galleries that demonstrate how human activities are affected by science and technology. *USS Requin*, moored in front of the center, is a World War II diesel electric submarine; 40-minute tours demonstrate the electronic, visual and voice communication devices on board. Henry Buhl Jr. Planetarium and Observatory is a technologically sophisticated interactive planetarium with control panels at every seat.

Admission: adults $14, seniors and children 3-12 $10. Sunday-Friday 10 a.m.-5 p.m., Saturday 10 a.m.-7 p.m.

THE FRICK ART AND HISTORICAL CENTER/ART MUSEUM
7227 Reynolds St., Pittsburgh, 412-371-0600; www.frickart.org
This museum complex built on grounds of the estate once belonging to industrialist Henry Clay Frick has numerous attractions. Be sure to visit Clayton, a restored four-story Victorian mansion with 23 rooms. It's the only remaining house in the area of East End once known as "Millionaire's Row". Some of the original décor remains and there are personal mementos of the Fricks inside. The art museum here houses the collection of Helen Clay Frick, daughter of Henry, which includes Italian Renaissance, Flemish and French 18th-century paintings and decorative arts. There are also gardens, the Car and Carriage

Museum, a greenhouse, and a café.

Admission: Free. Tuesday-Sunday 10 a.m.-5 p.m.

FRICK PARK

Beechwood Blvd. and English Lane, Pittsburgh, 412-422-6538; www.pittsburghparks.org

Covering 561 acres, Frick Park is Pittsburgh's largest regional park and it's largely in a natural state. Nature trails wind through ravines and over hills and there are over 100 species of birds. The park also includes tennis courts, picnic areas, baseballs fields and a popular playground.

Daily 6 a.m.-11 p.m.

MELLON ARENA

66 Mario Lemieux Place, Pittsburgh, 412-642-1800; www.mellonarena.com

This all-weather amphitheater accommodates more than 17,000 people. There is a retractable roof that can fold up within 2 ½ minutes. Many events take place here from concerts, to Penguins hockey games to Disney on Ice.

MONONGAHELA INCLINE

Pittsburgh, 412-442-2000; www.portauthority.org

Take this incline, which was built in 1870 and most recently renovated in 1994, to the top for panoramic views of the city from the observation deck.

Admission: adults $2, children 6-11 $1. Monday-Saturday 5:30 a.m.-12:45 a.m., Sunday 8:45 a.m.-midnight.

PHIPPS CONSERVATORY

700 Frank Curto Drive, Pittsburgh, 412-622-6914; www.conservatory.org

This conservatory has a constantly changing array of flowers; tropical gardens; and an outstanding orchid collection. There's also a children's Discovery Garden with interactive learning opportunities and seasonal flower shows. Check website for schedule.

Admission: adults $10, seniors and students $9, children 2-18 $7, children 1 and under free. Saturday-Thursday 9:30 a.m.-5 p.m., Friday 9:30 a.m.-10 p.m.

PITTSBURGH PIRATES (MLB)

PNC Park, 115 Federal St., Pittsburgh, 412-323-5000; www.pittsburghpirates.com

Pittsburgh's professional baseball team, the Pirates, play at PNC Park, which was opened in 2001. The Pirates played in the first modern World Series and have gone on to win five World Series titles. With alums such as Roberto Clemente, Jim Bunning and Burleigh Grimes, the Pirates have a great past to look back on. Unfortunately, they have not been good in some years, but it's always fun to catch a game at PNC Park.

PITTSBURGH STEELERS (NFL)

Heinz Field, 600 Stadium Circle, Pittsburgh, 412-432-7800; www.steelers.com

Everyone from Pittsburgh and the surrounding areas is a Steelers fan. The fans are known to be rather obnoxious, especially when it comes to playing their longtime rivals, the Baltimore Ravens. The Steelers have won six Super Bowls, the most recent in 2009. Pittsburgh has had an impressive roster over the years, including Terry Bradshaw, Jerome Bettis and Ben Roethlisberger. Catching a game at Heinz Field is quite an experience.

PITTSBURGH ZOO & AQUARIUM

1 Wild Place, Pittsburgh, 412-665-3640, 800-474-4966; www.pittsburghzoo.com

The zoo covers more than 70 acres containing more than 4,000 animals, a children's farm, reptile house, tropical and Asian forests, and an African savanna. The PPG Aquarium is 45,000 square feet and has more than 40 exhibits. Kids will enjoy the merry-go-round and train rides.

Admission: adults $12, seniors $11, children 2-13 $10, children 1 and under free. June-August, daily 9 a.m.-6 p.m.; September-December, daily 9 a.m.-5 p.m.; January-March, daily 9 a.m.-4 p.m.; April-May, daily 9 a.m.-5 p.m.

PPG PLACE

Market Square, Pittsburgh; www.ppgplace.com

Designed by Philip Johnson, this is Pittsburgh's most popular Renaissance II building. PPG Place consists of six separate buildings designed in a postmodern, Gothic skyscraper style. Shopping and a food court can be found in Two PPG Place. There is also a public ice skating rink.

Shops: Monday-Friday 10 a.m.-6 p.m. Food court: Monday-Friday 11 a.m.-3 p.m.

SCHENLEY PARK

5000 Forbes Ave., Pittsburgh, 412-687-1800; www.pittsburghparks.org

Covering 456 acres, Schenley Park offers trails, woods, picnic areas, an 18-hole golf course, lighted tennis courts, a swimming pool, an ice skating rink, softball fields, a running track, nature trails and a bandstand. There is also a café.

Daily 6 a.m.-11 p.m.

SENATOR JOHN HEINZ HISTORY CENTER

1212 Smallman St., Pittsburgh, 412-454-6000; www.pghhistory.org

Associated with the Smithsonian Institution, this history center has exhibits that preserve nearly 300 years of the region's history with artifacts and extensive collection of archives and photos. Check out the exhibit "Pittsburgh: A Tradition of Innovation", which tells the story of the history of the city through hands-on activities and displays. It also houses the Western Pennsylvania Sports Museum.

Admission: adults $10, seniors $9, students and children 4-17 $5, children 3 and under free. Daily 10 a.m.-5 p.m.

STATION SQUARE

125 W. Station Square, Pittsburgh, 412-471-5808, 800-859-8959; www.stationsquare.com

This 52-acre area located along the riverfront features shopping, dining and entertainment in and among the historic buildings of the P and LE Railroad. Shopping is available in warehouses that once held loaded railroad boxcars.

Monday-Saturday 10 a.m.-9 p.m., Sunday noon-5 p.m. Hours vary; see website for information.

TOUR-ED MINE AND MUSEUM

748 Bull Creek Road, Pittsburgh, 724-224-4720; www.tour-edmine.com

This mine and museum gives you the experience of a complete underground coal mining operation. There's a sawmill, furnished log house, old company store, a historical mine museum and shelters.

Admission: adults $8, children 12 and under $6.50. May-August, Wednesday-Monday 10 a.m.-4 p.m.

U.S. STEEL TOWER
Grant Street and Seventh Avenue, Pittsburgh

This is the tallest building in Pittsburgh, and the 35th tallest in the nation with ten exposed triangular columns and an exterior paneling of steel.

WHERE TO STAY

★★★HILTON PITTSBURGH
600 Commonwealth Place, Pittsburgh, 412-391-4600; www.hilton.com

Located in downtown Pittsburgh, this hotel offers comfortable accommodations nearby all the excitement of the city. Get a good night's rest in one of Hilton's signature Serenity Beds. Request views of the city or of the famous Three Rivers to make the most of your Pittsburgh stay. Grab some grub at Three Rivers Pub, a sports bar in the lobby.

713 rooms. Restaurant, bar. Business center. Fitness center. Pets accepted. $61-150

★★★HYATT REGENCY PITTSBURGH INTERNATIONAL AIRPORT
1111 Airport Blvd., Pittsburgh, 724-899-1234, 800-633-7313; www.hyatt.com

Whether you're in town for the day and need a place to clean up or have an early flight in the morning, this Hyatt is connected to the airport terminals and offers soundproof windows so you're guaranteed a restful night. A 24-hour business center ensures that no matter what time you arrive, you'll be able to get to work.

336 rooms. Restaurant, bar. Business center. Fitness center. Pool. $61-150

★★★MARRIOTT PITTSBURGH CITY CENTER
112 Washington Place, Pittsburgh, 412-471-4000, 888-456-6600; www.marriott.com

Located across the street from Mellon Arena and the downtown business district, you won't have to travel far to get a taste of the city. Guest rooms include pillow-top beds, thick down comforters and free Internet access. Make use of the onsite fitness center and Spa Uptown. Enjoy dinner and a glass of wine at Steelhead Brasserie and Wine Bar and grab coffee in the morning at the onsite Starbucks.

402 rooms. Restaurant, bar. Business center. Fitness center. Pool. Spa. $151-250

★★★OMNI WILLIAM PENN HOTEL
530 William Penn Place, Pittsburgh, 412-281-7100, 888-444-6664; www.omnihotels.com

This hotel, built in 1916, fuses historic charm with modern luxury in the heart of downtown Pittsburgh. The rooms and suites are tastefully and elegantly appointed with distinguished style. Executives on the go appreciate the hotel's complete business and fitness centers; families appreciate the Omni Kids Program; and leisure visitors enjoy the proximity to the city's leading stores. The hotel offers a variety of convenient and tempting dining choices, from Starbucks to pub food at the Palm Court and Tap Room, to fine dining at the Terrace Room.

596 rooms. Restaurant, bar. Business center. Fitness center. Spa. Pets accepted. $151-250

★★★RENAISSANCE PITTSBURGH HOTEL

107 Sixth St., Pittsburgh, 412-562-1200, 800-468-3571; www.marriott.com

Housed in the classic Fulton Building downtown, this hotel is an architectural stunner in the city's renowned Cultural District. Stroll across the Roberto Clemente Bridge to reach North Shore destinations. Guest rooms feature vintage furniture, and beds with pillow-top mattresses, featherbeds and comfortable duvets. Some rooms offer views of downtown or the Allegheny River. Head to the onsite Braddock's American Brasserie for dinner and then a cocktail at the Side Street Grill.

300 rooms. Restaurant, bar. Business center. Fitness center. Spa. $151-250

★★★SHERATON STATION SQUARE HOTEL

300 W. Station Square Drive, Pittsburgh, 412-261-2000, 800-325-3535; www.sheraton.com

In the heart of Station Square, a major nightlife destination, this riverfront hotel is convenient for sightseeing, North Shore destinations and the Gateway Clipper Fleet. Guest rooms are simple, yet comfortable and offer complimentary wireless Internet access. There's a fitness center, sauna and indoor pool so you can keep up with your workouts. Pittsburgh Rare, the hotel's restaurant serves up steaks and offers beautiful views of the city.

292 rooms. Restaurant, bar. Fitness center. Pool. Pets accepted. $151-250

★★★TARA COUNTRY INN

2844 Lake Road, Clark, 724-962-3535, 800-782-2803; www.tara-inn.com

Inspired by *Gone With the Wind*, this pillared inn brings Southern charm and hospitality to the northeast. All 27 rooms boast personalized décor and furnishings such as floral wallpaper, antique four-poster beds and hand-carved mantels. Ashley's Gourmet Dining Room continues the theme vibe.

27 rooms. Restaurant, bar. $251-350

★★★THE WESTIN CONVENTION CENTER PITTSBURGH

1000 Penn Ave., Pittsburgh, 412-281-3700; www.starwoodhotels.com

The Westin Convention Center is located in the heart of Pittsburgh's business and cultural districts, and is connected to the new David L. Lawrence Convention Center by a skywalk. Get a great night's rest in the Westin signature Heavenly Bed and gaze out the windows at a view of the business district. The Original Fish Market, the hotel's seafood restaurant, offers guests fresh seafood and sushi for lunch and dinner. In-room massage treatments and aerobics classes are offered so you can refresh after a day of business meetings or sightseeing.

616 rooms. Restaurant, bar. Business center. Fitness center. Pool. Pets accepted. $151-250

WHERE TO EAT

★★★COMMON PLEA

310 Ross St., Pittsburgh, 412-697-3100; www.commonplea-restaurant.com

With its dark paneling, glass wall and subdued lighting, this restaurant caters to the legal crowd. Start with prosciutto-wrapped scallops and then have the rainbow trout crab almondine with grilled asparagus and parsley potatoes or the housemade gnocchi with shrimp, roasted tomato and pinenuts in a herbed garlic butter and bomboloni sauce. Pair your meal with a wine offered on the extensive wine list.

Seafood. Lunch (Tuesday-Friday), dinner. Closed Sunday. Bar. $16-35

★★★GRAND CONCOURSE

100 W. Station Square Drive, Pittsburgh, 412-261-1717; www.muer.com

This converted railroad station offers a unique setting for a special occasion. The menu focuses on seafood, offering a raw bar and fresh fish like Chilean sea bass and Alaskan halibut. There are also a few non-seafood options like chicken Milano and filet mignon. On Sunday, they serve a legendary brunch offering everything from salads and seafood appetizers to hearty entrées and delicious pastries and desserts. Every Monday through Friday, there is a Happy Hour in the bar and patio with $5 martinis, cocktails and more.

International. Lunch (Monday-Saturday), dinner, Sunday brunch. Children's menu. Outdoor seating. Bar. $36-85

★★★HYEHOLDE

1516 Coraopolis Heights Road, Moon Township, 412-264-3116; www.hyeholde.com

Don a jacket and tie at this traditional outpost of English-country elegance 20 minutes from downtown Pittsburgh. The game and seafood menu and manor-like setting of rich tapestries, exposed wood beams and candlelight makes this a popular choice for special events.

International. Lunch, dinner. Closed Sunday. Outdoor seating. $36-85

★★★LE POMMIER

2104 E. Carson St., Pittsburgh, 412-431-1901; www.lepommier.com

Located in the oldest storefront in the area, cozy Le Pommier serves French-American bistro entrées such as cauliflower sautéed in brown butter with a roasted cauliflower-gruyere sauce and fresh oregano in puff pastry. Le Pommier is a great spot for a romantic dinner or a special occasion.

French. Dinner. Closed Sunday. Outdoor seating. Bar. $16-35

★★★SOBA

5847 Ellsworth Ave., Pittsburgh, 412-362-5656; www.bigburrito.com

A modern interior with a two-story waterfall, plush seating, tropical wood tones and mellow lighting serves as the perfect backdrop for Soba's sophisti-cated Asian fusion cuisine. Recent small-plate selections have included crispy tofu with lemongrass sauce and Vietnamese chicken spring rolls, while pad Thai, wok-seared sea scallops with sweet chili soy sauce, and filet mignon with chili-garlic mashed potatoes and Alaskan halibut have been featured as large plate choices. Soups and salads round out the menu. An ambitious wine list with selections that span the globe is also offered, along with a number of sakes, martinis and cocktails.

Pan-Asian. Dinner. Outdoor seating. Bar. $36-85

★★★STEELHEAD BRASSERIE AND WINE BAR

112 Washington Place, Pittsburgh, 412-394-3474; www.thesteelhead.com

This casual American brasserie features artistically prepared cuisine that high-lights fresh seafood like Prince Edward Island mussels, seared ahi tuna and oysters. The menu also includes certified Angus beef strip steak, filet mignon and a porterhouse pork chop. On a daily basis, a special soup, pasta, pizza and grilled fresh fish dish are offered, all of which can be perfectly paired with a selection from the adventurous wine list.

American. Breakfast, lunch (Monday-Friday), dinner. Children's menu. Bar. $36-85

THE POCONOS

The Poconos are a very popular winter and summer destination in Pennsylvania, with both mountains and lakes. Towns include Milford, which is located along the Pennsylvania-New Jersey border, not far from New York. Located southwest of Milford is Mount Pocono, which offers recreation year-round in nearby parks, lakes and ski areas.

WHAT TO SEE

MILFORD
CANOEING, RAFTING, KAYAKING AND TUBING
Kittatinny Canoes, River Beach Campsites, 378 Routes 6 & 209, Milford, 570-828-2338, 800-356-2852; www.kittatinny.com

Kittatinny Canoes provides trips down the Delaware River. Choose from a canoe trip, kayaking, rafting, tubing, paintball and camping.

Mid-April-October, daily.

GREY TOWERS
151 Grey Tower Drive, Milford, 570-296-6401; www.fs.fed.us

This is a 100-acre estate originally built in 1886 as a summer home for philanthropist James W. Pinchot. It then became the residence of his son, Gifford Pinchot, the "father of American conservation," governor of Pennsylvania and the first chief of USDA Forest Service. Now, it's the site of the Pinchot Institute for Conservation Studies.

Admission: adults $6, seniors $5, children 12-17 $3, children 11 and under free. Tours: June-August, daily 11 a.m.-4 p.m. (on the hour).

WHERE TO STAY

MILFORD
★★★CLIFF PARK INN
155 Cliff Park Road, Milford, 570-296-6491, 800-225-6535; www.cliffparkinn.com

The Cliff Park Inn (originally a farmhouse, built in 1820) is located on 500 acres overlooking the Delaware River. With 12 guest rooms, three restaurants, seven miles of hiking trails, a nine-hole golf course and complimentary wireless Internet access, all this inn has to offer might encourage you to extend your stay. Nearby activities include cross-country skiing, hiking trails, swimming and more.

12 rooms. Restaurant, bar. Complimentary breakfast. Reservations recommended. Golf. $61-150

HIGHLIGHT

WHAT ARE THE TOP THINGS TO DO IN THE POCONOS?

HIT THE SKI SLOPES
Head to one of the many ski resorts that dot the area.

HAVE AN ADVENTURE ON THE WATER
Strap on your helmets for a ride down the river through the rapids.

MOUNT POCONO

★★★CAESARS PARADISE STREAM
Highway 940, Mount Pocono, 570-226-2101, 800-432-9932; www.caesarsparadisestream.com

For that honeymoon experience the Poconos are so well known for, Caesars is the place to stay. These are all-inclusive resorts, with heart-shaped tubs, round beds and champagne glass-shaped whirlpools that offer a romantic getaway. Big-name entertainers often appear at Caesars.

164 rooms. Restaurant, bar. Pool. Spa. No children allowed. Tennis. $251-350

★★★CRESCENT LODGE
191 Paradise Valley, Mount Pocono, 570-595-7486, 800-392-9400; www.crescentlodge.com

Nestled in the heart of the Pocono Mountains, the Crescent Lodge is elegant and welcoming. Guests enjoy uniquely furnished guest rooms, with some rooms boasting sunken Jacuzzis, private patios and sundecks overlooking the well-maintained grounds.

31 rooms. Restaurant, bar. Complimentary breakfast. Pool. $61-150

★★★FRENCH MANOR
50 Huntington Road, South Sterling, 570-676-3244, 877-720-6090; www.thefrenchmanor.com

Each guest room in this elegant inn shines with personal touches and lots of space. But don't let the antique ambience fool you; modern amenities abound in the rooms including DVD players and complimentary high-speed Internet access. The Great Hall has two floor-to-ceiling fireplaces.

15 rooms. Restaurant, bar. Complimentary breakfast. Fitness center. Pool. Spa. No children under 12. $151-250

★★★THE INN AT POCONO MANOR
Highway 314, Pocono Manor, 570-839-7111, 800-233-8150; www.poconomanor.com

Less than two hours from New York, this "Grand Lady of the Mountains" has been in business since 1902. Its rooms are well appointed and tasteful, in keeping with its spot on the National Register of Historic Places. Golf, horseback riding, swimming and tennis are all available on the 3,000-acre estate, as are fishing, clay shooting and more. Pamper yourself at Laurel Spa, also onsite.

250 rooms. Restaurant, bar. Fitness center. Pool. Spa. Golf. $151-250

★★★SKYTOP LODGE
One Skytop, Mount Pocono, 570-595-7401, 800-345-7759; www.skytop.com

Skytop Lodge is the ultimate mountain getaway for outdoor enthusiasts, with an 18-hole golf course, seven tennis courts, a clay shooting range, indoor and outdoor pools and fly fishing in the natural streams found throughout the property. This retreat in the heart of the Poconos is easily accessed from New York or Philadelphia. Accommodations are offered within the historic hotel, four-bedroom cottages or the intimate golf-course inn. The American menu at the Windsor Dining Room draws a crowd, while more casual dining is available at the Lake View Dining Room and the Tap Room.

148 rooms. Restaurant, bar. Pool. Spa. Golf. Beach. $351 and up.

WHERE TO EAT

MOUNT POCONO
★★★POWERHOUSE
1 Powerhouse Road, White Haven, 570-443-4480; www.powerhouseeatery.net

This restaurant is popular for its Italian-American menu. Its brick walls and exposed pipes remind diners of when it was as a coal-fueled power plant.

American, Italian. Lunch (Tuesday-Sunday), dinner. Reservations recommended. Bar. $16-35

WELCOME TO VIRGINIA

FROM VIENNA TO VIRGINIA BEACH AND RICHMOND TO

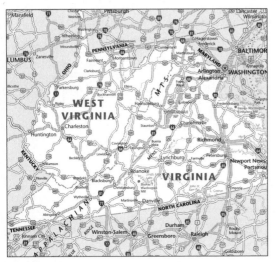

Roanoke, Virginia really is for lovers—of nature, history, art, fine dining and family fun. More than 1,600 historical markers dot its 55,000 miles of paved roads. And over 100 historic buildings are open all year; hundreds more welcome visitors during the statewide Historic Garden Week (usually the last week in April).

Permanent English settlement of America began in Jamestown in 1607 and started a long line of Virginia "firsts": the first legislative assembly in the Western Hemisphere; the first armed rebellion against royal government (Bacon's Rebellion, 1676); the first stirring debates, in Williamsburg and Richmond, which left pre-Revolutionary America echoing Patrick Henry's inflammatory "Give me liberty, or give me death". Records show that America's first Thanksgiving was held December 4, 1619, on the site of what is now the Berkeley Plantation. To Virginia, the nation owes its most cherished documents: Thomas Jefferson's Declaration of Independence, George Mason's Bill of Rights and James Madison's Constitution.

Ironically, the state so passionately involved in creating a new nation was nearly the means of its destruction. Virginia was the spiritual and physical capital of the Confederacy; the Army of Northern Virginia was the Confederacy's most powerful weapon, General Robert E. Lee its greatest commander. More than half the fighting of the Civil War took place in Virginia; and here, in the courthouse of the quaint little village of Appomattox, is where it finally came to an end. When chartered in 1609, the Virginia territory included about one-tenth of what is now the United States; the present state ranks 36th in size, but the area is remarkably diverse. For the vacationer today, the state offers colonial and Civil War history at every turn, seashore and mountain recreation year-round, the beautiful Shenandoah Valley and the Skyline Drive, one of the loveliest scenic drives in the East.

BEST ATTRACTIONS

VIRGINIA'S BEST ATTRACTIONS

CENTRAL VIRGINIA
Visit Monticello to tour Thomas Jefferson's home and gardens.

HAMPTON ROADS
Go back in time by exploring the colonial villages of Williamsburg and Jamestown. Each is rich in history and charm.

NORTHERN VIRGINIA
Pay your respects at the gravesites of President John F. Kennedy, Jacqueline Kennedy Onassis and others at Arlington Cemetery. The famous cemetery is located just across the Potomac River from Washington.

RICHMOND
While in town, be sure to check out the Executive Mansion—this colonial style home has been the residence of Virginia's governors and their families since 1813.

SHENANDOAH VALLEY
Go deep into the caverns of the Shenandoah Valley. These geological phenomena are something to see.

CENTRAL VIRGINIA

Made up of history and scenery, Central Virginia offers all kinds of activities. Popularly known as the number one small city in the South, Charlottesville is famous as the home of Thomas Jefferson, the third president of the United States, and the University of Virginia, which Jefferson founded and designed. The downtown pedestrian mall streetscape at the center of the historic district is alive with shops and restaurants, theaters and a skating rink. To the southwest of Charlottesville lies another college town. Lynchburg is perched on hills

HIGHLIGHT

WHAT ARE THE TOP THINGS TO DO IN CENTRAL VIRGINIA?

VISIT THE ESTATE ON THE HILLTOP

Monticello is considered one of the most beautiful places in Virginia. Explore Thomas Jefferson's home and gardens.

A LEGENDARY COURTHOUSE

Visit the site of the Civil War clashes between General Lee and General Grant.

overlooking the James River, which was for many years the city's means of growth. Petersburg, Lee's last stand before Appomattox (1864-1865), was settled in 1645 when the General Assembly authorized construction of Fort Henry at the falls of the Appomattox River. In 1784, three separate towns united to become the single city of Petersburg.

WHAT TO SEE

CHARLOTTESVILLE

ASH LAWN-HIGHLAND

1000 James Monroe Parkway, Charlottesville, 434-293-8000; www.ashlawnhighland.org

Built on a site personally selected by Thomas Jefferson in 1799, this 535-acre estate was the home of President James Monroe from 1799 to 1823. The estate is now owned by Monroe's alma mater, the College of William and Mary. Guided tours of the houses are offered.

Admission: adults $10, seniors $9, children 6-11 $5. April-October, daily 9 a.m.-6 p.m.; November-March, daily 11 a.m.-5 p.m.

HISTORIC MICHIE TAVERN

683 Thomas Jefferson Parkway, Charlottesville, 434-977-1234; www.michietavern.com

Visitors dine on hearty fare in the Tavern's Ordinary, where servers in period attire greet them. In the wintertime, you can warm up with hot mulled apple cider and lagers. Afterwards, a tour of the original tavern offers guests a chance to participate in 18th-century activities, including a lively Virginia dance.

Admission: Free. Tours: Daily 9 a.m.-5 p.m. Dining room: Daily, lunch.

LEWIS, CLARK AND SACAGAWEA STATUE

Midway Park, Ridge and Main streets, 434-293-6789, Charlottesville

This memorial honors the exploration of Meriwether Lewis, William Clark and Sacagawea in 1803-1806. Sculpted by Charles Keck in 1919, this statue dominates the brick walkway at the intersection of Ridge and Main streets. An inscription on the base of the statue commemorates the explorers and their farfetched, but accomplished mission.

MONTICELLO

931 Thomas Jefferson Parkway, Charlottesville, 434-984-9822; www.monticello.org

Located on a mountaintop, Monticello is one of the most beautiful estates in Virginia and is considered a classic of American architecture. The house was designed by Thomas Jefferson and built over the course of 40 years, symbolizing the pleasure he found in "putting up and pulling down". Jefferson moved into the first completed outbuilding of his new home in 1771, although construction continued until 1809. Most of the interior furnishings are original. Tours of the restored orchard, vineyard and vegetable garden are available. Jefferson died at Monticello on July 4, 1826, and was buried in the family cemetery. The Thomas Jefferson Memorial Foundation maintains the house and gardens.

Admission: adults $15 (November-February), $20 (March-October), children 6-11 $8, children 5 and under free. March-October, daily 8 a.m.-5 p.m.; November-February, daily 9 a.m.-4:30 p.m.

UNIVERSITY OF VIRGINIA

914 Emmet St. North, Charlottesville, 434-924-1019; www.virginia.edu

Founded by Thomas Jefferson and built according to his plans, the campus is made up of handsome red brick buildings with white trim and ancient trees. The serpentine walls, one brick thick, which Jefferson designed for strength and beauty, are famous. Room 13, West Range, occupied by Edgar Allan Poe as a student, is displayed for the public. Historical walking tours take place year-round except during a break in December and January and May, starting at the Rotunda.

Tours: Daily 10 a.m., 11 a.m., 2 p.m., 3 p.m., 4 p.m.

LYNCHBURG

APPOMATTOX COURT HOUSE NATIONAL HISTORICAL PARK

Highway 24, Appomattox, 434-352-8987; www.nps.gov

The series of clashes between General Ulysses S. Grant and General Robert E. Lee that started with the Battle of the Wilderness May 5, 1864 finally ended here on Palm Sunday, April 9, 1865, in the little village of Appomattox. A week earlier, Lee had evacuated besieged Petersburg and headed west in a desperate attempt to join forces with General Johnston in North Carolina. Ragged and exhausted, decimated by desertions, without supplies and beset by Union forces at every turn, the once-great Army of Northern Virginia launched its last attack on April 9 at dawn. By 10 a.m., it was clear that further bloodshed was futile; after some difficulty in getting a message to Grant, the two met in the parlor of the McLean House. By 3 p.m., the generous surrender terms had been drafted and signed. The war was over. Three days later, 28,231 Confederate soldiers received their parole here. The 1,743-acre park includes the village of Appomattox, restored and reconstructed to appear much as it did in 1865.

Admission: June-August, $4 ($10 maximum per vehicle), children 15 and under free; August-June, $3 ($5 maximum per vehicle), children 15 and under free. Visitor center: Daily 8:30 a.m.-5 p.m.

OLD COURT HOUSE MUSEUM
901 Court St., Lynchburg, 434-455-6226; www.lynchburgmuseum.org

This museum has been restored to its original 1855 Greek Revival appearance. Three galleries have exhibits on the early history of the area, highlighting Quaker settlement and the role of tobacco.

Admission: adults $6, seniors and students $5, children 6-17 $3, children 5 and under free. Monday-Saturday 10 a.m.-4 p.m., Sunday noon-4 p.m.

POINT OF HONOR
112 Cabell St., Lynchburg, 434-455-6226; www.pointofhonor.org

Dr. George Cabel Sr., who was the physician to Patrick Henry, built this mansion on Daniel's Hill above the James River in 1815. It's a Federalist style home with octagon bay façade and finely crafted interior woodwork with period furnishings and gardens.

Admission: adults $6, seniors and students $5, children 6-17 $3, children 5 and under free. Monday-Saturday 10 a.m.-4 p.m., Sunday noon-4 p.m.

PETERSBURG

PAMPLIN PARK CIVIL WAR SITE
6125 Boydton Plank Road, Petersburg, 804-861-2408; www.pamplinpark.org

This is the site of General Ulysses S. Grant's decisive victory over Confederate forces in 1865. The 422-acre park includes battle trails, reconstructed soldier huts and a plantation home. There is an interpretive center and museum.

Admission: adults $10, children 6-12 $5, children 5 and under free. Daily 9 a.m.-5 p.m.

PETERSBURG NATIONAL BATTLEFIELD
5001 Siege Road, Petersburg, 804-732-3531; www.nps.gov

At the price of 70,000 Union and Confederate casualties, the campaign that spelled doom for the Confederacy occurred in a huge, 40-mile semicircle around Richmond and Petersburg. After his unsuccessful attempt to take Richmond by frontal assault (at Cold Harbor, June 3, 1864), General Grant withdrew and attacked Petersburg. After four days of fighting and failing to capture the city, Grant decided to lay siege. Petersburg was the rail center that funneled supplies to Lee and Richmond. The siege lasted 10 months, from June 15, 1864 to April 2, 1865, with the two armies in almost constant contact. When Petersburg finally fell, Lee's surrender was only a week away. The park, at more than 2,700 acres, preserves Union and Confederate fortifications, trenches and gun pits. See the Crater, a hole remaining after Union troops tunneled beneath Confederate artillery position and exploded four tons of powder in 1864.

Daily 9 a.m.-5 p.m.

SIEGE MUSEUM
15 W. Bank St., Petersburg, 804-733-2404; www.petersburg-va.org

Located in the 1839 Exchange Building, the Siege Museum depicts the average life in Petersburg before, during and right after the Civil War. Focusing on the ten-month siege on Petersburg, the museum displays documents, photographs and artifacts. This was the longest period of time that an American city has ever been under military attack. Check out the film *The Echoes Still Remain*, a documentary about Petersburg involvement in the Civil War.

Admission: adults $5, seniors, military and children 7-12 $4, children 6 and under free. Daily 10 a.m.-5 p.m.

TRAPEZIUM HOUSE

Market and High Street, Petersburg, 804-733-2400; www.virginia.org

This house was built in 1817 in the form of a trapezium with no right angles and no parallel sides by eccentric Irish bachelor Charles O'Hara. O'Hara is said to have believed the superstitions of his West Indian servant, who thought that ghosts and evil spirits inhabited right angles. Because this house is privately owned, it is only open during events.

WHERE TO STAY

CHARLOTTESVILLE

★★★BOAR'S HEAD INN

200 Ednam Drive, Charlottesville, 434-296-2181, 800-476-1988; www.boarsheadinn.com

Located in the Blue Ridge Mountains, this resort welcomes guests to visit the past and enjoy the present. Guests can visit past presidential homes (a short drive away), stroll through local wineries or enjoy a panoramic view by hot-air balloon. Enjoy the many onsite amenities including a spa, golf course, swimming pools and numerous restaurants.

170 rooms. Restaurant, bar. Fitness center. Pool. Spa. Tennis. Golf. $151-250

★★★KESWICK HALL AT MONTICELLO

701 Club Drive, Keswick, 434-979-3440, 888-778-2565; www.keswick.com

Keswick Hall's 600-acre estate, set at the foot of the Blue Ridge Mountains, offers visitors individually designed guest rooms that reflect a modern inter-pretation of early American style, with overstuffed furniture, club chairs, Aubusson carpets and canopied four-poster beds. The rolling hills of the Shenandoah Valley invite exploration and the historic halls of Monticello are only minutes away, but this resort also entices its guests with a variety of recre-ational opportunities. The members-only Keswick Hall, adjacent to the hotel, presents an exclusive opportunity for guests to enjoy its indoor/outdoor pool, tennis courts, spa services and 18-hole Arnold Palmer golf course.

48 rooms. Restaurant, bar. Fitness center. Pool. Spa. Golf. Tennis. $351 and up.

★★★OMNI CHARLOTTESVILLE HOTEL

235 W. Main St., Charlottesville, 434-971-5500, 888-444-6664; www.omnihotels.com

Located on a downtown pedestrian mall, the Omni Charlottesville Hotel is within walking distance of the government buildings. Guest rooms offer views of the Blue Ridge Mountains and historic Charlottesville and are decorated in a traditional style. Enjoy cocktails at The Pointe Patio, overlooking the Downtown Mall.

208 rooms. Restaurant, bar. Business center. Fitness center. Pool. Pets accepted. $61-150

★★★SILVER THATCH INN

3001 Hollymead Drive, Charlottesville, 434-978-4686, 800-261-0720; www.silverthatch.com

Built in 1780, this clapboard home is full of history and is one of the oldest buildings in the area. Each guest room is named for a Virginia-born president. Rest comfortably on Egyptian cotton linens in your colonial room. Contemporary cuisine is served at the inn's restaurant.

7 rooms. Restaurant, bar. Complimentary breakfast. No children under 14. $151-250

WHERE TO EAT

CHARLOTTESVILLE

★★★FOSSETT'S RESTAURANT

Keswick Hall at Monticello, 701 Club Drive, Keswick, 434-979-3440; www.keswick.com

"A feast for the eyes" best describes the chef's classically inspired culinary creations, which are most appropriate given the formal dining room's trompe l'oeil wall murals and expansive garden views. The menu includes items such as fried green tomatoes with spring garlic prawns, spring pea risotto, poached salmon with curried cauliflower spring peas and shiitake bacon. Enjoy alfresco dining when the weather is warm, with views of the golf course.

American. Breakfast, dinner, Sunday brunch. Children's menu. Reservations recommended. Outdoor seating. Bar. $36-85

★★★OLD MILL ROOM

Boar's Head Inn, 200 Ednam Drive, Charlottesville, 434-972-2230, 800-476-1988; www.boarsheadinn.com

This dining room is located in the Boar's Head Inn at the University of Virginia. The menu features dishes such as grilled sea bass with cilantro-lime basmati rice and roasted peach salsa and pan-seared lamb loin with fresh rosemary and mint cous cous. Most ingredients are sustainable and organic.

American. Breakfast, lunch, dinner, Sunday brunch. Outdoor seating. Children's menu. Reservations recommended. Bar. $36-85

LYNCHBURG

★★★PORTERHOUSE RESTAURANT AND LOUNGE

126 Old Graves Mill Road, Lynchburg, 434-237-5655; www.theporterhouserestaurant.com

For more than 25 years, The Porterhouse has been cooking up delicious chops and fresh seafood. The red chairs draw customers into the classic steakhouse setting. Start off your memorable meal with baked mushrooms imperial, stuffed with crab and an alfredo sauce. Go with one of the house specialties such as The Porterhouse favorite, served with a glass of wine and dessert.

American. Dinner. Closed Sunday. Reservations recommended. Bar. $16-35

WHAT TO SEE

CHINCOTEAGUE

ASSATEAGUE ISLAND

8586 Beach Road, Chincoteague, 757-336-6577; www.nps.gov

A 37-mile barrier island, Assateague has stretches of ocean and sand dunes, forest and marshes that create a natural environment unusual on the East Coast. Sika deer, a variety of wildlife and countless birds, including the peregrine falcon, can be found here, but wild ponies occasionally roaming the marshes offer the most exotic sight for visitors. There are nature and auto trails,

HIGHLIGHT

WHAT IS THERE TO DO ON CHINCOTEAGUE ISLAND?

Oysters, wild ponies and good fishing are the stock in trade of this small island, connected with Chincoteague National Wildlife Refuge by a bridge and to the mainland by 10 miles of highway. The oysters, many of them grown on the hard sand bottoms off Chincoteague from seed or small oysters brought from natural beds elsewhere, are among the best in the East. Chincoteague's wild ponies are actually small horses, but when fully grown they are somewhat larger and more graceful than Shetlands. They are thought to have descended from horses that swam ashore from a wrecked Spanish galleon, their limited growth caused by generations of a marsh grass diet.

interpretive programs, swimming, lifeguards in summer, surf fishing, camping, hike-in and canoe-in camp sites and day-use facilities.
Daily.

CAPTAIN BARRY'S BACK BAY CRUISES & EXPEDITIONS
The Chincoteague Inn Restaurant, 6262 Marlin St., Chincoteague, 757-336-6508; www.captainbarry.net
Captain Barry's features cruises including a bird watch cruise, a back bay expedition, a champagne sunset cruise, moonlight excursions and a fun cruise.
Trips vary from one to four hours. Reservations recommended.

HAMPTON ROADS

Hampton Roads, Virginia's beach region, is filled with activities for everyone. Hampton is the oldest continuous English-speaking town in the United States. On May 13, 1607, in this unpromising setting, the first permanent English settlement in the New World, Jamestown, was founded. From the beginning, characteristics of the early United States were established: self-government, industry, commerce, the plantation system and a diverse populace. One of the three cities that make up the Port of Hampton Roads, Newport News has the world's largest shipbuilding company, Newport News Shipbuilding. Also in Newport News is Historic Hilton Village, which was built between 1918 and 1920 as a way to house workers during wartime. Today, it features 500 English cottage-style homes, restaurants and antique and specialty shops. Norfolk is part of the Port of Hampton Roads, and houses the largest naval facility in the world. It's headquarters for the United States Navy's Atlantic Fleet and NATO's Allied Command Atlantic. Across the river from Norfolk, Portsmouth is unrivaled for commercial shipping and shipbuilding activity. Portsmouth also has over 300 years of history represented by more than 20 examples of colonial, Federal-style and antebellum houses. The Historic Area of Williamsburg, approximately a mile long and a half-mile wide, encompasses most of the 18th-century capital. Eighty-eight of the original buildings have been restored; 50 major buildings, houses and shops and many smaller outbuildings have been reconstructed on their original sites. Yorktown's moment in history came at the Battle of the Capes on September 5, 1781 when the French defeated a British ship, marking the end of the Revolutionary War. Yorktown Battlefield, part of Colonial National Historical Park, surrounds the village.

WHAT TO SEE

HAMPTON
BUCKROE BEACH
22 Lincoln St., Hampton, 757-850-5134; www.hamptoncvb.com

Miles of coastline border the gentle waters of the Chesapeake Bay. The beach may not be on the ocean, but it's quiet and the water is warm. Just a few minutes from downtown Hampton, Buckroe Beach offers a place to lounge, windsurf, sail and eat along the beautiful Virginia coast. There are stands to rent umbrellas and chairs right on the beach to make the day worry-free. Catch the sunset on the Chesapeake horizon for a view you'll never forget.

June-August, daily 8 a.m.-6 p.m.

CASEMATE MUSEUM AT FORT MONROE
20 Bernard Road, Hampton, 757-788-3391; www.virginia.org

The first fort here was a stockade called Fort Algernourne; the second, Fort George, though built of brick, was destroyed by a hurricane in 1749. The present fort was completed about 1834. The museum provides insight on the heritage of the fort and offers access to a series of casemates. Jefferson Davis' casemate contains a cell in which the Confederacy's president was confined on false charges of plotting to kill Abraham Lincoln. The museum also features Civil War exhibits, military uniforms and assorted artwork, including three original Remington drawings, along with audiovisual programs. Scale models of coast artillery guns and dioramas represent the role of the coast artillery from 1901 to 1946.

Admission: Free. Daily 10:30 a.m.-4:30 p.m.

HAMPTON CAROUSEL
602 Settlers Landing Road, Hampton, 757-727-6381; www.virginia.org

This old-fashioned 1920 carousel is housed in its own pavilion and features 48 hand-carved horses. The Hampton Carousel is just one of only 200 antique carousels in the United States. This beautiful and rare display of American folk art is located downtown. Still dancing to its original band organ, this antique is one the kids will be begging to visit.

Admission: $2. June-mid-September, Monday-Wednesday noon-5 p.m., Thursday-Sunday noon-7 p.m.; Mid-September-December, Friday-Sunday noon-4 p.m.

JAMESTOWN COLONIAL NATIONAL HISTORIC PARK
GLASSHOUSE
Colonial National Historic Parkway and Jamestown Road, Jamestown Colonial National Historical Park; www.nps.gov

Colonists began producing glass here in 1608. See the remains of furnaces used for glassblowing and watch demonstrations of glassblowing as it's done today. There is also a gift shop here where you can purchase glass.

Daily 8:30 a.m.-5 p.m.

WHAT ARE THE TOP THINGS TO DO IN HAMPTON ROADS?

RELAX AND DIG YOUR TOES IN THE SAND
Head to Buckroe Beach for some fun in the sun. The beach is beautiful and the water is refreshing.

TOUR THE NEW JAMESTOWN
New Towne is the area where Jamestown expanded in the early 1600s.

GET A HISTORY LESSON WITH A SOUTHERN TWANG
Portsmouth boasts homes that are over 300 years old. From antebellum to federal-style architecture, these private homes are a sight to see.

GO BACK IN TIME TO THE COLONIAL ERA
Colonial Williamsburg offers more than just its wealth of history; however, the historic section of the town is a must-see when visiting the area.

JAMESTOWN MEMORIAL CHURCH
Colonial National Historic Parkway and Jamestown Road, Jamestown Colonial National Historical Park; www.historicjamestowne.org
The brick church that stands here was built in 1907 by the National Society of the Colonial Dames of America over the foundations of the original church built in 1639. In front of the church is a brick tower that was constructed in 1690 and is the only building from the 17th century that is still standing in Jamestown.

NEW TOWNE
1367 Colonial Parkway, Jamestown Colonial National Historical Park; www.nps.gov
This area where Jamestown expanded around 1620 may be toured along "Backstreete" and other original streets. The section includes reconstructed foundations indicating sites of the Governor's House, the homes of Richard Kemp (builder of one of the first brick houses in America), Henry Hartwell (a founder of the College of William & Mary) and Dr. John Pott and William Pierce, who led the "thrusting out" of Governor John Harvey in 1635.
Daily 8:30 a.m.-4:30 p.m.

NEWPORT NEWS
HISTORIC HILTON VILLAGE
Warwick Boulevard and Main Street, Newport News; www.shophiltonvillage.com

Listed on the National Register of Historic Places, this village was built between 1918 and 1920 as a way to house workers during wartime at Newport News Shipbuilding. This architecturally significant neighborhood features 500 English cottage-style homes, restaurants and antique and specialty shops.

NEWPORT NEWS PARK
13564 Jefferson Ave., Newport News, 757-886-7912, 800-203-8322; www.nnparks.com

Facilities in this 8,000-acre park include freshwater fishing, canoes and paddleboats rentals. There are history and nature trails, bicycle paths (along with bicycle rentals), an archery range, playgrounds, an arboretum, disc golf course, a discovery center, picnicking areas and campsites.
Daily dawn-dusk.

PENINSULA FINE ARTS CENTER
101 Museum Drive, Newport News, 757-596-8175; www.pfac-va.org

Changing bimonthly exhibits ranging from national traveling exhibitions to regional artists are featured at this arts center. There are also classes, workshops and special events, plus a children's hands-on activity area as well as a museum shop.
Admission: adults $7.50, seniors, military personnel, students and teachers $6, children 6-12 $4, children 5 and under free. Wednesday-Saturday 10 a.m.-5 p.m. Sunday 1-5 p.m. Tuesday 5:30-8 p.m. free.

VIRGINIA WAR MUSEUM
9285 Warwick Blvd., Newport News, 757-247-8523; www.warmuseum.org

More than 60,000 artifacts, including weapons, uniforms, vehicles, posters, insignias and accoutrements relating to every major U.S. military involvement from the Revolutionary War to the Vietnam War, are housed at this museum. There's also a military history library and film collection. Tours and educational programs are available.
Admission: adults $6, seniors $5, children $4, children under 3 and under free. Monday-Saturday 9 a.m.-5 p.m., Sunday 1-5 p.m.

NORFOLK
AMERICAN ROVER
Norfolk, 757-627-7245; www.americanrover.com

This 135-foot, three-mast topsail passenger schooner cruises the "smooth waters" of Hampton Roads historical harbor. The ship includes spacious sun decks, below-deck lounges and concessions. The tour passes historic forts, as well as merchant and U.S. Navy ships. Some tours also pass the naval base.
Mid-April-October, 1 ½- and 2-hour tours daily; see website for schedule and pricing.

CHRYSLER MUSEUM OF ART
245 W. Olney Road, Norfolk, 757-664-6200; www.chrysler.org

Art treasures representing nearly every important culture, civilization and historical period of the past 4,000 years can be found at this museum. There's a photography gallery, and a fine collection of Tiffany decorative arts and glass, which includes the 8,000-piece Chrysler Institute of Glass.

Admission: adults $7, seniors, military personnel $5, children $18 and under free. Wednesday 10 a.m.-9 p.m., Thursday-Saturday 10 a.m.-5 p.m., Sunday 1-5 p.m.

GENERAL DOUGLAS MACARTHUR MEMORIAL

City Hall Avenue and Bank Street, Norfolk, 757-441-2965; www.macarthurmemorial.org

The museum is housed in the restored former city hall where MacArthur is buried in a large rotunda with his wife, surrounded by inscriptions banners, flags and more. Nine galleries contain memorabilia of the general's life and military career. There are three other buildings on MacArthur Square: a theater where a film biography is shown, a gift shop and the library/archives.

Admission: Free. Monday-Saturday 10 a.m.-5 p.m., Sunday 11 a.m.-5 p.m.

HAMPTON ROADS NAVAL MUSEUM

1 Waterside Drive, Norfolk, 757-322-2987; www.hrnm.navy.mil

This naval museum interprets the extensive naval history of the Hampton Roads area through detailed ship models, period photographs, archaeological artifacts and a superior collection of naval prints and artwork.

Admission: Free. June-August, daily 10 a.m.-5 p.m.; September-May, Tuesday-Saturday 10 a.m.-5 p.m., Sunday noon-5 p.m.

NAUTICUS-THE NATIONAL MARITIME CENTER

1 Waterside Drive, Norfolk, 757-664-1000, 800-664-1080; www.nauticus.org

This center interprets aspects from marine biology and ecology to exploration, trade and shipbuilding. Interactive computer exhibits allow visitors to navigate a simulated ocean voyage, design a model ship, pilot a virtual reality submarine, and view actual researchers at work in two working marine laboratories. Active U.S. Navy ships and scientific research vessels periodically moor at Nauticus and open to visitors.

Admission: adult $11.95, seniors and military personnel $9.95, children 4-12 $9.50, children 3 and under free. June-August, daily 10 a.m.-5 p.m.; September-May, Tuesday-Saturday 10 a.m.-5 p.m., Sunday noon-5 p.m.

SPIRIT OF NORFOLK

109 E. Main Road, Norfolk, 757-625-1748, 866-304-2469, 866-451-3866; www.spiritofnorfolk.com

Enjoy a harbor cruise aboard a 600-passenger cruise ship. The captain's narration highlights the harbor's famous landmarks, including Waterside Festival Marketplace, Portsmouth Naval Hospital, Old Fort Norfolk, Blackbeard's hiding place, Norfolk Naval Base and the downtown area's dynamic skyline. There are lunch, midday and dinner cruises to choose from.

See website for schedules and ticket information.

TOWN POINT PARK

120 W. Main St., Norfolk, 757-441-2345; www.festeventsva.org

Town Point Park is the home to Norfolk Festevents and hosts more than 100 free outdoor concerts, parties, dances, movies and festivals each year. The park covers seven acres and is located on the Elizabeth River making it the perfect spot to enjoy a lovely spring or summer evening.

April-October; see website for schedules and ticket information.

VIRGINIA ZOOLOGICAL PARK

3500 Granby St., Norfolk, 757-441-2374; www.virginiazoo.org

This combination of a zoo, park and conservatory features plenty of fun things to do for the whole family. The zoo houses more than 350 animals ranging from lion cubs to red pandas to meerkats. A zoo train takes you around the property and is narrated by the engineer. There's also a playground, tennis courts, basketball courts, picnic areas and concessions within the park.

Admission: adults $7, children 2-11 $5, seniors $6, children 2 and under free. Train rides: $2. Daily 10 a.m.-5 p.m.

WATERSIDE FESTIVAL MARKETPLACE

333 Waterside Drive, Norfolk, 757-627-3300; www.watersidemarketplace.com

This waterfront pavilion features more than 90 shops, restaurants and bars. Bordering the Waterside are the city's marina and dock areas, where harbor tour vessels take on passengers.

Food Court: Monday-Saturday 11 a.m.-9 p.m., Sunday noon-6 p.m. Shops: Monday-Saturday 10 a.m.-9 p.m., Sunday noon-6 p.m.

PORTSMOUTH

COURTHOUSE GALLERIES

420 High St., Portsmouth, 757-393-5258; www.courthousegalleries.com

These galleries feature changing exhibits and provide lectures, classes, performances and other special events within an 1846 courthouse. Past exhibits have included Fairy Tale Art and Ceramic Art and Sculptures.

Admission: adults $5, children 2-17 $2, children under 2 free. Monday-Saturday 9 a.m.-5 p.m., Sunday 11 a.m.-5 p.m., first Friday of the month 9 a.m.-8 p.m.

HISTORIC HOUSES

Visitor Center, 6 Crawford Parkway, Portsmouth, 757-393-5111

Portsmouth has over 300 years of history represented by more than 20 examples of colonial, Federal-style and antebellum houses. Among them is the Nivison-Ball House, circa 1730-1750 (*417 Middle St.*), where Andrew Jackson and General Lafayette were entertained. These houses are private and may be viewed only from the exterior. Pick up walking tour brochures with maps and descriptions of churches, homes and old buildings from the Visitor Center.

NAVAL SHIPYARD MUSEUM

2 High St., Portsmouth, 757-393-8591; www.portsnavalmuseums.com

This shipyard museum features thousands of items of naval equipment, plus flags, uniforms, prints, maps and models, including one of the *CSS Virginia*; the U.S. Ship-of-the-line *Delaware*, which was built in Portsmouth; and the first ship dry-docked in the U.S.

Admission: adults $3, children 2-17 $1, children under 2 free. Monday-Saturday 10 a.m.-5 p.m., Sunday 1-5 p.m.

VIRGINIA BEACH

ADAM THOROUGHGOOD HOUSE

1636 Parish Road, Virginia Beach, 757-460-7588; www.virginiabeachhistory.org

This National Historic Landmark, built circa 1680, is one of the oldest remaining colonial homes in Virginia. The Department of Museum and Cultural

Arts operated the house until 2003 when the City of Virginia Beach took over. Special programs are offered in conjunction with the Francis Land House. The historic house museum is open six days a week and offers guided tours.

Admission: adults $4, seniors $3, students $2, children 5 and under free. Tuesday-Saturday 9 a.m.-5 p.m., Sunday 11 a.m.-5 p.m.

CONTEMPORARY ART CENTER OF VIRGINIA

2200 Parks Ave., Virginia Beach, 757-425-0000; www.cacv.org

This 32,000-square-foot facility is devoted to the presentation of 20th-century art through exhibitions, education, performing arts and special events. CAC, a non-profit and non-collecting institution, was created to promote the awareness, knowledge and study of art. This arts center holds annual fundraising events, such as Wine by Design and Boardwalk Art Show & Festival. Housed in a building owned by the city, the Contemporary Art Center of Virginia has more than 6,300 square feet of exhibition space.

Admission: adults $7, seniors, students and military personnel $5, children 3-14 $3. Tuesday-Friday 10 a.m.-5 p.m., Saturday 10 a.m.-4 p.m., Sunday noon-4 p.m.

FRANCIS LAND HOUSE HISTORIC SITE AND GARDENS

3131 Virginia Beach Blvd., Virginia Beach, 757-431-4000; www.virginiabeachhistory.org

Once a flourishing plantation near the Lynnhaven River, this 19th-century home is now owned by the City of Virginia Beach. The city purchased the property in 1975 with the intention of preserving the home and teaching others about the history of the land. A historic house museum since 1986, the Francis Land House provides activities such as "A Trip Through Time", created especially for students. Programs are also available to the general public six days a week.

Admission: adults $4, seniors $3, students $2, children 5 and under free. Tuesday-Saturday 9 a.m.-5 p.m., Sunday 11 a.m.-5 p.m.

LYNNHAVEN HOUSE

4405 Wishart Road, Virginia Beach, 757-431-4000; www.virginiabeachhistory.org

Built in 1725 by the Thelaball family, the Lynnhaven House is an example of the eighteenth century Tidewater Virginia vernacular architecture. Now owned by the City of Virginia Beach, the Lynnhaven house has been through its fair share of proprietors. The onetime owners, the Boush family, now dwell in the 19th-century burial site to the south of the house. Well maintained over the years, between 75 and 80 percent of the original construction material remains.

Admission: adults $4, seniors $3, children $2, children 5 and under free. Daily noon-4 p.m.

OCEAN BREEZE WATER PARK

849 General Booth Blvd., Virginia Beach, 757-422-4444; www.oceanbreezewaterpark.com

Take the plunge on the Paradise Pipeline and endure the twists and turns before plunging into the refreshing pool. Catch a few waves in Ocean Breeze Water Park's very own ocean—minus the beach—Runaway Bay Wave Pool. Reserve a private poolside cabana, where you can sit back and relax or grab a drink from Scallywags while the kids take on the slides. With plenty of water attractions for the whole group, it's a cool way to spend your day.

Admission: adults $24.99, seniors and children 3-9 $17.99, children 2 and under free. June-August, Daily; hours vary.

OLD CAPE HENRY LIGHTHOUSE AND MEMORIAL PARK

583 Atlantic Ave., Fort Story, Virginia Beach, 757-422-9421; www.apva.org

Built in 1792, Old Cape Henry Lighthouse guards the mouth of the Chesapeake Bay. Replaced by a new lighthouse in 1881, the Virginia antiquity is recognized for its architectural and historical significance. In 1896, it was marked as the location of the landing of the first English settlers on Virginian shores.

Admission: adults $4, children 3-12 $2, children 2 and under free. November-mid-March, daily 10 a.m.-4 p.m.; mid-March-October, daily 10 a.m.-5 p.m.

OLD COAST GUARD STATION

24th Street and Atlantic Avenue, Virginia Beach, 757-422-1587; www.oldcoastguardstation.com

This former Coast Guard Station displays visual exhibits of numerous shipwrecks along the Virginia coastline. "The War Years" exhibit relates United States Coast Guard efforts during World War I and World War II. There are photographs, ship models and artifacts.

Admission: adults $4, seniors and military personnel $3, children 6-18 $2, children 5 and under free. Monday-Saturday 10 a.m.-5 p.m., Sunday noon-5 p.m.

VIRGINIA AQUARIUM, A MARINE SCIENCE CENTER

717 General Booth Blvd., Virginia Beach, 757-385-3474; www.vmsm.com

Head to the aquarium to see live animals, interactive exhibits, a 300-seat IMAX 3-D theater and more. Exhibits include an ocean aquarium with sharks, a sea turtle aquarium, an aviary, a salt marsh preserve, a touch tank, a river room and more.

Admission: adults $11.95, seniors $10.95, children 3-11 $7.95, children 2 and under free. June-August, daily 9 a.m.-6 p.m.; September-May, Daily 9 a.m.-5 p.m.

WILLIAMSBURG

1700S SHOPPING

Williamsburg

Superior wares typical of the 18th century are offered in nine restored or reconstructed stores and shops. Items include silver, jewelry, herbs, candles, hats and books. Two craft houses sell approved reproductions of the antiques on display in the houses and museums.

Hours vary.

BUSCH GARDENS WILLIAMSBURG

1 Busch Gardens Blvd., Williamsburg, 757-253-3000, 800-343-7946; www.buschgardens.com

This European-style theme park on 360 acres features recreated 17th-century German, English, French, Italian, Scottish and Canadian villages. Attractions include more than 50 thrill rides, attractions and shows, including the Alpengeist roller coaster, one of the fastest and tallest in the world. Other attractions include live shows, an antique carousel and rides for small children. There are also theme restaurants and shops. Transportation around the grounds by sky ride or steam train is available. A computer-operated monorail links the park with the Anheuser-Busch Hospitality Center, where visitors can take a brewery tour.

Admission: adults $59.95, children 3-9 $49.95, children 2 and under free. Mid-April-August, daily; late March-mid-April and September-December, hours vary; see website for schedule.

THE COLLEGE OF WILLIAM & MARY
Richmond Road, Williamsburg, 757-221-4000; www.wm.edu

Established in 1693, William & Mary is America's second-oldest college (only Harvard is older). The school initiated an honor system, an elective system of studies and schools of law and modern languages. It was the second to have a school of medicine (established in 1779). The prestigious Phi Beta Kappa Society was founded here in 1776. Be sure to stop in the Muscarelle Museum of Art (*Jamestown Road and Phi Beta Kappa Circle, Williamsburg, 757-221-2700*). With past exhibitions ranging from women of Pamplona to Andy Warhol, the Museum of Art boasts quite a wide collection. There's also an impressive collection of Colonial American portraits.

Tours: Late May-early September, hours vary; see website for information. Museum: Admission: $5, students, children 11 and under free; special exhibits additional $5. Tuesday-Friday 10 a.m.-5 p.m., Saturday-Sunday noon-4 p.m.

FORD'S COLONY WILLIAMSBURG
1 Ford's Colony Drive, Williamsburg, 800-334-6033; www.fordscolony.com

This acclaimed Dan Maples-designed golf course features 54 holes, comprising the par-72 Marsh Hawk Course, the par-71 Blackheath Course and the par-72 Blue Heron Course. The course touts itself as a player's course that appeals to golfers of all levels. There's a dining room and country club where you can relax after a round of golf.

See website for schedule and pricing information.

MERCHANTS SQUARE
Williamsburg

One of the first planned shopping districts in the nation, you'll find a charming square featuring shops, restaurants and businesses along a pedestrian area filled with trees and brick sidewalks. Stores include Talbots, Scotland House Ltd. (featuring gifts from the U.K.), Chico's and Carousel Children's Clothier. There are also coffee shops, ice cream stores, bistros and more.

Stores: Monday-Saturday 10 a.m.-6 p.m., Sunday noon-5 p.m.

WATER COUNTRY USA
176 Water Country Parkway, Williamsburg, 757-253-3350, 800-343-7946; www.watercountryusa.com

With more than 30 water rides, attractions and live entertainment, this is a place for the whole family. Cool off in Surfer's Bay, the largest wave pool in Virginia, or head to Rampage and surf down the 60-degree waterslide before skidding across the 120-foot pool. Catch Aquabatics at the Caban-A-Rama Theater for all kinds of water stunts. Afterward, take a breather at one of the park's five restaurants.

Admission: adults $42.95, children 3-9 $35.95, children 2 and under free. Mid May-early September, hours vary; see website for schedule.

WILLIAMSBURG WINERY
5810 Wessex Hundred, Williamsburg, 757-229-0999; www.williamsburgwinery.com

Founded in 1985, the winery carries on a Virginia tradition that began with the Jamestown settlers in 1607. Located two miles from the Historic Area, it has 50 acres of vineyards. Visitors can take 30-45 minute guided walking tours, and tastings are available after the tour.

Admission (tour and tasting): $8. April-October, Monday-Saturday 10 a.m.-6 p.m., Sunday 11 a.m.-6 p.m.; November-March, Monday-Saturday 10 a.m.-5 p.m., Sunday 11 a.m.-5 p.m. Tours: Daily 11 a.m.-4 p.m. (every half hour).

YORK RIVER STATE PARK

5526 Riverview Road, Williamsburg, 757-566-3036; www.dcr.virginia.gov

Just 11 miles west of Colonial Williamsburg is this beautiful 2,550-acre state park along the York River. With more than 25 miles of hiking, biking and equestrian trails, York River State Park provides outdoor fun for everyone.

YORKTOWN

YORKTOWN BATTLEFIELD IN COLONIAL NATIONAL HISTORIC PARK

Colonial Parkway and Yorktown Visitor Center, Yorktown, 757-898-3400; www.nps.gov

The battlefield houses the remains of 1781 British fortifications, modified and strengthened by Confederate forces in the Civil War. See the Yorktown National Civil War Cemetery, which has 2,204 burials, most of which are unknown. Stop by the Visitor Center located at the Battlefield to pay the park admission fee, which includes access to the battlefield tour and other sights.

Admission: adults $10, children 15 and under free. Grounds: Daily dawn-dusk. Visitor center: Daily 9 a.m.-5 p.m.

YORKTOWN VICTORY CENTER

Route 1020, Williamsburg, 757-253-4838; www.historyisfun.org

This museum of the Revolutionary War chronicles the struggle for independence from the beginning of colonial unrest to the new nation's formation. There are exhibit galleries, a living history Continental Army encampment and late-18th-century farm. See website for a combination ticket with Jamestown Settlement available.

Admission: adults $9.25, children 6-12 $6.50, children 5 and under free. Daily 9 a.m.-5 p.m.

WHERE TO STAY

HAMPTON

★★★TIDES INN

480 King Carter Drive, Irvington, 804-438-5000, 800-843-3746; www.tidesinn.com

Water figures largely in the experience at this inn, which is bordered by the Chesapeake Bay, Potomac River and Rappahannock River, and includes its own marina. Golf, tennis, croquet, biking and exploring the nearby historic sites are just some of the ways guests fill their days. Dining runs the gamut from the elegant setting at the East Room dining room to the casual atmosphere of the Chesapeake Club.

106 rooms. Closed January-mid-March. Restaurant, bar. Business center. Fitness center. Pool. Spa. Pets accepted. Golf. Tennis. $151-250

NEWPORT NEWS

★★★OMNI NEWPORT NEWS HOTEL

1000 Omni Blvd., Newport News, 757-873-6664, 800-843-6664; www.omnihotels.com

Located minutes from historic Williamsburg, this suburban hotel is located in

HIGHLIGHT

COLONIAL WILLIAMSBURG

Visitor Center, 102 Information Center Drive, Williamsburg, 757-229-1000, 800-441-8679; www.colonialwilliamsburg.com

There is so much to see and do in Colonial Williamsburg, so your best bet is to go to the visitor center, where you can get information, make your selections and purchase tickets. An admission ticket is necessary to enjoy the full scope of Colonial Williamsburg, and there are different types to choose from, depending upon what you want to see and how long you want to spend here. Sights not to miss while you're visiting include the Courthouse, where county and city business was conducted from 1770 to 1932. The Magazine was an arsenal and military storehouse of the Virginia Colony. Stop by to see the authentic arms. The Capitol was the scene of Patrick Henry's speech against the stamp act. Swing by Raleigh Tavern, which was frequented by Jefferson, Henry and other Revolutionary patriots, then make time to see some of the historic buildings. The Wren Building is the oldest academic building in America. Historic homes include the Wythe House, home of George Wythe, America's first law professor, and the Peyton Randolph House, where the president of the First Continental Congress lived. The Public Gaol was where debtors, criminals and pirates (including Blackbeard's crew) were imprisoned, while the Public Hospital was the first public institution in the English colonies devoted exclusively to treatment of mental illness.

Visitor center: Daily 8:45 a.m.-5 p.m.

the Newport News central business district. Relax in comfortable guest rooms, which feature comfortable bedding and complimentary Internet. There are numerous dining options including Mitty's Ristorante, which serves seafood and Italian fare.

182 rooms. Restaurant, bar. Business center. Fitness center. Pool. $61-150

NORFOLK

★★★NORFOLK WATERSIDE MARRIOTT

235 E. Main St., Norfolk, 757-627-4200, 888-236-2427; www.marriott.com

In Norfolk's historic district, the Marriott Norfolk Waterside offers well-appointed guest rooms with Marriott's signature Revive beds. Upgrade to the Concierge Level to get more than just the standard amenities. The hotel is conveniently connected to the Waterside Convention Center. Shula's 347 is located in the hotel lobby and is a good option for a good steak dinner. For a great view, request a room overlooking the Elizabeth River.

405 rooms. Restaurant, bar. Fitness center. Pool. $151-250

★★★SHERATON NORFOLK WATERSIDE HOTEL

777 Waterside Drive, Norfolk, 757-622-6664, 800-325-3535; www.sheratonnorfolkwaterside.com

Adjacent to Waterside Marketplace on the Elizabeth River, this landmark hotel affords great views of the harbor and downtown skyline. The guest rooms are decorated with a comfortable, colonial palette. Each room is outfitted with Sheraton Sweet Sleeper beds and flat-screen TVs, and amenities include Shine by Bliss bath products.

468 rooms. Restaurant, bar. Fitness center. Pool. $61-150

PORTSMOUTH

★★★RENAISSANCE PORTSMOUTH HOTEL & WATERFRONT CONFERENCE CENTER

425 Water St., Portsmouth, 757-673-3000, 888-839-1775; www.marriott.com

Overlooking the water, this Portsmouth hotel has plenty of perks. Just steps from the historic Olde Towne Portsmouth district, you can relax in one of the inviting rooms adorned with rich linens and views of the shipyard or skyline. Outfitted in blues and yellows, the guest rooms boast a comfortable atmosphere with all the necessary amenities. Catch a meal at Foggy Point Bar & Grill, located in the lobby.

249 rooms. Restaurant, bar. Business center. Fitness center. Pool. $61-150

VIRGINIA BEACH

★★★CROWNE PLAZA HOTEL VIRGINIA BEACH-NORFOLK

4453 Bonney Road, Virginia Beach, 757-473-1700, 877-834-3613; www.cpvabeach.com

Just off Interstate 264, this traditional hotel is conveniently located in the Town Center Business District with easy access to downtown Virginia Beach, Norfolk, Chesapeake and many corporate offices. Guests are treated to comfortable rooms, a 24-hour fitness center, indoor pool and whirlpool and sauna. Golf courses and tennis courts are nearby.

149 rooms. Restaurant, bar. Business center. Fitness center. Pool. $151-250

★★★FOUNDERS INN

5641 Indian River Road, Virginia Beach, 757-424-5511, 800-926-4466; www.foundersinn.com

Sitting on 26 beautifully manicured acres, this Georgian-style inn has a southern-colonial décor and a unique combination of intimate charm and extensive meeting space. Unwind by the pool while kids enjoy the waterslide. Or head to the hot tub, which overlooks the lake. Pamper yourself at the Flowering Almond Spa with a hot stone massage or caviar facial. Then head to the Swan Terrace Restaurant for fresh seafood, or choose The Hunt Room, a more casual spot where you can also catch up on sports or shoot some pool.

240 rooms. Restaurant, bar. Business center. Fitness center. Pool. Spa. Pets accepted. Tennis. $61-150

WILLIAMSBURG

★★★KINGSMILL RESORT & SPA

1010 Kingsmill Road, Williamsburg, 757-253-1703, 800-832-2665; www.kingsmill.com

This playground for adults attracts golfers, tennis players and those seeking rest and relaxation to its 2,900 manicured acres along the James River. Three 18-hole golf courses and a nine-hole par-three course challenge players, while the Golf Academy provides clinics and individual instruction. Tennis players take their pick from fast-drying clay, Deco-Turf and hydro courts at the state-of-the-art facility, while other racquet sports and a fitness center are available at the Sports Club. After a day filled with activities, hearty appetites are always satisfied at the resort's six restaurants and lounges.

425 rooms. Restaurant, bar. Complimentary breakfast. Business center. Fitness center. Pool. Spa. Tennis. Golf. Beach. $251-350

★★★MARRIOTT WILLIAMSBURG
50 Kingsmill Road, Williamsburg, 757-220-2500; www.williamsburgmarriott.com

Conveniently located just three miles from Colonial Williamsburg and even closer to Busch Gardens, Marriott Williamsburg offers spacious and well appointed rooms for amusement park-goers. In town for business? Book a "Room That Works", adorned with all the latest amenities for the workaholic. For some extra amenities, opt for a room on the concierge level. After a day of thrill rides, grab a bite at one of the hotel's three restaurants.

295 rooms. Restaurant, bar. Business center. Fitness center. Pool. Tennis. $61-150

★★★★WILLIAMSBURG INN
136 E. Francis St., Williamsburg, 757-253-2277, 800-447-8679; www.colonialwilliamsburg.com

Furnished in English Regency style, the guest rooms have just the right amount of sophistication to appeal to adults while keeping children comfortable and satisfied. Blessed with a central location in the heart of this re-created 18th-century village, the inn is within a leisurely stroll of the blacksmith's shop, candle-maker and cobbler. After reliving history, guests reap the rewards of the inn's plentiful activities: play a round of golf, dive into the spring-fed pool, rally on the clay tennis courts or head to the gourmet restaurant.

62 rooms. Restaurant, bar. Business center. Fitness center. Pool. Golf. Tennis. $351 and up.

WHERE TO EAT

WILLIAMSBURG
★★★THE DINING ROOM AT FORD'S COLONY
240 Ford's Colony Drive, Williamsburg, 757-258-4107; www.fordscolony.com

Savor rich, imaginative American cuisine in this Georgian-style dining room. The dishes are made up of local farm products as often as possible. Located in the Ford's Colony Country Club, The Dining Room boasts a relaxing atmosphere. Surrounded by trees, lakes and a golf course, dining here is pleasurable. Add in fresh homemade bread and pastries and The Dining Room at Ford's Colony is a perfect spot for a quiet, picturesque meal.

American. Tuesday-Saturday, dinner. Reservations recommended. Outdoor seating. Bar. $36-85

★★★REGENCY DINING ROOM
136 E. Francis St., Williamsburg, 757-229-2141, 800-447-8679; www.colonialwilliamsburg.com

Set in the charming Williamsburg Inn, the Regency Dining Room offers diners a graceful setting in which to enjoy a leisurely dinner of contemporary Southern fare. The menu runs the gamut from dishes like citrus-glazed scallops and herbed prawns with butternut squash and Yukon Gold potatoes; salmon filet with crabmeat and corn risotto; and Berkshire pork tenderloin with almond bread pudding and braised cabbage. Live music and dancing are offered on Friday and Saturday night.

American. Breakfast, dinner, Sunday brunch. Bar. $36-85

★★★THE TRELLIS
403 Duke of Gloucester St., Williamsburg, 757-229-8610; www.thetrellis.com

This anchor of Historic Williamsburg's Duke of Gloucester Street opened its doors nearly 30 years ago and has yet to look back. Committed to serving local, healthy alternatives, The Trellis is what modern American dining is all about. Dine on the patio where you'll be surrounded by the namesake trellises. Chef/owner David Everett's dishes, including seared Hudson Valley duck and Idaho rainbow trout, bring nature to the table.

American. Lunch, dinner. Outdoor seating. Bar. $36-85

NORTHERN VIRGINIA

Not all of the tourist attractions are within the borders of D.C. Several key memorials and historic sites are across the Potomac in Northern Virginia. One of the most visited sites is the Arlington National Cemetery, where you'll see famous gravesites including that of President John F. Kennedy. Another tourist stop is in Alexandria at Mount Vernon, the home of President George Washington. Fredericksburg is often called a "middleman city" for its location between Richmond and Washington, D.C. Many buildings built before 1775 still stand in the historic part of the city. Leesburg is located in a scenic area of rolling hills and thoroughbred horse farms. Just fifteen miles from Washington D.C., Vienna has a small town feel to it with a historic district. The oldest of more than 25 American towns to be named after the first president, Washington was surveyed in 1749 by none other than George Washington himself. The streets remain laid out exactly as surveyed and still bear the names of families who owned the land on which the town was founded.

WHAT TO SEE

ALEXANDRIA
CARLYLE HOUSE
121 N. Fairfax St., Alexandria, 703-549-2997; www.nvrpa.org

This 1753 stately stone mansion built in the Palladian style was the site of a 1755 meeting between General Edward Braddock and five British colonial governors who planned the early campaigns of the French and Indian War.

Admission: adults $4, children 11-17 $2, children 10 and under free. Tuesday-Saturday 10 a.m.-4 p.m., Sunday noon-4 p.m.

FORT WARD MUSEUM AND HISTORIC SITE
4301 W. Braddock Road, Alexandria, 703-838-4848; oha.alexandriava.gov

One of the best-preserved Union forts in the nation, Fort Ward exhibits its importance in the Civil War. Visit the restored Northwest Bastion, a major defensive element of the fort. This oddly shaped fort provided major defense mechanisms in the fight to protect Washington. A museum, built in the 1960s, showcases various Civil War objects, such as weapons and uniforms. Tours of both the fort and the museum are available.

Museum: April-October, Tuesday-Saturday 9 a.m.-5 p.m., Sunday noon-5 p.m.; November-March, Tuesday-Saturday 10 a.m.-5 p.m., Sunday noon-5 p.m. Park: Daily 9 a.m.-dusk.

HIGHLIGHT

WHAT ARE THE TOP THINGS TO DO IN NORTHERN VIRGINIA?

VISIT WASHINGTON'S OTHER MEMORIAL
In addition to the Washington Monument, this area also boasts the George Washington Masonic National Memorial. The building is filled with relics from Washington's past.

CROSS THE RIVER TO HONOR OUR VETERANS
Arlington Cemetery strategically lies across from our nation's capital. The property is the resting place of men and women who served in the armed forces.

CHECK OUT WASHINGTON'S ESTATE
Head to Mount Vernon to see the estate designed by our first president himself. Now a museum, Mount Vernon is filled with Washington's history.

HEAD TO THE FIRST MAJOR CIVIL WAR BATTLEFIELD
Manassas is home to Bull Run Battlefield, where two major Civil War battles were fought. It was here that Andrew "Stonewall" Jackson won his infamous nickname.

FRANK LLOYD WRIGHT'S POPE-LEIGHEY HOUSE
9000 Richmond Highway, Alexandria, 703-780-4000; www.nationaltrust.org
Erected in Falls Church in 1940, the house was disassembled due to the construction of a new highway and rebuilt at the present site in 1964. Built of cypress, brick and glass, the house is an example of Wright's "Usonian" structures, which he proposed as a prototype of affordable housing for Depression-era middle-income families.
Admission: adults $8.50, children $4. April-December, Thursday-Monday 10 a.m.-5 p.m. Combination ticket for both houses available.

GADSBY'S TAVERN MUSEUM
134 N. Royal St., Alexandria, 703-838-4242; oha.alexandriava.gov
Gadsby's Tavern was frequented by Washington and other patriots. It combines two 18th-century buildings, the tavern and an old city hotel. Operated by Englishman John Gadsby between 1796 and 1808, this establishment was the center of social, political and business life in Alexandria. Now a museum, you can discover how to eat, drink and be merry as they did in those days.
Admission: adults $4, children 11-17 $2, children 10 and under free. November-March,

Wednesday-Saturday 11 a.m.-4 p.m., Sunday 1-4 p.m.; April-October, Tuesday-Saturday 10 a.m.-5 p.m., Sunday-Monday 1-5 p.m.

GEORGE WASHINGTON MASONIC NATIONAL MEMORIAL

101 Callahan Drive, Alexandria, 703-683-2007; www.gwmemorial.org

This 333-foot-tall structure houses a large collection of objects that belonged to George Washington, which were collected by his family or the Masonic lodge where he served as the first Master. Guided tours explore a replica of the lodge's first hall.

Admission: Free. April-September, daily 9 a.m.-4 p.m.; October-March, daily 10 a.m.-4 p.m.

KING STREET

Located within historic Old Town, Alexandria's main street is lined with trendy restaurants, shops, cafés, galleries and fine antique stores. The free King Street trolley operates up and down a one-and-a-half-mile route and will take you to the metro station if you're heading to D.C. Check out An American in Paris (*1225 King St.*) for European and American clothes and accessories for women, and pick up some books at Book Bank (*151 King St.*). After shopping, head to Vermilion (*1120 King St.*) restaurant for a delicious bite to eat.

Hours vary.

LEE-FENDALL HOUSE

614 Oronoco St., Alexandria, 703-548-1789; www.leefendallhouse.org

This house was built by Phillip Richard Fendall in 1785 and occupied by the Lee family for 118 years. Both George Washington and Revolutionary War hero "Light Horse Harry" Lee were frequent visitors to the house. The house is furnished with Lee family belongings.

Admission: adults $5, children 11-17 $3, children 10 and under free. Wednesday-Saturday 10 a.m.-4 p.m., Sunday 1-4 p.m.

MOUNT VERNON ESTATE & GARDENS

3200 Mount Vernon Memorial Highway, Alexandria, 703-780-0011; www.mountvernon.org

The home of America's first president, George Washington, is just a short drive from the eponymous city. Sitting high above the Potomac River, Mount Vernon is surrounded by a landscape designed by Washington himself. On the grounds of the 500-acre property, and former plantation, you can tour the historic mansion, visit the tomb of George and Martha and stroll through gardens. You can also witness 18th-century farming and cooking techniques at the four-acre Pioneer Farm, visit the blacksmith shop, and learn about Washington's life and his presidency at the Donald W. Reynolds Museum and Education Center. The new museum and education center has numerous interactive displays. Afterward, you can dine at the Mount Vernon Inn Restaurant and peruse the shops before heading back to the city. The estate sponsors a wine and jazz festival and sunset tour over one weekend in May. To learn more about what an innovative farmer and businessman Washington was, stop in at the George Washington Gristmill and Distillery, just three miles from Mount Vernon.

Admission: adults $15, seniors $14, children 6-11 $7, children under 6 free. (There is a separate charge for visiting the Gristmill). April-August, daily 8 a.m.-5 p.m.; March, September-October, daily 9 a.m.-5 p.m.; November-February, daily 9 a.m.-4 p.m.

SIGHTSEEING BOAT TOURS

Potomac Riverboat Company, 205 the Strand, Alexandria, 703-684-0580;
www.potomacriverboatco.com

Take a sightseeing boat tour of the Alexandria waterfront. Cruise down the Potomac River upon the *Admiral Tilp*. This 40-minute narrated tour livens the colorful history of Alexandria. Historic sights such as Admiral's Row, Founders Park and Old Town Yacht Basin charm you while on board. Tickets must be purchased 24-hours in advance.

Office: Monday-Friday 9 a.m.-5 p.m. See website for schedules and ticket information.

WALKING TOUR OF HISTORIC SITES

Ramsay House, 221 King St., Alexandria, 703-838-4200;
www.visitalexandriava.com

Start at the visitor center in Ramsay House, which is the oldest house in Alexandria and has been used as a tavern, grocery store and cigar factory. Here, you can obtain special events information and a free visitors' guide and purchase block tickets good for reduced admission to three of the city's historic properties. Guided walking tours depart from here. The bureau also issues free parking permits and maps.

Daily 9 a.m.-8 p.m.

WOODLAWN PLANTATION

9000 Richmond Highway, Alexandria, 703-780-4000; www.woodlawn1805.org

In 1799, George Washington gave 2,000 acres of land as a wedding present to Eleanor Parke Custis, his foster daughter, who married his nephew, Major Lawrence Lewis. Dr. William Thornton, first architect of the U.S. Capitol, then designed this mansion. The Lewises entertained such notables as Andrew Jackson, Henry Clay and the Marquis de Lafayette here. The house was restored in the early 1900s and later became the residence of a U.S. senator. The home has 19th-century period rooms with many original furnishings. The exterior houses formal gardens.

Admission: adults $8.50, children $4. April-December, Thursday-Monday 10 a.m.-5 p.m. Combination ticket for both houses available.

ARLINGTON

ARLINGTON FARMERS MARKET

N. Courthouse Road and N. 14th St., Arlington, 703-228-6423;
www.arlingtonfarmersmarket.com

Fresh berries, peaches and heirloom tomatoes are just some of the pleasures available at this lively market, which has been featuring the produce of farmers within 125 miles of Arlington since 1979. Don't miss the grass-fed meats, specialty goat cheeses and unusual varieties of familiar fruits and vegetables (one longtime vendor grows 35 different types of apples).

Mid-April-December, Saturday 8 a.m.-noon; January-mid-April, Saturday 9 a.m.-noon.

ARLINGTON NATIONAL CEMETERY/ARLINGTON HOUSE (CUSTIS-LEE MANSION)

214 McNair Road, Arlington, VA, 703-607-8000; www.arlingtoncemetery.org

The home and grounds of noted Confederate Robert E. Lee were essentially confiscated by the U.S. during the Civil War for failure to pay property taxes.

HIGHLIGHT

WHAT ELSE IS THERE TO SEE AND DO IN ALEXANDRIA, VIRGINIA?

Known as one of America's most historic destinations, Alexandria offers visitors a unique mix of colonial attractions, quaint neighborhoods with cobblestone streets and beautiful 18th- and 19th-century architecture.

Start your day by visiting a couple of historic buildings. The Old Dominion Bank Building (*201 Prince St.*) is an example of Classic Revival architecture. Also known as The Athenaeum, it was built for the Bank of the Old Dominion in 1852 and is where Robert E. Lee did his banking. To see where General Lee attended church services, visit Christ Church (*118 N. Washington St., 703-549-1450; www.historicchristchurch.org*), which has been in continuous use since it was built in 1773. George Washington was also a member and the family's bible was donated to the church after Martha Washington passed away.

Next, head to the waterfront of the Potomac River, which is filled with numerous shops, public parks and restaurants. Visit the Torpedo Factory Art Center (*105 N. Union St., Alexandria, 703-838-4565; www.torpedofactory.org*). This World War I munitions factory is now the largest visual arts center in the nation. The building boasts three floors with 82 working studios, six galleries and two workshops.

You'll find the ideal pit stop at Grape + Bean (*118 S. Royal St., Alexandria, 703-664-0214; www.grapeandbean.com*). This locally-owned business wears many hats. It's a retail wine shop, coffee spot and wine bar with a seasonal menu. Order some handmade cheese, fresh bread and organic chocolate as you sip wine from great independent wineries. Or try the shop's wide variety of fair trade and eco-friendly coffee.

After lunch, take some time to explore the Boutique District of Old Town Alexandria. This area offers a unique shopping experience with 19 shops featuring home décor, fashion, jewelry, beauty, children's apparel and gifts.

Before leaving Alexandria, enjoy an unforgettable meal at Restaurant Eve (*110 S. Pitt St., Alexandria, 703-706-0450; www.restauranteve.com*). This historic warehouse building was converted into a quaint, 100-seat restaurant.

They were later returned to the family in 1877 after a Supreme Court ruling, and then resold to the U.S. for $150,000 by heir Custis Lee. Lee's house is decorated and furnished with period pieces and is open for self-guided tours. The more than 600-acre property includes gravesites for approximately 300,000 veterans and members of their families. The most famous gravesites are those of President John F. Kennedy (highlighted by an eternal flame) and Jacqueline Kennedy Onassis. There are also memorials to both Space Shuttle tragedies (Challenger and Columbia), a cairn for the victims of the Lockerbie Pan-Am Flight 103 terrorist bombing, a memorial to the victims of the 9/11 attack on the Pentagon, the mast of the *USS Maine* and the Tomb of the Unknown, which contains the remains of unidentified soldiers from both World Wars and the Korean War. The Tomb of the Unknown for the Vietnam War remains empty as the remains originally interred were later identified and re-interred at a different location.

Admission: free. April-September, daily 8 a.m.-7 p.m.; October-March, daily 8 a.m.-5 p.m.

THE PENTAGON

Arlington, 703-697-1776; pentagon.afis.osd.mil

The massive five-sided headquarters for the U.S. Department of Defense includes over 17 miles of corridors. One-hour tours of one of the world's largest office buildings are available for free by contacting a member of congress or by booking on the Pentagon website. There are two memorials relating to 9/11—the American Heroes Memorial is within the building at the site where American Airlines Flight 77 crashed into the Pentagon. Outside, in a patio shaded by maple trees, a series of 184 lighted benches honors the 184 victims of the plane crash.

Admission: free. Monday-Friday 9 a.m.-3 p.m.

UNITED STATES AIR FORCE MEMORIAL

1 Air Force Memorial Drive, Arlington, 703-979-0674; www.airforcememorial.org

This sweeping tribute honoring Air Force servicemen and women features three stainless steel arcs stretching more than 200 feet into the sky. Built on top of a hill, the design reflects the pattern of the contrails of the Thunderbird Demonstration Team forming a "bomb burst" maneuver. At the base of the spires is the Air Force "star" insignia engraved in granite. Four bronze statues at one side of the structure represent the Memorial's Honor Guard.

April-September, daily 8 a.m-11 p.m.; October-March, daily 8 a.m.-9 p.m.

THE U.S.M.C. WAR MEMORIAL

George Washington Memorial Parkway, 1 N. Marshall Drive, Arlington; www.virginia.org

The Iwo Jima Memorial depicts one of the most captivating images in history—the Pulitzer Prize-winning photograph from Joe Rosenthal of the raising of the flag by Marines in Iwo Jima during World War II. The 60-foot bronze sculpture is located near Arlington National Cemetery in Rosslyn, Virginia and next to the Netherlands Carillon, a bell tower with 50 bells that was a gift from the Netherlands to thank the U.S. for support during the war.

DULLES INTERNATIONAL AIRPORT AREA

SMITHSONIAN NATIONAL AIR & SPACE MUSEUM ANNEX (STEVEN F. UDVAR-HAZY CENTER)

14390 Air and Space Museum Parkway, Chantilly, VA, 703-572-4118; www.nasm.si.edu

There wasn't enough room at the Air and Space Museum on the National Mall for the collection of cool planes, rockets and spacecraft. So the Smithsonian built this enormous annex in Virginia. The complex includes the Space Shuttle Enterprise, the SR-71A Blackbird (the world's fastest jet-propelled aircraft) and the Enola Gay, which dropped the A-bomb on Hiroshima. The Donald D. Engen Observation Tower allows visitors to watch flights take off and land from nearby Dulles International Airport. There are also flight simulators and an IMAX Theater. Don't miss the collection of antique hang gliders.

Admission: free. September-May, daily 10 a.m.-5:30 p.m.; June-August, daily 10 a.m.-6:30 p.m.

FAIRFAX

ALGONKIAN REGIONAL PARK

47001 Fairway Drive, Sterling, 703-450-4655; www.nvrpa.org/park/algonkian

This 800-acre park on the Potomac River features a par-72 golf course, miniature golf, a water park, picnic areas and vacation cottages.

The hours for the pool and golf courses vary; see website for information. Daily.

FREDERICKSBURG

CONFEDERATE CEMETERY

Willliam St. and Washington Ave., Fredericksburg; 540-373-6122; www.nps.gov

The Ladies Memorial Association purchased this land in 1867 to create the Confederate Cemetery. Soldiers buried elsewhere were reinterred in the new location. Of the 3,300 Confederate soldiers who were laid to rest here, six were generals and 2,184 are unknown. The association still cares for the cemetery. An observance is held each Memorial Day in remembrance of those buried here.

THE GARI MELCHERS HOME AND STUDIO AT BELMONT

224 Washington St., Fredericksburg, 540-654-1015; www.umw.edu

The Belmont Estate was the residence from 1916 to 1932 of American-born artist Gari Melchers (1860-1932), best known for his portraits of the famous and wealthy, including Theodore Roosevelt, William Vanderbilt and Andrew Mellon, and as an important impressionist artist of the period. The artist's studio comprises the nation's largest collection of his works, housing more than 1,800 paintings and drawings. The site is a registered National and State Historic Landmark and includes a 27-acre estate, frame house built in the late 18th century and enlarged over the years, and a stone studio built by Melchers. Owned by the state of Virginia, Belmont is administered by Mary Washington College.

Admission: adults $10, seniors $9, children 6-18 $5. Monday-Saturday 10 a.m.-5 p.m.

FREDERICKSBURG AND SPOTSYLVANIA NATIONAL MILITARY PARK

1013 Lafayette Blvd., Fredericksburg, 540-373-6122; www.nps.gov

See the battlefield where the Battle of Fredericksburg was fought in 1862. Visit Chatham Manor (*120 Chatham Lane*), a Georgian brick manor house, which was converted to Union headquarters during two of the battles of Fredericksburg. The house was eventually used as a hospital where Clara Barton and Walt Whitman nursed the wounded. Near Chatham Manor, there's the Stonewall Jackson Shrine in front of the plantation office where Confederate General Jackson, ill with pneumonia and with his shattered left arm amputated, murmured, "Let us cross over the river, and rest under the shade of the trees", and died on May 10, 1863. Visit the Fredericksburg National Cemetery where more than 15,000 are buried and almost 13,000 are unknown.

Admission (to park): Free. Visitor center: September-October, Monday-Friday 9 a.m.-5 p.m., Saturday-Sunday 9 a.m.-6 p.m.; November-mid-April, daily 9 a.m.-5 p.m.

GEORGE WASHINGTON'S HOME AT FERRY FARM

268 Kings Highway, Fredericksburg, 540-370-0732; www.kenmore.org

It was on this 80-acre plantation that George Washington received his formal schooling. Deriving its name from the ferry that ran from the farm across the Rappahannock River, the plantation was known for fishing and farming. The farm has gone through its fair share of occupants, including Native Americans, English settlers, the Washingtons, brigadier general Dr. Hugh Mercer and Winter Bray. In the mid-twentieth-century, the George Washington Boyhood Home Foundation was formed to preserve the childhood of the father of this nation. Archeologists continue to work on the plantation in hopes of uncovering more details about Washington's life.

Admission: adults $5, students $3, children 5 and under free. March-October, daily 10 a.m-5 p.m.; November-December, daily 10 a.m.-4 p.m.

JAMES MONROE MUSEUM AND MEMORIAL LIBRARY

908 Charles St., Fredericksburg, 540-654-1043; www.umw.edu

As a young lawyer, James Monroe lived and worked in Fredericksburg from 1786 to 1789 and even served on Fredericksburg's City Council. This museum houses one of the nation's largest collections of Monroe memorabilia, articles and original documents. Included are the desk bought in France in 1794 during his years as ambassador and used in the White House for signing the Monroe Doctrine, formal attire worn at the Court of Napoleon, and more than 40 books from Monroe's library. There is also a garden. The site is a national historic landmark owned by the Commonwealth of Virginia and administered by Mary Washington College.

Admission: adults $5, children $1. Monday-Saturday 10 a.m.-5 p.m., Sunday 1-5 p.m.

KENMORE PLANTATION

1201 Washington Ave., Fredericksburg, 540-373-3381; www.kenmore.org

Considered one of the finest restorations in Virginia, Kenmore is the former home of Colonel Fielding Lewis, commissioner of Fredericksburg gunnery, who married George Washington's only sister, Betty. On an original grant of 863 acres, Lewis built a magnificent home in 1752; three rooms have full decorative molded plaster ceilings.

Admission: adults $8, students $4, children 5 and under free. March-October, daily 10 a.m.-5 p.m.; November-December, daily 10 a.m.-4 p.m.

MARY WASHINGTON HOUSE

1200 Charles St., Fredericksburg, 540-373-1569; www.apva.org

George Washington bought this house for his mother in 1772; she lived here until her death in 1789. Here, General Lafayette visited her. Some original furnishings are still here as well as the boxwood garden she loved.

Admission: adults $5, children 6-18 $2, children 5 and under free. March-October, Monday-Saturday 11 a.m.-5 p.m., Sunday noon-4 p.m.; November-December, Monday-Sunday noon-4 p.m.

STRATFORD HALL PLANTATION

Highway 3 E. and Highway 214, Montross, 804-493-8038;
www.stratfordhall.org

The birthplace of General Robert E. Lee features a monumental Georgian house built circa 1735, and famous for its uniquely grouped chimneystacks. Interiors span approximately a 100-year period and feature a Federal-era parlor and neoclassical paneling in the Great Hall. The grounds include a boxwood garden, 18th- and 19th-century carriages, a working mill, and a visitor center with a museum.

Admission: adults $10, seniors and military personnel $9, children 6-11 $5, children 5 and under free. Visitor center: Daily 9:30 a.m.-4 p.m.

LEESBURG

BALL'S BLUFF BATTLEFIELD

Ball Bluff Road, Leesburg, 703-737-7800; www.nvrpa.org

One of the smallest national cemeteries in the U.S. marks the site of the third armed engagement of the Civil War. On October 21, 1861, four Union regiments suffered catastrophic losses while surrounded by Confederate forces; the Union commander, a U.S. senator and presidential confidant, was killed here along with half his troops, while attempting to cross back over the Potomac River. Oliver Wendell Holmes, Jr., later to become a U.S. Supreme Court justice, was wounded here.

Daily dawn-dusk. Tours: April-October, Saturday-Sunday 11 a.m.-1 p.m.

OATLANDS

20850 Oatlands Plantation Lane, Leesburg, 703-777-3174;
www.oatlands.org

The 261-acre estate includes a Classical Revival mansion built by George Carter. The house was partially remodeled in 1827, which was when the front portico was added. Most of the building materials, including bricks and wood, came from or were made on the estate. The interior is furnished with American, English and French antiques reflecting the period between 1897 and 1965 when the house was owned by Mr. and Mrs. William Corcoran Eustis, prominent Washingtonians. The formal garden has some of the finest boxwoods in the U.S. There are equestrian areas for races and horse shows.

Admission: adults $10, seniors and children 6-16 $9, children 5 and under free. Admission (to garden and grounds only): $7. April-December, Monday-Saturday 10 a.m.-5 p.m., Sunday 1-5 p.m. Tours: on the hour.

VINEYARD AND WINERY TOURS

Loudon County Visitor Center, 112-G South St. S.E., Leesburg, 703-771-2617, 800-752-6118;
www.visitloudoun.org

Stop into the Loudon County Visitor Center to get information on the surrounding wineries to plan a tour of your own. You can take part in a winery and vineyard tour chauffeured by a limousine. In Leesburg alone, there are numerous wineries to visit including Casanel Vineyards, Dry Mill Vineyard and Winery, Fabbioli Cellars and more.

Visitor center: Daily 9 a.m.-5 p.m.

WATERFORD

15609 High St., Waterford, 504-882-3018; www.waterfordva.org

This eighteenth-century Quaker village, designated a National Historic Landmark, has been restored as a residential community. An annual homes tour (first full weekend in October) has craft demonstrations, exhibits and traditional music. The Waterford Foundation has brochures outlining self-guided walking tours. If the Waterford Foundation is closed, visit the Waterford Market (*15487 Second St.*) where you can also grab a bite to eat, as there are no restaurants in Waterford.

Waterford Foundation: Monday-Friday 10 a.m.-3 p.m. Waterford Market: Monday-Friday 10 a.m.-7 p.m., Saturday 10 a.m.-5 p.m.

MANASSAS
THE MANASSAS MUSEUM

9101 Prince William St., Manassas, 703-368-1873; www.manassascity.org

This museum features collections dealing with Northern Virginia Piedmont history up to modern times, with an emphasis on the Civil War. The museum's permanent collection is very large, allowing a rotation of objects through-out the year. Discover documents, exhibitions, publications and programs depicting the history of the area. The collection includes a flax wheel dating back to 1830 and a Saltillo Sarape from between 1800 and 1825. Past exhibits include the Civil War Espionage Exhibit, focusing on the spies of the Civil War, and range from civilian life to spies.

Admission: adults $5, seniors and children $4, children 5 and under free. Tuesday-Sunday 10 a.m.-5 p.m.

MANASSAS (BULL RUN) NATIONAL BATTLEFIELD PARK

6511 Sudley Road, Manassas, 703-361-1339; www.nps.gov

This 5,000-acre park was the scene of two major Civil War battles. More than 26,000 men were killed or wounded here in struggles for control of a strategi-cally important railroad junction. The war's first major land battle was fought here on July 21, 1861, between poorly trained volunteer troops from both the North and South. The battle finally evolved into a struggle for Henry Hill, where "Stonewall" Jackson earned his nickname. Thirteen months later in the second battle of Manassas, General Robert E. Lee outmaneuvered and defeated Union General John Pope and cleared the way for a Confederate invasion of Maryland. While here, be sure to check out the Battlefield Museum, which has exhibits that reflect incidents of battles. The Chin House Ruins served as a field hospital in both engagements and marked the left of the Confederate line at First Manassas; it was also the scene of Longstreet's counterattack at Second Manassas. The Stone Bridge is where Union artillery opened the Battle of First Manassas; it afforded an avenue of escape for the Union troops after both First and Second Manassas.

Park: Daily dawn-dusk. Visitor center: Daily 8:30 a.m.-5 p.m.

MCLEAN

COLVIN RUN MILL HISTORIC SITE

10017 Colvin Run Road, Great Falls, 703-759-2771; www.fairfaxcounty.gov

Take a tour of this historical gristmill as it operated in the 19th century. The Colvin Run Mill General Store, which still operates today, sells old-fashioned items including penny candy. Miller's House also displays an exhibit about milling, and there's a barn and grounds to explore.

Admission (to park): free. March-December, Wednesday-Monday 11 a.m.-5 p.m.; January-February, Wednesday-Monday 11 a.m.-4 p.m. Tours: adults $6, students $5, seniors and children 15 and under $4

GREAT FALLS PARK

George Washington Memorial Parkway, McLean, 703-285-2965, 703-285-2513; www.nps.gov

Spectacular natural beauty can be found only 15 miles from the nation's capital at this park, where the usually peaceful Potomac River narrows into a series of dramatically cascading rapids and 20-foot waterfalls before heading through Mather Gorge. Enjoy the view from a scenic overlook and then explore some of the park's 15 miles of trails, which take you past the remains of the Patowmack Canal, part of an 18th-century engineering project backed by George Washington, among others.

Park: Daily 7 a.m.-dusk. Visitor center: Daily 10 a.m.-4 p.m.

THEODORE ROOSEVELT ISLAND

GW Memorial Parkway, Mclean, 703-289-2500; www.nps.gov

On an island in the Potomac, a towering 17-foot high statue of Teddy Roosevelt resembles a Macy's Thanksgiving Parade Balloon. Upon appropriately named Theodore Roosevelt Island, he stands bulbous on a pedestal with one arm outstretched over his head in a grand gesture. The 88-acre island includes numerous trails through the woods, two fountains and four stone monoliths featuring quotes by Teddy. The island is accessed by a footbridge from George Washington Memorial Parkway in Virginia.

Admission: free. Daily 6 a.m.-10 p.m.

VIENNA

BARNS OF WOLF TRAP

1645 Trap Road, Vienna, 703-938-8463; www.wolf-trap.org

A gift from Wolf Trap's founder, Catherine Filene Shouse, the site includes two eighteenth century barns. The larger of the two, the German Barn, was built in 1730 and seats 284 on the threshing floor with another 98 in the hayloft. This is where the performances take place. The other, smaller barn, the English Barn, built in 1791, serves as the reception area, keeping the tradition of the barn as the gathering place. The intimate performances range from operas, including Mozart's *Zaide*, to classic plays, such as Shakespeare's *A Midsummer Night's Dream*.

See website for schedules and ticket information.

FILENE CENTER AT WOLF TRAP PARK FOR THE PERFORMING ARTS

1624 Trap Road, Vienna, 703-255-1900; www.wolf-trap.org

This performance venue was built for Catherine Filene Shouse, who donated

100 acres of farmland to the U.S. Government. In warmer weather, varied concerts and programs include ballet, musicals, opera, classical, jazz and folk music among others. Filene Center has an open theater seats, 3,800 under cover and 3,000 on the lawn. For those with lawn seats, you can picnic on the grounds. Past performers include Diana Krall, Huey Lewis & the News, Buddy Guy, Michael McDonald and more.

Late May-September.

MEADOWLARK BOTANICAL GARDENS
9750 Meadowlark Gardens Court, Vienna, 703-255-3631; www.nvrpa.org

This 95-acre park is a nice escape. Filled with lilac, wildflower, native plants and landscaped gardens, the botanical perfume is enough to make your day. There are more than twenty varieties of cherry trees, a fantastic sight on its own come springtime. The foliage is gorgeous in the fall, covering the ground with leaves of various reds, oranges and yellows.

Admission: adults $5, seniors and children 7-17 $2.50, children 6 and under free. May, daily 10 a.m.-7:30 p.m.; June-August, daily 10 a.m.-8 p.m.; September, April, daily 10 a.m-7 p.m.; October, March, daily 10 a.m.-6 p.m.; November-February, daily 10 a.m.-5 p.m.

WHERE TO STAY

ALEXANDRIA
★★★HILTON ALEXANDRIA MARK CENTER
5000 Seminary Road, Alexandria, 703-845-1010; www.hilton.com

The lakeside Hilton Alexandria Mark Center is situated near the central business district of Washington, D.C., and the shops and galleries of Old Town. This elegant atrium hotel sits adjacent to a 43-acre botanical preserve and offers views of the Capitol. Guests looking for onsite activities can work out in the 24-hour fitness center or take a swim in the heated indoor/outdoor pool.

496 rooms. Restaurant, bar. Complimentary breakfast. Business center. Fitness center. Pool. Pets accepted. $61-150

★★★HILTON SPRINGFIELD
6550 Loisdale Road, Springfield, 703-971-8900, 800-445-8667; www.hilton.com

The Hilton Springfield is located just 15 minutes from Washington, D.C. and offers complimentary shuttle service to the Springfield/Franconia Metro station. This modern, welcoming hotel puts every comfort at your fingertips. Accommodations are streamlined and stylish. Guest rooms feature complimentary wireless Internet access. Unwind and grab a drink and a bite at the hotel's restaurant, Houlihan's.

244 rooms. Restaurant, bar. Business center. Fitness center. Pool. Pets accepted. $61-150

★★★MORRISON HOUSE BOUTIQUE HOTEL
116 S. Alfred St., Alexandria, 703-838-8000, 866-324-6628; www.morrisonhouse.com

Just down the river from the Capitol, this Federal-style mansion presents visitors with a peaceful alternative to the bustling city. Decorative fireplaces, four-poster mahogany beds and silk sofas fill the guest rooms, all furnished in early American décor. But the amenities are all 21st century, with oversized marble bathrooms and luxurious Frette linens. The Grille attracts a smart,

HIGHLIGHT

ARLINGTON HOUSE, THE ROBERT E. LEE MEMORIAL

Arlington National Cemetery, Arlington, 703-235-1530; www.nps.gov

This national memorial to Robert E. Lee was built between 1802 and 1818 by George Washington Parke Custis, Martha Washington's grandson and the step-grandson/foster son of George Washington. In 1831 his daughter, Mary Anna Randolph Custis, married Lieutenant Robert E. Lee; six of the seven Lee children were born here. As executor of the Custis estate, Lee took extended leave from the U.S. Army and devoted his time to managing and improving the estate. It was the Lee homestead for 30 years before the Civil War. On April 20, 1861, following the secession of Virginia, Lee made his decision to stay with Virginia. Within a month, the house was vacated. Some of the family possessions were moved for safekeeping, but most were stolen or destroyed when Union troops occupied the house during the Civil War. In 1864, when Mrs. Lee could not appear personally to pay property tax, the federal government confiscated the estate; a 200-acre section was set aside for a national cemetery. There is some evidence that indicates this was done to ensure the Lee family could never again live on the estate. G. W. Custis Lee, the general's son, later regained title to the property through a Supreme Court decision and sold it to the U.S. government in 1883 for $150,000. Restoration of the house to its 1861 appearance began in 1925. The Classic Revival house is furnished with authentic pieces of the period, including some Lee family originals. From the grand portico with its six massive, faux-marble Doric columns, there is a panoramic view of Washington, D.C.

Admission: Free. Daily 9:30 a.m.-4:30 p.m.

casual set with its clubby ambience and live piano music. Don't miss the exceptional Dining Room, where menus are banished and the dishes are determined by the chef's conversations with each diner.

45 rooms. Restaurant, bar. Pets accepted. $151-250

★★★SHERATON SUITES OLD TOWN ALEXANDRIA

801 N. St. Asaph St., Alexandria, 703-836-4700, 800-325-3535; www.sheratonsuitesalexandria.com

Offering the comfort of home in Old Town Alexandria, this hotel provides all the amenities. Enjoy a good night's rest on the signature Sweet Sleeper Beds. The suites are comfortably decorated with blues and reds and French doors. Views of the Potomac River, Washington and Alexandria add a nice touch. Grab a bite at The Fin and Hoof Bar and Grill, the in-house restaurant.

247 rooms. Restaurant, bar. Business center. Fitness center. Pool. Pets accepted. $151-250

ARLINGTON

★★★CROWNE PLAZA WASHINGTON NATIONAL AIRPORT HOTEL

1480 Crystal Drive, Arlington, 703-416-1600, 800-227-6963; www.cpnationalairport.com

Stay close to Reagan National Airport at this Washington hotel. The guest rooms have flat-screen televisions and wireless Internet. Grab a bite to eat at

Potomac Bar and Grille. Have an early flight? There is a complimentary shuttle to Reagan National.

308 rooms. Restaurant, bar. Business center. Fitness center. Pool. $151-250

★★★HILTON ARLINGTON

950 N. Stafford St., Arlington, 703-528-6000, 800-695-7487; www.hiltonarlington.com

This centrally located hotel is connected by a sky bridge to the Ballston Common Mall and National Science Foundation Office Complex. The contemporary guest rooms feature Hilton's Serenity Bed and amenities such as Crabtree & Evelyn toiletries.

209 rooms. Restaurant, bar. Complimentary breakfast. Business center. Fitness center. Pets accepted. $151-250

★★★HYATT ARLINGTON

1325 Wilson Blvd., Arlington, 703-525-1234, 800-233-1234; www.arlington.hyatt.com

This hotel is located in the Rosslyn neighborhood across the bridge from Washington, D.C. and close to the Arlington National Cemetery. Sitting among businesses, shops and restaurants, the Hyatt Arlington is within walking distance of the Metro and Georgetown.

317 rooms. Business center. Fitness center. $151-250

★★★MARRIOTT CRYSTAL CITY AT REAGAN NATIONAL AIRPORT

1999 Jefferson Davis Highway, Arlington, 703-413-5500; www.crystalcitymarriott.com

This conveniently located, boutique-style hotel has an underground walkway that gives guests access to the Metro system, the Crystal City shopping mall and the surrounding metropolitan area. A curved staircase in the lobby leads you to guest rooms that feature Revive, Marriott's signature bed with 300 thread-count linens, and wireless Internet access.

343 rooms. Restaurant, bar. Fitness center. Pool. $151-250

★★★★THE RITZ-CARLTON, PENTAGON CITY

1250 S. Hayes St., Arlington, 703-415-5000, 800-241-3333; www.ritzcarlton.com

Five minutes from Washington National Airport, the Ritz-Carlton, Pentagon City offers tailored elegance with feather beds, Egyptian cotton linens, updated technology and luxurious club-level accommodations. Service is polished and professional. Massages and personal fitness assessments are available at the fitness center. Enjoy afternoon tea at Fyve Restaurant Lounge or enjoy their American fare for breakfast, lunch or dinner.

366 rooms. Restaurant, bar. Complimentary breakfast. Business center. Fitness center. Pool. Pets accepted. $251-350

★★★SHERATON CRYSTAL CITY HOTEL

1800 Jefferson Davis Highway, Arlington, 703-486-1111, 800-325-3535; www.sheratoncrystalcity.com

Relax in one of the comfortable guest rooms decorated in browns and tans. You don't have to skip out on your workout at this hotel as it is outfitted with a state of the art fitness center. Just across the river from Washington, D.C., the Sheraton Crystal City Hotel offers complimentary shuttle service to and from local businesses and Ronald Reagan Washington National Airport.

217 rooms. Restaurant, bar. Business center. Fitness center. Pets accepted. $151-250

DULLES INTERNATIONAL AIRPORT AREA

★★★HYATT REGENCY RESTON

1800 Presidents St., Reston, 703-709-1234; www.hyatt.com

Located in the heart of Fairfax County's technology hub, this property offers a resort-like ambience in a suburban setting. The oversized guest rooms offer flat screen TVs, ergonomic desk chairs and wireless Internet access.

518 rooms. Restaurant, bar. Business center. Fitness center. Pool. $151-250

★★★SHERATON RESTON HOTEL

11810 Sunrise Valley Drive, Reston, 703-620-9000, 800-325-3535; www.sheratonreston.com

Located just 20 minutes from Washington, D.C., and near shopping, various corporate headquarters and Reston Town Center, this contemporary hotel is a smart choice for both business and leisure travelers. Each spacious guest room features the famous Sheraton Sweet Sleeper Bed with a pillow-top mattress, individual climate control and a large work area. Golf lovers can get a game in at the adjacent Reston National Golf Course.

301 rooms. Restaurant, bar. Business center. Fitness center. Pool. Pets accepted. $151-250

★★★WASHINGTON DULLES MARRIOTT SUITES

13101 Worldgate Drive, Herndon, 703-709-0400, 800-228-9290; www.marriott.com

This all-suite hotel located in the Dulles Technology Corridor is just minutes from the airport and corporate offices. After a long day at the office or at play, guests can relax in their spacious suites with luxury bedding. The hotel and surrounding area offer an indoor/outdoor pool, biking and jogging trails, tennis, squash, bowling and miniature golf.

253 rooms. Restaurant, bar. Fitness center. Pool. $151-250

★★★WESTFIELDS MARRIOTT WASHINGTON DULLES

14750 Conference Center Drive, Chantilly, 703-818-0300; www.marriott.com

This Marriott looks more like a manor than a hotel. With a circular driveway and pillars lining the front entrance, step inside a relaxing setting. Sleep on the signature Marriott Revive bed with soft linens and fluffy pillows for the best night's rest before that big conference in the morning. The hotel is only 10 miles from the National Air and Space Museum.

336 rooms. Restaurant, bar. Fitness center. Pool. $151-250

FAIRFAX

★★★HYATT FAIR LAKES

12777 Fair Lakes Circle, Fairfax, 703-818-1234; www.hyatt.com

Hyatt Fair Lakes provides a comfortable setting with large guest rooms featuring pillow-top mattresses and decorated in hues of blue and brown. Book a suite (there are 22 of these) for panoramic views of the Fair Lakes area. Just a few minutes from Washington Dulles Airport, the property features a column-free ballroom and a towering atrium lobby.

316 rooms. Restaurant, bar. Business center. Fitness center. Pool. $151-250

LEESBURG

★★★LANSDOWNE RESORT

44050 Woodridge Parkway, Leesburg, 703-729-8400, 877-509-8400; www.lansdowneresort.com

The stylishly streamlined Lansdowne Resort, which comprises a nine-story tower and two five-story wings, underwent a $55 million renovation. Guest rooms are reminiscent of a country manor—elegant but casual, with woodland views.

296 rooms. Restaurant, bar. Fitness center. Pool. Spa. Golf. Tennis. $151-250

MANASSAS

★★★POPLAR SPRINGS INN

9245 Rogues Road, Casanova, 540-788-4600, 800-490-7747; www.poplarspringsinn.com

This pretty inn is a lovely country getaway. Rooms are kitted out in colonial-style furnishings. If you don't want to enjoy lounging around in plush robes or sleeping under luxe duvets, take a calming walk around the 200 acres.

21 rooms. Complimentary breakfast. Restaurant, bar. Fitness center. Pool. Spa. Tennis. $251-350

MCLEAN

★★★HILTON MCLEAN TYSONS CORNER

7920 Jones Branch Drive, McLean, 703-847-5000, 800-445-8667; www.mclean.hilton.com

Just steps away from the superb Tysons Corner Center, this atrium-style hotel is a great spot to stay outside of Washington. The guestrooms are comfortably adorned with down comforters and the basic amenities. Catch a good night's sleep on the signature Hilton Serenity Bed outfitted with plush linens. Enjoy a meal in one of the three restaurants located in the hotel. At Opus 88, enjoy live jazz every Friday and Saturday night.

458 rooms. Restaurant, bar. Business center. Fitness center. Pool. Pets accepted. $151-250

★★★★THE RITZ-CARLTON, TYSONS CORNER

1700 Tysons Blvd., McLean, 703-506-4300, 800-241-3333; www.ritzcarlton.com

Only 15 miles from Washington, D.C., this northern Virginia hotel is a luxurious retreat from the bustle of the city center. Guestrooms feature luxurious fabrics, flat screen TVs and down duvet-covered beds. The Ritz-Carlton Day Spa offers unique treatments such as a coffee anti-cellulite wrap and the bamboo lemongrass body scrub. Opt for a Club Level room for extra amenities, including a private lounge with complimentary snacks throughout the day and concierge service. The adjacent Tysons Galleria and Tysons Mall have more than 300 shops and a movie theater.

398 rooms. Restaurant, bar. Business center. Fitness center. Pool. Spa. Pets accepted. $351 and up.

VIENNA

★★★MARRIOTT TYSONS CORNER

8028 Leesburg Pike, Vienna, 703-734-3200, 800-228-9790; www.marriott.com

This property is located in the heart of Tysons Corner. Guest rooms feature down comforters and duvets, flat-screen TVs, marble bathrooms and Internet access. You don't have to miss your workout while you're on vacation; the Marriott offers a 24-hour fitness center and indoor pool. Grab a bite to eat and relax with a cocktail at Shula's Steak House.

396 rooms. Restaurant, bar. Fitness center. Pool. $151-250

WASHINGTON

★★★BLUE ROCK INN

12567 Lee Highway, Washington, 540-987-3190; www.thebluerockinn.com

This turn of the century farmhouse boasts five beautifully appointed rooms and great views of the Blue Ridge Mountains. Enjoy your morning coffee on the balcony while taking in the fresh Appalachian air. Satisfy your appetite at the restaurant overlooking the Inn's vineyards and pond. Curl up with a good book in the library or wander the property with your camera in hand. The Blue Rock Inn is perfect for a quiet, romantic getaway.

5 rooms. Complimentary breakfast. $151-250

★★★★★THE INN AT LITTLE WASHINGTON

309 Main St., Washington, 540-675-3800; www.theinnatlittlewashington.com

Savvy epicureans book a room—and a table—at the Inn at Little Washington. Tucked away in the foothills of the Blue Ridge Mountains, the inn offers visitors a taste of the good life, complete with afternoon tea with scones and tartlets. As tempting as it may be to indulge, guests save their appetites for the evening's cuisine. Many make special trips just for the talented chef's award-winning meals, though lucky guests recount their memorable feasts while ensconcing themselves in one of the inn's lovely guest rooms. The surrounding area provides opportunities for hiking, fly-fishing, hot air ballooning, antiquing and wine tasting.

18 rooms. Restaurant, bar. Complimentary breakfast. Closed Tuesday in January-March and July. $351 and up.

WHERE TO EAT

ALEXANDRIA

★★★CHEZ ANDRÉE

10 E. Glebe Road, Alexandria, 703-836-1404; www.chezandree.com

Chez Andrée, family-owned for more than 40 years, offers country French cuisine in three different dining rooms. Originally a railroad bar that catered to the Potomac Yards, the restaurant now serves specials such as duck l'orange and rack of lamb to hungry diners.

French. Lunch (Monday-Friday), dinner. Closed Sunday. Reservations recommended. Bar. $16-35

★★★THE GRILLE

Morrison House, 116 S. Alfred St., Alexandria, 703-838-8000; 800-367-0800; www.morrisonhouse.com

The Grille in the Morrison House Boutique Hotel

allows diners create their very own flight of food based on what the chef has purchased from local markets and farmers that day. Instead of a dinner menu, you'll be presented with a wine list, followed by a personal visit from the chef to discuss what you're in the mood to eat. He'll give you the list of ingredients, and you work together to develop the menu. After dinner, a butler will escort you to the parlor for an after-dinner drink or an aromatic pot of special-blend loose tea made for the Morrison House Boutique Hotel.

International. Breakfast, dinner, Sunday brunch. Bar. $36-85

★★★LA BERGERIE
218 N. Lee St., Alexandria, 703-683-1007; www.labergerie.com

In a historic brick warehouse, La Bergerie serves up French dishes, including roasted wild rockfish on mussel and salmon caviar risotto with a saffron vanilla sauce, roasted wild boar chop with kimchi cabbage, burgundy carrots and a sweet and sour sauce, along with a daily prix fixe menu.

French. Lunch (Monday-Saturday), dinner. Reservations recommended. Bar. $16-35

ARLINGTON
★★★FYVE RESTAURANT LOUNGE
Ritz-Carlton, Pentagon City, 1250 S. Hayes St., Arlington, 703-415-5000; www.ritzcarlton.com

Fyve Restaurant Lounge at the Ritz-Carlton Pentagon City offers upscale American classics in a warm, clubby dining room decked out in mahogany wood. The seasonal menu features dishes such as lobster, filet mignon, foie gras, caviar and oysters. On Sunday, Fyve hosts one of the best champagne brunches in the area and on weekends, afternoon tea is also offered.

American. Breakfast, lunch, dinner, brunch. Children's menu. Reservations recommended. Bar. $36-85

DULLES INTERNATIONAL AIRPORT AREA
★★★PALM COURT
Westfields Marriott Washington Dulles, 14750 Conference Center Drive, Chantilly, 703-818-3520; www.westfieldspalmcourt.com

In the Westfields Marriott hotel, this restaurant offers a buffet-style Sunday brunch with tuxedo-clad waiters, mimosas and an unending array of sweets. Each meal is a culinary experience when dining at Palm Court. Enjoy the signature lobster bisque. Accompany your meal with a glass of wine from the list of more than 200 wines from 13 countries.

American. Breakfast (Saturday-Sunday), lunch (Monday-Saturday), dinner (Tuesday-Saturday), Saturday-Sunday brunch. Children's menu. Reservations recommended. Bar. $16-35

FAIRFAX
★★★LARUE 123 AT BAILIWICK INN
4023 Chain Bridge Road, Fairfax, 703-691-2266; www.larue123.com

This Federal-style inn and restaurant, on the National Register of Historic Places, offers French-American cuisine in a quaint, romantic space. Visit for one of the seasonal wine dinners or for traditional English high tea in one of the intimate parlors.

French. Lunch (Tuesday-Friday), dinner. Reservations recommended. Outdoor seating. Bar. $36-85

MANASSAS

★★★CARMELLO'S AND LITTLE PORTUGAL

9108 Center St., Manassas, 703-368-5522; www.carmellos.com

At Carmello's and Little Portugal, Italian and Portuguese cuisines are beautifully combined to create generous contemporary dishes. The restaurant's intimate atmosphere makes it a popular spot to celebrate special occasions.

Italian, Spanish. Lunch (Monday-Friday), dinner. Bar. $16-35

★★★PANINO

9116 Mathis Ave., Manassas, 703-335-2566; www.girasole-panino.com

Although off the beaten path, this chef-owned and operated restaurant has for the past decade offered perhaps the best regional Italian cuisine outside the Beltway. Only the freshest ingredients are used.

Italian. Lunch (Monday-Friday), dinner. Closed Sunday. Reservations recommended. $16-35

MCLEAN

★★★DANTE RISTORANTE

1148 Walker Road, Great Falls, 703-759-3131; www.danterestaurant.com

A historic Victorian home (previously a dairy farm and "lying-in" hospital) is the setting for this romantic restaurant. There are several small dining areas, each with its own unique décor, but all are charming—one room has an entire wall displaying wine bottles. The authentic northern Italian menu offers items such as rabbit legs, ossobuco and homemade ravioli. Don't leave without trying the layered chocolate cake (filled with a chocolate mousse) with a cup of espresso.

Italian. Lunch (Monday-Friday), dinner. Closed Sunday. Reservations recommended. Outdoor seating. Bar. $36-85

★★★FIORE DI LUNA

1025-I Seneca Road, Great Falls, 703-444-4060; www.fiorediluna.com

Fiore di Luna is a simple but elegant Northern Italian restaurant, serving dishes such as butternut squash gnocchi with a robiola cheese sauce, julienne celery, amaretti cookies and parmesan cheese, or Grimaud farm-raised Muscovy duck breast with baby green and red Brussels sprouts, white polenta timbale and parsley purée.

Italian. Lunch (Tuesday-Friday), dinner. Closed Monday. Reservations recommended. Outdoor seating. Bar. $36-85

★★★L'AUBERGE CHEZ FRANCOIS

332 Springvale Road, Great Falls, 703-759-3800; www.laubergechezfrancois.com

Dirndl-clad servers in red vests with gold buttons deliver rich, hearty dishes at this Alsatian-themed restaurant. Located outside the Great Falls area, this charming farmhouse restaurant is set along a winding, two-lane road. Outside, the restaurant is surrounded by flowers and an herb garden, a gazebo and fountains on the terrace. The inside is cozy with wood beams, wood burning fireplaces and stained glass panels. The Haeringer family focuses on traditional Alsatian French cuisine and offers a prix fixe menu.

French. Lunch (Tuesday-Friday), dinner. Closed Monday. Children's menu. Reservations recommended. Outdoor seating. $36-85

★★★SERBIAN CROWN

1141 Walker Road, Great Falls, 703-759-4150; www.serbiancrown.com

Russian and French cuisines are fearlessly combined to create an elegant menu at this special-occasion restaurant. Beef stroganoff, stuffed cabbage rolls, marinated wild boar, and duck braised in sauerkraut are just a few of the items that keep diners coming back for more. Various live entertainments such as a violinist, Gypsy music and a piano bar add to the ambience.

French, Russian. Lunch (Wednesday-Friday), dinner, late night. Closed Monday. Reservations recommended. Bar. $36-85

VIENNA

★★★NIZAM'S

523 Maple Ave. West, Vienna, 703-938-8948

Doner kebob, a forebear of the gyro, is the legendary mainstay of this refined Turkish restaurant. Thin, tender slices of marinated, spit-roasted lamb nestle inside soft pita bread in a dish that rivals anything Istanbul could turn out. Service is friendly and attentive.

Turkish. Dinner. Closed Monday. Reservations recommended. Bar. $16-35

WASHINGTON

★★★BLUE ROCK INN

12567 Lee Highway, Washington, 540-987-3190; www.thebluerockinn.com

This country-inn farmhouse is located on 80 acres of rolling hillside overlooking the Blue Ridge Mountains and adjoining vineyards. It is a great place to stop between Harrisonburg and Washington, D.C. Enjoy seared duck breast with a port cherry reduction, grilled pork loin with mango chutney or Thai-style scallops with Thai green chili sauce. For dessert, try the homemade pumpkin pie.

French. Dinner, Sunday brunch. Closed Monday-Tuesday. Reservations recommended. Outdoor seating. Bar. $36-85

★★★★★THE INN AT LITTLE WASHINGTON

309 Main St., Washington, 540-675-3800; www.theinnatlittlewashington.com

Chef Patrick O'Connell has amassed almost every culinary award in existence. Seasonal dishes include a crab cake "sandwich" with fried green tomatoes and tomato vinaigrette; prosciutto-wrapped pan roasted veal loin with spinach raviolini and parmesan broth; salmon in lemon butter sauce with spring vegetables and Louisiana crawfish tails; and for dessert, a southern butter pecan ice cream sandwich with hot caramel sauce. The atmosphere is no less enticing, with rose-colored lampshades, high-backed chairs and gilded mirrors.

American. Dinner. Closed Tuesday. Reservations recommended. Bar. $86 and up.

WHERE TO SHOP

ARLINGTON

CRYSTAL CITY SHOPS

Crystal Drive, Arlington, 703-922-4636; www.thecrystalcityshops.com

Crystal City, a mixed-use residential and commercial development, is a bustling downtown area with more than 200 stores and restaurants. Tree-lined sidewalks are filled with outdoor cafés, shops, parks, hotels and more. You will find jewelry and gift shops, men and women's apparel, books and home furnishings, and a variety of dining options.

Monday-Friday 10 a.m.-7 p.m., Saturday 10 a.m.-6 p.m. Shops at 2100: Monday-Saturday 10 a.m.-6 p.m.

THE FASHION CENTRE AT PENTAGON CITY

1100 S. Hayes St., Arlington, 703-415-2400; www.fashioncentrepentagon.com

The Ritz-Carlton Hotel's presence dictates a glamorous tone at this huge, glittering mall, anchored by Macy's and Nordstrom and home to more than 170 other tantalizing shops and restaurants. Women's fashion and accessories stores include Kenneth Cole and MAC Cosmetics. For home furnishings, check out Brookstone and Williams-Sonoma.

Monday-Saturday 10 a.m.-9:30 p.m., Sunday 11 a.m.-6 p.m.

LE VILLAGE MARCHE

4150 Campbell Ave., Arlington, VA, 703-379-4444; www.levillagemarche.com

Le Village Marché, which translates to "the village shop," possesses a Parisian flea market environment and is a great place to purchase gifts or to buy something lovely for yourself. You'll find charming trinkets, beautiful antique armoires and unique vintage furniture. Great gifts include Paddywax soy candles, fleur-de-lis glasses, and blocks of soap. It's like a trip to France just outside D.C.

Monday-Saturday 11 a.m.-9 p.m., Sunday noon-7 p.m.

DULLES INTERNATIONAL AIRPORT AREA

RESTON TOWN CENTER

11900 Market St., Reston, 703-689-4699; www.restontowncenter.com

A 20-acre urban development incorporating elements of a traditional town square includes more than 50 retail shops and 30 restaurants, a movie theater complex, office space and a hotel. There are also special events and concerts held in the Pavilion, along with ice-skating in the winter.

Hours vary; see website for details.

MCLEAN

TYSONS GALLERIA

2001 International Drive, Mclean, 703-827-7730; www.tysonsgalleria.com

This high-end shopping center features more shops than you can imagine, ranging from Saks Fifth Avenue to Sur La Table and De Beers to Godiva. Tysons Galleria is a prime destination for shopping in the Washington area. Take a lunch break at one of the various restaurants including The Cheesecake Factory and Wildfire. For more shopping, wander over to Tysons I, located just across the street.

Monday-Saturday 10 a.m.-9 p.m., Sunday noon-6 p.m.

RICHMOND

Located at the falls of the James River, Richmond had to wait 170 years before becoming the state capital. Four hundred years later, with a history almost as old as Jamestown, the city blends its heritage with vibrant, contemporary commerce and trade. Its location, equidistant from the plantations of Tidewater Virginia and the Piedmont of central Virginia, gives the city a unique mix of heritage, culture and geography. There have been few dull moments in Richmond's history. Native Americans and settlers fought over the ground on which it now stands. In 1775, Patrick Henry made his famous "liberty or death" speech in St. John's Church, and in 1780, the city was named capital of the state. British soldiers plundered it brutally during the Revolutionary War. And as the capital of the Confederacy from 1861 to 1865, it was constantly in danger. Finally, in 1865, the city was evacuated and retreating Confederate soldiers burned the government warehouse. A portion of the rest of the city also went up in flames. Richmond survived, and it now proudly exemplifies the modern South: industrially aggressive yet culturally aware, respectful of its own historical background yet receptive to new trends in architecture and modes of living.

WHAT TO SEE

17TH STREET FARMERS' MARKET

17th and Main Street, Richmond, 804-646-0477; www.17thstreetfarmersmarket.com

This farmers' market is built at the site of a Native American trading village and features seasonal local produce, baked goods and homemade products.

April-early-December, Thursday 8:30 a.m.-4 p.m., Saturday-Sunday 9 a.m.-4 p.m.; also late May-early September, Friday 4-8 p.m.

AGECROFT HALL

4305 Sulgrave Road, Richmond, 804-353-4241; www.agecrofthall.com

This half-timbered Tudor manor built in the late 15th century near Manchester, England was disassembled, brought here and rebuilt during the late 1920s in a spacious setting of formal gardens and grassy terraces overlooking the James River. It has English furnishings from 16th and 17th centuries.

Tuesday-Saturday, 10 a.m.-4 p.m., Sunday 12:30-5 p.m.

BLACK HISTORY MUSEUM AND CULTURAL CENTER

3 E. Clay St., Richmond, 804-780-9093; www.blackhistorymuseum.org

Founded in 1981, this museum is dedicated to commemorating the lives and accomplishments of Blacks in Virginia through displaying exhibits featuring limited editions, prints, art, photographs, memorabilia and more. There are collections from artists such as Sam Gilliam, John Biggers and P.H. Polk.

Admission: adults $5, seniors, students and teachers $4, children 12 and under free. Tuesday-Saturday 10 a.m.-5 p.m.

CANAL CLUB

1545 E. Cary St., Richmond, 804-643-2582; www.thecanalclub.com

Catch live music, especially blues and rock, or shoot a game of pool in Shockoe Bottom. A bonus: there's a tasty menu at The Downstairs Lounge (featuring

HIGHLIGHT

WHAT ARE THE TOP THINGS TO DO IN RICHMOND?

GO SHOPPING
Visit Richmond's urban retail district of Carytown. With plenty of shops and restaurants, you'll find an entire afternoon's worth of diversions.

SEE THE GOVERNOR'S MANSION
Better known as the Executive Mansion, this residence has served as the home of Virginia's governors and families for nearly 200 years.

TAKE A CRUISE DOWN THE JAMES RIVER
Hop aboard one of the canal cruisers for a ride through the canal and into the river. It's a great way to see the city.

bar food such as chicken wings, burgers and nachos), which is the smaller room below the Canal Club upstairs. See website for schedules and tickets.
Downstairs Lounge: Wednesday-Sunday.

CANAL WALK
Enter at S. Fifth, Seventh, 14th, 15th, or 17th streets; 804-788-6466
The Canal Walk will take you 1 ¼ miles through downtown and features a pedestrian bridge to Brown's Island. You'll see historic monuments and more on your walk.
Brown's Island: Daily dawn-dusk.

CARYTOWN
West Cary Street, between Boulevard and Thompson streets, Richmond, 804-422-2279; www.carytownrva.org
More than 300 shops and restaurants in this area include quirky clothing boutiques, antique shops, the city's best music store and collectibles ranging from Christmas decorations to glass and dolls. It covers nine blocks, so you'll find plenty of fun things to buy.
Monday-Saturday 10 a.m.-6 p.m.; some shops open on Sunday.

CHILDREN'S MUSEUM OF RICHMOND
2626 W. Broad St., Richmond, 804-474-7000, 877-295-2667; www.c-mor.org
Although designed for children, this museum is fun for the whole family. Children and grown-ups alike can discover stalagmites and stalactites in the

newly renovated cave. Check out the sun tubes at the Dominion Solar Energy Exhibit and learn about sensory airways and solar energy. Float on over to the James River Water Play where toy boats can sail down actual features of the James River.

Admission: adults $8, children under 1 free. Daily after 4 p.m. $4. Tuesday-Saturday 9:30 a.m.-5 p.m., Sunday noon-5 p.m.

CHURCH HILL HISTORIC AREA
Main and 21st streets, bounded by Broad, 29th, Main, and 21st streets,
East of Capitol Square, Richmond

This neighborhood is filled with 19th-century houses, more than 70 of which predate the Civil War. Some Church Hill houses are open for viewing during Historic Garden Week. You'll also find Chimborazo Park, which is the site of the largest military hospital in the Civil War.

CITY HALL OBSERVATION DECK
901 E. Broad St., Richmond, 804-646-7000; www.richmondgov.com

The eighteenth-floor observation deck at city hall offers a panoramic view of the city, including the Capitol grounds, James River and Revolutionary and Civil War-era buildings contrasted with modern skyscrapers.

Admission: Free. Monday-Friday 8 a.m.-5 p.m.

CIVIL WAR VISITOR CENTER
490 Tredegar St., Richmond, 804-780-1865; www.tredegar.org

Begin your exploration of Richmond's Civil War heritage at the National Park Service Center at the restored Tredegar Iron Works near the James River. On the bottom floor, a continuously running film orients you to the 12 battlefields in the area. Park Service guides explain to kids how to fire the kind of cannon that Tredegar Iron Works made for the war.

Admission: adults $8, seniors and students $6, children 7-12 $2, children 6 and under free. Daily 9 a.m.-5 p.m.

EDGAR ALLAN POE MUSEUM
1914-1916 E. Main St., Richmond, 804-648-5523, 888-213-2763; www.poemuseum.org

Housing the world's finest collection of Edgar Allan Poe manuscripts, memorabilia and personal belongings, this museum honors the life of "America's Shakespeare." Poe lived and worked in Richmond in the early nineteenth century. Located in The Old Stone House, the museum is just a few blocks away from the author's former home. Discover treasures such as the Poe Family Bible, passed down through the family, his childhood bed and even a lock of Edgar Allan Poe's hair.

Admission: adults $6, seniors and students $5. Tuesday-Saturday 10 a.m.-5 p.m., Sunday 11 a.m.-5 p.m.

EQUESTRIAN STATUE OF WASHINGTON
Ninth and Grace streets, Richmond

Created by Thomas Crawford, this statue was cast in Munich over an 18-year period. The base features allegorical representations of six famous Revolutionary War figures from Virginia. Standing 60 feet tall, this statue of George Washington dominates the area around it. Randolph Rogers completed the statue after Crawford's death. The full memorial was revealed on Washington's Birthday, February 22, 1858.

THE FAN DISTRICT AND MONUMENT AVENUE

Main and Belvidere streets, Richmond; www.fandistrict.org

Named for the layout of streets that fan out from Monroe Park toward the western part of town, this historic neighborhood has restored antebellum and turn-of-the-century houses, museums, shops, restaurants and the famed Monument Avenue. The fashionable Boulevard, between Lombard and Belmont streets, is dotted with imposing statues of Generals Lee, Stuart and Jackson.

GOVERNOR'S MANSION

Ninth and Grace streets, Richmond, 804-371-8687; www.executivemansion.virginia.gov

Built during the War of 1812, this is the oldest Governor's Mansion built for that purpose in the nation. The Governor's Office, restored in 1999, appears as it did in the nineteenth century. Virginia governors took up residence here after the capital was moved from Williamsburg in 1813. This Federal style home has a long history, from fires to visits by Queen Elizabeth. The beautiful mansion features stunning architecture inside and out.

Tours: Tuesday-Thursday 10 a.m.-noon, 2-4 p.m.

HISTORIC RICHMOND TOURS

1015 E. Clay St., Richmond, 804-649-0711; www.richmondhistorycenter.com

Explore this historical city on a tour with the Valentine Richmond History Center. Whether walking, seated on a bus, or riding on a Segway, these tours are fun for everyone. See the diversity that this Virginian city has to offer. Choose between several different tours that guide you to different spots of the city. City Center Walks lead you through the historic streets of Richmond, passing by the National Theatre, St. Paul's Church and more. Bus through the Civil War sites in Richmond as you learn the important role this city played in the defining war.

Admission: Prices vary by tour. Walking tour: April-October. Bus tour: Monday-Saturday; see website for schedule.

HOLLYWOOD CEMETERY

412 S. Cherry St., Richmond, 804-648-8501; www.hollywoodcemetery.org

Overlooking the James River, this cemetery is the resting place of James Monroe, John Tyler, Jefferson Davis and more than 18,000 Confederate soldiers. Designed in 1847 by John Notman, this cemetery covers 135 acres. The breathtaking setting of Hollywood Cemetery complements the impressive architecture. As is often the case with graveyards, there are plenty of ghost stories and legends that have haunted Hollywood Cemetery for years. Listen to the legends during the tours offered.

Daily 8 a.m.-5 p.m. Walking tour: April-October, Monday-Saturday 10 a.m.

JACKSON WARD

Broad and Belvidere streets, Richmond; www.richmondgov.com

This historic downtown neighborhood was home to many famous black Richmonders, including Bill "Bojangles" Robinson, Duke Ellington and others.

The Maggie Walker House is also located here. It's where Maggie Walker, the nation's first female bank president lived. The area has numerous 19th-century, Greek Revival and Victorian buildings with ornamental ironwork that rivals the wrought iron of New Orleans.

JAMES RIVER PARK

West 22nd Street and Riverside Drive, Richmond, 804-646-8911; www.jamesriverpark.org

This unique park is the largest in the James River Park System. With more than 550 acres located in the heart of Richmond, James River Park offers activities such as hiking, fishing and canoeing. Comprised of eleven unique parts, you'll find islands, beaches, woodlands and rapids.

JOHN MARSHALL HOUSE

818 E. Marshall St., Richmond, 804-648-7998; www.apva.org

This beautiful brick home, built between 1788 and 1790, was where John Marshall lived until his death in 1835. Known as a "plantation in town", the property is located on Court End, a square owned by Marshall. Marshall also had his law office, a laundry, kitchen, garden, carriage house and stable on the property. The home, which remained in the Marshall family until 1911, when the City of Richmond bought it, hasn't been changed much. Today, the John Marshall Courthouse occupies the majority of the square. The home is managed by Preservation Virginia and has been open to the public since 1913

Admission: adults $10, seniors $6, students $4, children 3 and under free. March-December, Friday-Saturday 10 a.m.-5 p.m., Sunday noon-5 p.m.; January-February, by appointment only

KANAWHA CANAL CRUISES

14th Street and Virginia Street, Richmond, 804-649-2800; www.venturerichmond.com

Cruise the Kanawha Canal and James River in a covered boat. These impressive stone locks that control the canal were part of the nation's first canal system, planned by George Washington. It was Washington's vision to connect the ports of the east to the trade opportunities of the west, ideally all the way to the Rocky Mountains. A 40-minute narrated tour guides you on the canal along Richmond's Canal Walk. Private charters are also available.

Admission: adult $5, children 5-12, seniors $4, children 4 and under free. Check website for tour hours.

KINGS DOMINION

16000 Theme Park Way, Dosewell, 804-876-5000; www.kingsdominion.com

Over 400 acres of thrill rides and attractions make up this kingdom of fun. The park includes 15 roller coasters—hop aboard the Grizzly, the wooden coaster that was modeled after the infamous Coney Island Wildcat. There are also plenty of family rides. Go back in time on the Blue Ridge Tollway in an antique car, or cool off at the water park.

Admission: adults $56.99, seniors and children 3-18 $34.99. Hours vary; see website for calendar.

MAGGIE L. WALKER NATIONAL HISTORIC SITE

110 ½ E. Leigh St., Richmond, 804-771-2017; www.nps.gov

This site commemorates the life and career of Maggie L. Walker, daughter of former slaves, who overcame great hardships to become successful in banking and insurance and was an early advocate for women's rights and racial equality. This two-story, red brick house was home to her family from 1904 to 1934. Head to the visitor center first (*600 N. Second St.*) and watch a film on Walker's life and take a guided tour (leaving from the visitor center).

Monday-Saturday 9 a.m.-5 p.m.

MONTPELIER

11407 Constitution Highway, Montpelier Station, 540-672-2728; www.montpelier.org

The former residence of James Madison, fourth president of the United States, is a must-stop when you're in the area. Madison was the third generation of his family to live on this extensive plantation. He inherited Montpelier and expanded it twice. After his presidency, he and Dolley Madison retired to the estate, which Mrs. Madison sold after the president's death to pay off her son's gambling debts. In 1901, the estate was bought by William DuPont, who enlarged the house, added many outbuildings (including a private railroad station) and built greenhouses and planted gardens. Head out on your own self-guided tour of the arboretum, nature trails and formal garden. For a guided tour of the mansion and grounds, check in at the visitor center to start with a 15-minute video presentation.

Admission: adults $14, children 6-14 $7, children 5 and under free. April-October, daily 9:30 a.m.-5:30 p.m.; November-March, daily 9:30 a.m.-4:30 p.m.

MUSEUM OF THE CONFEDERACY

1201 E. Clay St., Richmond, 804-649-1861; www.moc.org

The museum features the world's largest collection of Confederate artifacts, including uniforms, weapons, tattered flags and daguerreotypes. Exhibits feature artifacts from Confederate officers with descriptions of their demise.

Admission: adults $8, seniors $7, children 7-13 $6, children 6 and under free. Monday-Saturday 10 a.m.-5 p.m., Sunday noon-5 p.m.

PLANTATIONS

Visitor Center, 405 N. Third St., Richmond, 804-783-7450; www.visitrichmondva.com

Plantations played a huge role in the history of Virginia. Just as you'd imagine, these southern farms are outfitted with gorgeous homes. Visit Thomas Jefferson's boyhood home at Tuckahoe Plantation, which has a beautiful house built between 1733 and 1740. Trek to Eppington Plantation to see a traditional plantation home. This Georgian style house was built in 1768 by Francis Eppes VI, the brother-in-law of Jefferson. The Richmond-Petersburg-Williamsburg area has many fine old mansions and estates. Some are open most of the year, while others are only open during Historic Garden Week.

RICHMOND NATIONAL BATTLEFIELD PARK

Civil War Visitor Center, 470 Tredegar St., Richmond, 804-226-1981; www.nps.gov

The Union made a total of seven drives on Richmond, the symbol of secession, during the Civil War. Richmond National Battlefield Park, 770 acres in ten different units, preserves the sites of the two efforts that came close to success: McClellan's Peninsula Campaign of 1862 and Grant's attack in 1864. Of McClellan's campaign, the park includes sites of the Seven Days' Battles at Chickahominy Bluffs, Beaver Dam Creek, Gaines' Mill (Watt House) and Malvern Hill. Grant's campaign is represented by the battlefield at Cold Harbor, where on June 3, 1864, Grant hurled his army at fortified Confederate positions, resulting in 7,000 casualties in less than one hour. Confederate Fort Harrison, Parker's Battery, Drewry's Bluff (Fort Darling) and Union-built Fort Brady are also included. Stop by the Civil War Visitor Center at Tredegar Iron Works first to pick up a park map.

Admission: Free. Daily 9 a.m.-5 p.m.

SHOCKOE SLIP DISTRICT

11 S. 12th St., Richmond; www.shockoeslip.org

Named after the Indian name for the stones at the mouth of the creek that once flowed through it, Shockoe Slip was the commercial center of Richmond and much of western Virginia back in the days of George Washington. Entrepreneurs and architects rejuvenated the neighborhood in the 1970s, making it a prime example of urban restoration and historic preservation. Now a prime shopping district, Shockoe Slip boasts a unique collection of boutiques throughout the neighborhood's restored warehouses. Offering plenty of restaurants, shops, galleries and hotels, Shockoe Slip is worth a visit.

STATE CAPITOL

Ninth and Grace streets, Richmond, 804-698-1788; www.virginiacapitol.gov

Modeled after La Maison Carre, an ancient Roman temple at Némes, France, the Capitol was designed by Thomas Jefferson. In this building, where America's oldest continuous English-speaking legislative bodies still meet, is the famous Houdon statue of Washington. The rotunda features the first interior dome in the United States.

Admission: Free. Monday-Saturday 9 a.m.-4 p.m., Sunday 1-4 p.m. Tours: 9 a.m.-4 p.m.

ST. JOHN'S EPISCOPAL CHURCH

2401 E. Broad St., at 24th St., Richmond, 804-648-5015, 877-915-1775;
www.historicstjohnschurch.org

St. John's boasts as much history as it does spirituality. Gaining its fame from the Second Virginia Convention, when Patrick Henry delivered his stirring "give me liberty or give me death" speech in March 1775, the church was the only building in Richmond suitable at the time to hold the delegates. Throughout the summer, professional actors reenact the unforgettable day each Sunday.

Admission: adults $6, seniors $5, students 7-18 $4, children 6 and under free. Tours: Monday-Saturday 10 a.m.-4 p.m., Sunday 1-4 p.m. (last tour leaves at 3:30 p.m.)

VIRGINIA HISTORICAL SOCIETY

428 N. Boulevard St., Richmond, 804-358-4901; www.vahistorical.org

The Virginia Historical Society, founded in 1831, thrives to collect, preserve and teach as much of the Virginian past as possible. The society has a comprehensive collection of Virginia history housed in its museum with permanent and changing exhibits. The Library of Virginia History offers historical and genealogical research facilities. With exhibitions such as "Solving History's Mysteries: The History Discovery Lab" and "Virginians at Work", the Virginia Historical Society showcases various aspects of life in Virginia.

Admission: adults $5, seniors $4, students $3, children 18 and under free. Free Sunday. Tuesday-Sunday 10 a.m.-5 p.m., Sunday 1-5 p.m.

VIRGINIA MUSEUM OF FINE ARTS

200 N. Blvd., Richmond, 804-340-1400; www.vmfa.state.va.us

America's first state-supported museum of art has collections of paintings, prints and sculpture from major world cultures. Of note are the Russian Imperial Easter eggs and jewels by Fabergé. The museum also features decorative arts of the Art Nouveau and Art Deco movements, and includes a sculpture garden.
Wednesday-Sunday 11 a.m.-5 p.m.

VIRGINIA WAR MEMORIAL

621 S. Belvidere St., Richmond, 804-786-2060; www.vawarmemorial.org

The Virginia War Memorial honors Virginians who died in World War II, the Korean War, the Vietnam War, Persian Gulf, Afghanistan and Iraq. More than 11,600 names are engraved on glass and marble walls in memory of those Virginians who died for their country. An eternal flame, the Torch of Liberty, burns constantly in remembrance of these soldiers.
Admission: Free. Monday-Saturday 9 a.m.-4 p.m., Sunday noon-4 p.m.

WHITE HOUSE OF THE CONFEDERACY

1201 E. Clay St., Richmond, 804-649-1861; www.moc.org

Next door to the Museum of the Confederacy, this Classical Revival house was used by Jefferson Davis as his official residence during the period when Richmond was the capital of the Confederacy. Abraham Lincoln met with troops here during the Union occupation of the city. A National Historic Landmark, it has been restored to its prewar appearance with many of its original furnishings.
Admission: adults $8, seniors $7, children 7-13 $4, children 6 and under free. (A combination ticket with the Confederacy Museum is available.) Monday-Saturday 10 a.m.-5 p.m., Sunday noon-5 p.m.

WILTON HOUSE MUSEUM

215 S. Wilton Road, Richmond, 804-282-5936; www.wiltonhousemuseum.org

Once the center of a 2,000-acre tobacco plantation, Wilton was built in 1753 for William Randolph III. This eighteenth century Georgian home is an exquisite example of Colonial American architecture. It was at Wilton that the Randolphs entertained George Washington, Thomas Jefferson and Marquis de Lafayette. Opened to the public in 1952, Wilton House Museum showcases 18th- and 19th-century textiles, furnishings, glass, and ceramics.
Admission: adults $10, seniors $8, children 6 and under free. Tuesday-Saturday 10 a.m.-4:30 p.m., Sunday 1:30-4:30 p.m.

WHERE TO STAY

★★★THE BERKELEY HOTEL

1200 E. Cary St., Richmond, 804-780-1300, 888-780-4422; www.berkeleyhotel.com

Located at the crossroads of the business district and Shockoe Slip, this hotel opened in 1988, but its stylish look seems much more historic. Dark wood paneling adorns the lobby and dining room. Dramatic windows to the ceiling give the hotel a European appearance. Diners at the hotel's restaurant get a view of the Slip's cobblestones and lamplights.

55 rooms. Restaurant, bar. $151-250

★★★CROWNE PLAZA

555 E. Canal St., Richmond, 804-788-0900, 888-444-0401; www.crowneplaza.com

Just nine miles from Richmond International Airport, this hotel is situated in the heart of the historic district on the Canal Walk. Its higher floors have a spectacular view of the James River. The hotel is located minutes from area attractions such as Shockoe Slip, Sixth Street Market Place, museums, theaters and fine dining. Brown's Island, a concert and special-events venue, is located behind the hotel. Richmond Ballet is adjacent to the hotel, and ballet packages are available.

298 rooms. Restaurant, bar. Business center. Fitness Center. Pool. $61-150

★★★★★THE JEFFERSON HOTEL

101 W. Franklin St., Richmond, 804-788-8000, 800-424-8014; www.jeffersonhotel.com

The Jefferson Hotel is an institution in the heart of Richmond. A historic Beaux-Arts landmark dating back to 1895, the hotel offers elegant guest rooms furnished in a traditional style with antique reproductions and fine art. Pedigreed residents take afternoon tea here. TJ's provides a casual setting for fine dining with local dishes like oyster chowder and peanut soup, while the hotel's restaurant, Lemaire, offers a sparkling ambience and a farm-to-table inspired menu. The hotel's location is ideal, putting you in close proximity to the city's financial district, museums and shopping. If you don't feel like walking, a complimentary car service will transport you to these and other destinations within a three-mile radius.

262 rooms. Restaurant, bar. Business center. Fitness center. Pool. Pets accepted. $251-350

★★★RICHMOND MARRIOTT

500 E. Broad St., Richmond, 804-643-3400, 800-228-9290; www.marriott.com

Attached to the Convention Center via skywalk, this high-rise hotel in the heart of the city is close to the Coliseum and both the historic and river districts. Business travelers will appreciate access to the concierge lounge, while families will love the

---

WHICH RICHMOND HOTEL IS THE MOST HISTORIC?

The Jefferson Hotel: A historic Beaux-Arts landmark dating back to 1895, the hotel offers elegant guest rooms furnished in a traditional style with antique reproductions and fine art.

spacious rooms, indoor pool and downtown location. The hotel offers complimentary shuttle service to Shockoe Slip, as well as to all major businesses within three miles.

410 rooms. Restaurant, bar. Business center. Fitness center. Pool. $151-250

★★★OMNI RICHMOND HOTEL

100 S. 12th St., Richmond, 804-344-7000, 888-444-6664; www.omnihotels.com

This contemporary hotel is conveniently located in the center of the financial and historic districts in the James Center and features scenic river views. It's across the street from the famous Tobacco Company restaurant, and a great place to stay if you intend to explore Shockoe Slip and Shockoe Bottom.

361 rooms. Restaurant, bar. Business center. Pool. Pets accepted. $61-150

WHERE TO EAT

★★★THE DINING ROOM AT THE BERKELEY HOTEL

The Berkeley Hotel, 1200 E. Cary St., Richmond, 804-225-5105, 888-780-4422; www.berkeleyhotel.com

Located in a European-style hotel, this handsomely decorated dining room serves elegant meals in a sophisticated and tranquil atmosphere. Entrée selections include shrimp and grits, the chef's signature crab cake and grilled New York Strip with Chesapeake Bay blue crab meat stuffed Atlantic shrimp.

American. Breakfast, lunch (Monday-Saturday), dinner, Sunday brunch. Reservations recommended. Bar. $36-85

★★★LEMAIRE

The Jefferson Hotel, 101 W. Franklin, Richmond, 804-788-8000, 800-424-8014; www.jeffersonhotel.com

Located in the historic Jefferson Hotel, Lemaire has evolved from Old World fine dining to a more casual atmosphere serving innovative cuisine, but with its rich history still intact. The restaurant is named for Etienne Lemaire, who served as maître d' to President Jefferson and was widely credited with introducing the fine art of cooking with wines to America. His love of food and wine is continued at Lemaire, where local seasonal ingredients are used by chef Walter Bundy, himself inspired by the farm-to-table philosophy. Enjoy small plates, wine and cocktails in the new bar and lounge.

American. Breakfast, lunch, dinner. Reservations recommended. Bar. $36-85

★★★THE OLD ORIGINAL BOOKBINDER'S

2306 E. Cary St., Richmond, 804-643-6900; www.bookbindersrichmond.com

The first Bookbinder's to open outside of Philadelphia is located in a historic building that was once a Philip Morris manufacturing plant. Menu selections include high-quality seafood and homemade desserts. There is an outdoor courtyard area for alfresco dining.

Seafood. Dinner. Reservations recommended. Outdoor seating. Bar. $36-85

★★★THE TOBACCO COMPANY

1201 E. Cary St., Richmond, 804-782-9555; www.thetobaccocompany.com

The Tobacco Company, the restaurant that helped pioneer the renaissance of Richmond's Shockoe Slip neighborhood, is carved from a former tobacco

warehouse. Its centerpiece is a dramatic, sky-lit atrium with an antique cage elevator servicing three floors of dining. The menu is extensive if not inventive: steaks, prime rib, lobster, veal, shrimp, scallops, salmon, rainbow trout, chicken, crab, Virginia ham and pasta. Enjoy live music every Friday and Saturday night and cigars in the bar.
American. Lunch, dinner, Sunday brunch. Reservations recommended. Bar. $36-85

SHENANDOAH VALLEY

Once known as "Hell Town" for all the wild and reckless spirits it attracted, Front Royal was a frontier stop on the way to eastern markets. Set in rolling country between the Blue Ridge and Allegheny mountains, Lexington is known for attractive homes, fine old mansions and two of the leading educational institutions in the Commonwealth. Luray's name is of French origin, and its fame comes from the caverns discovered here in 1878. New Market gained its niche in Virginia history on May 15, 1864, when, in desperation, Confederate General Breckinridge ordered the cadets from Lexington's Virginia Military Institute to join the battle against the forces of General Franz Sigel. Tucked in the valley's center, the city of Roanoke itself evolved from a thriving, industrial railroading nexus in the late 1800s to a state-of-the-art destination.

About 450 million years ago, the Blue Ridge was at the bottom of a sea. Today, it averages 2,000 feet above sea level, and some 300 square miles of the loveliest Blue Ridge area are included in Shenandoah National Park. To historians, Staunton is known as the birthplace of Woodrow Wilson, and to students of government it is the place where the City Manager plan was adopted. The first western Virginia town to be served by two railroads, Strasburg became a prominent railroad town, manufacturing center, and home of printing and publishing businesses after 1890. Today, Strasburg calls itself the "antique capital of Virginia." Nestled at the foot of Little Mountain, the spring wildflowers and groves of fall foliage make Warm Springs a very scenic spot for sightseeing, hiking and water activities. Winchester is the oldest colonial city west of the Blue Ridge and is sometimes called the "apple capital of the world."

WHAT TO SEE

FRONT ROYAL
SKYLINE CAVERNS
10344 Stonewall Jackson Highway, Front Royal, 540-635-4545, 800-296-4545; www.skylinecaverns.com

Explore these caverns to see extensive, rare, intricate flowerlike formations of calcite. Tours include a sound and light presentation and a trip via miniature train through the surrounding wooded area. The caverns are electrically lit and kept at a temperature of 54 Fahrenheit year-round (so bring a jacket). There's a snack bar and gift shop here. Cavern tours start every few minutes.
Admission: adults $16, children 7-13 $8, children 5 and under free. Mini-train: adults and children 3-18 $3, children 2 and under free. Mid-March-mid-June and September-mid-November, Monday-Friday 9 a.m.-5 p.m., Saturday-Sunday 9 a.m.-6 p.m.; mid-June-August, daily 9 a.m.-6 p.m.; mid-November-mid-March, daily 9 a.m.-4 p.m.

HIGHLIGHT

WHAT ARE THE TOP THINGS TO DO IN THE SHENANDOAH VALLEY?

EXPLORE THE CAVERNS
The Shenandoah Valley boasts many caverns to discover. These geological formations are quite impressive, especially when you hear the acoustics.

SEE THE CADETS
Virginia Military Institute is situated right next to Washington & Lee University. This state military, engineering and liberal arts school is filled with 1,300 cadets.

WARREN RIFLES CONFEDERATE MUSEUM
95 Chester St., Front Royal, 540-636-6982; www.vaudc.org

Everything from relics to cavalry equipment is on display at this Civil War museum. Designed to preserve these treasures from the War Between the States, the museum is a tribute to Confederate soldiers and civilians. The museum houses some of the most bizarre remains from the Civil War, including a human hipbone with a bullet embedded in it and a wreath made of human hair. You can also see pieces of the Pegram Battery battle flag and the spurs of Colonel John Singleton Mosby.

Mid-April-November, Monday-Friday 9 a.m.-4 p.m., Sunday noon-4 p.m.;
December-mid-April, by appointment.

HOT SPRINGS
THE HOMESTEAD SKI AREA
Highway 220, Hot Springs, 540-839-3860, 866-354-4653; www.thehomestead.com

The beautiful 45-acres of The Homestead Ski Resort has been a destination for skiers and snowboarders since 1959. Beginners can attend The Sepp Kober Ski School while the more advanced fly down the more challenging trails. Enjoy snowmobiling, ice-skating and snow tubing on the mountain when you've gotten enough of the slopes.

Mid-December-March, daily 10 a.m.-5 p.m.

LEXINGTON
GEORGE C. MARSHALL MUSEUM
Virginia Military Institute Parade Ground, Lexington, 540-463-7103;
www.marshallfoundation.org

This museum features displays on the life and career of George C. Marshall, the illustrious military figure and statesman (1880-1959). Exhibits include a World War I electric map and recorded narration of World War II.

Admission: adults $5, seniors $3, children 13-18 $2, children 12 and under and military personnel free. Tuesday-Saturday 9 a.m.-5 p.m.

LEE CHAPEL AND MUSEUM

Washington and Lee University campus, Lexington, 540-458-8768; www.leechapel.wlu.edu

It is only fitting that the tomb of General Robert E. Lee is located on the lower level of this chapel. It was built upon the request of General Lee in 1867 during his presidency of the former Washington College. Following Lee's death in 1870, a crypt was added to the church where he and his relatives are buried. The lower level of the chapel, which was once Lee's office, is now a museum in which many family possessions are on display. This Victorian chapel is a National Historic Landmark and remains an integral part of the campus of Washington and Lee University.

April-October, Monday-Saturday 9 a.m.-5 p.m., Sunday 1-5 p.m.; November-March, Monday-Saturday 9 a.m.-4 p.m., Sunday 1-4 p.m.

STONEWALL JACKSON HOUSE

8 E. Washington St., Lexington, 540-463-2552; www.stonewalljackson.org

This is the only home owned by Confederate General Thomas J. "Stonewall" Jackson, restored to its appearance from 1859 to 1861. Jackson once owned many of the furnishings. There's an interpretive slide presentation, guided tours, restored gardens and a gift shop.

Admission: adults $6, children 6-17 $3, children 5 and under free. Monday-Saturday 9 a.m.-5 p.m., Sunday 1-5 p.m.

STONEWALL JACKSON MEMORIAL CEMETERY

White and Main streets, Lexington; www.lexingtonvirginia.com

Originally a burial ground for the old Presbyterian Church, this cemetery has quite the notable residents. General Stonewall Jackson rests here along with 144 of his Confederate soldiers, two Virginia governors and Margaret Junkin Preston, the Civil War Poet Laureate of the South. A statue, sculpted in 1891 by Edward V. Valentine, resides in this famous cemetery, keeping watch over Jackson's grave.

Admission: Free. Daily dawn-dusk.

VIRGINIA MILITARY INSTITUTE

Letcher Avenue, Lexington, 540-464-7207; www.vmi.edu

Founded in 1839, this was the first state military college in the nation, and it became coeducational in 1997. Stonewall Jackson taught here, as did Matthew Fontaine Maury, the famed naval explorer and inventor. George Catlett Marshall, an army general and author of the Marshall Plan, was a graduate. Mementos of these men are on display in the VMI museum.

Tours: Daily noon. Museum: Daily 9 a.m.-5 p.m.

WASHINGTON AND LEE UNIVERSITY

West Washington Street, Lexington, 540-463-8400; www.wlu.edu

This liberal arts university with 2,189 students is situated on an attractive campus with white colonnaded buildings. It also includes Washington and Lee Law School. Founded as Augusta Academy in 1749, it became Liberty Hall in 1776 and then the Washington Academy in 1798, after the school was given

200 shares of James River Canal Company stock from George Washington, and then become Washington College. General Robert E. Lee served as president from 1865-1870. Soon after Lee's death in 1870, it became Washington and Lee University.

LURAY
LURAY CAVERNS
970 Highway 211 W., Luray, 540-743-6551; www.luraycaverns.com

At one of the largest caverns in the East, huge underground rooms (one is 300-feet wide, 500-feet long, with a 140-foot ceiling) are connected by natural corridors and paved walkways which are encrusted with colorful rock formations. In one chamber is the world's only "stalacpipe" organ, which produces music of symphonic quality from stone formations. Indirect lighting permits taking of color photos within caverns. The temperature in the caverns is 54 F (so bring a jacket). One-hour guided tours start about every 20 minutes.

Admission: adults $21, seniors $18, children 6-12 $10.

LURAY SINGING TOWER
970 Highway 211/340 W., Luray, 540-743-6551; www.luraycaverns.com

Officially known as the Belle Brown Northcott Memorial, the tower houses a 47-bell carillon with the largest bell weighing 7,640 pounds. Come for one of the 45-minute recitals by the celebrated carillonneur. The tower is in the park adjacent to caverns.

April-May, Saturday-Sunday 2 p.m.; June-August, Tuesday, Thursday, Saturday-Sunday 8 p.m.; September-October, Sunday 2 p.m.

NEW MARKET
SHENANDOAH CAVERNS
261 Caverns Road, New Market, 540-477-3115, 888-422-8376; www.shenandoahcaverns.com

An elevator lowers visitors 60 feet underground to large subterranean rooms filled with fascinating rock formations. The caverns stay at a constant 54 F. There's also a café here with an original 1957 soda fountain. After your tour, grab a burger and a milkshake or homemade cherry coke.

Admission: adults $22, seniors $20, children 6-14 $10, children 5 and under free. Tour times vary; see website for information.

ROANOKE
GEORGE WASHINGTON AND JEFFERSON NATIONAL FORESTS
5162 Valleypointe Parkway, Roanoke, 540-265-5100; www.southernregion.fs.fed.us

The forests consist of approximately two million acres, which offer many different outdoor activities including swimming, fishing, hunting, horseback riding, camping and picnicking. There are scenic drives past Crabtree Falls, hardwood forests and unusual geologic features. Be sure to check out the beautiful overlooks of the Shenandoah Valley. There are also trails for the visually impaired.

Beach: Daily 6 a.m.-8 p.m.

SHENANDOAH NATIONAL PARK
BLUE RIDGE PARKWAY
828-298-0398; www.nps.gov

Winding 469 mountainous miles between the Shenandoah and Great Smoky Mountains national parks (about 217 miles are in Virginia), the Blue Ridge Parkway represents a different concept in highway travel. It is not an express highway but a road intended for leisurely travel—travelers in a hurry would be wise to take state and U.S. routes, where speed limits are higher. The parkway follows the Blue Ridge Mountains for about 355 miles, then winds through the Craggies, Pisgahs and Balsams to the Great Smokies. Overlooks, picnic and camp sites, visitor centers, nature trails, fishing streams and lakes, and points of interest are numerous and well-marked. Accommodations are plentiful in cities and towns along the way. Food availability is limited on the parkway. The parkway is open all year, but the best time to drive it is between April and November. Some sections are closed by ice and snow for periods in winter and early spring. Fog may be present during wet weather. The higher sections west of Asheville to Great Smoky Mountains National Park and north of Asheville to Mount Mitchell may be closed January through March due to hazardous driving conditions.

STAUNTON
WOODROW WILSON BIRTHPLACE AND PRESIDENTIAL MUSEUM
24 N. Coalter St., Staunton, 540-885-0897; www.woodrowwilson.org

This restored Greek Revival manse has period furnishings and Wilson family mementos from the 1850s. The museum building on the grounds houses a seven-gallery presidential exhibit, "The Life and Times of Woodrow Wilson", and his 1919 Pierce-Arrow limousine.

Admission: adults $12, seniors, military personnel $10, students $5, children 6-12 $3, children 5 and under free. November-February, Monday-Saturday 10 a.m.-4 p.m., Sunday noon-4 p.m.; March-October, Monday-Saturday 9 a.m.-5 p.m., Sunday noon-5 p.m.

STRASBURG
BELLE GROVE PLANTATION
336 Belle Grove Road, Strasburg, 540-869-2028; www.bellegrove.org

This 1797 limestone mansion's design reflects Thomas Jefferson's influence. It was used as Union headquarters during the Battle of Cedar Creek on October 19, 1864. Positioned on 283 acres of the original 483 acres, this plantation house features unique hand carved woodwork and restored interiors. Built by Major Isaac Hite, the brother-in-law of President James Madison, this planta-tion, in addition to another 7,000 acres, was used for growing wheat, raising cattle and sheep, and operating a distillery.

Admission: adults $8, seniors $7, children 6-12 $4, children 5 and under free. Guided tours: April-October, Monday-Saturday 10:15 a.m.-3:15 p.m., Sunday 1:15-4:15 p.m. (depart 15 minutes after each hour). Self-guided tours: Late March-December, Monday-Friday 10 a.m.-4 p.m., Saturday 10:15 a.m.-3:15 p.m., Sunday 1:15-4:15 p.m.

STONEWALL JACKSON MUSEUM AT HUPP'S HILL
33229 Old Valley Pike, Strasburg, 540-465-5884; www.stonewalljacksonmuseum.org

Discover this Civil War battlefield through all kinds of hands-on activities.

Unlike so many museums, this one is almost completely filled with hands-on artifacts. Try on Civil War costumes and role-play in the Civil War "camp".

Admission: adults $5, seniors, students, military personnel and children 6-18 $4, children 4 and under free. Daily 10 a.m.-5 p.m.

WINCHESTER
STONEWALL JACKSON'S HEADQUARTERS
415 N. Braddock St., Winchester, 540-667-3242; www.winchesterhistory.org

During the winter of 1861 and 1862, General Stonewall Jackson used this Gothic Revival house as his headquarters. Today, this National Historic Landmark functions as a museum. With the largest collection of Jackson memorabilia, like his initialed prayer book and his staff's personal objects, this museum honors Stonewall Jackson as one of Robert E. Lee's most valuable officers.

Admission: adults $5, seniors $4.50, students $2.50. April-October, Monday-Saturday 10 a.m.-4 p.m., Sunday noon-4 p.m.

WASHINGTON'S OFFICE-MUSEUM
Cork and Braddock streets, Winchester, 540-662-4412; www.winchesterhistory.org

The small log building, now the middle room of the museum, was George Washington's military office from 1755 through 1756 during the construction of Fort Loudoun. The property is filled with artifacts ranging from a limestone well to a cannon. A statue of young Washington, dedicated in 2004, honors the fort where he spent much of his time during a crucial couple of years.

Admission: adults $5, seniors $4.50, children 7-15 $2.50, children 6 and under free. April-October, Monday-Saturday 10 a.m.-4 p.m., Sunday noon-4 p.m.

WHERE TO STAY

HOT SPRINGS
★★★THE HOMESTEAD
Highway 220, Hot Springs, 540-839-1766, 866-354-4653; www.thehomestead.com

Founded 10 years before the American Revolution, The Homestead is one of America's finest resorts. For more than two centuries, presidents and other notables have flocked to this idyllic mountain resort on 15,000 acres in the scenic Allegheny Mountains. From the fresh mountain air and natural hot springs to the legendary championship golf, this Georgian-style resort is the embodiment of a restorative retreat. A leading golf academy sharpens skills, while three courses challenge players. America's oldest continuously played tee is located here at the Old Course. Guests take to the waters as they have done for 200 years, while the spa incorporates advanced therapies for relaxation and rejuvenation.

483 rooms. Restaurant, bar. Fitness center. Pool. Spa. Golf. Tennis. $151-250

SHENANDOAH NATIONAL PARK
★★★L'AUBERGE PROVENÇALE
13630 Lord Fairfax Highway, Boyce, 540-837-1375, 800-638-1702; www.laubergeprovencale.com

Located in Virginia Wine Country, L'Auberge Provençale is surrounded by beautiful views of the Shenandoah Valley. This French-style inn, decorated with Victorian and European antiques, brings France to small-town Virginia. The rooms are adorned with authentic French style. The Main Manor House, built in 1753, boasts attractive rooms with an elegant Old World feel. Enjoy a full gourmet breakfast in the morning featuring homemade pastries.

11 rooms. No children under 10. Complimentary breakfast. Restaurant. $151-250

WARM SPRINGS

★★★INN AT GRISTMILL SQUARE

Highway 619, Warm Springs, 540-839-2231; www.gristmillsquare.com

Wake up to the smell of fresh-baked muffins every morning at the Inn at Gristmill Square, a village-like collection of restored 19th-century buildings. Tucked into picturesque Warm Springs, the inn offers guest rooms with comfortable, country décor. After exploring the area, end your day with a dinner of fresh local trout at the inn's restaurant in a converted mill.

19 rooms. Restaurant, bar. Complimentary breakfast. $61-150

WHERE TO EAT

ROANOKE

★★★LIBRARY

3117 Franklin Road, Roanoke, 540-985-0811; www.thelibraryrestaurantroanoke.com

Not only is this 1785 New England-style mansion a historic landmark, but it has also served the likes of George Washington and a host of other presidents. The service and ambiance is what sets it apart from other fine dining experiences. With the piano playing in the background, books surrounding you and the candle-lit tables glowing, dinner at Library is pleasingly romantic. It's perfect for a special occasion or just a nice dinner.

French, American. Dinner. Closed Monday-Sunday. Reservations recommended. $36-85

SHENANDOAH NATIONAL PARK

★★★L'AUBERGE PROVENÇALE

13630 Lord Fairfax Highway, Boyce, 540-837-1375, 800-638-1702; www.laubergeprovencale.com

This country inn has earned a reputation for fine cuisine served with detailed, personal attention. Innkeeper/chef Alain Borel, from Avignon, with his wife, Celeste, provides an authentic, garden-inspired menu. Choose from the three-, five- or six-course prix fixe menu, each guaranteeing an authentic taste of Provence. Dishes, such as the steamed Prince Edward Island mussels with fennel, capers and country ham in a white wine broth, transport you to a small town in France.

French. Lunch (Sunday), dinner. Closed Tuesday. Outdoor seating. Reservations recommended. Jacket requested. Bar. $36-85

STRASBURG

★★★HOTEL STRASBURG

213 S. Holliday St., Strasburg, 540-465-9191, 800-348-8327; www.hotelstrasburg.com

Originally a private hospital, this Victorian home was built in 1902. The inn's ornate lobby gives way to an invitingly cozy country restaurant, where locals and travelers alike dine on fine wines and elegant cuisine, including seasonal seafood dishes. Dine by candlelight for a truly romantic Victorian feel. Try the Shenandoah Valley chicken cordon bleu for a real taste of the region.

Mediterranean. Lunch, dinner. Reservations recommended. Bar. $61-150

SPA

HOT SPRINGS

★★★THE HOMESTEAD SPA

Highway 220, Hot Springs, 540-839-1766; www.thehomestead.com

The Homestead Spa at the Homestead Resort grows out of a healing tradition nearly as old as the local mountains themselves: taking the waters that bubble up from the ground in Hot Springs. For thousands of years, people have soaked in these mineral-rich waters to ease aches and ailments. The Homestead is a National Historic Landmark, and has been a spa since 1766. The octagonal wooden building atop the Hot Springs is even older, built in 1761 and essentially unchanged. Thomas Jefferson came to the Gentleman's Pool House to soak several times a day during his Homestead visit in 1818. Today, men can still retreat to the Jefferson Pools, while women have their own Ladies' Pool House atop another spring. Treatments have become more exotic over time, encompassing reflexology and Ayurvedic head massage, alpha-beta skin peels and banana-and-coconut hair therapy. But the spa still values the time-tested mineral baths and salt scrubs of the past, often combined with fresh-picked flowers and herbs from the mountains that hug the Homestead.

WELCOME TO WASHINGTON, D.C.

THERE IS SIMPLY NO PLACE LIKE WASHINGTON, D.C. FOR sightseeing. You could visit year after year and still not see all the fascinating exhibits at the nearly 70 museums—most of which taxpayers will be happy to learn are free. As jaded as you may be about government or disagree over current politics, you still can't help getting goose bumps on a visit to the White House or the Capitol. Hundreds of years of history are meticulously preserved within these confines, which date back to December 1790, when

President George Washington signed an Act of Congress declaring that the federal government would reside in a district "not exceeding ten miles square...on the river Potomac". There is no disagreement between liberals and conservatives over the beauty of the city, which at its heart is dominated by a wide expanse of grass called the National Mall, lined with some of the best museums in the world and breathtaking memorials. The city's ethnic and international diversity also gives it a cosmopolitan feel that is best experienced in the various neighborhoods.

Beyond all the great sites, D.C. is emerging as a culinary destination. Washington, D.C., used to be the overlooked culinary stepsister to big shots like New York and Los Angeles, but those days are gone for good. In the last 10 years, visionaries such as José Andrés have made the city their home base, paving the way for a thriving restaurant scene that is today much more than Southern fare or seafood, both regional staples of the city's epicurean history. From Penn Quarter to Dupont Circle and beyond, we've compiled the best the city has to offer for intrepid travelers who seek the mystery of molecular

BEST ATTRACTIONS

WASHINGTON, D.C.'S BEST ATTRACTIONS

THE CAPITOL
Touring the majestic workplace of Congress and the Senate has been made vastly easier with the addition of the Capitol Visitor Center in 2008. If they are in session, you can also see the House and Senate while at work.

GEORGETOWN
The upscale neighborhood features a harbor on the river, high-end galleries, ritzy restaurants and fashionable shops. The beautiful red brick buildings give the area an old town, colonial feel not found in other parts of the city.

NATIONAL AIR AND SPACE MUSEUM
It is no wonder the museum is the most visited in the world. The vast museum has exhibits on the planets, the Wright Brothers, the Apollo moon program and famous aircraft.

gastronomy, the comfort of a burger, eclectic international fare or just the chance to imbibe with a frosty beverage after a long day of hitting the monuments and museums. These D.C. restaurants are becoming national treasures all on their own.

Great shopping has hardly been associated with the nation's capital. D.C.'s style has long been personified in pearls, boxy suits and proper pumps dyed to match. But like a lot of things in Washington, D.C. these days, the fashion scene is changing. With First Lady Michelle Obama leading the charge, it's safe to say the typical, straight-laced Washingtonians are making way for a stylish new crowd. Head to the U Street Corridor to uncover fabulous finds for both your wardrobe and your home. Of course, you'll still find enough preppy fashion if that suits your taste. In today's D.C., it's about making your own mark.

NATIONAL MALL

The Mall, a park that extends from Capitol Hill to the Potomac River and includes the Tidal Basin, is the heart and soul of the city. The long and wide grassy expanse is bordered by the Smithsonian Museums and includes a majority of the memorials in the city. The White House straddles the Mall and D.C.'s Downtown. The Mall is also the site of concerts on national holidays, as well as a great place to just have a picnic, toss a Frisbee or fly a kite. Don't miss taking a stroll from the West side of the Mall down to the Tidal Basin Park, a small body of water next to the Potomac River, where you can rent paddleboats, see the Jefferson Memorial reflected from the water or stroll along paths under Cherry Trees that were given to the United States by the Japanese. In the spring, the Cherry Blossom Festival is one of the major events in the city, attracting tourists from all over the world to see the beautiful white and pink blossoms.

WHAT TO SEE

ARTHUR M. SACKLER AND FREER GALLERY OF ART

1050 Independence Ave., S.W., National Mall, 202-633-1000; www.asia.si.edu

One half of a multi-level underground maze connected with the National Museum of African Art, the Sackler and Freer collections focus on Asian and Middle Eastern cultures, which includes everything from Egyptian sculptures to Japanese porcelain and Korean ceramics to Buddhist images and other artworks of the Himalayan region. Many of the pieces are small and intricate and easily overlooked. But if you are a patient devotee of jade, bronze, glassware and finely decorated objects of subtle variation, then a visit will require more than a quick and cursory afternoon.

Admission: free. Daily 10 a.m.-5:30 p.m.

BUREAU OF ENGRAVING AND PRINTING

14th and C streets, S.W., National Mall, 202-874-2330; www.moneyfactory.gov

It won't cost you a dime to see millions of dollars being printed—that is, unless you want to purchase some money in the gift shop. Free tickets are available on a first-come, first-serve basis during the week from March through August (from September through February, tickets are not required) for a 40-minute guided tour that shows you how money is made. Displays include a $100,000 note used by the Federal Reserve Bank, as well as a collection of counterfeit bills. Just be sure to arrive early as tickets go on sale at 8 a.m. and usually are gone by 9 a.m. (the facility is closed on weekends and holidays). You can also contact your representative to request a special tour. The gift shop includes items such as a two-dollar note, on sale here for $7.95.

Admission: free. Visitor Center: March, Monday-Friday 8:30 a.m.-3:30 p.m.; April-August, Monday-Friday 8:30 a.m.-7:30 p.m.

HIRSHHORN MUSEUM AND SCULPTURE GARDEN

Independence Avenue, S.W. and Seventh Street, S.W., National Mall, 202-633-1000; www.hirshhorn.si.edu

The circular edifice houses a permanent collection of modern art from the late 19th century to the end of the 20th century as well as rotating exhibits

that include the works of current artists. There isn't much in the way of middle ground in this modern art museum—visitors either love the pieces or hate them. The eclectic mix includes paintings, sculptures, photographs and mixed media artworks from noted artists such as Willem de Kooning and Alberto Giacometti. The adjacent outdoor sculpture garden is terraced into the ground to provide a contemplative space that feels open and un-crowded even on the busiest days.
Admission: free. Daily 10 a.m.-5:30p.m.

NATIONAL AIR AND SPACE MUSEUM

Independence Avenue, S.W. and Sixth Street, S.W., National Mall, 202-633-1000; www.nasm.si.edu

Walking into the grand entry hall, visitors are overwhelmed by the rockets reaching to the sky and famous aircraft suspended from cables above. You'll see the Apollo 11 Command Module, Sputnik 1, Charles Lindbergh's Ryan NYP "Spirit of St. Louis", and the Bell X-1, which Chuck Yeager used to break the sound barrier, as well as other historic air and spacecraft. It is no wonder the museum is the most visited in the world. The vast museum has exhibits on the planets, the Wright Brothers, the Apollo moon program (see the original space suits worn by Neil Armstrong and Buzz Aldrin on the Moon) and much more. See a movie in one of the two theaters (one being IMAX) or take a virtual trip into the sky in one of the robotic flight simulators. Just don't forget to touch a piece of moon rock in the entry hall before you go.
Admission: free. September-March, daily 10 a.m.-5:30 p.m.; April-August, daily 10 a.m.-7:30 p.m.

NATIONAL GALLERY OF ART

401 Constitution Ave., National Mall, 202-737-4215; www.nga.gov

Created in 1937, the National Gallery of Art is actually two museums in one. The West building, opened in 1941, exemplifies classic Greek and Roman influences, featuring a marble rotunda fronted by a colonnade. The permanent collection features paintings and sculptures spanning the 13th through 20th centuries, particularly the French Impressionist period and the Italian Renaissance, which includes the *Ginevra de' Benci* by Leonardo da Vinci. The angular East Building, designed by I.M. Pei, houses works by modern artists such as Matisse, Picasso, Jackson Pollock and Alexander Calder. The two buildings are connected via an underground concourse that receives natural light from a grand window, which looks out onto a curtain of water tumbling down from a fountain at street level. The Pavilion Café located here is a perfect spot for a quick lunch while enjoying the view of the cascade. The enclosed outdoor sculpture garden features 17 works including Roy Lichtenstein's colorful, perspective-changing *House 1* and Claes Oldenburg's *Typewriter Eraser, Scale X.*
Admission: free. Monday-Saturday 10 a.m.-5 p.m., Sunday 11 a.m.-6 p.m.

NATIONAL MUSEUM OF AFRICAN ART

950 Independence Ave., S.W., National Mall, 202-633-4600; www.nmafa.si.edu

The large and bold wooden masks and African carvings are a striking contrast to many of the exhibits within the Arthur M. Sackler and Freer Gallery of Art, which the museum is connected to underground. The highlight here is the Walt Disney-Tishman African Art Highlights Collection, which features more than 80 pieces, including masks, carved figures and crowns from the 525-piece

Tishman private collection. The Tishmans, husband and wife private collectors, acquired African art for twenty years from the mid- 1960's to the mid-1980s and then gave the collection—which represents over 20 countries within sub-Saharan Africa—to the Walt Disney Company. In 2005 the Walt Disney World Company donated the collection to the Smithsonian.

Admission: free. Daily 10 a.m.-5:30 p.m.

NATIONAL MUSEUM OF AMERICAN HISTORY

14th Street and Constitution Avenue, N.W., National Mall, 202-633-1000; www.americanhistory.si.edu

The museum completed an 85 million dollar renovation in 2006, adding a five-story sky-lit atrium, a new grand staircase and a new environmentally-controlled display for the Star Spangled Banner, the flag that flew over Fort McHenry and inspired Francis Scott Key to write the poem that became our National Anthem. You can also see an exhibit of inaugural dresses donated to the museum by the first ladies, including First Lady Michelle Obama's white Jason Wu-designed gown. And that's just the tip of the iceberg of all you can see at this American treasure. The museum, which opened in 1964, has collected over three million artifacts relating to American history, from food to photographs to coins to old computers. While emphasizing the often-staid subject of American history, this museum is full of fun exhibits, such as the Electricity Hall, which houses an Edison light bulb and early electrical appliances, and Power Machinery, which features all sorts of engines, including the Holloway 10-horsepower engine from 1819, the oldest surviving parts of an American-built stationary steam engine. The National Treasures of Popular Culture features Dorothy's Ruby Slippers from *The Wizard of Oz*, Kermit the Frog, Archie Bunker's Chair from *All in the Family* and Mohammad Ali's Boxing Gloves.

Admission: free. September-May, daily 10 a.m.-5:30 p.m.; June-August, daily 10 a.m.-7:30 p.m.

NATIONAL MUSEUM OF THE AMERICAN INDIAN

Independence Avenue and Fourth Street, S.W., National Mall, 202-633-1000; www.nmai.si.edu

The first museum devoted solely to Native Americans has a beautiful, golden sandstone exterior that resembles the windblown bluffs and canyon walls of the American Southwest. Inside, the 120-foot high Potomac Atrium faces east towards the rising sun. Permanent exhibits feature Native American artworks and artifacts and tell the story of Native Americans from three main perspectives—Our Lives, which reveals how people in Native American communities live today; Our Peoples, which shares how Native Americans have survived in the last 500 years and kept their culture alive; and Our Universes, which focuses on Native American philosophies and the spiritual relationship between man and the natural world. The Return to a Native Place exhibit includes ceremonial artifacts and objects of the Algonquian Peoples of the Chesapeake Bay area, what is now Washington, D.C., Maryland, Virginia and Delaware. The Mitsitam Café serves Native foods such as traditional fry bread.

Admission: free. Daily 10 a.m.-5:30 p.m.

NATIONAL MUSEUM OF NATURAL HISTORY

Tenth Street and Constitution Avenue, N.W., National Mall, 202-633-1000; www.mnh.si.edu

You could spend days examining skeletons, bugs, fossils, rocks, plants and more at this more than 100-year-old museum which houses a massive collection of natural science specimens and cultural artifacts. Check out the Tyrannosaurus Rex in the dinosaur hall; watch a tarantula feeding demonstration in the Insect Zoo, which includes live insects from around the world; and see how close you resemble your pre-historic relatives in the new David H. Koch Hall of Human Origins. If you're into gems, you'll love the Hall of Geology and Gems where you can peer into the 45.52 carat deep-blue Hope Diamond and the Star of Asia Sapphire, one of the largest sapphires in the world. If forensic science is more your thing, head to the Written in Bone exhibit, where you can play *CSI* while examining bones and other forensic evidence from the 17th century. The museum also houses extensive displays on life in the oceans.

Admission: free. September-March, daily 10 a.m.-5:30 p.m.; April-August, daily 10 a.m.-7:30 p.m.

RIPLEY CENTER

1100 Jefferson Drive, S.W., National Mall, 202-633-1000; www.si.edu/ripley

This very small, domed building which resembles a kiosk is often over-looked. It's actually the entrance to the underground International Gallery, which features regularly changing exhibits from the Smithsonian's Traveling Exhibition Service, such as the display of works by contemporary Argentinean artists. The center also houses the Discovery Theatre, a live show for children covering a variety of subjects relating to science, the arts and history. Past shows at Discovery Theatre have included Seasons of Light and Lions of Industry, Mothers of Invention.

Admission: free. Daily 10 a.m.-5:30 p.m.

SMITHSONIAN INSTITUTION BUILDING, THE CASTLE

1000 Jefferson Drive, S.W., National Mall, 202-633-1000; www.si.edu

Built in 1855, this distinctive red brick castle was the original Smithsonian Institution Building. Designed by architect James Renwick Jr., who also designed St. Patrick's Cathedral in New York City and the Smithsonian's Renwick Gallery in Washington, D.C., the red sandstone used to construct the building came from Maryland. The landmark building, popularly known as the Castle, now houses the administrative offices of the Smithsonian and functions as the Visitor's Center with videos and displays, including one which features objects representing all of the Smithsonian museums (there are 19) to give you an idea of the how vast the collection actually is. So this is a good place to begin sightseeing. Though you'll want to make time to tour the castle as well. A recent exhibit showcased pins from former Secretary of State Madeleine Albright's collection. There's also a marvelous 4.2 acre rooftop park and, in season, the magnificent Haupt Garden.

Admission: free. Daily 8:30 a.m.-5:30 p.m.

UNITED STATES HOLOCAUST MEMORIAL MUSEUM

100 Raoul Wallenberg Place, S.W., National Mall, 202-488-0400; www.ushmm.org

This searing museum tells the story of the Holocaust in three parts: Nazi Assault, Final Solution and Last Chapter. Self-guided tours allow you to view the more than 900 artifacts and watch the many video and film clips at your own pace in the permanent exhibit. The powerful films and video clips include eyewitness testimonies and historic footage. (The permanent exhibit is not recommended for children under the age of 11. A separate exhibit conveys the history of the Holocaust in manner more suitable to younger audiences.) The Children's Tile Wall is a permanent memorial created by thousands of children who were asked to record their impressions of the Holocaust on ceramic tiles. The Hall of Remembrance allows visitors to light memorial candles. The building itself also tells a story through several architectural allusions that set an emotional stage.

Admission: free. Daily 10 a.m.-5:20 p.m., until 6:30 April-May. No passes are required from September-February. Passes are required March-August for the permanent exhibition.

THE WHITE HOUSE
1600 Pennsylvania Ave., National Mall, 202-456-7041; www.whitehouse.gov

You can only see the White House by calling or writing your local congressman (request passes through a congressional representative up to six months in advance and no less than 30 days before your visit), and only a small portion of the building is accessible with most rooms roped off so you can only view the interiors from afar, but it's worth it for just a peak inside the President's House. The self-guided tour allows you to see the East Room, often used by the President for speeches; the Blue Room, known for its oval shape and views of the South Lawn; and the Red Room, a small room decorated in shades of red which functions as a reception room. The White House Visitor Center provides a great orientation prior to your tour. You can watch an informative video and see exhibits on the White House's architecture, furnishings, first families and social events. Next door to the White House you'll notice the Eisenhower Executive Office Building, also called the Old Executive Office Building. The grand and highly ornate architecture is of a French Second Empire style that some consider spectacular and others find garish. The six-story building has 900 exterior columns and took 17 years to construct. It has served many functions and is now used as offices for the White House Staff.

Admission: free (with passes from congressional representative). Tours: Tuesday-Thursday 7:30 a.m.-11 a.m., Friday 7:30 a.m.-noon, Saturday 7:30 a.m.-1 p.m. Visitor Center: daily 7:30 a.m.-4 p.m.

CAPITOL HILL AND NORTHEAST D.C.

Dominated by the Capitol, the neighborhood is a grid of street after street of historic row houses. The vibrant political area includes numerous shops and restaurants and the eclectic H Street, with a mix of trendy bars, tattoo parlors, theatres and take-out joints. It's the largest neighborhood in the city and home to numerous congressional staffers. As the home of the Congress, Senate and the Supreme Court, the talk never strays far from politics, and the community even has it's own monthly newspaper, the Hill Rag. On warm evenings in the spring through fall, the streets are filled with young and old alike, dining in outside cafes and restaurants or simply sitting on porch steps discussing the political climate. The Barracks Row Main Street (*Eighth St., S.E.*) is Capitol Hill's latest example of revitalization with even more shops and restaurants for D.C.'s urbane crowd.

HIGHLIGHT

WHAT IS THE SMITHSONIAN?

The Smithsonian is actually a collection of 19 museums, nine research centers and a zoo, eight of which are located on the National Mall. It's the world's largest museum complex and features everything from art to rockets and dinosaurs to precious books and documents. Each year, more than 30 million people visit the various museums and the zoo, including the African Art Museum, Air and Space Museum, American History Museum, Freer Gallery of Art, Natural History Museum, Portrait Gallery, Postal Museum and much more. Admission is free for all the museums and the zoo.

BASILICA OF THE NATIONAL SHRINE

400 Michigan Ave., N.E., Northeast, 202-526-8300; www.nationalshrine.com

The blue and gold dome of this Roman Catholic church— the largest in North America— can be seen from miles away. Free one-hour guided tours of the astounding art and architecture are available every day of the week. The Byzantine-Roman architecture is exemplified by thick stonewalls and high arches that do not include support from columns or internal steel framework. Sculptures of saints abound within the church, as well as numerous intricate mosaics and stained glass windows. The tour includes a visit to the church crypt, which is modeled after the Christian Catacombs.

Tours: Monday-Saturday 9 a.m., 10 a.m., 11 a.m., 1 p.m., 2 p.m., 3 p.m., Sunday 1:30 p.m., 2:30 p.m., 3:30 p.m.

FOLGER SHAKESPEARE LIBRARY

201 E. Capitol St., S.E., Capitol Hill, 202-544-4600; www.folger.edu

The library contains one of the world's largest collections of Shakespearean writings and materials, as well as a collection of other works written during the Renaissance. The Folger also hosts plays by the Bard, such as *Henry VIII* and *Hamlet*, and speakers come from all over to talk about the infamous Brit. Past lectures have included Stories at Sea: At the Bottom of Shakespeare's Ocean and Discovering Hamlet. Each year, the library celebrates Shakespeare's birthday in late April with all kinds of activities such as stories of 16th-century England, sonnet contests and arts and crafts.

Monday-Saturday 10 a.m.-5 p.m.

LIBRARY OF CONGRESS

101 Independence Ave., S.E., Capitol Hill, 202-707-5000; www.loc.gov

The largest library in the world is used for research by Congress and includes millions of books, manuscripts, films and recordings, as well as interesting exhibits on American history. Read over early drafts of the Declaration of Independence; see the first map to include America from 1507; view a historic collection of bibles, and much more. Other exhibits may examine such interesting topics as the role entertainers have played in politics. The Library houses the world's largest collection of films, legal materials, maps and sound recordings. The Thomas Jefferson Library is a reconstruction of the third president's library and holds 6,487 volumes. If you are looking for a particular book, the friendly librarians are there to help.

Admission: free. Monday-Saturday 8:30 a.m.-4:30 p.m. No prior reservation necessary.

NATIONAL ARBORETUM

3501 New York Ave., N.E., Northeast, 202-245-2726; www.usna.usda.gov

The 446-acre garden and agricultural research center, with its wide open green spaces and wooded trails, is great place to escape the throngs of tourists. The arboretum is at its best in the spring, when the cherry blossoms, dogwood trees, azaleas and beds of perennials are in full bloom. The site also includes a collection of bonsai trees, an herb garden and a mix of boxwoods. To make the most of your visit, picnic and head to the National Grove of State Trees, which includes all 50 state trees. The Capitol Column Collection is a series of freestanding Corinthian columns from the Capitol that were removed during a renovation in 1958. The columns are made more photogenic by being placed next to a reflecting pool.

Daily 8 a.m.-5 p.m.

NATIONAL POSTAL MUSEUM

2 Massachusetts Ave., N.E., Capitol Hill, 202-633-5555; www.postalmuseum.si.edu

You've got mail—the old-fashioned kind, that is. Learn about the history of mail services and postal delivery, and gain an appreciation of how it has binded the nation and played a role in our democracy. Avid philatelists love the rare collections of stamps. The Pony Express exhibit features maps and displays of the various routes, while the Art of Cards and Letters Gallery displays a collection of correspondences sent and received during wars. The exhibit also includes working models of innovative envelope making machines.

Admission: free. Daily 10 a.m.-5:30 p.m.

TAFT MEMORIAL

Constitution Avenue, between First Street, N.W. and New Jersey Avenue, N.W., Capitol Hill; www.aoc.gov

The bronze statue and a 100-foot-tall marble bell tower near the Capitol is a tribute to Senator Robert A. Taft, son of President Taft. The Senator, nicknamed Mr. Republican, had a long history of opposition—opposing U.S. involvement in WWII, the New Deal, the Nuremberg Trials and labor unions. The statue honors the prominent conservative spokesman and his contributions to the United States.

UNION STATION

50 Massachusetts Ave., N.E., Northeast, 202-289-1908; www.unionstationdc.com

A hub for rail travel, the grand Beaux-Arts building with 96-foot-high ceilings is a throwback to a time when riding by rail was elegant and sophisticated. After a massive restoration in the late 1980s, Union Station was transformed into an upscale mall with a variety of shops, restaurants, a movie theater and of course, a train station. It's one of the most popular sites in the city due its close proximity to the Capitol and because its a terminal for Amtrak, MARC and Virginia Railway Express lines, plus being a stop on the Metro subway system.

Mall: Monday–Saturday 10 a.m.-9 p.m., Sunday noon-6 p.m.

U.S. BOTANIC GARDEN AND NATIONAL GARDEN

100 Maryland Ave., S.W., Capitol Hill, 202-225-8333; www.usbg.gov

Even if it's cold outside, it's always hot in this beautiful Victorian-style greenhouse conservatory. More than 26,000 plants are on display in different ecological zones—a desert with cacti, a tropical rainforest within the 93-foot-high main dome, an orchid display and the newest permanent exhibit that showcases the plants and grasses of Hawaii. The building is adjoined by the small National Garden outside, which includes a rose garden and a butterfly garden, and Bartholdi Park—a splendid English style garden with seasonal flowers and paths leading to the grand Bartholdi Fountain in the center.

Admission: free. Daily 10 a.m.-5 p.m.

THE U.S. CAPITOL

100 Constitution Ave., N.E., Capitol Hill, 202-226-8000; www.visitthecapitol.gov

Touring the majestic workplace of Congress and the Senate has been made vastly easier with the addition of the Capitol Visitor Center in 2008. The underground, three-level complex is the starting point for all tours. Here you can learn all about the history of Congress and the Capitol. Touch a model of the dome; watch a film on Congress as well as live feeds of chamber proceedings when in session in the House and Senate theaters. You can also see exhibits on slavery, women's fight to win the right to vote and more. Tours of the Capitol itself include visits to the towering main Rotunda, the old representative's chamber with its quirky acoustics that allow you to hear even the faintest whisper anywhere in the chamber, and the National Statuary Hall, which features a statue donated from each state. If they are in session, you can also see the House and Senate while at work. For a real treat, contact one of your Senators and request passes to the Senate Dining Room for a chance to rub elbows with our elected representatives. Tickets are available online or by contacting a member of congress. It is also possible to pick up tickets on-site based upon availability.

Visitor center: Monday-Saturday 8:30 a.m.-4:30 p.m. Tours: Monday-Saturday 8:50 a.m.-3:20 p.m.

DOWNTOWN/CHINATOWN/PENN QUARTER

As D.C.'s business center, downtown Washington is home to office buildings, the Washington Convention Center, restaurants that focus on lunch, department stores and shopping malls, including The Shops at National Place and the Old Post Office Pavilion. The area is also home to the Verizon Center, Warner Theater and the National Theatre. Downtown includes Chinatown and a section along Pennsylvania Avenue north of the National Mall called Penn Quarter, which has been redeveloped to include new restaurants and several private museums. Spanning across the intersection of H and Seventh streets, the intricate and grand Friendship Archway showcases Chinatown. The mostly gold archway is decorated with 272 stylistic dragons from the Ming and Qing dynasties and is the largest arch of its kind in the world.

HIGHLIGHT

WHAT IS THERE TO SEE ON CAPITOL HILL?

To get a real local flavor of the historic Capitol Hill neighborhood, head to the 100-year-old Eastern Market (*225 Seventh St., S.E.*), Washington's oldest and continuously operated fresh food public market and a favorite of locals. After suffering from a fire in 2007, the eclectic local market re-opened in the summer of 2009 and is bigger and better than ever. D.C. inhabitants flock to this market for fresh produce, flowers and jewelry.

The indoor/outdoor market is not only a community hub, but a cultural must-see for visitors from all over. The indoor market is open during the week (Tuesday-Friday 7 a.m.-7 p.m.) while the outdoor market operates on weekends (Saturday 7 a.m.-6 p.m., Sunday 9 a.m.-5 p.m.). Merchants in the indoor market offer everything from fresh produce to seafood. A majority of the produce is grown locally, with much of it coming from the Eastern Shore in Maryland or from rural parts of Virginia. The outdoor market bustles with various vendors selling beautiful handmade arts and crafts. Be sure to visit Doris Little and check out her handmade dolls "Beeks Button Babies", which have been purchased by people from all over the world. Almost everything you find in the outdoor market is local. The venue boasts more than 20 food vendors and 100 arts and crafts vendors, which are constantly changing, so that you can always find something new. This is a good place to find a unique piece of jewelry or a nice gift to take home. Once you've had a chance to browse, head over to South Hall Market to sample delicious foods from around the world. And be sure to nab a delicious homemade donut from the donut robot (the fryer they're cooked in) at popular Migue's Magnificent Mini Donuts on Sundays at the Flea Market (*Seventh and C Streets, S.E.*) at Eastern Market. On weekends, you can also enjoy live music (*see website for calendar of events; www.easternmarket-dc.org*).

INTERNATIONAL SPY MUSEUM
800 F St., N.W., Penn Quarter, 202-393-7798; www.spymuseum.org

After an initial explosion of James Bond-style gadgets in the main exhibit hall, the rest of the exhibits might not live up. Nevertheless, there is certainly much to see here if you're curious about espionage or secretly wish you had become a spy. Opened in 2002, the museum contains the largest collection of espionage artifacts on public display in the world. The School for Spies area showcases over 200 gadgets, many from the Cold War era, including photographic equipment, listening devices and weapons. An exhibit on the history of spying covers the use of espionage as far back as Biblical times. There is also an exhibit on code breaking.

Admission: adults $18, seniors, military and intelligence $17, children 5-11 $15. Daily 10 a.m.-6 p.m.

NATIONAL ARCHIVES
700 Pennsylvania Ave., N.W., Penn Quarter, 202-357-5000; www.archives.gov/nae

You will feel proud to be an American while viewing the Constitution, the

Declaration of Independence and the Bill of Rights. Free, guided tours are offered on a first come, first served basis (or may be booked online for a convenience fee of $1.50). However, unless they are American history buffs, most people stick to the rotunda, which houses the three famous documents collectively called the Charters of Freedom. The tour adds historic documents such as Presidential Orders and Declarations of War. The rotunda can be a madhouse on weekends, making it difficult to view the documents. Go early on weekends or during the week.

Admission: free. Monday-Tuesday, Saturday, 9 a.m.-5 p.m., Wednesday-Friday, 9 a.m.-9 p.m. Rotunda: Mid-March-Labor Day, daily 10 a.m.-7 p.m.; Labor Day-mid-March, daily 10 a.m.-5:30 p.m.

NATIONAL LAW ENFORCEMENT OFFICERS MEMORIAL

400 Seventh St., N.W., Downtown 202-737-3400; www.nleomf.com

On two curved waist high, gray marble walls located in Judiciary Square, the names of nearly 19,000 United States police officers who have died in the line of duty since 1792 are inscribed. The walls are along pathways in a small three-acre tree-lined park. Sculptures of a lion protecting her cubs, symbolizing the protective nature of law enforcement, adorn the pathway entrances. This memorial is ever changing in that new names of fallen officers are added every spring, coinciding with National Police Week.

NATIONAL GEOGRAPHIC MUSEUM

1145 17th St., N.W., Downtown, 202-857-588; www.nationalgeographic.com

Dedicated to the ideals of The National Geographic Society, the museum showcases an ever-changing array of exhibits based upon the fieldwork and research of the world-renowned magazine. The museum housed a collection of the Terra Cotta Warriors from China's First Emperor in 2009 that drew over 280,000 visitors. Many of the displays relate to photography; however, a recent exhibit included 15 species of live geckos.

Admission: free, unless otherwise specified (prices for exhibits vary). Daily 9 a.m.-5 p.m.

NATIONAL MUSEUM OF CRIME AND PUNISHMENT

575 Seventh St., N.W., Downtown, 202-621-5550; www.crimemuseum.org

Visiting this museum is a bit like walking onto the sets of TV's *Law and Order*, *CSI* and *NYPD Blue*, with a bit of the *Sopranos* and *Bonnie and Clyde* thrown in as you learn about the history of crime in America. Visitors can test their shooting skills or safe-cracking dexterity, as well as drive in a high-speed police chase in one of the simulators. The interactive CSI Lab includes a morgue and DNA testing equipment displays. The full-scale model police station includes a booking room, a jail cell and a police line-up. One level of the museum functions as the filming studio for the television program *America's Most Wanted*.

Admission: adults $19.95, military, law enforcement and seniors $16.95, children 5-11 $14.95, children under 5 free. Discounted tickets available online. Daily 9 a.m -7 p.m.

NATIONAL MUSEUM OF WOMEN IN THE ARTS

1250 New York Ave., N.W., Penn Quarter, 202-783-5000; www.nmwa.org

Housed within an airy and exquisite space that was once a Masonic Lodge, the museum showcases over 3,000 works by women's artists from the 16th century to present day, mostly from the private collection of founders Wilhelmina Cole Holladay and Wallace F. Holladay. Artists include Camille Claudel, Georgia O'Keeffe and Frida Kahlo. Temporary exhibits highlight the work of women artisans from around the globe. The art is displayed on four floors and a mezzanine within this Renaissance Revival style building. The museum also includes a performance hall, a charming café and the grand hall, which may be rented for weddings and other receptions.

Admission: adults $10, seniors and students $8, children under 18 free. Monday-Saturday 10 a.m.-5 p.m., Sunday noon-5 p.m. Tours: reservations required four weeks in advance.

NATIONAL PORTRAIT GALLERY

800 F St., N.W., Penn Quarter, 202-633-8300; www.npg.si.edu

See the portraits of American presidents, sports champions and legendary performers. The Struggle for Justice displays over 40 paintings, buttons, sculptures and photographs of Americans who were integral in the civil rights and women's rights movements, such as Martin Luther King, Jr., Frederick Douglass and Betty Friedan. The "American Origins, 1600-1900" exhibit is housed within 17 galleries and covers the time from the colonization of America to the Civil War and includes a collection of daguerreotypes, the first commercially successful type of photography. The "Jo Davidson: Biographer in Bronze" exhibition includes 14 sculptures of renowned Americans such as FDR and Gertrude Stein. In the "Americans Now" exhibit, you can view portraits of famous Americans from today such as Toni Morrison, President Obama, Martha Stewart and Willie Nelson among others. There's a museum shop as well as a Courtyard Café where you can enjoy fresh seasonal cuisine under a canopied courtyard.

Admission: free. Daily 11:30 a.m.-7 p.m.

NEWSEUM

555 Pennsylvania Ave., N.W., Penn Quarter, 888-639-7386; www.newseum.org

Billed as Washington's most interactive museum, the privately run Newseum immerses visitors in the news. The Great Hall of News is a 90-foot-high atrium with features an Electronic Window on the World media screen with constant updates and uncensored news and headlines. With more than 250,000 square feet of exhibition space, Newseum takes visitors behind the scenes to experience why and how news is created. The News Corporation News History Gallery features a display of historic newspaper and magazine stories. The NBC News Interactive Newsroom allows you to enact the role of a journalist or step in front of the camera to play a TV reporter. There are also galleries on the 911 Terrorist Attacks, the Berlin Wall, the First Amendment to the Constitution, Pulitzer Prize winning photographs and a memorial to journalists who died while covering the news.

Admission: adults $19.95, seniors, military and students $17.95, children 7-18 $12.95, children 6 and under free. Daily 9 a.m.-5 p.m.

THE OLD POST OFFICE PAVILION AND CLOCK TOWER

1100 Pennsylvania Ave., N.W., Penn Quarter, 202-289-4225; www.oldpostofficedc.com

The 315-foot-tall clock tower offers a panoramic view of the city and houses the official United States Bells of Congress, which ring Thursday evenings between 7 and 9 p.m. The bells were a gift from the Ditchley Foundation of Great Britain in 1976 as a symbol of friendship between the United States and England. The Romanesque building was built in 1899 and is the former head-quarters of the United States Postal Service. Visit the pavilion, which today is the home to shops, restaurants, musical performances and more. You can also pick up segway tours (*www.segsinthecity.com*), trolley tours (*www.royaltrolleys.com*) and bike tours (*www.bikeandroll.com*) here.

Admission: free. Pavilion: Labor Day-mid-March, Monday-Saturday 10 a.m.-7 p.m., Sunday noon-6 p.m.; mid-March-Labor Day, Monday-Saturday 10 a.m.-8 p.m., Sunday noon-7 p.m. Clock Tower Tours: Labor Day-Memorial Day, Monday-Saturday 9 a.m.-5 p.m., Sunday 10 a.m.-6 p.m.; Memorial Day-Labor Day, Monday-Saturday 9 a.m.-8 p.m., Sunday 10 p.m.-6 p.m.

RENWICK GALLERY

1661 Pennsylvania Ave., N.W., Downtown, 202-633-7970; www.americanart.si.edu

Designed by James Renwick Jr., who also designed the Smithsonian Castle and St. Patrick's Cathedral in New York City, the gallery is part of the American Art Museum and features an eclectic collection of crafts and decorative arts from the 19th and 20th centuries. The unique pieces are fashioned from anything and everything—clay, wood, metal, paper, glass and textiles. *Game Fish* by Larry Fuente is a sculpture of a swordfish fashioned from badminton birdies, poker chips, dice and a wide assortment of other game pieces. The George Ault exhibit, on display from March 11, 2011 through September 5, 2011, will feature the striking surrealistic paintings by the artist, who lived from 1891 to 1948.

Admission: free. Daily 10 a.m.-5:30 p.m.

UNITED STATES NAVY MEMORIAL

701 Pennsylvania Ave., N.W., Penn Quarter, 202-737-2300; www.navymemorial.org

Built in the style of an amphitheater, a 100-foot diameter granite map of the world forms the patio of a plaza, which is ringed by fountains and a wall featuring 26 bronze relief plaques depicting historic and important scenes of U.S. Naval history. The stone courtyard also includes a ship's mast and a statue of The Lone Sailor, who solemnly stands waiting with his duffle bag at his side. The adjacent Naval Heritage Center includes a small theater, interactive exhibits and a gift shop.

Heritage Center: daily 9:30 a.m.-5 p.m.

U STREET CORRIDOR AND ADAMS MORGAN

These two neighborhoods are both culturally diverse and have fantastic ethnic restaurants, bars and nightlife. The neighborhoods intersect at the conjunction of Florida Avenue, U Street and 18th Street. Adams Morgan is the more estab-lished of the two and is considered by many to be the hub for nightlife in the city. U Street rivaled Harlem in the early twentieth century as a center for African American culture and music. The neighborhood fell into decline in the late 1960s. However, an influx of new condominiums in the 90s revitalized the area and it now rivals Adams Morgan as the top spot in D.C. for nightlife. At the corner of U Street and Vermont Avenue, don't miss the African American Civil War Memorial, a poignant sculpture that honors the over 200,000 African-American soldiers and sailors who fought for the Union. The ethnic diversity of these two neighborhoods comes alive with a variety of cuisines from the numerous Ethiopian restaurants to Belgian ale bars and Asian and South American restaurants. Check out Madam's Organ Blues Bar and Soul Food Restaurant (*2461 18th St., N.W.*), named after the neighborhood, where you can listen to live blues and jazz every night while enjoying soul food such as fried chicken, collard greens, fried okra, barbecue ribs and fried catfish. You'll also find art galleries and funky shops in this neighborhood.

AFRICAN AMERICAN CIVIL WAR MEMORIAL & MUSEUM
1200 U St. N.W., Washington D.C., U Street, 202-667-2667; www.afroamcivilwar.org

This sculpture pays tribute to the more than 200,000 African-American soldiers who fought in the Civil War. Permanent exhibits at the museum give visitors insight into African Americans' struggle for freedom, including the documentary Fight for Freedom, replicas of the uniforms that soldiers wore, and the Glorious March to Liberty which features photographs and documents from the soldiers and sailors telling of their experiences. There is also a registry for visitors to find information on their ancestors.

Admission: free (donations accepted). Monday-Friday 10 a.m.-5 p.m., Saturday 10 a.m.-2 p.m.

DUPONT CIRCLE/UPPER NORTHWEST

The art-centric area includes over a dozen small galleries, plus bookshops, cafes, bars, yoga studios, funky shops and boutique hotels. Residents strive to keep the neighborhood unique and open-minded, lending a vibrant air to the area. The neighborhood that prides itself on its gay history and activism is the hangout for much of the LGBT population of Washington. A large number of Foreign Embassies are located amongst the old brownstone townhouses and mansions in a stretch labeled Embassy Row. The embassies host frequent events, adding an international flare to the neighborhood.

DUPONT CIRCLE FOUNTAIN
DuPont Circle NW., Dupont Circle

The fountain is located within a large traffic circle and gives the area its name. It's a memorial to Samuel Francis Du Pont, a rear admiral for the Union during the Civil War. The circle also includes parkland and numerous benches, and is always bristling with activity.

HILLWOOD ESTATE MUSEUM AND GARDENS
4155 Linnean Ave., N.W., Upper Northwest, 202-686-5807; www.hillwoodmuseum.org

Most Washingtonians don't know about this hidden gem. Tucked into the woods next to Rock Creek Park, the Hillwood Estate is the home of heiress and celebrated businesswoman Marjorie Merriweather Post (1887-1973). Originally called Arbremont, Post quickly changed the name to Hillwood Estate, the name of her former property on Long Island. During her lifetime, Post collected French and Russian porcelain, a wide variety antiques, 18th century French tapestries and a beautiful bejeweled pink Catherine the Great

Fabergé Egg. She bequeathed her home to become a museum so that everyone would have the opportunity to enjoy her unique collection. The mansion is surrounded by 25 acres with woods and manicured landscaping, the highlight of which is the Japanese Garden designed by Shogo J. Myaida.

Admission: adults $12, seniors $10, students $7, children $5. Tuesday-Saturday 10 a.m.-5 p.m. Reservations are required.

THE KREEGER MUSEUM

2401 Foxhall Road, N.W., Upper Northwest, 202-337-3050; www.kreegermuseum.org

This private museum is D.C.'s hidden gem. The former home of collectors David and Carmen Kreeger, the museum is remarkable in both its collection and setting. Monet, van Gogh, Picasso, Renoir, Kandinsky, Cezanne and other greats from the modern period are on display inside the futuristic post-modern house with its gleaming white travertine walls and perfectly proportioned rooms. Every room is a cube of approximately 22' by 22' by 22', a proportional system used by the ancient Greeks in buildings such as the Parthenon. Needless to say, the home was designed specifically to house artworks; more than 14,000 square feet of the 24,000-square-foot mansion was set aside as gallery space. The home also includes a great hall where concerts and lectures are held.

Admission: adults $10, seniors and students $7. Tuesday-Friday 10:30 a.m.-1:30 p.m., Saturday 10 a.m.-4 p.m. Closed August.

NATIONAL ZOO

3001 Connecticut Ave., N.W., Upper Northwest, 202-633-4800; www.nationalzoo.si.edu

Though it has gotten some bad press over the last couple of years due to mismanagement, everybody loves the zoo. With an entrance at the top of a hill on Connecticut Avenue and another entrance (and parking area) down in the valley in Rock Creek Park, there's no avoiding getting a good workout walking up and down the hill to see all of the habitats and exhibits (and the zoo has it's own Metro stop, making it easy to get to without driving). See the world famous Giant Pandas, walk through an aviary, experience a rainforest, enjoy the antics of otters and watch the apes swing from trees and climb overhead on suspended ropes. As part of the Smithsonian, the zoo prides itself on educating the public on the plight and importance of animals from all over the world. The well-rounded complex includes invertebrates, reptiles and amphibians, hippos, elephants, farm animals, lemurs and other small mammals as well as lions and tigers and bears.

Admission: free. April–October daily 10 a.m. to 6 p.m.; November–March daily 10 a.m. to 4:30 p.m.

THE PHILLIPS COLLECTION

1600 21st St., N.W., Dupont Circle, 202-387-2151; www.phillipscollection.org

After the death of his father and his brother, Duncan Phillips, an author and art collector, created this modern art museum as a way to memorialize his loved ones and also find a will to live through his passion of art. With nearly 3,000 impressive works of art, The Phillips Collection features masterpieces such as Renoir's *Luncheon of the Boating Party* and Matisse's *Studio, Quai St. Michel*. In addition to paintings by Renoir, van Gogh, Mark Rothko and Georgia O'Keeffe, the gallery houses a small but significant array of photographs, including works by O'Keeffe's husband Alfred Steigletz.

Admission: Tuesday-Friday, donations accepted; Saturday-Sunday, adults $10, seniors and students $8. Tuesday-Wednesday, Friday-Saturday 10 a.m.-5 p.m., Thursday 10 a.m.-8:30 p.m., Sunday 11 a.m.-6 p.m.

ROCK CREEK PARK

3545 Williamsburg Lane, N.W., Upper Northwest, 202-895-6070; www.nps.gov.rocr

Meandering through the center of the city, the 1,754-acre park (more than twice the size of Central Park in New York City) is a true respite from city life. Down in a forested valley, following the rocky and aptly named creek, there are no signs of urban commotion. The park includes a nature center, planetarium, horseback riding center, amphitheatre, golf course, tennis stadium and over 25 miles of trails. On weekends, a large section of the park's main vehicle thoroughfare is closed to traffic.

Daily dawn-dusk.

THE TEXTILE MUSEUM

2320 S St., N.W., Upper Northwest, 202-667-0441; www.textilemuseum.org

This small gallery includes a learning center where visitors are encouraged to learn about various forms of textiles through touch. Past exhibits have included The "Art of Living" exhibit, which recently showcased textiles from around the world. Temporary exhibits range from the use of textiles in fashion to tapestries to rare silks and unique fabrics from Asia, the Middle East and South America. Fashion lovers, crafts people and anyone who has ever put a needle to thread will have a great time. Even if you think this isn't your scene, it is still interesting to see the various fabrics and discover the difference in texture between each one.

Admission: $5 suggested donation. Tuesday-Saturday 10 a.m.-5 p.m., Sunday 1-5 p.m.

WASHINGTON NATIONAL CATHEDRAL (CHURCH OF SAINT PETER AND SAINT PAUL)

Massachusetts and Wisconsin avenues, N.W., Upper Northwest, 202-537-6200; www.nationalcathedral.org

As magnificent as any cathedral in Great Britain, the Gothic style structure features flying buttresses, vaulted ceilings, and a 300-foot-high tower. A kaleidoscope of colors illuminates the church from the light that streams through the more than 200 stained glass windows, including the futuristic Space Window, which honors the Apollo Moon Landing. As the sixth largest cathedral in the world, it took over 83 years to construct. In fact, the structure was only recently completed in 1990. No matter what your religion, it's hard not to be awestruck when entering this Episcopal house of worship that Congress designated "the national house of prayer for all people". The State funerals of Presidents McKinley, Theodore Roosevelt, Harding, Wilson, Taft, Coolidge, FDR, Kennedy, Hoover, Eisenhower, Truman, Johnson, Nixon, Reagan and Ford have all been held at the Cathedral.

Admission: requested donation $5. Monday-Friday 10 a.m.-5:30 p.m., Saturday 10 a.m.-4:30 p.m., Sunday 8 a.m.-5 p.m.

GEORGETOWN AND FOGGY BOTTOM

Once an instrumental port of commerce, this upscale neighborhood still features a harbor on the river and thriving commerce, only these days it's more in the form of high-end galleries, ritzy restaurants and fashionable shops. The beautiful red brick buildings give the area an old town, colonial feel not found in other parts of the city. It's also home to the prestigious Georgetown University and the starting point of the 184.5-mile long C&O Canal and towpath. The C&O Canal was once a major route for coal transportation, but is now a park complete with a towpath that makes a great walk along the water. The entrance to the canal from the Potomac River is controlled by a gate, called the Watergate. The infamous office and condominium complex, 'The Watergate', nearby is named after this starting point for the canal. In addition to the waterfront and the main street of shops and restaurants (M Street), the area extends to the northwest along Wisconsin Avenue and MacArthur Boulevard. Take some time to stroll around the Georgetown campus (37th and O streets). The famous Catholic and Jesuit University founded in 1789 by John Carroll features beautiful gothic stone buildings along with some of the newer Georgian brick buildings. The Foggy Bottom neighborhood is situated between Georgetown and the National Mall and is home to George Washington University.

CORCORAN GALLERY
1801 35th St., N.W., Foggy Bottom, 202-333-3034; www.corcoran.org

Founded in 1869, this so-called gallery is a rather extensive museum and one of the oldest art museums in the country. It's also the largest privately operated museum in the city. The collection consists mostly of 18th through 20th century American Art, yet also includes many works by European Masters, such as Picasso, Monet and Degas. Within the classic Beaux-Arts style building, an ever-changing series of high caliber, and somewhat controversial exhibits, including the infamous photographs by Robert Mapplethorpe, attracts art lovers from around the nation. The gallery is affiliated with Corcoran College of Art and Design.

Admission: adults $10, seniors and students $8, children 12 and under free. Free programs Saturday. Wednesday, Friday-Sunday 10 a.m.-5 p.m., Thursday 10 a.m.-9 p.m.

DUMBARTON OAKS
1703 32nd St., N.W., Georgetown, 202-339-6410; www.doaks.org

This private museum at the highest point in Georgetown houses an exhibit of pieces from the Byzantine Empire, including jewelry and mosaics, and gold, silver and bronze vessels utilized during the Eucharist. There's also a collection of Pre-Columbian artworks featuring stone sculptures and polished jades. But it is most famous for its beautiful 10-acre formal garden, which includes fountains, rose and herb gardens, flowering trees and expansive lawns. Expect to spend at least two hours marveling at the well-maintained works of Mother Nature while winding along the many pathways within the garden.

Admission: Museum: adults $8, seniors, students and children $5; Museum: free. Museum: Tuesday-Sunday 2-5 p.m. Gardens: Tuesday-Sunday 2-6 p.m.

HIGHLIGHT

WHAT ARE D.C.'S BEST WATER-BASED TOURS?

CAPITAL RIVER CRUISES

Washington Harbour, Georgetown, 301-460-7447; www.capitolrivercruises.com

This popular cruise company runs 45-minute tours on the Potomac from the harbor to see the sights of the city reflected in the water. There's also a bar where you can purchase cocktails and snacks. Purchase tickets online to receive a discount.

Admission: adults $14, children 3-12 $7; online tickets: adults $11, children 3-12 $6. April-October, daily noon-9 p.m.

JACK'S BOATHOUSE

Washington Harbour, 3500 K St. N.W., Georgetown, 202-337-9642; www.jacksboathouse.com

If you'd like to paddle down the Potomac, head to Jack's, where you can rent canoes and kayaks. Guided sunset tours on the river to see the memorials and monuments from the water's edge are also offered. See the website for pricing.

Tuesday-Sunday 10 a.m.-8 p.m., Monday noon-8 p.m.

WASHINGTON HARBOUR

30th-31st streets and K St., N.W. Georgetown

The large plaza features several restaurants with outdoor seating and a boardwalk offering views of the Potomac River, Kennedy Center and Key Bridge. The harbour has been a popular hangout for years. Located at the bottom of Georgetown, it makes for a great waterfront dining spot. With restaurants such as Nick's Riverside Grille (*3050 K St., N.W., Georgetown, 202-342-3535; www.nicksriversidegrille.com*) and Farmers & Fishers (*3000 K St., N.W., Georgetown, 202-298-0003; www.farmersandfishers.com*), the Washington Harbour is an experience to be had.

WHERE TO STAY

CAPITOL HILL/NORTHEAST D.C.

★★★THE HOTEL GEORGE

15 E St. N.W., Capitol Hill, 202-347-4200; www.hotelgeorge.com

George Washington takes center stage at this Kimpton hotel on Capitol Hill. The lobby nods to the area's white-washed federal buildings, but mod furniture and Andy Warhol-style artwork—stylized images of the Washington Monument and one dollar bill, naturally—lend a hip vibe. Guest rooms are clean and bright, with white bed linens and beige walls; color is introduced in the rich cherry furniture, a striped cobalt chair and ottoman, and fuchsia throw. The 32-inch flat-screen TV is smartly hidden with the dresser, safe and minibar in a built-in armoire. Marble bathrooms have large vanity mirrors and built-in speakers that can pipe through TV audio. Take advantage of the complimentary wine bar in the lobby weekdays from 5 to 6 p.m., and be sure to dine in the

HIGHLIGHT

WHAT'S THE BEST WAY TO SEE D.C. IN ONE DAY?

The best way to get around the monuments, memorials and museums is via the Tourmobile, the official franchise of the National Park Service. The hop-on/ hop-off bus allows you to take as much time as you want at each site and then board one of the regularly running buses at your leisure. Each bus includes a live narrator who serves up interesting facts and stories about the city. Spend the morning riding the bus and getting off at the most famous memorials—Lincoln, Washington, Jefferson, FDR, Vietnam and Korean and Arlington Cemetery.

Grab lunch at the café beneath the wings of the National Gallery of Art. Then, depending on your interests, tour the art galleries, the National Museum of Natural History, the National Air and Space Museum, National Museum of American History or any of the other Smithsonian Museums. Be sure to stop in at the National Archives to see the Constitution, Bill of Rights and the Declaration of Independence. Tourmobile tickets may be purchased at Arlington National Cemetery, Union Station and at a kiosk on the National Mall (*1401 Jefferson Drive, N.W., 202-554-5100; www.tourmobile.com, $13-27*).

For dinner, take the Metro to Foggy Bottom and walk about a mile (or grab a taxi) to one of Georgetown's numerous restaurants. After dinner, take a stroll along the boardwalk at Washington Harbour and cap off an evening with a show at Blues Alley (*1073 Wisconsin Ave., N.W., 202-337-4141; www.bluesalley.com*).

WHAT'S THE BEST WAY TO SEE D.C. IN THREE DAYS?

Begin your second day in D.C. at the National Zoo (*3001 Connecticut Ave. N.W., 202-366-4800; www.nationalzoo.si.edu*). This will take most of the morning. The zoo is easily accessed via the Metro's Red Line. Return to the Red Line and go south for one stop to Dupont Circle for lunch at Kramerbooks and Afterwards Café (*1517 Connecticut Ave., N.W., 202-387-1400; www.kramers. com*). The independently owned bookstore attracts bibliophiles from around the world. From Dupont Circle, hail a cab or take one of several buses to Washington National Cathedral (*3101 Wisconsin Ave., N.W., 202-537-6200; www.nationalcathedral.org*) to see the gothic architecture and gorgeous stained glass windows that make this one of the most beautiful cathedrals in the nation. Stroll along Embassy Row, just steps from National Cathedral, to take in some of the 144 embassies located in Washington. In the evening, venture to U Street for Ethiopian cuisine at Dukem Restaurant (*1114 U St., N.W., 202-667-8735; www.dukemrestaurant.com*). The city abounds with Ethiopian restaurants and Dukem is one of the best. If Ethiopian food isn't your thing, head to Ben's Chili Bowl (*1213 U St., N.W., 202-667-0909; www.benschilibowl.com*), a Washington legend known for its chili. Then it's time to be a night owl, and stay up late at Bohemian Caverns (*2001 11th St., N.W., 202-299-0800; www.bohemiancaverns. com*), the historical jazz club.

For your final day, book a late morning tour of the Capitol. Grab lunch at Good Stuff Eatery (*303 Pennsylvania Ave., S.E., 202-543-8222;*

HIGHLIGHT *continued*

www.goodstuffeatery.com), a burger joint run by former *Top Chef* contestant Spike Mendelsohn. Walk lunch off with a visit to the U.S. Botanic Garden (*100 Maryland Ave., S.W., 202-225-8333; www.usbg.gov*) and Bartholdi Park and Fountain (*Independence and Washington avenues*) in Capitol Hill. Continue north past the Capitol to Union Station (*50 Massachusetts Ave., N.E., 202-289-1908; www.unionstationdc.com*) for a bit of shopping and souvenir hunting. For dinner, head over to Bistro Bis (*15 E St. N.W., 202-661-2700; www.bistrobis.com*) in The Hotel George, which is about a block and a half away, for delicious French cuisine, a glass of wine and a possible celebrity sighting.

hotel's adjacent French restaurant, Bistro Bis. Other good nearby dining bets are Johnny's Half Shell and Charlie Palmer Steak.

139 rooms. Restaurant, bar. Business center. Fitness center. Pets accepted. $151-250

RECOMMENDED

THE LIAISON CAPITOL HILL, AN AFFINIA HOTEL

415 New Jersey Ave. N.W., Capitol Hill, 202-638-1616; www.affinia.com

Washington's only Affinia branch, this Capitol Hill hotel balances modern sophistication with a good dose of comfort. The running theme here is "transformative ideals," seen in artist Randy Slack's six-foot portraits of world leaders adorning the lobby, and it is carried through to the restaurant and bar. Guest rooms don't pack much punch in terms of décor—you'll find standard-issue blue carpets and beige wallpaper—but a mohair-and-wood headboard adds some interest. Beds are dressed in Egyptian-cotton sheets, a down comforter and a soft throw; you have a choice of six pillows ranging from Swedish memory foam to sound pillows, which include headphones to plug in your iPod. The bathrooms have separate vanity and sink areas, black granite countertops, sleek fixtures and textured walls. One of the main draws of the Liaison is the restaurant, Art and Soul, helmed by Oprah's former personal chef, Art Smith. Enjoy southern-inspired regional cuisine and have a cocktail afterward at the adjacent ArtBar. The hotel also has a chic rooftop pool, where a daily complimentary yoga class takes place, and a well-equipped gym. For extra perks, set up a My Affinia guest profile before you stay and you can get customized amenities like a guitar, cupcakes or a fitness kit delivered to your room, many of which are free.

343 rooms. Restaurant, bar. Business center. Fitness center. Pool. Pets accepted. $151-250

DOWNTOWN/CHINATOWN/PENN QUARTER

★★★DONOVAN HOUSE

1155 14th St. N.W., Downtown, 202-737-1200; www.thompsonhotels.com

Hip travelers in search of modern luxury flock to this Thompson Hotels outpost on D.C.'s Thomas Circle. The lobby features stark-white walls and cool mod furniture—Eames-style chairs; plush, low benches; and Lucite bubble seats suspended from the ceiling. The rooms are equally sleek with clean, light walls that contrast the dark woods, heavy draperies, and purple, maroon and

WHICH D.C. HOTELS HAVE THE BEST VIEWS?

Mandarin Oriental, Washington D.C.:
Located near the Potomac Tidal Basin, this luxe hotel overlooks the Jefferson Memorial.

The Hay Adams:
One of D.C.s' most revered landmarks offers unmatched views of the White House and St. John's Church, the "Church of the Presidents".

beige accents. Guest rooms also feature large windows, 400-thread-count SFERRA linens, iPod docking stations, C.O. Bigelow bath products, mini-bars stocked with snacks from Dean & Deluca, and spiral-shaped "cocoon" showers that blend seamlessly with the rest of the room. Relax beside the rooftop pool and dine at one of Washington's best Asian-fusion restaurants, Zentan, helmed by Hong Kong-born chef Susur Lee, who's also an alum from *Top Chef Masters*. If you feel like venturing from the hotel, Donovan House is within easy walking distance of the traditional tourist destinations, such as the White House and National Mall, as well as more off-the-beaten-path stops, like hip U Street and Logan Circle.

193 rooms. Restaurant, bar. Business center. Fitness center. Pool. $151-250

★★★THE FAIRMONT WASHINGTON, D.C.
2401 M St. N.W., Downtown, 202-429-2400, 866-540-4505; www.fairmont.com

A 10-minute walk from both K Street power players and Georgetown shops, this West End hotel is a good fit for business and leisure travelers alike. Built in 1985, the 10-story hotel shed much of its outdated décor during a massive renovation in 2000. The light-swathed lobby, which feels more greenhouse than check-in, overlooks a sunny courtyard garden that features a marble fountain and umbrella-covered tables—the perfect spot for early-evening cocktails. Inside, tasteful guest rooms are decorated in warm earth tones and florals, and some have courtyard-facing balconies that bring the outdoors in. There are also 30 one- and two-bedroom suites, including the eco-swank Lexis Hybrid Living Suite, which features a kitchen, three bathrooms, and spacious sitting and dining areas, plus environmentally-friendly touches like white bamboo floors, recycled-glass-and-cement countertops, and reclaimed birch trees for decoration. Health nuts can make use of the newly upgraded fitness center ($15 a day), complete with TV-mounted cardio equipment, Technogym weight machines, access to personal trainers and group-exercise classes, and ball courts; use of the 50-foot lap pool is free. If exercising alfresco is more your bag, take a jog in D.C.'s Rock Creek Park—access to a paved trail is just three blocks away.

415 rooms. Restaurant, bar. Business center. Fitness center. Pool. Pets accepted. $151-250

★★★GRAND HYATT WASHINGTON

1000 H St. N.W., Penn Quarter, 202-582-1234;
www.grandwashington.hyatt.com

This Penn Quarter hotel feels mammoth inside, thanks to a glass-ceilinged 12-story atrium lobby. With more than 40,000 square feet of function space and 32 state-of-the-art meeting rooms, the place caters to the business set. Simple yet welcoming guest rooms are decorated in earth-tone solids and include large work desks with Herman Miller chairs, 42-inch flat-panel TVs, and iPod-ready alarm clocks. Worker bees can put in a full day, burn off steam in the health club and meet clients for cocktails at Cure Bar & Bistro—all without leaving the premises. But touring Washington's sites and sounds is easy, too: The Grand Hyatt's center-city location means that you're just a short walk from the National Archives, the National Portrait Gallery, the Old Post Office Pavilion and the White House. Theater lovers might want to check out performances at nearby Sidney Harman Hall, Woolly Mammoth Theatre, National Theatre or Warner Theatre. Or if obscure foreign flicks are more your speed, indie art-house E Street Cinema is only three blocks away.

888 rooms. Restaurant, bar. Business center. Fitness center. Pool. $151-250

★★★★THE HAY-ADAMS

1 Lafayette Square, Downtown, 800-853-6807;
www.hayadams.com

Once part of the White House grounds, Lafayette Square contains a number of important, historic buildings, including the White House, the Old Executive Office Building, the Department of the Treasury, the Decatur House and, of course, The Hay-Adams—named for John Milton Hay, Abraham Lincoln's private assistant and secretary of state, and Henry Brooks Adams, author and descendent of Presidents John Adams and John Quincy Adams. This hotel has hosted a number of the nation's presidents, along with many other important figures, such as Amelia Earhart and Sinclair Lewis. You will even feel like royalty upon stepping through the doors into this Italian Renaissance-style building. The guest rooms have a regal vibe with ornamental ceilings, fireplaces, European linens, marble bathrooms and some have balconies with views of the White House or Lafayette Square Park. One of the best spots in the hotel is the luxurious rooftop

---

WHAT ARE D.C.'s MOST LUXURIOUS HOTELS?

Four Seasons Hotel Washington, D.C.: Dignitaries, royalty and celebrities who regularly travel to the nation's capital know that this is one of the most luxurious and spacious hotels in the city. Inside the contemporary brick façade, you'll find stunning artwork, high-end design and views of Georgetown.

The Jefferson, Washington D.C.: A major renovation made this boutique hotel one of the city's best, with stylish interiors, an outstanding restaurant and generous amenities.

The Ritz-Carlton, Washington D.C.: This West End hotel is Ritz-Carlton at its finest: sophisticated, traditional décor; attentive service; comfortable rooms; and a great location.

The St. Regis Washington, D.C.: This historic property in the heart of Washington, D.C., offers luxury and modern-day comfort in a regal setting.

WHAT ARE GEORGETOWN'S BEST HOTELS?

Four Seasons Hotel Washington, D.C.:
The contemporary brick hotel on the edge of Georgetown offers some of the largest rooms in the city and views of Georgetown, Rock Creek Park or the C&O Canal.

The Ritz-Carlton Georgetown, Washington, D.C.:
This upscale Ritz-Carlton property sits on a quiet side street in the heart of Georgetown between the C&O Canal and the Potomac River. It occupies the turn-of-the-century Georgetown Incinerator building and has retained much of the industrial feel.

terrace. Its panoramic views of the city, monuments and Capitol make it an excellent choice for private parties and events.

144 rooms. Restaurant, bar. Business center. Fitness center. $351 and up

★★★HOTEL MONACO WASHINGTON D.C.

700 F St. N.W., Penn Quarter, 202-628-7177; www.monaco-dc.com

If you feel like you're entering a museum at this stylish Kimpton hotel, there's a reason: Its Greek-revival architecture resembles the National Portrait Gallery and Smithsonian American Art Museum, which are right across the street. Hotel Monaco occupies the former U.S. General Post Office building, a one-block-square, 19th-century construct that's been dubbed a National Historic Landmark. The hotel has retained some of the historic elements, including 20-foot ceilings, curved marble stairways and a side-entrance carriageway that leads to the hotel's restaurant and bar, Poste Moderne Brasserie. If you go, be sure to try one of the tasty seasonal cocktails and order the truffle fries, which are only $5 during happy hour (Monday-Friday, 4-7 p.m.). Inside the hotel, there's an elegant yet playful lobby and a marble fireplace. Rooms are awash in patterns and colors, which manage to tie together without feeling too busy. In the small but adequate white-tiled bathrooms, you'll find Aveda products. Call ahead before you arrive and request a goldfish in your room. A staffer will hand-pick a fish from the hotel's massive tank and put a finned companion in your room—for free.

183 rooms. Restaurant, bar. Business center. Fitness center. Pets accepted. $151-250

★★★JW MARRIOTT WASHINGTON, D.C.

1331 Pennsylvania Ave. N.W., Downtown, 202-393-2000, 800-393-2503; www.marriott.com

Just blocks from the White House, Department of Justice and FBI headquarters, this downtown hotel is truly at the power center of the city. From the outside, the 15-story brown-brick building is rather nondescript, but inside you'll encounter a cheery palette of reds and golds and a recently renovated two-story atrium. The standard brown-and-gold guest rooms could use a punch of color, but Marriott's comfy Revive bed—an extra-thick mattress with 300-count sheets, a down duvet and fluffy pillows—is the real draw. An easy dining option is the hotel's 1331 Bar & Lounge, but for a uniquely Washington experience, head to Old Ebbitt Grill a few blocks away. The clubby, Victorian-accented dining room has been a favorite of presidents, lobbyists and Washington power players for more than 150 years.

772 rooms. Restaurant, bar. Business center. Fitness center. Pool. $351 and up

★★★THE MADISON

1177 15th St. N.W., Downtown, 202-862-1600; www.loewshotels.com

An upscale hotel in Washington's business center, The Madison is conveniently located for business travelers and tourists alike—it lies within walking distance to the White House, Dupont Circle and a number of restaurants and bars. The ritzy, timeless lobby décor with high ceilings, chandeliers and velvet furniture creates an air of luxury where guests may relax and read or socialize. Rooms are decorated in earthy tones and dark wood furniture, with framed photographs depicting classic Washington scenes. The professional, friendly staff assists with any questions or needs, including planning tours or outings around the city. Palette Restaurant & Bar offers breakfast, lunch and dinner in an elegant, modern setting and PostScript is the perfect place to meet for a drink.

366 rooms. Restaurant, bar. Business center. Fitness center. Spa. Pets accepted. $151-250

★★★★THE RITZ-CARLTON, WASHINGTON D.C.

1150 22nd St. N.W., Downtown, 202-835-1588; www.ritzcarlton.com

This West End hotel is Ritz-Carlton at its finest: sophisticated, traditional décor; attentive service; comfortable rooms; and a great location. The wood-paneled lobby is decorated with muted canvas paintings, fresh flowers, elegant chandeliers and parlor-style furniture. Walk through the Lobby Bar and Café—you'll find a cocktail hour here daily from 5 to 9 p.m. with wines by the glass and cheese galore—to get to Westend Bistro, an Eric Ripert restaurant serving delicious modern-American fare. Rooms, which are large by Washington standards, feature down duvets, Frette linens and fully stocked minibars with champagne, wine, liquor, sodas and sweet and savory snacks. In the bathrooms, you'll find separate showers and soaking tubs; gilded over-the-sink mirrors; marble countertops and tile; and Ritz-Carlton or Bulgari bath products. You

WHAT ARE THE BEST HOTELS NEAR THE NATIONAL MALL?

The Hay Adams:
Once part of the White House grounds, Lafayette Square contains a number of important, historic buildings, including the White House, the Old Executive Office Building, the Department of the Treasury, the Decatur House and, of course, The Hay-Adams.

Mandarin Oriental, Washington D.C.:
A view of the water is rather unusual for a hotel in this town, but the Mandarin Oriental boasts an impressive one of the Tidal Basin, the southwest waterfront and the Jefferson Memorial.

can work on your fitness ($15 a day) at the adjacent Sports Club/L.A., which has an indoor pool and full basketball court, among other perks. Or if you want to do some sightseeing, you are within walking distance of Georgetown and downtown D.C., and can hop on the Metro's Orange Line via the Foggy Bottom stop, which offers direct transportation to the White House, Smithsonian museums on the National Mall and the U.S. Capitol Building.

300 rooms. Restaurant, bar. Business center. Fitness center. Pool. Spa. Pets accepted. $351 and up

★★★SOFITEL WASHINGTON D.C.

Lafayette Square, 806 15th St. N.W., Downtown, 202-730-8800; www.sofitel.com

Next door to the White House, this hotel occupies a historic building, with modern and Art Deco-style interior décor. The hotel radiates urban chic, stylish ambience without snobbery and a soothing overall atmosphere. Its French restaurant, iCi Urban Bistro lures anyone with an appetite for world-class French dishes and homemade desserts made from fresh, local ingredients. If you have a sweet tooth, try the mini-crème fraîche panna cotta with mixed berries. Rooms are decorated in warm hues and contain a range of modern paintings; marble bathrooms have glass-enclosed showers and separate tubs. The Smithsonian, downtown D.C. and Chinatown are all nearby, but if you want something different, ask the exceedingly helpful and pleasant staff to offer suggestions for outings.

237 rooms. Restaurant, bar. Business center. Fitness center. Pets accepted. $251-350

★★★★THE ST. REGIS WASHINGTON, D.C.

923 16th St. N.W., Downtown, 202-638-2626; www.stregis.com

This historic property in the heart of Washington, D.C., has hosted most of our nation's presidents as well as an assortment of royalty and prime ministers. President Calvin Coolidge cut the grand-opening ceremony ribbon in 1926, and since then the hotel has been renovated with modern amenities and furniture while retaining its original Palladian windows and Italian Renaissance chandeliers. The tasteful, sophisticated atmosphere appeals to business travelers and couples, but families are welcome—it's quite normal to find well-behaved children lounging in the lobby, reading or browsing the Web on their laptops. You won't need

HIGHLIGHT

WHAT ARE D.C.'S BEST BOUTIQUE HOTELS?

DONOVAN HOUSE
Hip travelers in search of modern luxury flock to this Thompson Hotels outpost on D.C.'s Thomas Circle. From the sleek lobby to the mod rooms and the sexy Asian-fusion restaurant run by *Top Chef Master* alum Susur Lee, you're guaranteed a good stay.

HOTEL MONACO
Hotel Monaco occupies the former U.S. General Post Office building, a one-block-square, 19th-century construct whose Greek-revival architecture resembles the National Portrait Gallery and Smithsonian American Art Museum, which are right across the street. Rooms are awash in patterns and colors.

THE HOTEL GEORGE
George Washington takes center stage at this Kimpton hotel on Capitol Hill. The lobby nods to the area's white-washed federal buildings, but contemporary furniture and Andy Warhol-style artwork lend a hip vibe. Guest rooms are clean and bright, and there's a complimentary wine bar in the lobby on weekdays from 5 to 6 p.m.

THE JEFFERSON, WASHINGTON D.C.
With only 99 rooms, this luxurious hotel has an intimate scale that allows the polished staff to lavish guests with attention. Rooms are freshly renovated and have an elegant French deco flair.

to worry about a thing while you're here; the signature St. Regis butlers will do everything from unpack and pack your belongings to make dinner and tour reservations. Rooms have contemporary touches, such as the supremely comfortable signature St. Regis beds, writing desks and Bose sound systems.
182 rooms. Restaurant, bar. Business center. Fitness center. $351 and up

★★★THE WESTIN WASHINGTON, D.C. CITY CENTER
1400 M St. N.W., Downtown, 202-429-1700; www.starwoodhotels.com
A mere five blocks from the convention center and close to two Metro stations, this hotel often hosts many business travelers. Nearby bars, nightclubs and restaurants appeal to those interested in checking out the trendy side of D.C. Those attempting to maintain their workout schedules will adore this establishment, with its 24-hour fitness facility, complimentary use of a jogging stroller for parents and nearby tennis courts. Rooms feature modern décor,

muted tones, oversized desks and ergonomic chairs alongside Heavenly beds and Heavenly showers and baths. Even pets get the all-star treatment with Heavenly dog beds upon request.

406 rooms. Restaurant, bar. Business center. Fitness center. Pets accepted. $151-250

★★★WILLARD INTERCONTINENTAL
1401 Pennsylvania Ave. N.W., Penn Quarter, 202-628-9100;
www.washington.intercontinental.com

Martin Luther King Jr., wrote his "I Have a Dream" speech while staying at the Willard InterContinental in the days before his march on Washington. Many other famous people have found inspiration, or at least a luxurious pillow on which to rest their heads for a night, in this hotel, including Mark Twain, Walt Whitman and Charles Dickens. And throughout the years, many foreign dignitaries and celebrities have stayed here as well. The elegant lobby has regal décor in red and gold tones, classic furniture, high ceilings and marble columns. Suites have standout features such as dual entrances, parlors with dining tables, elegant custom-made furniture, two bathrooms and many have views of Pennsylvania Avenue.

335 rooms. Restaurant, bar. Business center. Fitness center. Spa. Pets accepted. $351 and up

RECOMMENDED

CAPITAL HILTON
1001 16th St. N.W., Downtown, 202-393-1000; www.hilton.com

This Hilton is just a stone's throw from the White House. The Neoclassical-style hotel was built in 1943 and is listed on the National Register of Historic Places. From the outside, it looks a bit dated, but inside you'll find a regal lobby with soaring ceilings, ornate carpets, marble-accented mahogany columns and crystal chandeliers. The newly updated guest rooms feature rich blue carpeting with gold fleurs-de-lis, cherry furniture and accents, and a plush headboard with built-in reading lights. Photographs of Washington scenes adorn the walls, and beds are dressed in Hilton Serenity Collection bedding. In the bathrooms, you'll find a long granite vanity with plenty of storage and counter space. If a workout is on your itinerary, you're in luck: The hotel is attached to the Capital City Club & Spa, a top-of-the-line gym that you can use for $15 a day. The health club offers cardio and weight equipment plus classes, such as spinning, cardio-boxing and yoga.

544 rooms. Restaurant, bar. Business center. Fitness center. Spa. Pets accepted. $61-150

THE HENLEY PARK HOTEL
926 Massachusetts Ave. N.W., Downtown, 202-638-5200; www.henleypark.com

A quaint garden leads up to the elegant entrance of The Henley Park Hotel, just off Massachusetts Avenue, where you're greeted with gargoyles perched on the façade and lovely stained-glass windows. Inside, the English-style decor and antique furniture evoke a storybook ambience. It'll make you want to have the formal afternoon tea service in the Wilkes Room. Although the rooms also echo an Old World feel, they have every modern convenience, including complimentary WiFi and in-room spa services. The Blue Bar Cocktail Lounge attracts guests with live piano and signature cocktails, such as the Gingered Tequila Sunrise; though if you're looking for a meal, Coeur de Lion is a

HIGHLIGHT

WHICH D.C. HOTELS ARE THE MOST HISTORIC?

THE ST. REGIS WASHINGTON, D.C

This property in the heart of Washington, D.C., has hosted most of our nation's presidents as well as an assortment of royalty and prime ministers. President Calvin Coolidge cut the grand-opening ceremony ribbon in 1926.

THE HAY ADAMS

Named for John Milton Hay, Abraham Lincoln's private assistant and secretary of state, and Henry Brooks Adams, author and descendent of Presidents John Adams and John Quincy Adams, this hotel has hosted a number of the nation's presidents, along with many other important figures, such as Amelia Earhart and Sinclair Lewis.

THE HENLEY PARK HOTEL

This hotel has been a classic in downtown Washington, D.C. since 1918. It was once an apartment building where many senators, congressmen and other high-society Washingtonians lived.

THE MAYFLOWER RENAISSANCE

Walking through the grand lobby of The Mayflower is like stepping into the 1920s. The hotel, right near Dupont Circle and the White House, hosted every U.S. presidential inaugural ball from Calvin Coolidge through Ronald Reagan.

THE JEFFERSON, WASHINGTON, D.C.

Built in 1923 as the Jefferson Apartment, this property transformed into a hotel in 1955. The décor and art throughout the hotel echo the taste of Thomas Jefferson—most of the furniture consists of custom-built replicas of pieces from Monticello, Jefferson's home.

renowned D.C. restaurant serving contemporary American cuisine. If want to do some sightseeing, this historic hotel is near the convention center, Capitol Hill, Chinatown and the Smithsonian.

96 rooms. Restaurant, bar. Business center. Fitness center. $61-150

HOTEL ROUGE

1315 16th St. NW, Downtown, 202-232-8000; www.rougehotel.com

Hotel Rouge emits an urban atmosphere that lures a cool crowd to its Bar Rouge at happy hour. The lobby's sleek, chic décor is sophisticated, with rich reds, dark wood and modern, stylish furniture, and the daily complimentary wine and beer happy hour allows guests to get the evening started before heading out on the town. Like all Kimpton hotels, the Rouge is an eco-friendly and pet-friendly property, and it offers free in-room yoga programs and signature spa therapies, including organic massage treatments. Rooms follow the hotel's style and have enormous mirrors, large beds and animal print robes. Just a short walk from many local sites, this vibrant hotel appeals to hip, adult travelers looking to add some spice to their vacation or business trip.

137 rooms. Restaurant, bar. Business center. Fitness center. Pets accepted. $251-350

THE MAYFLOWER RENAISSANCE
1127 Connecticut Ave. N.W., Downtown, 202-347-3000; www.mariott.com

Walking through the grand lobby of The Mayflower is like stepping into the 1920s, as the building's high, gold-accented ceilings, chandeliers and marble floors evoke a more glamorous era. The hotel, right near Dupont Circle and the White House, hosted every U.S. presidential inaugural ball from Calvin Coolidge through Ronald Reagan. The swanky Town and Country Bar and Lounge regularly reels in D.C.'s nightlife with entertainment and its signature martinis. Recently renovated, the hotel's 650 guest rooms have classic décor and muted tones, pillow-top mattresses and marble bathrooms.

650 rooms. Restaurant, bar. Business center. Fitness center. $251-350

W WASHINGTON D.C.
515 15th St. N.W., Downtown, 202-661-2400; www.starwoodhotels.com

From the outside, the W Washington has the classic, historic look you would expect from a place just steps from the White House. But inside, visitors are treated to a glammed-up lobby with whitewashed walls, checkerboard floors, chic chandeliers and retro-mod black, red and cream furniture. Rooms have the same classic-modern feel, while the bathrooms have stall-style showers and vanity mirrors that reflect the glow from recessed and pendant lighting. If you want someone else to pamper you, visit the onsite Bliss spa for a blissage massage or a triple oxygen treatment, its signature facial. With a rooftop bar with a great view of the city's monuments and chef Jean-Georges Vongerichten's excellent J&G Steakhouse, the W will take care of most of your needs, and you won't even have to leave the premises.

317 rooms. Restaurant, bar. Business center. Fitness center. Spa. Pets accepted. $251-350

DUPONT CIRCLE/UPPER NORTHWEST

★★★★THE FAIRFAX AT EMBASSY ROW
2100 Massachusetts Ave. N.W., Dupont Circle, 202-293-2100; www.starwoodhotels.com

The country-club set would feel at home in this classy 1920s-era hotel. Guests are greeted with an eight-story, red-brick exterior trimmed with white molding and anchored by a well-manicured garden. Inside, a wood-paneled lobby leads to the Fairfax Lounge, the hotel bar and Jockey Club, a dining room with old-guard French service where you can order such classics as Dover sole and lobster Thermidor. Both spaces continue the country-club-chic look, with paintings of hunting and sailing scenes, vaulted tray ceilings, dark woods and touches of plaid. Guest rooms receive a classic English-countryside treatment and feature two-poster wood headboards, floral drapes, papered walls and settees. Pillow-top beds are covered in 300-thread-count Fili D'oro linens and a colorful floral throw. In the bathroom, you'll find Frette robes and slippers, marble floors and countertops and Gilchrist & Soames amenities. Some rooms have lovely views of the mansions along Embassy Row, but you should get out and explore the area for yourself. Head west from the hotel to reach wooded Rock Creek Park and Georgetown, or go east to Dupont and Logan circles. The Dupont Circle stop on the Red Line is just two blocks away, so it's easy to get just about anywhere in the city.

259 rooms. Restaurant, bar. Business center. Fitness center. Pets accepted. $251-350

★★★HILTON WASHINGTON EMBASSY ROW

2015 Massachusetts Ave. N.W., Dupont Circle, 202-265-1600; www.hilton.com

This Hilton outpost—one of three within city limits—is a natural choice for diplomats and international visitors, since it neighbors the embassies of Portugal, Indonesia, Morocco and India, and employs an international staff versed in dozens of languages. Set between quiet Q Street and busy Massachusetts Avenue, the hotel literally straddles D.C.'s residential and political identities. Its simple concrete façade and red-brick driveway blend in with the neighborhood's aesthetics, but inside the place takes European cues. White ceilings and floors in the lobby are set off by rich, dark-wood accents. Modest guest rooms repeat the light-and-dark décor; they're outfitted with down comforters and pillows, 250-thread-count sheets and Crabtree & Evelyn's La Source bath amenities. A rooftop pool with food and drink service provides a place to kick back, or you can work up a sweat in the 24-hour fitness room. Just be sure to take full advantage of the hotel's best feature: its location. The hotel is close to some of Washington's best restaurants, art galleries, museums and nightlife spots in the Dupont Circle and Adams Morgan neighborhoods.

231 rooms. Restaurant. Business center. Fitness center. Pool. Pets accepted. $251-350

★★★HOTEL PALOMAR WASHINGTON D.C.

2121 P St. N.W., Dupont Circle, 202-448-1800; www.hotelpalomar-dc.com

You can see the "Art in Motion" theme of this upscale Kimpton hotel in almost everything, from the artwork-studded lobby to the "Sculpting Room"—a.k.a. fitness center—right down to the staff members, who are called "artists." The dimly-lit guest corridors feature funky striped wallpaper, and the rooms are wild with animal prints, including faux-lynx-fur throw blankets, leopard bathrobes and taupe rugs with textured giraffe spots. The beds—which come with down duvets, Frette linens and tall leather headboards—are the center-pieces here. The small bathrooms are a mix of modern and dated—a voguish square sink sits near a cramped motel-style tub/shower combo—but they are stocked with Aveda products. The 40-foot outdoor pool is one of the prettiest features of the hotel, with a brick privacy wall that includes mirrored archways; a curtain-covered cabana with pillows and cushions that invite lounging. The hotel's restaurant and bar, Urbana, is a solid dining option, but don't overlook the plentiful restaurants in nearby Dupont Circle.

335 rooms. Restaurant, bar. Business center. Fitness center. Pool. Pets accepted. $251-350

★★★★THE JEFFERSON, WASHINGTON, D.C.

1200 16th St. N.W., Dupont Circle, 202-448-2300; www.jeffersondc.com

Built in 1923 as the Jefferson Apartment, this property transformed into a hotel in 1955 and to this day it retains its original mixture of European and American décor. The hotel underwent a major renovation before reopening in 2009, when the lobby was updated and an arched skylight dating back to the 1920s was unveiled. The décor and art throughout the hotel echo the taste of Thomas Jefferson—most of the furniture consists of custom-built replicas of pieces from Monticello, Jefferson's home. The lounge, Quill, serves herbal-infused alcohols—try the signature Pisco Rabano—and an extensive wine list inspired by Jefferson's travels and favorites. In Plume, the hotel's fine dining restaurant, you can dine on fresh regional cuisine inspired by the gardens of Jefferson's home and gaze at the hand-painted mural of the south vineyard of Monticello on the walls. Framed maps throughout the hotel depict areas where the third president traveled to and which he was fond of, and some rooms have framed quotes from the leader. The hotel staff are incredibly knowledgeable and passionate about Jefferson's life and the history of the hotel; they'll happy share many fascinating stories if you ask. Rooms have skylights or city views, Italian marble bathrooms, antique-style furniture custom built to work with modern technology and accents that nod to Jefferson's life, such as a throw detailed with subtle green drawings of Monticello. A personal butler greets every guest and will assist with any needs.

99 rooms. Restaurant, bar. Business center. Fitness center. Spa. $351 and up

★★★OMNI SHOREHAM HOTEL

2500 Calvert St. N.W., Upper Northwest, 202-234-0700; www.omnihotels.com

Located on 11 wooded acres overlooking D.C.'s Rock Creek Park, the Omni Shoreham Hotel has been in operation since 1930. Part of the National Trust for Historic Preservation's Historic Hotels of America, the Omni has played host to presidents, dignitaries, visiting celebrities and even ghosts, if you believe local lore. The property has retained the grandiose feel of its time period, with manicured gardens, high vaulted ceilings, ornate columns and archways, sweeping tapestries and crystal chandeliers. Guest rooms are equally stately yet a bit more accessible—you'll find simpler, cleaner colors with serene floral flourishes. Rooms range from about 200 square feet to more than 1,700 and have marble bathrooms, robes, iPod alarm clocks and desks; larger suites have balconies and separate living areas. With the Woodley Park Metro Stop (Red Line) just a block away, you have easy access to both the city's residential and downtown neighborhoods. The National Zoo and Washington National Cathedral are also nearby.

836 rooms. Restaurant, bar. Business center. Fitness center. Pool. Pets accepted. $151-250

★★★WASHINGTON MARRIOTT WARDMAN PARK

2660 Woodley Road N.W., Upper Northwest, 202-328-2000; www.marriott.com

Finding a hotel in Washington, D.C. set on acres of land seems unlikely, especially one in a convenient location. But the Washington Marriott Wardman Park lies on 16 lovely garden acres right next to Woodley Park, within an easy walk of the Metro, the National Zoo and the National Cathedral. It isn't in the center of downtown, which is a plus for families who want to be a bit removed from the commotion but want spacious rooms and an outdoor pool with a sundeck. Rock Creek Park is steps away—there's a beautiful path through the woods for jogging, walking or bicycling and taking in the green side of D.C.

Foodies will salivate over the numerous excellent restaurants nearby, including Lebanese Taverna, Petits Plats and Ardeo. Catch a movie at the Uptown in Cleveland Park, a one-screen, old-time theater with a balcony; it's a moviegoing experience you won't forget.

1,335 rooms. Restaurant, bar. Business center. Fitness center. Pool. Pets accepted. $351 and up

RECOMMENDED

THE DUPONT HOTEL

1500 New Hampshire Ave. NW., Dupont Circle, 202-483-6000; www.doylecollection.com

Dupont Circle bustles constantly with locals and visitors roaming the streets, shopping, eating at the numerous restaurants, admiring the city's beautiful architecture, sipping a drink in a trendy bar or relaxing and reading a newspaper in the park. This neighborhood offers a never-ending assortment of attractions and a paradise for people-watching. The Dupont Hotel stands strong in the midst of this tree-lined neighborhood, an elegant hotel with modern décor and French ambience. Ask for one of the Level Nine rooms, which have floor-to-ceiling windows, hardwood floors, glass balconies and top-of-the-line amenities, such as Kiehl amenities, Sferra bathrobes and an iPad with customized apps to use for the duration of your stay. All rooms feature contemporary, comfortable furniture, 300 thread-count bed linens, heated tiles in the bathroom and iPod docking stations. Café Dupont's menu is inspired by the neighborhood markets, where chefs shop for ingredients to whip up the organic, French cuisine.

327 rooms. Restaurant, bar. Business center. Fitness center. $151-250

THE TABARD INN

1739 N St. NW., Dupont Circle, 202-785-1277; www.tabardinn.com

On a quiet street just off Dupont Circle, The Tabard Inn invites passers-by to duck in and explore the historic property or enjoy a cocktail in the cozy lounge, decorated with antique furniture. Depending on the night, you could catch a local jazz musician performing there. The winter draws crowds eager to huddle by the fireplace, whereas the patio beckons people during the warmer months. This is the quintessential boutique hotel—originally three rowhouses built in the late 19th century, each slowly merged to become The Tabard Inn. The rooms were individually designed to emanate the historic character of the hotel; all of them lack televisions (although they do have a few to loan out) and some share bathrooms. Make reservations for brunch, lunch or dinner at the hotel's Restaurant, a not-to-be-missed upscale establishment featuring tasty contemporary American cuisine made from local, seasonal ingredients.

40 rooms. Restaurant, bar. Complimentary breakfast. Pets accepted. $151-250

WASHINGTON HILTON

1919 Connecticut Ave. NW., Dupont Circle, 202-483-3000; www.hilton.com

This Dupont Circle hotel just completed a top-to-bottom, $150 million renovation—everything from the lobby to guest rooms to the elevator bank got a face-lift. The place looks much more modern, with a consistent color scheme and design throughout the building. The warm brown, gold and cream rooms have tall, plush headboards, 250-thread-count sheets, Hilton Serenity beds, glass table lamps and a lime-colored throw. In the bathrooms, you'll find space-saving pocket doors, granite countertops, dark-wood cabinets and Crabtree & Evelyn products. The 110,000-square-foot conference center includes the 30,000 square-foot Columbia Hall, the newest addition to the meeting space. It features nine meeting rooms fitted with ergonomic chairs, whiteboards, recessed projection screens and credenzas. Also new is an outdoor courtyard and event space, which features fire pits, sitting areas, a garden, and fountain; there's also an outdoor pool and state-of-the-art fitness center. Getting around D.C. from the hotel is easy: You're just four blocks from the Dupont Circle Metro station on the Red Line, which takes you directly to destinations such as Union Station and the National Zoo. And in the Dupont Circle neighborhood, there are dozens of shops, restaurants and bars to suit a range of tastes.

1,070 rooms. Restaurant, bar. Business center

FOGGY BOTTOM

★★★PARK HYATT WASHINGTON D.C.

1201 24th St. N.W., Foggy Bottom, 800-633-7313; www.parkhyattwashington.com

The Park Hyatt Washington D.C. is known for its great staff, as the service at this hotel is personal and consistent, catering to guests' every need. Tony Chi designed the interior using contemporary décor and a subtle, sophisticated American spirit theme by including pieces of American folk art in the rooms and a glass sculpture etched with images of cherry blossoms in the lobby. The elegant, modern ambience mixes well with the inviting feeling that fills this property, ensuring return visits. Spacious rooms with warm limed oak, gray limestone and black walnut offer soothing escapes from the city and have aromatic bath amenities made exclusively for the hotel by Parisian artisan perfumer Blaise Mautin. The Blue Duck Tavern, one of D.C.'s most highly regarded restaurants, serves modern American cuisine and the Tea Cellar steeps teas from all over the world, from $8 to $300 per pot.

216 rooms. Restaurant, bar. Business center. Fitness center. Pool. Spa. Pets accepted. $251-350

★★★THE WESTIN GRAND, WASHINGTON, D.C.

2350 M St. N.W., Foggy Bottom, 202-429-0100; www.starwoodhotels.com

A luxurious spot with an international ambience, The Westin Grand is a posh hotel with flair—natural wood and clean lines along with Art Deco-style carpeting merge to create the modern atmosphere in this property. The running concierge leads three- and five-mile runs through the city each morning (on Wednesdays, the General Manager leads the run), encouraging you to exercise, breathe fresh air and view some of the sights—part of the Westin's goal to help enhance its guests' mind, body and spirit. The outdoor pool offers another opportunity to be outside—but this time relaxing rather than running—and to enjoy the beautiful, tranquil deck area. For a more quiet respite, bring a book or magazine to the European-style courtyard. The nice-sized rooms are a big perk, and the hotel's signature Heavenly shower and bed both live up to the hype.

267 rooms. Restaurant, bar. Business center. Fitness center. Pool. Pets accepted. $151-250

GEORGETOWN

★★★★★FOUR SEASONS HOTEL WASHINGTON, D.C.

2800 Pennsylvania Ave. N.W., Georgetown, 202-342-0444; www.fourseasons.com

Dignitaries, royalty and celebrities who regularly travel to the nation's capital know that this is one of the most luxurious and spacious hotels in the city, especially since its $40 million renovation in 2009 by designer Pierre-Yves Rochon, who created an oasis of the lobby, library and grand staircase using an art and garden theme. Upon entering the contemporary brick façade on the edge of Georgetown, you are immersed in marble, stunning artwork from the hotel's 2,000-piece collection and a lobby area with comfortable furniture, books and seasonal plants. The rooms are some of the largest in the city, with lavender, mauve or sage color schemes; contemporary furniture; limestone or marble bathrooms; and views of Georgetown, Rock Creek Park, or the C&O Canal. Premier suites offer separate bedrooms and sitting rooms for entertainment or meetings. The 12,500-square-foot spa and fitness club features new exercise equipment, a saltwater pool, a whirlpool, a sauna, fitness classes, a complimentary juice bar, indoor and outdoor sitting areas and more. The Four Seasons strikes a perfect balance between comfort and high-end design with this one-of-a-kind resort within D.C.

222 rooms. Restaurant, bar. Business center. Fitness center. Pool. Spa. Pets accepted. $351 and up

★★★THE GEORGETOWN INN

1310 Wisconsin Ave., Georgetown, 202-333-8900, 888-587-2388; www.georgetowninn.com

Located along a main artery in D.C.'s upscale shopping corridor, this 40-year-old inn is just steps from dozens of local boutiques. The hotel keeps up with its affluent surroundings with its classic European design—dramatic tapestries, muted paisley wallpaper, rich wood floors, antique-style furniture—and rooms with a similarly regal feel. Guest rooms are outfitted with pillow-top mattresses, soft duvets, robes and more. The hotel has an onsite restaurant, the Daily Grill, which is open for breakfast, lunch and dinner, but adventurous diners might be better off exploring some of Georgetown's other options, such as chef Michel Richard's French dining room, Citronelle—one of the best restaurants in the city. If you want to check out some of the other neighborhoods and attractions D.C. has to offer, it's a bit of a hike to the nearest Metro stop (Foggy Bottom on the Orange and Blue lines), but the Circulator bus picks up a block from the hotel at Wisconsin Avenue and O Street. It makes stops near the White House, National Mall and Union Station.

96 rooms. Restaurant, bar. Business center. Fitness center. $151-250

★★★LATHAM HOTEL

3000 M St. N.W., Georgetown, 800-583-7591; www.thelatham.com

For many travelers, convenience and location hover somewhere at the top of the list of hotel requirements. The Latham Hotel scores high in these categories. Just off the main drag in the center of Georgetown, it features affordable, clean rooms suited for all types. Foodies will love that Michel Richard's excellent Citronelle restaurant is attached to the hotel and caters business functions. Even better: The restaurant does room service. Standard rooms are decorated in muted tones and have all the basics: comfortable beds and linens, eco-friendly amenities and some have views of Georgetown or the quaint courtyard. If you are here for pleasure, head up to the small rooftop pool, a rare attraction for this area. It has plenty of lounge chairs for sunbathing.

133 rooms. Restaurant. Business center. Fitness center. Pool. $151-250

★★★★THE RITZ-CARLTON GEORGETOWN, WASHINGTON, D.C.

3100 South St. N.W., Georgetown, 202-912-4100; www.ritzcarlton.com

This upscale Ritz-Carlton property sits on a quiet side street in the heart of Georgetown between the C&O Canal and the Potomac River. It occupies the turn-of-the-century Georgetown Incinerator building and has retained much of the industrial feel, including a red-brick façade, black ironwork and a 130-foot smokestack. Inside, the place is all about modern comfort. The spacious lobby boasts exposed-brick walls, large windows with dramatic draperies and a wood-burning fireplace; you can gorge on the complimentary s'mores here each night from 6:30 to 7 p.m. Guest rooms have beds covered in down duvets, feather pillows and 400-thread-count Frette linens. Floor-to-ceiling windows, some of which have views of the Potomac River, are softened with cheerful yellow curtains. You can admire the view at sunrise while donning one of the provided plush robes. The spa and fitness center are good places to blow off steam, but serious runners should venture out of the hotel and jog along the waterfront. You can do a five-mile loop on the Rock Creek Trail going from the hotel, around the Tidal Basin and back.

86 rooms. Restaurant, bar. Business center. Fitness center. Spa. Pets accepted. $351 and up

NATIONAL MALL

★★★L'ENFANT PLAZA HOTEL

480 L'Enfant Plaza S.W., National Mall, 202-484-1000; www.lenfantplazahotel.com

The concrete exterior of this Southwest D.C. hotel feels distinctly Soviet era, but inside is a surprisingly light-and-airy lobby with clean midcentury touches. The guest rooms are refreshingly sunny, and all the rooms have pillow-top beds, 310-thread-count linens and marble bathrooms. A great choice for museum hoppers, the hotel is just blocks from the National Air and Space Museum, Freer and Sackler Galleries, the United States Holocaust Memorial Museum and more. But it's also a nice place to relax. The neighborhood is dominated by office buildings, so it's quiet on the weekends, and the hotel has a pretty rooftop pool and offers in-room massages. If you get hungry, L'Enfant has an onsite steak-and-seafood restaurant, but the nearby Maine Avenue Fish Market is a don't-miss. It's an open-air market with a carnival atmosphere where Washingtonians go for fresh-off-the-boat seafood and some of the best crab cakes around.

382 rooms. Restaurant, bar. Business center. Fitness center. Pool. Pets accepted. $61-150

★★★★MANDARIN ORIENTAL, WASHINGTON D.C.

1330 Maryland Ave. S.W., National Mall, 202-554-8588; www.mandarinoriental.com

A view of the water is rather unusual for a hotel in this town, but the Mandarin Oriental boasts an impressive one of the Tidal Basin, the southwest waterfront and the Jefferson Memorial. Towering nine stories above the water, the hotel's neoclassical architecture reflects the original plans intended for Washington dating back to the 1700s, and with a limestone façade and ornate columns, it stands out against nearby government buildings. The Mandarin Oriental's interior is a whole different story. It follows the principles of feng shui in an East-meets-West design—the spacious lobby features massive American walnut columns, marble floors and Asian art. The sizable rooms and suites, also with an East/West theme, have flat-screen televisions encased in Japanese chests, custom-built furniture, deep soaking tubs and many have unbeatable views of the cherry blossoms, if you happen to be traveling at the right time to catch sight of these precious buds. A team of traditional Chinese medicine specialists and aromatherapists developed signature spa treatments such as the Oriental Harmony, where two massage therapists work together, offered in the 10,500-square-foot spa and fitness center. The Smithsonian, Capitol Hill and many National Monuments are just a short stroll away, making this a good base for those who are lobbying on the hill as well as those who just want to do the tourist thing.

400 rooms. Restaurant, bar. Business center. Fitness center. Pool. Spa. $251-350

WHERE TO EAT

NATIONAL MALL
★★★★CITYZEN
Mandarin Oriental Washington D.C., 1330 Maryland Ave. S.W., National Mall, 202-787-6006; www.mandarinoriental.com

Tucked inside the Mandarin Oriental hotel, CityZen's main dining room oozes decadence, yet the restaurant's vaulted ceilings, dramatic lighting and hushed atmosphere are reminiscent of an exclusive Zen Buddhist retreat. Diners are bathed in golden candlelight reflected in the buttery tones of rich velveteen banquettes punctuated by dots of red table-top votives. The menu offerings at this temple of gastronomy change frequently to honor the seasons. Chef Eric Ziebold's menu can include everything from beer-battered Chesapeake Bay soft-shell crabs to sweet butter-poached Maine lobsters. But the menu always demonstrates his commitment to sourcing the best local ingredients. One standout is the vegetarian tasting menu. Items such as black radish tempura and russet potato bone marrow would surely make even the most hardcore meat lovers' taste buds happy. Luckily, carnivores can devour a range of meat dishes as well, including the herb-roasted Elysian Fields lamb rib-eye with green chickpeas, piquillo peppers, merguez garlic confit and turmeric broth.

Contemporary American. Dinner. Closed Sunday-Monday. Reservations recommended. Jacket required. Bar. $86 and up

RECOMMENDED

J&G STEAKHOUSE
W Washington D.C., 515 15th St. N.W., National Mall, 202-661-2440; www.jgsteakhousewashingtondc.com

The District's first W hotel has become a hot see-and-be-seen spot because of its rooftop bar with spectacular views of the Washington Monument and this restaurant from celebrity chef Jean-Georges Vongerichten. While J&G is billed as a steakhouse, there is definitely another dimension to this restaurant's personality. Executive chef Philippe Reininger heads the kitchen that is devoted to superb cuts of beef as well as fresh selections of fish and produce. Regulars consistently rave about the crispy calamari, pickled chilies and yuzu dip starter as well as the seared halibut with scallion-chili sauce, basil and cherry. Pristine

HIGHLIGHT

WHICH D.C. RESTAURANTS ARE THE MOST HISTORIC?

MICHEL RICHARD CITRONELLE

Chef Michel Richard has traded California for the brackish waters of the Potomac, and Citronelle in Washington, D.C., emerged as his flagship restaurant. He and his cuisine are an affable amalgamation of frolicking Californian whimsy and technical precision.

MARCEL'S

This may be the best restaurant in D.C. out-of-towners have never heard of. Marcel's was chef Robert Wiedmaier's first foray into the D.C. dining scene, and it consistently draws accolades for its upscale Franco-Belgian cuisine.

1789

This stalwart of the D.C. restaurant scene is largely steeped in traditional, continental European cuisine, but relatively young upstart chef Dan Giusti has managed to wake up the menu a bit and experiment with seasonal ingredients.

CORDUROY

A former apprentice of culinary star Michel Richard, Tom Power lets the ingredients in his deftly executed dishes quietly speak for themselves at Corduroy. It's safe to say that the main themes of Corduroy do not owe themselves to any culinary region, but to the philosophy of understated elegance and a commitment to seasonality.

oysters on the half shell whet your appetite for the more substantial beef dishes, like the six peppercorn prime New York steak. Warm chocolate cake with vanilla bean ice cream is a sweet ending to an evening of political stargazing at this reputed hangout for younger Obama administration staffers. If you haven't had your fill of supping amid the political stars by meal's end, ride the elevator and take in the ceiling, which forms the constellations as they appeared in the sky on July 4, 1776.

Steakhouse. Breakfast, lunch (Monday-Friday), dinner, Saturday-Sunday brunch. Reservations recommended. Bar. $36-85

SOU'WESTER

Mandarin Oriental, Washington D.C., 1330 Maryland Ave. S.W., National Mall, 202-787-6140; www.mandarinoriental.com

Chef de Cuisine Rachael Harriman puts a slight Southern accent on her offerings at Sou'Wester, located at the Mandarin Oriental. Utilizing farm-fresh ingredients that the restaurant sources from farms of the Shenandoah Valley and the waters of the nearby Chesapeake Bay, she turns out traditional as well as interpretive spins on American classics. Sou'Wester skillet fried chicken (it's dark meat only) with iceberg salad and ranch dressing, chicken and dumplings, and sautéed red snapper with buttermilk mashed potatoes all pay homage to cuisine steeped in sweet tea history, while entrées such as seafood stew with mussels, smoked blue fish and squid in a tomato broth pay tribute to the North. Pastry chef Matthew Petersen's desserts take it full circle with homegrown Southern favorites, such as red velvet cake with cream cheese frosting, upside-down pineapple cake and chocolate French silk pie.

Contemporary American. Breakfast, lunch, dinner. Reservations recommended. Bar. $16-35

CAPITOL HILL/NORTHEAST D.C.

★★★BISTRO BIS

The Hotel George, 15 E St. N.W., Capitol Hill, 202-661-2700; www.bistrobis.com

Unlike Los Angelinos or New Yorkers, Washingtonians aren't accustomed to run-ins with the rich and famous so much as the powerful and corrupt. This restaurant adjacent to the Hotel George, however, provides an unusual treat to diners among eateries in the District because of its proximity to Capitol Hill: celebrity sightings. When Congress is in session it's not uncommon to experience D.C.'s version of a TMZ episode as policy-promoting celebrities like George Clooney and U2 frontman Bono dine among celebrity-seeking politicians. The menu at Bistro Bis speaks with a proper French accent, but acts contemporary in form. No doubt this dichotomy plays well to more stoic members of the Senate and House, and also in dishes like the classic duck liver parfait that arrives in three uniform squares topped with strips of toasted brioche and punctuated with three pickled Morello cherries.

Contemporary American, French. Breakfast, lunch, dinner, Saturday-Sunday brunch. Reservations recommended. Bar. $36-85

RECOMMENDED

CAVA

527 Eighth St. S.E., Capitol Hill, 202-543-9090; www.dc.cavamezze.com

The owners of Cava bucked the usual trend in the D.C. restaurant scene by actually opening a D.C. outpost on Capitol Hill after the birth of

---

WHAT ARE D.C.'S BEST STEAKHOUSES?

Bourbon Steak:
Acclaimed chef Michael Mina raises the "steaks" at this upscale steakhouse in the Four Seasons hotel. Mina's method of butter-poaching meat and poultry creates dishes that are succulent and sinfully decadent.

J&G Steakhouse:
The District's first W hotel has become a hot see-and-be-seen spot thanks to its rooftop bar with spectacular views of the Washington Monument and this restaurant from celebrity chef Jean-Georges Vongerichten. Executive chef Philippe Reininger heads a kitchen that is devoted to superb cuts of beef, as well as fresh selections of fish and produce.

Prime Rib:
Settle into an executive-style leather chair and start with an order of the Maine lobster bisque before attacking the restaurant's eponymous signature item: a 45-ounce roasted prime rib, aged four to five weeks.

WHAT ARE D.C.'S BEST PLACES FOR BRUNCH?

Café Atlántico:
The Saturday brunch is delicious, but the Sunday Latino dim sum is out of this world. The chef's dim sum tasting menu is available from 11:30 a.m. until 1:30 p.m. and is $35 per person for 14 dishes. Order a pisco sour or a mango mimosa and then sit back as an array of delicious bites come your way.

Seasons:
Seasons is the spot for power breakfasts and Sunday brunch. Get your morning metabolism going with the black truffle skillet with truffle cheese, scrambled eggs, cremini mushrooms and roasted potatoes. Extensive brunch options never fail to impress Washingtonians and tourists alike.

their flagship restaurant in the suburbs of Rockville, Maryland. Some diners will associate the word "cava" with Spanish sparkling wine, but it is also used to describe high-quality Greek table wine, and Greek cuisine is what this mezzeria is all about. They create mezze-sized plates that are larger than small plates but not as ,big as entrées. The sleek décor and industrial ceilings of the establishment speak to modernity, but the restaurant has an old soul. It's not uncommon to see older Greek men in black fishing hats sipping ouzo at the bar alongside younger D.C. professionals, who are staples of the bar scene on Capitol Hill. The kitchen turns out pitch-perfect avgolemono, a Greek standard of pulled chicken with orzo in a tangy lemon broth soup. Spicy lamb sliders and messy "disco" fries with braised pork and veal are also not to be missed. The simple finisher of Greek yogurt with honey and walnuts is probably the cheapest way you'll be transported to the Greek islands this year.

International. Lunch (Tuesday-Saturday), dinner, Sunday brunch. Reservations recommended. $86 and up

DOWNTOWN/CHINATOWN/PENN QUARTER

★★★★ADOUR

The St. Regis Washington, D.C., 923 16th and K streets N.W., Downtown, 202-509-8000; www.adour-washingtondc.com

Adour has wine in mind, and it's no wonder. The restaurant is the brainchild of French oenophile and culinary master Alain Ducasse, so diners can choose from among 400 wines by the bottle, smaller formats by the half decanter, and if you're feeling especially celebratory, by the magnum and jeroboam as well. The eatery gets its moniker from a river near a town near Ducasse's birthplace, and the menu takes its culinary cues from France. Halibut garnished with grapes and foie gras-stuffed squab breast perched on a bed of cabbage are favorites, but look for seasonal offerings like the summer vegetable cookpot, the establishment's signature dish that appears on every menu throughout Ducasse's restaurant empire. Save room for the complimentary housemade truffles and macaroons; the delicious calling cards of the restaurant can be purchased separately year round in flavors reflective of the season. Steeped in brown, cream and gold tones, as well as original hand-blown glass spheres that dangle from the ceiling, Adour is crisply modern.

Contemporary French. Breakfast, dinner. Closed Sunday-Monday. Reservations required. Bar. $36-85

★★★BOMBAY CLUB

815 Connecticut Ave. N.W., Downtown, 202-659-3727;
www.bombayclubdc.com

Harboring a bar decked out in burnt orange and browns and seating that mimics wicker furnishings prepared to withstand the heat and humidity of the tropics, this restaurant seems like an unlikely sibling to the ultra-hip Rasika in Penn Quarter. That is, until you order from the menu. Though the dining area is adorned with kitschy paintings of romanticized, palm-filled Indian countryscapes, the fare at Bombay Club pays homage to traditional Indian cuisine. There are unexpected dishes, too, like spicy duck kabob with a ginger-chili kick, and venison korma spiced with onion, yogurt, almond and nutmeg. Bombay Club is not afraid to shout out its ethnic heritage either—dishes like the Goa fish curry, which features halibut bathed in coconut milk, coriander and onion, can be found under the section "Unabashedly Indian Curries" on the menu. *Indian. Lunch (Monday-Friday), dinner, Sunday brunch. Reservations recommended. Bar. $36-85*

★★★BRASSERIE BECK

1101 K St. N.W., Downtown, 202-408-1717; www.beckdc.com

If you couldn't guess from chef Robert Wiedmaier's last name, he is half Belgian, and no doubt his affinity for Flemish cuisine and beer craft stem from his ancestry. Brasserie Beck's atmosphere is lively and fits the bill nicely for upscale, traditional brasserie fare: Quintessential moules in white wine garlic and parsley and Belgian frites accompanied by a mayonnaise trio, a charcuterie plate, a classic croque monsieur, and lamb shank with white beans are just a few of the bistro staples you'll find on Wiedmaier's menu. Tie-clad locals and t-shirted tourists alike gather around tables and the bar to sip on a dizzying array of Belgian brews, or park themselves in the outdoor-seating area to people-watch along K Street. The restaurant boasts the most comprehensive Belgian beer collection in the District with nine on draft and more than 100 by the bottle. While the crowd is a good mix of Washingtonians and out-of-towners, locals may be able to take better advantage of the daily half-price draft specials that occur from 5 to 7 p.m.; on Tuesdays select bottles of wine are half price. Wine Steward Jaime Lang doesn't let vino take a backseat to suds. Brasserie Beck's wine list claims 50-plus selections by the glass and the bottle.

WHAT ARE D.C.'S BEST PLACES FOR A CASUAL LUNCH?

Cava:
It's not uncommon to see older Greek men in black fishing hats sipping ouzo at the bar alongside younger D.C. professionals at this Greek mezzeria. The kitchen turns out simple and delicious mezze-sized plates that are larger than small plates but not as big as entrées.

Jaleo:
José Andrés' flagship restaurant is steeped in the small-plates tradition of Spain with tapas like spicy patatas bravas and the legendary jamón Ibérico from the black-footed pigs.

WHICH D.C. RESTAURANTS SERVE THE BEST BURGERS?

Palena:

The burgers on Palena's café menu have been touted as the best the nation's capital has to offer in terms of the quintessential American sandwich, probably because of the truffle cheese and housemade kaiser rolls. In any case, the burgers beg to be accompanied by the restaurant's elevated version of a side of fries: a mix of shoestring-style fries, dauphine potatoes, onion rings and Palena's signature fried lemon slices.

Central Michel Richard:

Ironically, the buzz about this Franco-American alliance in comfort food has to do with the decidedly un-Francophone, all-American hamburger. Cheese is optional, but if you request to dress your burger with such dairy finery, it arrives as a thick, gooey blanket topped with paper-thin, crispy potato tuiles.

Belgian, French. Lunch (Monday-Friday), dinner, Saturday-Sunday brunch. Bar. $36-85

★★★CAFÉ ATLANTICO

405 Eighth St. N.W., Penn Quarter, 202-393-0812; www.cafeatlantico.com

José Andrés has made the culinary science fiction of molecular gastronomy accessible to the American palate. Café Atlantico is part of his multi-ethnic, small-plates empire in the District of Columbia. The restaurant's décor, as well as its drink list and menu, are an homage to pan-Latin national identity, as well as the whimsy of molecular cooking. Everything from Brazilian caipirinhas to Peruvian pisco sours, to a deconstructed Cuban Magic Mojito made from cotton candy grace the fancy cocktails list. Unlike most of Andrés' other establishments, however, entrées are the norm here, though small plates are given their 15 minutes of fame on Sundays when the restaurant's version of Latino dim sum blasts off. This is space-age Latino cuisine, where you will find your plates embellished with banana foam, and Chihuahua cheese is just as revered as soy-yuzu vinaigrette. Even humble street vendor victuals like Salvadoran pupusas are adorned with elegant foie gras fondant. For a real out-of-this-world meal, head upstairs to the second-floor minibar, Andrés' micro-restaurant and homage to experimental cuisine. It's only for those who are brave enough to pass through the decompression chamber into the culinary unknown.

Latin American. Lunch (Tuesday-Friday), dinner, Saturday brunch. Closed Monday. Bar. $16-35

★★★CENTRAL MICHEL RICHARD

1001 Pennsylvania Ave., Penn Quarter, 202-626-0015; www.centralmichelrichard.com

Don't let the cartoonish display of oversized plates at Central's entrance fool you into thinking you've stepped into a cutesy themed culinary outpost of Richard's more upscale destination, Citronelle in Georgetown. Though a Warhol-esque portrait of the affable chef hangs in the main dining area. This is a culinary venue for the masses, but the cuisine is executed with the precision and attention to detail of its Georgetown sibling. Ironically, the buzz about this Franco-American alliance in comfort food has to do with the all-American hamburger. Cheese is optional, but if you request to dress your burger with such dairy finery, it arrives as a thick, gooey blanket topped with paper-thin, crispy potato tuiles. Fried chicken is moist, dunked in unusually crispy panko-style breading and is paired with delicately whipped mashed potatoes with generous helpings of cream and butter. The French part of this equation is traditional bistro fare that includes nibbles like French onion soup, frog's legs, many iterations of charcuterie and chocolate mousse. Keeping the American balance of the menu in check, the foil to the classic chocolate mousse in the dessert department is Le Kit Kat, a decadent study in the various states of chocolate: liquid, solid and wafer; it's also Frenchman Richard's nod to his adopted D.C. home. *American, French. Lunch (Monday-Friday), dinner. Reservations recommended. Bar. $36-85*

★★★DC COAST

1401 K St. N.W., Downtown, 202-216-5988; www.dccoast.com

The owners of this Beaux Arts restaurant played up the Art Deco stylings of the downtown space during its renovation more than 10 years ago. While the space pays respect to the roaring 1920s, the food is contemporary cuisine with a subtle splash of Southern inspiration. Seafood-focused fare highlights classic local favorites, such as the fried Chesapeake oysters with tomato horseradish jam and watercress. Menu surprises include the poisson cru, a Tahitian-style tuna tartare in fresh lime juice and coconut milk, but you can still settle into your chair with a comfy roasted chicken entrée or a DC Coast burger with housemade pickles. Any self-respecting flapper will find herself at the bar, however, sipping on a refreshing K Street martini with Ciroc vodka, white grape juice and a frozen grape garnish. *Contemporary American. Lunch (Monday-Friday), dinner. Bar. $16-35*

★★★ICI URBAN BISTRO

Sofitel Lafayette Square Washington D.C., 806 15th St. N.W., Downtown, 202-730-8700;
www.iciurbanbistro.com

Ici has perfected what the French refer to as the "art de vivre," or the art of living. Located in the Sofitel at Lafayette Square, this bistro is home to a lively bar scene. Its aptly named watering hole, Le Bar, offers a good selection of globally procured wines and beer, as well as signature cocktails. Try a Napoleón, a ladylike libation consisting of muddled strawberries,

---

WHAT ARE D.C.'S BEST PLACES FOR A POWER LUNCH?

Bistro Bis:
Washingtonians aren't accustomed to run-ins with the rich and famous so much as the powerful or corrupt. This restaurant adjacent to the Hotel George, however, provides an unusual treat to diners among eateries in the District because of its proximity to Capitol Hill: celebrity sightings.

Teatro Goldini:
This eatery dedicated to Italian fare is a consistent favorite among the locals and a power spot for Washington's elite. Pasta and risotto are favorites, but unexpected small plates make appearances with updated Italian classics.

HIGHLIGHT

WHAT ARE THE BEST PLACES IN D.C. TO SATISFY A SWEET TOOTH?

BLUE DUCK TAVERN

A slice of the signature cinnamon-crusted apple pies is a must. And what's pie without ice cream? Here, it comes in a large family-style receptacle with a wooden spoon. It's so good you'll want to lick the velvety vanilla ice cream off the serving paddle.

CENTRAL MICHEL RICHARD

Keeping the American balance of the menu in check, the foil to the classic chocolate mousse in the dessert department is Le Kit Kat, a decadent study in the various states of chocolate: liquid, solid and wafer; it's also Frenchman Richard's nod to his adopted D.C. home.

COCO SALA

It is definitely all about decadence at this chocolate lover's hideaway. Chocoholics will want to choose a three-course menu of chocolaty concoctions or five-course tasting menu that includes a cheese plate with items like German chocolate and warm milk chocolate variants of the original black and white whoopie pie filled with bourbon and pecan gelato and raspberry sauce, respectively.

HOOK

Hook's longtime pastry chef Heather Chittum's was featured on the inaugural season of *Top Chef: Just Desserts*. Chittum turns out summertime sweets like a lingonberry linzertorte with Taleggio ice cream, and a caramel pine nut tart that comes with four dollops of gorgonzola dolce and topped with rosemary ice cream. In the fall and winter, expect creations that utilize the season's bounty, like walnuts and apples.

Emperor's vodka, crème de cassis and lime juice. But iCi has more to offer than just fun cocktails at Le Bar. Chef Olivier Perret is dedicated to incorporating locally sourced ingredients and regularly crafts his Fresh Farm Fridays fare around produce gathered from the Freshfarm Market in Penn Quarter. The bistro's regular dinner offerings include French and American dishes with a smattering of the requisite cheese plates and pasta dishes, including entrées such as Muscovy duck breast with couscous and vegetables dotted with orange confit; penne and prosciutto with shallot confit and Comté cheese; or the hamburger with Emmentaler cheese.

Contemporary American, contemporary French. Breakfast, lunch (Monday-Friday), dinner. Reservations recommended. Bar. $36-85

★★★JALEO
480 Seventh St. N.W., Penn Quarter, 202-628-7949; www.jaleo.com

José Andrés' flagship restaurant is steeped in the small-plates tradition of Spain with tapas like spicy patatas bravas and the legendary jamón Ibérico from black-footed pigs (or try a less expensive version of the melt-in-your-mouth cured ham: the jamón serrano). While these will transport you back to your favorite tapas spot on the Plaza Mayor, other dishes owe more to Washington, D.C., for their inspiration than Andrés' Spanish heritage, like butifarra casera con mongetes "Daniel Patrick Moynihan," a tasty a sausage treat named after the former U.S. senator. Start with the gazpacho estilo Algeciras to refresh your palate or ward off muggy D.C. summers. Peruse the wine list for a nice smattering of jerez, vino tinto, rosé and cava, Spain's answer to sparkling wine. The by-the-glass selections will complement what is sure to be a round robin of eating enjoyment.

Spanish. Lunch, dinner, Saturday-Sunday brunch. Bar. $36-85

★★★MIO
1110 Vermont Ave. N.W., Washington, D.C.Downtown, 202-955-0075; www.miorestaurant.com

Mio dubs itself a showcase for urban Latin American cuisine, but think of the pan-Latino concept as more of a reference point that cannibalizes other culinary traditions, most notably Italian and Spanish. That explains why you'll find summer vegetable risotto alongside roasted pork dishes garnished with plantains. At Mio, current chef de cuisine Vicente Torres masterfully combines the flavors and textures of haute cuisine with traditional peasant fare. The rich duck liver pâté paired with candied papaya becomes carnavalesque fusion. Depending on the day you pay a visit to Mio, you might also be treated to the talents of a guest chef from Venezuela or Puerto Rico. Friday nights spotlight Puerto Rican cuisine, featuring classic victuals from the Caribbean island like lechón con escabeche de yucca, whole roasted pig served with yucca, and sorullitos con queso, Puerto Rican-style corn fritters.

International. Lunch (Monday-Friday), dinner. Closed Sunday. Reservations recommended. Bar. $36-85

★★★PROOF
775 G St. N.W., Penn Quarter, 202-737-7663; www.proofdc.com

Chances are, if you are visiting from out of town and ask around about a D.C. wine bar worthy of breaking out your wine key, you'll be directed to this steel-and-wood-wrought enoteca. The crowd here is just as pretty as the carefully plated prosciutto. In fact, you'll find a healthy selection of charcuterie, including Arlington-based Nathan Anda's Red Apron line with rossette de Lyon, bresaola, coppa, speck and pistachio-and-cherry-flecked pâté de campagne. The ever-changing wine list's more than 1,000 bottles and 40 by-the-glass selections will surely please oenophiles, wine newbies and everyone in between; you're just as likely to find an esoteric sauvignon from Slovenia as a standout California cabernet. Foodies also will be sated at Proof, as chef Haidar Karoum peppers his seasonal modern American menu with a dash of internationale. Boutique domestic cheese offerings like creamy, tangy Humboldt Fog share the bill with wood-smoke-infused French Blue de Causses. More substantial wine-friendly dishes include seared Hudson Valley foie gras, and a spicy duck breast dressed in pomegranate emulsion.

Contemporary American. Lunch (Monday-Friday), dinner. Reservations recommended. Bar. $36-85

RECOMMENDED

AGAINN

1099 New York Ave. N.W., Downtown, 202-639-9830; www.againndc.com

You might think that there's a typo on the signage of this D.C. gastro-pub. It's pronounced "a-gwen," a Gaelic term loosely translated as "with us". You'll find familiar pub fare at Againn, like fish and chips with a side of mushy peas, but the restaurant prides itself on using sustainable seafood, organic meats, and sourcing from select local farms in Pennsylvania and the Shenandoah Valley. The attention to sustainability; uncommon touches such as personal Scotch lockers where patrons can store up to three bottles of their favorite malted beverage for a minimum annual fee; and an extensive single-malt Scotch whiskey, beer and fine wine list make Againn appropriate for a well-deserved stretch after a day of sightseeing or an intimate get-together. Pub favorites like bangers and mash and black pudding are housemade, and even quintessential pub grub like shepherd's pie and onion mash are raised to new heights in the hands of executive chef Wes Morton. But the food is still approachable enough that you'll likely visit again and again.

British. Lunch (Monday-Friday), dinner. Closed Sunday. Reservations recommended. Bar. $36-85

CAFÉ DU PARC

1401 Pennsylvania Ave. N.W., Penn Quarter, 202-942-7000; www.cafeduparc.com

This traditional French bistro is next to a D.C. classic, the Willard InterContinental Hotel. French fare is the order of the day at Café du Parc. Travelers and Washington natives alike can pop in for breakfast, lunch or dinner, as the café serves all three meals seven days a week. If the weather is favorable, head outside to the patio to enjoy bistro classics like French onion soup or tarte flambée Alsacienne, a riff on quiche Lorraine in the form of an Alsatian-style tart with smoked bacon, onions and fromage blanc. Try the pan-seared rib-eye steak with béarnaise sauce and roasted organic chicken and you'll feel like you're on the Champs-Élysées rather than at the InterContinental.

Contemporary French. Breakfast, lunch, dinner. Outdoor seating. Bar. $36-85

CARMINE'S DC

425 Seventh St. N.W., Penn Quarter, 202-737-7770; www.carminesnyc.com

Late founder Artie Cutler took the Italian expression "Abbondanza", which means "plenty," to heart when he conceived of Carmine's culinary mission to feed diners on a daily basis as if they were at a large Italian wedding. New Yorkers have been familiar with the family-style Southern Italian fare from Alicart Restaurant Group for decades. Now the recently opened D.C. location has diners south of the Mason-Dixon Line hankering for Carmine's famous meatballs, shrimp scampi, chicken parmigiana and veal Marsala that come in generous portions made for sharing among four to six of your closest amici. Speaking of large, at nearly 700 seats, Carmine's is D.C.'s second-largest dining room (Clyde's is bigger by square footage).

Italian. Lunch, dinner. Reservations recommended. Bar. $36-85

CEIBA

701 14th St. N.W., Downtown, 202-393-3983; www.ceibarestaurant.com

The mythical ceiba tree has a storied place in Latin American culture because of its impressive above ground root system, as well as a canopy of branches that stretches as wide as the trees are tall. Chef/owner Jeff Tunks' menu extends across Latin America like the fabled tropical tree, grasping at far-flung regions like Venezuela and Brazil to create an eclectic, modern menu. Ceiba's drink list boasts twists on traditional libations, including the Hemingway mojito, made with a splash of sparkling wine and Mount Gay Extra Old Rum. Or try Brazil's famous export, the caipirinha, an unfettered, classic concoction made with Pitu Cachaça, muddled fresh lime and sugar. In another nod to the land of sun and samba, the slow-braised pork shank is Ceiba's riff on feijoada, the Brazilian national dish that's a base of leftover porcine parts, black beans, manioc flour and bitter greens. The restaurant's signature version of the dish showcases a pork shoulder that sits atop a mountain of rice and delicately flavored black beans. Other crowd-pleasers come in the form of ceviche, with seafood running the gamut from shrimp to wild striped bass to yellow fin tuna marinated in citrus juice.

International. Lunch (Monday-Friday), dinner. Reservations recommended. Bar. $36-85

COCO SALA

929 F St. N.W., Penn Quarter, 202-347-4265; www.cocosala.com

It's not all about chocolate at Coco Sala, though you can sate that craving in the chocolate salon (open Monday-Friday). It definitely is all about decadence at this chocolate lover's hideaway. The main dining area serves a variety of small plates for those occasions when you need to satisfy something beyond your sweet tooth. Veggie options include a tart of creamy artichoke hearts, tomato confit and truffle with tarragon vinaigrette, and an arugula salad of caramelized walnuts decorated with dates, apples, oranges and even a coffee-based vinaigrette, so you can get your caffeine fix in lieu of the chocolate. The heavier plates of lamb and chicken sliders have an Asian bent, with the lamb bathed in curry and coconut while the chicken is cooked in a tandoor oven and comes with a side of cardamom carrots and greens. Chocoholics will want to choose a three-course menu of chocolaty concoctions or five-course tasting menu that includes a cheese plate with items like German chocolate and warm milk chocolate variants of the original black and white whoopie pie filled with bourbon and pecan gelato and raspberry sauce, respectively. Coco Sala also offers naturally decaffeinated organic Mexican coffee.

International. Afternoon tea (Monday-Friday), dinner, Saturday-Sunday brunch. Reservations recommended. Bar. $16-35

CORDUROY

1122 Ninth St. N.W., Downtown, 202-589-0699; www.corduroydc.com

A former apprentice of culinary star Michel Richard, Tom Power lets the ingredients in his deftly executed dishes quietly speak for themselves at Corduroy. Though you won't find overly flowery descriptions of entrées on his vaguely

French-inspired menu, it's safe to say that the main themes of Corduroy do not owe themselves to any culinary region, but to the philosophy of understated elegance and a commitment to seasonality. Summer tomato salad is prepared simply but teems with heirloom, green and cherry tomatoes in one small three-dimensional tower. A main of scallops with cubanelle pepper sauce requires only a carefully timed sear to let the mollusks sing. Power's training under Richard, a master pastry chef, is also evident in his desserts as well. He conjures ice creams and sorbets with perfectly crafted textures. Other noteworthy sweets include a deeply rich chocolate tart accompanied by caramelized bananas as well as a flourless chocolate cake. Even among Washingtonians, Corduroy is still a well-kept secret, so go there while you can still snag a reservation.

Contemporary American. Dinner. Closed Sunday. Reservations recommended. Bar. $36-85

LA TABERNA DEL ALABARDERO

1776 I St. N.W., Downtown, 202-429-2200; www.alabardero.com

The azulejos, or Spanish tiles, that border the kitchen, as well as the hanging tapestries and the garnet walls of the main dining room will make you want to break out your fan and don a mantilla like the elegant ladies of Old Castilla. Spanish highlights feature various regions of the Iberian Peninsula: from the South, paella de langosta with scallops, squid and shrimp is a highlight, while the jamón ibérico al corte (cured meat from the highly prized black-footed pig) appetizer is quintessential Spanish noshing. An interesting locavore note on the wine list: It includes a Spanish varietal, Albariño, from Virginia producer Chrysalis Vineyards, which has taken a shine to the grape and made it uniquely prolific in the foothills of the Blue Ridge Mountains.

International. Lunch (Monday-Friday), dinner. Closed Sunday. Reservations recommended. Bar. $36-85

MINIBAR

405 Eighth St. N.W., Penn Quarter, 202-393-0812; www.cafeatlantico.com

As Ferran Adrià's protégé, José Andrés is no stranger to pushing the culinary envelope, so expect the unexpected when dining at minibar. Tucked away on the second floor of Café Atlantico, minibar is like Andrés' laboratory where diners are invited in small batches to bear witness to cutting-edge culinary experimentations. Menu items are deceptively simple in description and at times pay respect to Andrés' Iberian roots and his penchant for whimsy. Sweet peas Catalan-style is a wink to Northwestern Spain, but other items like "Guacamole"—a sushi-style roll of tomato sorbet encased in gossamer-thin slices of chilled avocado topped with Fritos—are an indicator of Andrés' sense of humor and eagerness to challenge your palate. Since its inception, minibar has offered some iteration of cotton candy. It has been paired with foie gras or accompanied by eel—another example of Andrés' boyish zeal for creating whimsical dishes that would be suitable for tea with Alice and the White Rabbit. Despite the reverence for highly crafted morsels, minibar is meant to be a fun dining experience. Just ask Anderson Cooper, who looked like a fire-breathing dragon exhaling "smoke" out of his nose with the help of some liquid nitrogen during a visit. Tricks aside, Andrés is serious about his craft and also seriously good at getting his patrons to reconsider the very notion of food.

Contemporary American. Dinner. Closed Sunday-Monday. Reservations required. $86 and up

OCEANAIRE SEAFOOD ROOM

1201 F St. N.W., Penn Quarter, 202-347-2277; www.theoceanaire.com

The Oceanaire chain is known for its belly-busting servings of fresh seafood and sides, so come hungry. Larger portions and the vintage 1930s décor make this eatery feel like a seafood-steak house, and there are offerings of rib-eye, filet mignon, New York strip and a double-cut pork chop, if you're feeling more turf than surf. Specialties from the sea include pan-seared Georgia Island sea bass with wilted spinach and horseradish brown butter, grilled Rhode Island rockfish and roasted squash with lemon, and whole oven-roasted Greek branzini with Mediterranean vinaigrette and charred lemon. Other Oceanaire takes on seafood include the black and bleu Costa Rican mahi mahi, which can be ordered "dirty" with caramelized onions and bleu cheese butter.

Seafood. Lunch (Monday-Friday), dinner. Reservations recommended. Bar. $36-85

OYAMEL

401 Seventh St. N.W., Penn Quarter, 202-628-1005; www.oyamel.com

Small plates still reign at Oyamel, but Mexican cuisine is the order of the day. Another one of José Andrés' adventures in victuals, the menu draws heavily from Mexico and, in pure Andrés fashion, swaps the concepts of low and haute cuisine. Dishes from the Mexican outback like grilled cactus paddles (which taste surprisingly like green beans) with tomatillos, grilled tomatoes, green onions, cilantro and green chiles are menu mainstays at Oyamel. Other dishes—such as the six ceviches of red snapper, Australian yellow tail, shrimp and crab, Hawaiian Pacific blue, bay scallops and tuna—may be more familiar, but don't shy away from more adventurous plates, like the taco de chapulines (grasshoppers, shallots, tequila and guacamole). The dining room is draped with playful Day of the Dead skeletons in jaunty hats and occasionally holding musical instruments. Two delicate sculptures of butterflies in flight grace the ceiling in the main dining area.

Mexican. Lunch, dinner, Saturday-Sunday brunch. Bar. $36-85

POSTE

Hotel Monaco, 555 Eighth St. N.W., Penn Quarter, 202-783-6060; www.postebrasserie.com

The aptly named Poste was the original 1841 General Post Office in days of yore, but it now houses a dining room inside the Hotel Monaco. If the weather is favorable, follow the doors through the lounge to the European-style outdoor patio and mingle with a crowd that can turn from international travelers to local imbibers in a split second. Back indoors, the restaurant is a testament to sustainability: Used coffee grounds stand in for fertilizer in the significantly sized onsite garden; the restaurant regularly composts about 500 pounds of food per month; even the menus are made from recycled paper and are printed with soy-based ink. Chef Robert Weland incorporates much of the produce from Poste's garden into French-inspired dishes like summer vegetable crêpes and French onion soup with garden heirloom tomato salad. Once a week, Weland also hosts Market to Market dinners where he shops with diners for fresh produce, introduces guests to local farmers and takes them back to the restaurant to prepare a meal with their purchases. No time for a shopping trip? Just enjoy the classics, like steak tartare with sea salt and housemade brioche or beef bourguignon paired with a biodynamic wine.

Contemporary American. Breakfast (Monday-Friday), lunch (Monday-Friday), dinner, Saturday-Sunday brunch. Reservations recommended. Outdoor seating. Bar. $36-85

RASIKA

633 D St. N.W., Penn Quarter, 202-637-1222; www.rasikarestaurant.com

Forget everything you think you know about Indian food. Indian food buffets and even that fine dining Indian place you frequent are inadequate reference points for what awaits you at this upscale temple of curry-infused fare. Rasika in Sanskrit means many flavors, and those flavors are masterfully controlled by chef Vikram Sunderam. Even the bread basket doesn't go untouched by his culinary prowess; it includes several different iterations of naan. Entrées touch on all regions of India, from the tandoori chicken in Kashmiri chili and mint chutney to the tawa (griddle) ahi tuna with mustard corn chaat. The restaurant also offers a full vegetarian roster of morsels, like the eggplant pepper fry featuring baby eggplant curry leaves and black pepper.

Indian. Lunch (Monday-Friday), dinner. Closed Sunday. Reservations recommended. Bar. $16-35

SIROC

915 15th St. N.W., Downtown, 202-628-2220; www.sirocrestaurant.com

Tourists dining at Siroc should consider themselves lucky. The restaurant is a bit of a sleeper hit that offers a great fine dining value for modern Italian-influenced cuisine in the District. Like traditional and memorable Italian cuisine, dishes at Siroc are unfussy, and preparation doesn't get in the way of letting the flavors speak for themselves. Here, salads are as elegant and fretted over as much as any establishment touting haute cuisine in D.C., and even the standard mixed baby field greens with tomato, cucumbers and radishes drizzled with a roasted shallot vinaigrette is sure to delight your tastebuds. The Italian-influenced menu means that pasta is housemade and true to its roots. Try the black pepper tagliatelle with sweet garlic, red pepper flakes and seared scallops. The tender, fresh pasta ribbons have a slight kick, and the seafood lends a sweetness that comes from being perfectly executed and neither too dry nor undercooked. Desserts are classic affairs as well, and the Bosc pear poached in red wine and ginger served with mascarpone ice cream and ginger cream is a sleeper hit all on its own.

Italian. Lunch (Monday-Friday), dinner. Reservations recommended. Bar. $36-85

THE SOURCE BY WOLFGANG PUCK

575 Pennsylvania Ave. N.W., Penn Quarter, 202-637-6100; www.wolfgangpuck.com

You don't have to be a journalist to enjoy the Asian-inspired fare at Wolfgang Puck's The Source, but you'll want to do some investigative reporting at this eatery attached to the Newseum. The three Kobe sliders from the casual lower-level Izakaya menu are good enough for the likes of a grizzled sports reporter on the go, but if you fancy yourself more of an international correspondent, try the Hong Kong-style steamed wild king salmon with bok choy in the upper dining room, where the floor-to-ceiling glass windows will help you keep an eye out for breaking news along Pennsylvania Avenue. Experience D.C.'s Asian connection with a signature cocktail like the Asian pear drop, made of Absolut Pears vodka, sake and pear purée. Take a tour of the Newseum Tuesday to Saturday after the three-course prix fixe lunch for an additional $7, a substantial discount from the usual $20 admission.

Asian. Lunch (Monday-Friday), dinner, Saturday brunch. Closed Sunday. Reservations recommended. Bar. $86 and up

ZOLA

800 F St. N.W., Penn Quarter, 202-654-0999; www.zoladc.com

Located next to the International Spy Museum, Zola is a no-nonsense dining experience. And while you won't unlock any secrets in the food, you will find backlit panels of coded KGB documents decorating this restaurant. The straightforward American menu features popular starters like a lobster cobb salad of romaine hearts, tomato caviar, crispy avocado, pancetta crisps, slow-cooked egg yolks and egg white dressing, or the pineapple heirloom tomato salad with sorbet, gelée, preserved ravioli and olive oil mousse. A main of Miller Farms pork and peaches is the perfect disguise for blending into the local Southern scene. Vegetarians won't feel double-crossed while noshing on an entrée of maitake mushrooms and sweet onions, either. If your cover is blown like Valerie Plame, bury your face in an order of the Zola lobster mac and cheese.

Contemporary American. Lunch (Monday-Friday), dinner. Reservations recommended. Bar. $36-85

U STREET CORRIDOR/ADAMS MORGAN

RECOMMENDED

CASHION'S EAT PLACE

1819 Columbia Road N.W., Adams Morgan, 202-797-1819; www.cashionseatplace.com

Travel to Europe via Mississippi at Cashion's Eat Place. This eatery has changed hands from Mississippi native and longtime D.C. chef Ann Cashion (she sold it to her long-time sous chef, John Manolatos), but the menu has remained largely powered by items at home in both the Gulf Coast and the Cote d'Azur. A solid roast chicken, dorade with lime dipping sauce and New Orleans-style file gumbo are all part of the multicultural symphony at Cashion's Eat Place. The updated menu extends the restaurant's European bent to Greece with a ragoût of wild mushrooms with artisanal polenta and Tuscan liver sauce. The European vibe at Cashion's also allows for dawdling over your food, so come here for a leisurely meal (and on Fridays and Saturdays, you can enjoy a late-night menu from midnight to 2 a.m.).

Contemporary American. Dinner, late-night, Sunday brunch. Closed Monday. Reservations recommended. Bar. $36-85.

CORK RESTAURANT AND WINE BAR

1720 14th St. N.W., U Street Corridor, 202-265-2674; www.corkdc.com

Cork Restaurant and Wine Bar originally opened as a place to not only imbibe, but also learn about oenology and viticulture. Cork offers wine education classes on a monthly basis, so stop by to enjoy a pour from its collection of more than 50 wines by the glass and 160 bottles from small producers around the globe. Specialties such as wine-braised lamb with pomegranate; the famously crispy duck confit; and fries dusted with parsley, lemon zest and garlic served with a faintly spicy housemade ketchup make for excellent noshing with or without wine. The chalkboard by the bar offers tasting suggestions that compare three wines of similar grapes, styles or regions.

International. Dinner. Closed Monday. Reservations recommended. Bar. $16-35

ESTADIO

1520 14th St. N.W., U Street Corridor, 202-319-1404; www.estadio-dc.com

Warm ceramic azulejo tiles in orange and red decorate this house of Spanish cuisine, which is reminiscent of a courtly medieval castillo. The same team behind Proof powers this small-plate establishment, where you'll find regional Spanish classics that bring to mind Castilian fare that is somewhat pork-centered, with jamón croquetas and blood sausage bocadillos, as well as the essential tortilla Española with aioli and sweet and hot peppers. Northern Spain is represented in Basque dishes such as grilled octopus with potato-caper salad. The restaurant leaves classic cuisine behind with fun, fresh takes on imbibing, like the "slushitos", adult Slurpees that come in grown-up flavors like fresh strawberries with basil-lime Campari and gin, or lemon-paprika Scotch and sherry.

International. Dinner. Reservations recommended. Bar. $16-35

MARVIN

2007 14th St. N.W., U Street Corridor, 202-797-7171; www.marvindc.com

Restaurateur Eric Hilton has a soft spot for soul singer Marvin Gaye, who also happens to be a native son of the nation's capital, and that explains where this U Street establishment gets its moniker. Marvin's other claim to fame is its rooftop deck and omnipresent DJs who spin an engaging mix of retro soul and funk hits every night of the week. The rooftop that rocks all week long and the more subdued restaurant below give Marvin's a bit of a split personality, as well as a menu that's part Southern charm and Belgian brewhouse. Be sure to order the Southern crispy fried chicken and waffles or the shrimp and grits. The Belgian moules frites with white wine and shallot sauce are equally as good. Another favorite offered at Marvin's is waterzooi, a Belgian dish brimming with lobster, shrimp and mussels and a cream sauce spiked with wine that makes a tasty pool for the carrots and potatoes. Marvin's might have a split personality, but it definitely has soul.

Belgian, Southern. Dinner (Monday-Saturday), Sunday brunch. Reservations recommended. Bar. $16-35

DUPONT CIRCLE/UPPER NORTHWEST
★★★GEORGIA BROWN'S

950 15th St. N.W., Dupont Circle/Upper Northwest, 202-393-4499; www.gbrowns.com

People sometimes don't remember that D.C. is essentially a Southern town. But Georgia Brown's brandishes its Southern and Low Country pedigree with so much ballyhoo that you can't forget this is a place where Louisianan Emeril Lagasse would be equally comfortable. The restaurant makes no apologies for the high calorie count of its down-home Southern cooking, with savory-sweet dishes such as sweet-tea-infused fried chicken and sugar-and-spice pork loin. The calorie-packed cuisine didn't deter fit first lady Michelle Obama from dining here. Low Country staples like Charleston she crab soup, shrimp and grits and Louisiana "devil" shrimp are a precious reminder of this region's reliance on the sea.

Southern, soul food. Lunch, dinner. Reservations recommended. Bar. $16-35

★★★★THE JOCKEY CLUB

The Fairfax at Embassy Row, 2100 Massachusetts Ave. N.W., Dupont Circle, 202-835-2100; www.thejockeyclub-dc.com

The Jockey Club maintains a storied place in Washington, D.C.'s history, having hosted some of the most iconic figures of our time. The restaurant that was born to accommodate JFK's inaugural entourage became one of the first seen-and-be-seen places to dine when the District was still a sleepy Southern outpost of the culinary cultured. Nestled in Embassy Row, the Jockey Club catered to the likes of Jackie Kennedy and other notable names of the era, and after a multimillion dollar renovation in 2008, the Club continues to be the stomping ground of social and political bigwigs like Hillary Clinton and General David Petraeus, who enjoy the restaurant's impeccable service. As for the food, an elegant appetizer is the classic steak tartare, made from hand-cut filet mignon, capers and anchovies and served with grilled ciabatta. Diners rave about the local fish of the day, and a specialty of the house is chef Ralf Hofman's Dover sole lemon meunière, which is prepared tableside.

Contemporary American, contemporary French. Breakfast, lunch, dinner (Tuesday-Saturday). Reservations recommended. Bar. $36-85

★★★KOMI

1509 17th St. N.W., Dupont Circle, 202-332-9200; www.komirestaurant.com

Save for the 3-hour tasting menu ($125) feast at Komi, everything about this restaurant is a study in minimalism. From the sparsely furnished dining area to the cuisine, Komi is pure and unfettered. Chef Johnny Monis celebrates his family's Greek heritage with pristine ingredients that are made to stand on their own with minimal tweaking by the chef. Greek goes global with signature dishes like mascarpone-stuffed Medjool dates that are slow roasted, touched with olive oil and intricately decorated with sea salt crystals. Roasted baby goat is another signature of Monis' and also a nod to his Greek ancestry. While the chef has a reputation for shying away from the press, his restaurant does not. Washingtonians agree that the local and national buzz surrounding the ultra-modern concept of Komi is well-deserved.

Contemporary American, Mediterranean. Dinner. Closed Sunday-Monday. Reservations recommended. $86 and up

★★★NAGE

1600 Rhode Island Ave. N.W., Dupont Circle, 202-448-8005; www.nagerestaurant.com

If you thought that an affordable fine dining experience without the stuffiness of a snobby waitstaff only existed in your dreams, this restaurant will be an awakening. Nage (French for "swimming") may seem targeted to grownup hipsters with their own kids in tow, but all are welcome. Executive chef and owner Glenn Babcock sets the tone for the laidback attitude that permeates the dining room as well as the kitchen. The restaurant combines seafood with comfort in dishes like lobster mac and cheese, truffle fries and ancho-braised short ribs with sweet corn succotash, fava beans and fried green tomatoes. Kids can munch on a flatbread pizza or a prime rib burger. The restaurant is like a relaxing spot you'd go for a meal on the weekend, though every day feels like Saturday at Nage.

Contemporary American, French. Breakfast, lunch (Monday-Friday), dinner, Sunday brunch. Reservations recommended. Bar. $16-35

★★★★PALENA

3529 Connecticut Ave. N.W., Upper Northwest, 202-537-9250; www.palenarestaurant.com

Palena's earth-tone interior is as much an homage to the Medieval Abruzzi town for which it's named as it is a Mediterranean escape complete with statuesque figurines and trellised greenery. The classic dining room serves a two-, three-, and four-course seasonal prix fixe tasting menu featuring dishes like pan-roasted squab with spices, zucchini and a black currant and juniper sauce. The burgers on Palena's café menu have been touted as the best the nation's capital has to offer, probably because of the truffle cheese and housemade kaiser rolls. Others rave about the 45-minute half roasted chicken, and the restaurant's elevated version of a side of fries: a mix of shoestring-style fries, dauphine potatoes, onion rings and Palena's signature fried lemon slices. Washingtonians' real passion is for chef Frank Ruta's take on Italian-inspired morsels, including the uniquely complex potato gnocchi that anchors a rotating list of pastas made fresh daily. In the works is Palena Market, which will feature more seating for the café so more people can indulge in the delicious burgers.

Italian, contemporary American. Dinner. Closed Sunday (dining room also closed Monday). Bar. $86 and up

★★★★PLUME

The Jefferson, Washington, D.C., 1200 16th St. N.W., Dupont Circle, 202-448-2300; www.plumedc.com

Plume finds inspiration in its surroundings at the stately Jefferson hotel, and specifically the hotel's namesake. In accordance with Thomas Jefferson's passion for wine, the restaurant pays homage to the oenophile inclinations of the founding father with a hefty number of wines from the world over, as well as a real-time, online wine list that allows you to plan your evening's imbibing up to the nanosecond of your arrival. The room is a jewelbox of a space, bedecked in blue hues and dazzling antique crystal chandeliers; the confident waitstaff can just as easily explain Jefferson's favorite wines as they can the dishes on the night's menu. Though chef Damon Gordon's offerings, like slow-roasted magret of duck with carrot and cardamom risotto, lean heavily on classic French execution, dishes such as navarin of Maine lobster remind us that we still have one foot on this side of the Atlantic at Plume. It is possible, however, to be transported back to colonial America with a wine list that also includes rare finds Jefferson might have indulged in himself, including a 1780 Borges Madeira Bual.

Contemporary American, contemporary French. Dinner. Closed Sunday-Monday. Reservations recommended. Bar. $36-85

★★★RESTAURANT NORA

2132 Florida Ave. N.W., Dupont Circle, 202-462-5143; www.noras.com

The New American cuisine at Restaurant Nora is just as comforting as the quilts that hang from the dining room's walls. Wrap yourself in culinary Americana with starters like sweet and succulent Maine peekytoe crab salad, local tempura squash blossoms and beef tenderloin tartare. While the diverse fare is a celebration of regional and seasonal ingredients, the thread that connects Nora's menu is a commitment to sustainability. Restaurateur Nora Pouillon pioneered the organic food movement in Washington, D.C., and in 1999 Nora's became the first eatery in the country to have the certified organic designation bestowed upon it. It's little wonder that this slow food paradise dedicates half the dinner menu to a lengthy narrative of sustainable agriculture and is written with the same attention to detail that's used to designate European wines by quality and region.

Contemporary American, vegetarian. Dinner. Closed Sunday. Reservations recommended. Bar. $36-85

★★★SAM AND HARRY'S

1200 19th St. N.W., Dupont Circle, 202-296-4333; www.samandharrys.com

Steak is the main attraction at this upscale chain that celebrates beef in its many iterations from North to South. Three variations of center-cut filet mignon grace the menu, two of which come topped with sauce béarnaise and a third "à la Oscar" with a side of asparagus and jumbo lump crab. Try the 16-ounce USDA prime-aged Cajun rib-eye crowned with horseradish cream and grated horseradish, or take a bite of the Big Apple with a cut of New York strip in béarnaise sauce. Make any of these dishes Sam and Harry's classics by getting them covered with grilled prawns, asparagus and béarnaise. Seafood here is fresh and unfettered. Preparations don't stray far from seared and just plain raw, and include oysters served with lemon, shallot and fresh peppercorn mignonette and fresh horseradish cocktail sauce, or choose between an icy or hot seafood sampler featuring crab, tuna scallops and shrimp.

Steakhouse. Lunch (Monday-Friday), dinner. Reservations recommended. Bar. $36-85

★★★TEATRO GOLDINI

1909 K St. N.W., Dupont Circle, 202-995-9494; www.teatrogoldoni.com

Wearing the colors of a Florence cityscape, the space at Teatro Goldini is awash in terra-cotta-hued furnishings and flecked with blue-accented light fixtures. This eatery dedicated to Italian fare is a consistent favorite among the locals and a power spot for Washington's elite. Pasta and risotto are favorites, but small plates, like tuna pizza with wasabi cream cheese, arugula and ginger sauce, make appearances with updated Italian classics such as Italian sausage with creamy polenta and blueberry sauce. The restaurant takes a similarly unconventional tact on presentation; plates like branzino carpaccio come in the cigar box in which they were smoked. If you're a sucker for more traditional Italian dishes, a newer menu lets you indulge your need for classic comfort food.

Italian. Lunch (Monday-Friday), dinner. Closed Sunday. Reservations recommended. $36-85

★★★VIDALIA

1990 M St. N.W., Dupont Circle, 202-659-1990; www.vidaliadc.com

A Vidalia is, of course, a variety of onion with a Southern disposition. And with entrées like carpetbagger's steak, Vidalia's American menu is not subtle about waving its Southern-cuisine flag. While there are many allium-based dishes on the menu—Vidalia onion with shiitake mushrooms and capers—other signature dishes do without the pungent herb, such as the baked macaroni with Amish cheddar, and Low Country greens with bacon and spicy vinegar. You can also try other iterations of Low Country cuisine, such as the shrimp and grits with tasso ham in a shellfish emulsion. Charming endings include watermelon gazpacho as well as Georgia pecan and tangy lemon chess pies, all of which are thankfully onion-free.

Contemporary American, Southern. Lunch, dinner. Reservations recommended. Bar. $36-85

RECOMMENDED

BIRCH AND BARLEY/CHURCHKEY
1337 14th St. N.W., Upper Northwest, 202-567-2576; www.birchandbarley.com

When Birch and Barley opened in 2009 beer "knurds" in the District finally had a place to call home. A gastro-pub below and a craft beer sanctuary above (named ChurchKey), Birch and Barley offers 50 draught beers that are categorized by tasting notes: crisp, hop, smoke, malt, roast, fruit and spice, and tart and funky. There's also a 500-bottle beer list. The menu here steals a little from both Mediterranean and American classics, including in one of the house specials, port-glazed figs flatbread, a perfect balance of sweet and savory with tangy gorgonzola, prosciutto and fig preserves. The grilled pork tenderloin comes with spaetzle, mustard greens and haricot verts. Of course a gastro-pub wouldn't be a gastro-pub without a burger, and the brat burger gets a thumbs-up. Pastry chef Tiffany MacIsaac's housemade cookies and confections dessert plate is a signature finish to a meal. It features an assortment of sweet nostalgia, including an oatmeal cream pie and a housemade Hostess cupcake.

American. Dinner, Sunday brunch. Closed Monday. Bar. $36-85

FIREFLY
1310 New Hampshire Ave. N.W., Dupont Circle, 202-861-1310; www.firefly-dc.com

Reclaimed wood tables, a stunning floor-to-ceiling tree dotted with candle lanterns and an intimate backlit bar set a cozy scene for executive chef Daniel Bortnick's American comfort food. True to the restaurant's commitment to respect seasons and local purveyors, Bortnick has made an effort to procure local artisanal cheeses like the creamy Monocacy Ash from Cherry Glen Goat Farm in Maryland. Seasonal dishes such as crispy soft-shell crab with Anson Mills grits, roasted asparagus, tomato tarragon puree and pickled ramps will make you feel like you're on a twilight picnic instead of sitting inside a brick-and-mortar restaurant. Don't miss the signature mini pot roast with Yukon Gold mashed potatoes, braised baby carrots and roasted shallot; it's comforting like a blanket on a cool, late fall evening.

Contemporary American. Breakfast (Monday-Friday), lunch (Monday-Friday), dinner, Saturday-Sunday brunch. Reservations recommended. Bar. $36-85

SUSHI TARO
1503 17th St. N.W., Dupont Circle, 202-462-8999; www.sushitaro.com

After an extensive renovation of its interior in 2009, Sushi Taro emerged with fewer seats and a revamped menu to claim the title of most authentic sushi dining experience in D.C. Owner Nobu Yamazaki wanted to create a dining experience for Washingtonians that was faithful to dining in a sushi bar in Japan. To this end,

Yamazaki receives regular shipments of fish from the famed Tsukiji market in Tokyo; you won't want to miss any dish that has the o-toro, or blue fin fatty tuna. He also uses authentic condiments in preparing dishes like nikiri, a sauce of soy, sake and carp that's painted on strips of fish and commonly used by Japanese sushi chefs. The restaurant has quite a collection of sake as well as shochu, Japan's other alcoholic beverage made from barley, sweet potatoes or rice. Stick with the housemade desserts, like the mochi, which are pounded sticky rice sweets molded into shapes that are really addictive.

Japanese. Lunch (Monday-Friday), dinner. Closed Sunday. Reservations recommended. $86 and up

GEORGETOWN

★★★1789

1226 36th St. N.W., Georgetown, 202-965-1789; www.1789restaurant.com

From the Kennedys to Madeleine Albright, Georgetown has been home to its fair share of American royalty and political heavyweights. And 1789 is just as much a grande dame as Jackie O. ever was. Don't dismiss 1789 as a haughty dining experience stuck in the past. This stalwart of the D.C. restaurant scene is largely steeped in traditional, continental European cuisine, but relatively young upstart chef Dan Giusti has managed to wake up the menu a bit and experiment with seasonal ingredients. He still offers the quintessentially European lamb dishes but procures meat sourced from the Shenandoah Valley. The rack is prepared as lamb three ways—in a loin, a leg and a rack—with New World sides of roasted squash and salsa verde.

Contemporary American. Dinner. Reservations recommended. Bar. $36-85

★★★MENDOCINO GRILLE AND WINE BAR

2917 M St. N.W., Georgetown, 202-333-2912; www.mendocinodc.com

Mendocino's executive chef Sam Whitcomb is Washington, D.C.'s answer to Berkeley-based Alice Waters, who pioneered the local-food movement. His dedication to procuring locally sourced and seasonal items here in the mid-Atlantic has been compared to the zeal with which the aforementioned queen of sustainability has championed high-quality food on the Left Coast. In fact, California transplants to the D.C. area revel in the 200-plus-bottle wine list that draws heavily from California, as well as Washington State and Oregon. The flagstone walls of varying shades of gray echo the laidback attitude of the cuisine, and though the restaurant is decidedly casual, it's elegant enough for a special outing. Locals indulge in the Francophone-influenced housemade pâté plate of brandied chicken liver and country-style pork accompanied by an assortment of mustards and country bread.

Contemporary American. Dinner. Reservations recommended. Bar. $36-85

★★★★MICHEL RICHARD CITRONELLE

Latham Hotel, 3000 M St. N.W., Georgetown, 202-625-2150; www.citronelledc.com

Michel Richard's culinary sojourn to the United States had its beginnings in California, far from the power-tie-wearing pundits in the nation's capital. Eventually he traded sea and sand for the brackish waters of the Potomac, and Citronelle in Washington, D.C., emerged as his flagship restaurant. He and his cuisine are an affable amalgamation of Californian whimsy and technical precision. Dishes such as traditional châteaubriand are joined by those much-loved cafeteria-lunchroom staples, tater tots. The fried chicken appetizer at the bar is a haute version of chicken nuggets; the golden-fried morsels are plated with a zippy mayonnaise. Other highlights include the spoon-tender 72-hour sous vide short ribs in raisin-peppercorn sauce, or suckling pig garnished with sweet potato gratin and barley for two. A closet painter, Richard uses those skills to deliver plates with dramatic visual presentations. Diners will see a kaleidoscope of colors in a mosaic-like dish that includes finely sliced eel and Kobe beef. Signature eye candy like the garnet-and-white-striped tuna napoleon niçoise should not be missed, either.

Contemporary American. Dinner. Closed Sunday-Monday. Jacket required. Reservations recommended. Bar. $86 and up

★★★SEASONS

Four Seasons Washington, D.C., 2800 Pennsylvania Ave. N.W., Georgetown, 202-342-0444; www.fourseasons.com

Located on the edge of the boutique-lined streets of Georgetown in the Four Seasons hotel, Seasons is the spot for power breakfasts and Sunday brunch. Get your morning metabolism going with the black truffle skillet with truffle cheese, scrambled eggs, cremini mushrooms and roasted potatoes. Besides the weekday breakfast offerings, extensive brunch options never fail to impress Washingtonians and tourists who come back again and again to spend lazy Sundays chatting or reading an engrossing book on one of the restaurant's complimentary Kindles while enjoying executive chef Doug Anderson's plates of pulled pork sliders with slaw, homemade bread and butter pickles in a cast-iron skillet; green lip mussels with Thai vinaigrette; or the crowd-pleasing smoked pastrami and dill-marinated salmon bagel. Floor-to-ceiling windows bring the pretty gardens in sight as you enjoy your leisurely morning meal.

Contemporary American. Breakfast, lunch (Saturday), Sunday brunch. Reservations recommended. Bar. $36-85

RECOMMENDED

2 AMYS

3715 Macomb St. N.W., Georgetown, 202-885-5700; www.2amyspizza.com

This pizzeria, classically adorned with Mediterranean butter-yellow walls and black-and-white-tiled floors, is popular with locals for its authentic Neapolitan pies. It's tucked away in a Georgetown neighborhood, but don't expect watered-down American versions of Italian eats while dining here. At 2 Amys, it's the real deal, right down to the mozzarella di bufala. Everything created in this Neapolitan pizzeria is handmade or officially D.O.C.-approved. The owners abide by the strict regulations of the Italian Denominazione di Origine Controllata: Their dough is yeasty, and pies are cooked in a wood-fired oven and arrive uncut to your table. Pizza toppings include uncommon varieties like cockles, which arrive with the shells open and ready for the sweet flesh to be slurped out. If you're there on a Friday, try the weekly special sfogliatelle, a handmade pastry dough that is stretched into a cone shape and filled with a ricotta and semolina mixture and served with latte ice cream.

Pizza. Lunch (Tuesday-Sunday), dinner. Bar. $16-35

BOURBON STEAK

Four Seasons Washington, D.C., 2800 Pennsylvania Ave. NW., Georgetown, 202-944-2026; www.bourbonsteakdc.com

Acclaimed chef Michael Mina raises the "steaks" at this upscale steakhouse in the Four Seasons hotel. Mina's method of butter-poaching meat and poultry creates dishes that are succulent and sinfully decadent. According to Mina, the butter seals the meat, rendering beef and poultry super moist. Diners will find a carefully selected array of cuts, ranging from USDA prime-aged beef to Wagyu, as well as evidence of Mina's deference to culinary classics like seared Hudson Valley foie gras, both as a starter and a main accompanied by a scallion pancake and confit rillet. Finish with an upgraded candy bar for adult palates: a sinful bar of coconut, milk chocolate, gooey praline caramel and Marcona almonds.

Steakhouse. Lunch (Monday-Friday), dinner. Reservations recommended. Bar. $86 and up

HOOK

3241 M St. NW., Georgetown, 202-625-4488; www.hookdc.com

Hook gets kudos for its commitment to sourcing sustainable seafood. Its efforts were noticed in 2007, when the Blue Ocean Institute honored the restaurant for its dedication to incorporating sustainably raised and caught seafood into its menu. Chef Faisal Sultani showcases the seafood in dishes like barramundi fish tacos and yellow fin tuna. The focus on sustainability and deference to seasonality extends to Hook's longtime pastry chef Heather Chittum's desserts. Featured on the inaugural season of *Top Chef: Just Desserts*, Chittum turns out summertime sweets like a lingonberry linzertorte with taleggio ice cream, and a caramel pine nut tart that comes with four dollops of gorgonzola dolce and topped with rosemary ice cream. In the fall and winter, expect creations that utilize the season's bounty, like walnuts and apples. Don't ignore the suggested wine pairings for Chittum's sweet endings, either. Chittum's desserts matched with sommelier Jamie Smith's wine recommendations alone are reason enough to cast your culinary net at Hook.

Seafood. Lunch (Tuesday-Friday), dinner, Saturday-Sunday brunch. Reservations recommended. Bar. $36-85

MIE N YU

3125 M St. NW., Georgetown, 202-333-6122; www.mienyu.com

Mie N Yu is not so much a restaurant as an anthropological tour de force of the cultures that dot the Silk Road. The restaurant touts partnerships with legacy institutions like the National Geographic Museum in the form of sponsored menus to make this cultural connection to the culinary offerings of executive chef Tim Miller, who is himself a trained anthropologist. Part Tibetan lounge, Moroccan bazaar and Italian drawing room, this restaurant features movie-set-worthy décor—like a chef's table enclosed in an iron-wrought birdcage—that's just as bold as the flavors. Among the panoply of Asian-inspired fare are the eponymous Mie N Yu dim sum appetizer with sweet shrimp-stuffed bean curd, organic beef shumai and tea-smoked barbecue pork buns with soy ginger vinaigrette. For heavier starters, try the mixed grill of sweet soy and ginger beef sausage, tandoori chicken kabobs, raita sauce, lamb merguez sausage, and grilled pita bread; or let your taste buds travel to Vietnam for entrées like caramel-chili duck with purple basil rice porridge. At Mie N Yu, the choices are virtually endless, and hopping continents is just a matter of picking up your fork.

Contemporary American. Dinner, Friday-Sunday brunch. Reservations recommended. Bar. $36-85

SUSHIKO

2309 Wisconsin Ave. N.W., Georgetown, 202-333-4187; www.sushikorestaurants.com

Don't let the gentleman's club next door deter you from dining at Sushiko. As D.C.'s oldest sushi bar, Sushiko is doing something right. Unlike other sushi joints, it doesn't try to replicate recipes that call for unobtainable ingredients stateside; rather, it cleverly integrates the best the East and West have to offer. Order highlights such as wild mushroom soup or salmon ceviche with ikura and yuzu vinaigrette. Intrepid eaters can go "Osakame," or chef's choice, and see what sushi surprises the chef conjures up. Enjoy the knife skills show at the sushi bar. Owner Daisuke Utagawa maintains a wine list that is decidedly on the French side, a result of regularly scouring vineyards in France to fulfill his quest for choice burgundies that draw out the flavors of raw fish.

Japanese. Lunch (Tuesday-Friday), dinner. Reservations recommended. Bar. $36-85

FOGGY BOTTOM
★★★KINKEAD'S

2000 Pennsylvania Ave. N.W., Foggy Bottom, 202-296-7700; www.kinkead.com

Bob Kinkead helms this bastion of fine seafood located just steps from the White House. The 240-seat restaurant is outfitted in slatted wooden chairs and feels like the deck of a ship, as blue fishscapes flank the main walls of the dining room. A New Englander, Bob Kinkead wanted to create an American brasserie featuring fresh seafood, and while the victuals here are reminiscent of the old seafood standbys—New England seafood chowder and jumbo lump crab cakes garnished with mustard crème fraîche among them—Kinkead's does not lack in creativity. Grilled squid with tomato fondue on polenta, and cod lavished with crab imperial, spoon bread and Virginia ham are Kinkead's classics. Dip your toe in the deep end with uncommon seafood specialties that draw on Latin flavors, including the cumin, cocoa nib, pepper and sea salt-crusted rare tuna on a tortilla with mole, chayote chile relish and guacamole. If you're more of a turf than surf person, fear not. Kinkead's has a New York strip served with green peppercorn sauce and fries as well as a pan-roasted organic chicken breast and thigh accompanied by mushroom duxelle.

Contemporary American. Lunch (Monday-Friday), dinner. Bar. $36-85

★★★PRIME RIB

2020 K St. N.W., Foggy Bottom, 202-466-8811; www.theprimerib.com

This traditional surf-and-turf establishment is culled straight from Manhattan steakhouses from the 1940s, when dames were dames and men were men (yes, a jacket is required to sup in the main dining room). Settle into an executive-style leather chair and start with an order of the Maine lobster bisque before attacking the restaurant's eponymous signature item: a 45-ounce roasted prime rib, aged four to five weeks. Smaller, but just as tasty, beef dishes are the steak au poivre broiled with cracked peppercorns and a loin veal chop served in its natural juices. Not in the mood for beef? The surf side of this menu is just as

HIGHLIGHT

WHICH D.C. RESTAURANTS HAVE CELEBRITY CHEFS?

ADOUR
Adour has wine in mind, and it's no wonder. The restaurant is the brainchild of French oenophile and culinary master Alain Ducasse, so diners can choose from among 400 wines by the bottle, smaller formats by the half decanter, and if you're feeling especially celebratory, by the magnum and jeroboam as well.

BOURBON STEAK
Acclaimed chef Michael Mina raises the "steaks" at this upscale steakhouse in the Four Seasons hotel. Mina's method of butter-poaching meat and poultry creates dishes that are succulent and sinfully decadent. Diners will find a carefully selected array of cuts, ranging from USDA prime-aged beef to Wagyu.

J&G STEAKHOUSE
The District's first W hotel has become a hot see-and-be-seen spot because of its rooftop bar with spectacular views of the Washington Monument and this restaurant from celebrity chef Jean-Georges Vongerichten.

THE SOURCE BY WOLFGANG PUCK
You don't have to be a journalist to enjoy the Asian-inspired fare at Wolfgang Puck's The Source, but you'll want to do some investigative reporting at this eatery attached to the Newseum.

WEST END BISTRO BY ERIC RIPERT
Culinary Zen master Eric Ripert's Westend Bistro is a sanctuary of calm, dressed in dark wood and red-cushioned chairs that look out over large glass windows onto Georgetown's bustling streets. While this Le Bernardin offshoot is simple in its approach to bistro food, it's not simplistic.

hefty. Try the award-winning jumbo lump crabcakes or a whopping two-pound Maine lobster stuffed with imperial crab. If you still have room for dessert, classics make a comeback in the sweets department with sweet-toothed favorites like apple and key lime pie, cheesecake with strawberries, or a hot fudge sundae.

Steakhouse. Lunch (Monday-Friday), dinner. Closed Sunday. Jacket Required. Reservations recommended. Bar. $36-85

★★★WESTEND BISTRO BY ERIC RIPERT
1190 22nd St. N.W., Foggy Bottom, 202-974-4900; www.westendbistrodc.com
Culinary Zen master Eric Ripert's Westend Bistro is a sanctuary of calm, dressed

in dark wood and red-cushioned chairs that look out over large glass windows onto Georgetown's bustling streets. Though the food-writer cognoscenti argue over whether the *Top Chef* judge makes appearances at this Washington, D.C., outpost attached to the Ritz-Carlton, the staff swears he is there a couple of times a month. It's no matter with chef de cuisine Joe Palma handling affairs in the kitchen. Palma's known for elevating bistro fare like roasted chicken to heights so satisfyingly rich, you'll feel like you've been transported to a French sidewalk café. While this Le Bernardin offshoot is simple in its approach to bistro food, it's not simplistic. The menu is equally divided with dishes from both sea and land. One of the restaurant's signatures, tuna carpaccio, is pounded into a large, thin, perfectly pink disc and garnished with olive oil, chive, shallot and lemon, and soft-shell crab is served atop a raft of asparagus spears in a creamy black pepper sauce with lemon. Other sea-based favorites include the fish burger and the skate done up in braised artichokes, fennel, tomatoes and black olives.

French, American. Lunch (Monday-Friday), dinner. Reservations recommended. Bar. $16-35

RECOMMENDED

BLUE DUCK TAVERN
Park Hyatt Washington D.C., 1201 24th St. N.W., Foggy Bottom, 202-419-6755; www.blueducktavern.com

Thomas Jefferson was known for his political prowess as well as a penchant for fine food and wine, which he developed during his tenure as minister to France. That Jeffersonian joie de vivre and Federalist-era farm-to-table cooking philosophies have been injected into various eateries in the nation's capital, including Blue Duck Tavern. The restaurant is a Jeffersonian take on fine dining, and nods to America's third president are visible throughout the space, from the wooden Federalist-era furnishings to the family-style menu. In addition to the view of the open kitchen from the dining room, visitors are treated to a close-up look at the pastry station, where they can see the signature cinnamon-crusted apple pies being made. The creative cuisine is just as accessible. Entrées of roasted chicken, a fish of the day and braised beef get imaginative in McBride's hands. The braised short rib arrives with the bone serving as a decorative surfboard for the pristine cubes of meat. Sides are family style at the tavern, so consider that when ordering entrée accompaniments. Save lots of room for the ice cream, which comes in a large family-style receptacle with a wooden spoon. You'll want to lick the velvety vanilla ice cream off the serving paddle.

Contemporary American. Breakfast (Monday-Friday), Lunch (Monday-Friday), dinner, Saturday-Sunday brunch. Reservations recommended. Bar. $36-85

MARCEL'S
2401 Pennsylvania Ave. N.W., Foggy Bottom, 202-296-1166; www.marcelsdc.com

Marcel's may be the best restaurant in D.C. out-of-towners have never heard of. Though chef Robert Wiedmaier helms two other properties (Brasserie Beck in the District and Brabo in Old Town, Alexandria), Marcel's was his first foray into the D.C. dining scene, and it consistently draws accolades for its upscale Franco-Belgian cuisine. Don't miss the boudin blanc, a white pork sausage with pearl onions, wild mushrooms and Madeira sauce, as well as the lamb trio wrapped in phyllo. An avid hunter and outdoorsman, Wiedmaier also gets points from locals for doing game, and dishes like the roasted saddle of rabbit with a cumin rabbit leg farce should be on your checklist when considering the restaurant's prix fixe menus. If you are catching a show at the nearby Kennedy Center, Marcel's offers a convenient pre-theater menu, and executive car service to the venue is included with dinner.

International. Dinner. Reservations recommended. Bar. $36-85

SPA

★★★★THE SPA AT THE MANDARIN ORIENTAL, WASHINGTON, D.C.

Mandarin Oriental, Washington, D.C., 1330 Maryland Ave. S.W., National Mall, 202-787-6100; www.mandarinoriental.com

Long considered one of the country's top hotel destinations, the Mandarin Oriental brand has also gained acclaim for its Asian-inspired spas. The D.C. outpost is no exception. Boasting an oversized lounge, hot-and-cold-water experiences and a crystal steam room, the Zen-like ambience doesn't stop in the relaxation room. Rather than reserving specific treatments, book two- or three-hour Time Rituals, where programs are designed to accommodate the unique needs of a client on a specific day. Each journey begins with a detoxifying foot bath and massage to cleanse the body, mind and spirit. Also popular is the 110-minute Thai massage, a light stretching technique performed while you are fully clothed.

WHERE TO SHOP

GEORGETOWN
FORNASH

The Shops at Georgetown Park, 3222 M St. N.W., Georgetown, 202-338-0774; www.fornash.com

From the popped collars to the bright colored bags, Georgetown has been home to the prepster. This boutique celebrates that with custom fabric handbags that are all the rage in the DelMarVa (Delaware, Maryland, Virginia) region. Inspired by a post-grad extended vacation in the Caribbean, owner Stephanie Fornash Kennedy's designs now including clothing, jewelry and accessories perfect for the preppy fashionista or even for a trip in the tropics. You can't help but smile when you walk into Fornash, with its splash of tropical colors from all the fabulous accessories, clothing and jewelry this store has to offer.

Monday-Saturday 10 a.m.-8 p.m., Sunday noon-6 p.m.

GEORGETOWN FLEA MARKET

1819 35th St. N.W., Georgetown, 202-775-3532; www.georgetownfleamarket.com

Around since 1973, the flea market attracts a large crowd every weekend when more than 100 vendors gather to showcase everything from antique furnishings to vintage clothing to handcrafted jewelry you won't find elsewhere. The market attracts area collectors, decorators and antiques dealers, and is definitely worth a visit if you're looking for a piece of antique furniture or a one-of-a-kind painting. It's also a great way to get a flavor of the neighborhood—for many locals, a trip the flea market is a Sunday ritual.

Sunday 8 a.m.-4 p.m.

HU'S SHOES

3005 M St. N.W., Georgetown, 202-342-0202; www.husonline.com

Owner Marlene Hu Aldaba spends her days traveling to New York, Paris and Milan to find the perfect new additions to her luxurious collection of designer footwear. The result is a delicate assortment of handpicked shoes that will thrill any shoe lover. The minimalist interior puts the straight-off-the-runway designs center stage. Designers include Alexander McQueen, Lanvin and Sergio Rossi, a favorite of well-heeled Washingtonians, it's definitely worth a visit while in town. *Monday-Saturday 10 a.m.-7 p.m., Sunday noon-5 p.m.*

HU'S WEAR

2906 M St. N.W., Georgetown, 202-342-2020; www.husonline.com

The perfect pair of shoes only works with an equally perfect outfit. Marlene Hu Aldaba, owner of Hu's Shoes, has expanded her eclectic sense of style into a boutique filled with both fashion-forward and up-and-coming brands devoted to luxury clothing. What makes Hu's Wear stand out is that almost all of the clothing lines are regionally exclusive to the store. You'll also find pieces from big-name designers including Jean Paul Gaultier, dsquared and Viktor & Rolf. *Monday-Saturday 10 a.m.-7 p.m., Sunday noon-5 p.m.*

LOST BOYS

1033 31st St. N.W., Georgetown, 202-333-0093; www.lostboysdc.com

Within this converted Federal-era row house, modern glass walls and flat-screen televisions mingle with rustic flea market curios. You'll find a similarly chic mix of clothing, all geared toward comfort and quality. Shop for super-soft cashmere Theory hoodies, tailored shirts from Band of Outsiders and jeans from Earnest Sewn. Men who hate to shop will appreciate the Style Bar, which offers one-on-one appointments with style expert and owner, Kelly Muccio, who can help any man upgrade his style, get ready for a hot date or just stock up on staples. Call ahead to schedule and make shopping as quick and painless as possible. *Tuesday-Thursday 11 a.m.-7 p.m., Friday-Saturday 11 a.m.-9 p.m., Sunday noon-7 p.m.*

THE MAGIC WARDROBE

1663 Wisconsin Ave. N.W., Georgetown, 202-333-0353; www.themagicwardrobe.com

Have you ever seen a childhood picture of yourself and thought, 'I will never dress my child like that'? The Magic Wardrobe is the store that allows you to keep that promise to yourself. Ranging from chic sundresses to sharp blazers, the kids whose parents shop here for them are the most stylish on the block. Scoop up custom cotton sweaters complete with a personalized monogram, Seven jeans and beautiful special occasion dresses and outfits for little guys. You can also pick up great gifts from cuddly receiving blankets to a custom made rocking horse, which actually looks like a real horse. *Monday-Saturday 10 a.m-5 p.m., Sunday noon-5 p.m.*

MAJOR

1426 Wisconsin Ave. N.W., Georgetown, 202-625-6732; www.majordc.com

A line is often seen snaking out the door at Major, D.C.'s premium sneaker boutique which stocks limited edition Air Jordans, Chuck Taylors, and other brands, as well as unusual brands such as Knowledge, Orisue, and Freshjive. These are definitely not your ordinary sneakers, as top-notch styles can run upwards of $200.

Monday-Thursday 11 a.m.-8 p.m., Friday 11 a.m.-9 p.m., Saturday 11 a.m.-9 p.m., Sunday noon-7 p.m.

RANDOM HARVEST

1313 Wisconsin Ave. N.W., Georgetown, 202-333-5569; www.randomharvesthome.com

The interior of Random Harvest is so beautiful you may want to move in, or at least design your home to look the same. With the perfect blend of old and new, the store boasts refreshingly affordable home furnishings sourced from around the world. With a classic elegance and cozy vibe, shoppers can browse pieces that range from formal to rustic and casual. Unique pieces to add to your home include a solid mahogany bureau from the late 1800s, rolltop desks made in France, and antique lift top benches made by families in Eastern Europe in the mid-to-late 1800s.

Monday-Saturday 11 a.m.-6 p.m., Sunday noon-6 p.m.

RELISH

3312 Cady's Alley N.W., Georgetown, 202-333-5343; www.relishdc.com

You will indeed relish all the modern and comfortable clothing from Marni, Jil Sander and Dries Van Noten and other designers found at this hidden treasure in Cady's Alley. Relish's clothing philosophy focuses on modern classics that are meant to last. The simplistic store is airy with natural light flooding throughout its two floors of women's clothing, shoes, jewelry and accessories.

Monday-Saturday 10 a.m.-6 p.m.

URBAN CHIC

1626 Wisconsin Ave. N.W., Georgetown, 202-338-5398; www.urbanchiconline.com

Located at the end of Wisconsin Avenue, the original location of this mini-chain (there are four other locations) is that place you love to shop with an incredible selection—Rebecca Taylor to Rag & Bone—that never feels overwhelming. Don't be afraid to mess up the meticulously organized stacks of jeans and rifle through the statement-making jewelry in Urban Chic's two airy rooms. And keep an eye out for unique events like fashion shows and fundraisers, where you can check out some of the store's featured fashion along with live music and more.

Monday-Saturday 10 a.m.-7 p.m., Sunday noon-5 p.m.

WINK

3109 M St. N.W., Georgetown, 202-338-9465; www.shopwinkdc.com

Blink and you'll miss it—the contemporary boutique is hidden under the Steve Madden store. Wink has an eclectic selection that will appeal to conservatives looking to dress for an event, artsy types who want to be more casual and fashionistas who pride themselves on being daring. Designers range from House of Harlow to Milly and Trina Turk, and include popular items such as yoga pants from local designers.

Monday-Saturday 11 a.m.-7 p.m., Sunday noon-6 p.m.

U STREET CORRIDOR

MISS PIXIE'S

1626 14th St. N.W., U Street, 202-232-8171; www.misspixies.com

Acquiring all her knick-knacks from auctions, Miss Pixie's has an ever-changing inventory of antiques. Which means you never know what you might find at this antiques store. You might just walk out with a fabulous Deco cedar chest, a vinyl wrought iron bench from the 1950s, or cash register from the 1920s. The store also carries vintage shoes and clothing, such as Chanel, Gucci and Lilly Pulitzer. Talk about a score.

Tuesday-Sunday noon-7 p.m.

MULÉH

1831 14th St. N.W., U Street, 202-667-3440; www.muleh.com

With its beautiful collection of modern Asian furniture, there is no doubt that Muléh fits in with the home-design of stores on 14th Street. Merchandise focuses on designs by Bali-based Warisan and Filipino Kenneth Cobonpue. The store also has a fantastic selection of lighting and an equally covetable selection of clothing, with racks full of hard-to-find pieces by designers such as 3.1 Phillip Lim and Rozae Nichols.

Tuesday-Saturday 11 a.m.-7 p.m., Sunday noon-5 p.m.

NANA

1528 U St. N.W., U Street, 202-667-6955; www.nanadc.com

This independently owned boutique located on U Street has become a fixture for its modern-vintage mix. The boutique contains two sections: the first part offers a diverse selection of rare labels such as Kasil, House of Spy and Magnes Sisters handbags. The second showcases carefully selected vintage items and accessories, many of which have been repurposed by Toronto-based design house Preloved. Between the new and the old, Nana provides stylish women's clothing and accessories you won't find anywhere else like Mary Green lingerie, Fashion Doll hats and vintage treasures such as Pucci skirts.

Wednesday-Saturday noon-7p.m., Sunday noon-6 p.m.

RCKNDY

1515 U St. N.W., U Street, 202-332-5639; www.rckndy.com

Pronounced "rock candy," this U Street destination specializes in contemporary furniture suited for small spaces, and also offers unique housewares and gifts. The light-filled showroom is stocked with exclusives pieces. Members of the trendy U Street crowd use this as their go-to spot for one-of-a kind gifts, including kooky games, coffee-table books and barware. To make a trip here even sweeter, each customer is given a stick of rock candy with their purchase.

Monday-Saturday noon-8 p.m., Sunday noon-6 p.m.

DOWNTOWN

APRÈS PEAU

1430 K St. N.W., Downtown, 202-783-0022; www.aprespeau.com

Renowned local cosmetic dermatologist Tina Alster created her downstairs boutique, meaning "after skin," as a side project to her practice to make finding the perfect gift easy and fun. Pick from exotic perfume and unique, handcrafted jewelry, such as cufflinks made from seats removed from RFK Stadium during a renovation. Patriotic and D.C. themes are prevalent including marble vintage D.C. map coasters, exclusive Washington Monument note cards and chocolate bars with flavors like Washington Monumint.

Monday-Friday 10 a.m.-6 p.m.

WELCOME TO WEST VIRGINIA

JOHN DENVER SAID IT BEST: WEST VIRGINIA IS ALMOST HEAVEN.

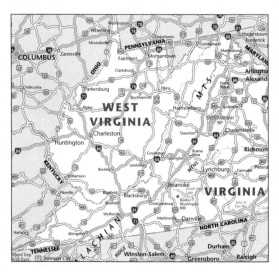

For nature lovers and outdoor sports enthusiasts, the Mountain State is a natural paradise of rugged mountains and lush, lyric-inspiring countryside. With the highest total altitude of any state east of the Mississippi River, West Virginia's ski industry has opened several Alpine and Nordic ski areas. Outfitters offer excellent whitewater rafting on the state's many turbulent rivers. Rock climbing, caving and hiking are popular in the Monongahela National Forest. And West Virginia's state parks and areas for hunting and fishing are plentiful.

West Virginia is also a land of proud traditions, with many festivals held throughout the year as tributes to the state's rich heritage. These events include celebrations honoring the state's stern-wheel riverboat legacy, its spectacular autumn foliage and even its strawberries, apples and black walnuts.

Archaeological evidence indicates that some of the area's very first settlers were the Mound Builders, a prehistoric Ohio Valley culture that left behind at least 300 conical earth mounds. Many have been worn away by erosion, but excavations in some have revealed elaborately adorned human skeletons and artifacts of amazing beauty and utility. Centuries later, pioneers who ventured into western Virginia in the 18th century (West Virginia did not break away from Virginia until the Civil War) found fine vistas and forests, curative springs and beautiful rivers. George Washington and his family frequented the soothing mineral waters of Berkeley Springs, and White Sulphur Springs later became a popular resort among the colonists. But much of this area was still considered the "Wild West" in those days, and life here was not easy.

The Commonwealth of Virginia largely ignored its western citizens—only one governor was elected from the western counties before 1860. When the western counties formed their own state during the Civil War, it was the result of many

BEST ATTRACTIONS

WEST VIRGINIA'S BEST ATTRACTIONS

EASTERN PANHANDLE
Visit the oldest spa in the country and then get in some gambling at the Charles Town Races & Slots. This venue attracts people from all over for the horse races and slot machines.

SOUTHERN WEST VIRGINIA
If you've always wanted to challenge the rapids, take an adventure down the New and Gauley rivers. For extreme pampering afterward, book a room at The Greenbrier, which has a top-notch spa.

years of strained relations with the parent state. The war finally provided the opportunity the counties needed to break away. Although many sentiments in the new state remained pro-South, West Virginia's interests were best served by staying with the Union. The war left West Virginia a new state, but like other war-ravaged areas, it had suffered heavy losses of life and property and the recovery took many years. West Virginians eventually rebuilt their state. New industry was developed, railroads were built and resources like coal, oil and natural gas brought relative prosperity. For visitors, West Virginia offers warm springs, beautiful scenery and whitewater rafting, historic sights and much more.

EASTERN PANHANDLE

Popularized by George Washington, who surveyed the area for Lord Fairfax in 1748, Berkeley Springs is the oldest spa in the nation. The town is officially named Bath, for the famous watering place in England, but the post office is Berkeley Springs. The waters, which are piped throughout the town, are fresh and slightly sweet, without the medicinal flavor of most mineral springs. Charles Town is serene, aristocratic and full of tradition, with orderly, tree-shaded streets and 18th-century houses. It was named for George Washington's youngest brother, Charles, who laid out the town and named most of the streets after members of his family. Scene of abolitionist John Brown's raid in 1859, Harpers Ferry is at the junction of the Shenandoah and Potomac rivers, where West Virginia, Virginia and Maryland meet. When war broke out, Harpers Ferry was a strategic objective for the Confederacy, which considered it the key to Washington. In

1944, Congress authorized a national monument here, setting aside 1,500 acres for that purpose. In 1963, the same area was designated a National Historical Park. In 1787, Shepherdstown was the site of the first successful public launching of a steamboat. This is the oldest continuously settled town in the state.

WHAT TO SEE

BERKELEY SPRINGS
BERKELEY SPRINGS STATE PARK
2 S. Washington St., Berkeley Springs, 304-258-2711; www.berkeleyspringssp.com

This famous resort features health baths and five warm springs. There are Roman baths with mineral water heated to 102 F, and you can enjoy a relaxing bath or a Swedish massage. There are also steam cabinets heated to 124 F, which can be included with a bath or massage treatment.

Daily 10 a.m.-6 p.m. (last appointment at 4:30 p.m.); April-October, Friday 10 a.m.-9 p.m. See website for rates.

PROSPECT PEAK
Highway 9, Berkeley Springs

The Potomac River winds through what the National Geographic Society has called one of the nation's outstanding vistas.

CHARLES TOWN
CHARLES TOWN RACES AND SLOTS
Flowing Springs Road, Route 340 North, Charles Town, 304-725-7001, 800-795-7001; www.ctownraces.com

Head to the Charles Town Races and Slots for a day full of fun; you can also enjoy thoroughbred racing year round. There are over 5,000 slot machines here and plenty of other machines to play. There are also numerous restaurants.

Slots: Daily 7 a.m.-4 a.m. racing: Wednesday-Sunday.

JEFFERSON COUNTY COURTHOUSE
100 E. Washington, Charles Town, 304-728-7713; www.nps.gov

This red brick, Georgian colonial structure (1836) was the scene of John Brown's trial, one of three treason trials held in the U.S. before World War II. The courthouse was shelled during the Civil War but was later rebuilt; the original courtroom survived both the shelling and fires and is open to the public. In 1922, leaders of the miners' armed march on Logan City were tried here; one, Walter Allen, was convicted and sentenced to 10 years.

Tours: April-November; call for schedule.

HARPERS FERRY
HARPERS FERRY NATIONAL HISTORICAL PARK
Shenandoah and High streets, Harpers Ferry, 304-535-6029; www.nps.gov

The old town has been restored to its 19th-century appearance; exhibits and interpretive presentations explore the park's relation to the Civil War. The visitor center is located off Highway 340 at 171 Shoreline Drive. From there, a bus will take visitors to Lower Town. There is also a shop for books and gifts.

Admission: vehicle $6, individual (on foot or bicycle) $4. Park: Daily 8 a.m.-5 p.m. Store: Daily 9 a.m.-5 p.m.

HIGHLIGHT

WHAT ARE THE TOP THINGS TO DO IN THE EASTERN PANHANDLE?

HIT THE SPRINGS
People have been coming to the healing baths of Berkeley Springs for centuries. Enjoy a warm bath, followed by a soothing massage.

RIDE THE RIVER
Go on a river adventure on the rapids of the Shenandoah and Potomac rivers.

JEFFERSON ROCK
Harpers Ferry; www.nps.gov

In 1783, it was from this rock that Thomas Jefferson pronounced the view to be "one of the most stupendous scenes in nature". Hike up to the Jefferson Rock where you'll enjoy a beautiful vista where the Potomac and Shenandoah Rivers connect. Stone steps lead up to the rock.

WHITEWATER RAFTING
Harpers Ferry, 800-225-5982; www.wvriversports.com

Many outfitters offer guided trips on the Shenandoah and Potomac rivers.

SHEPHERDSTOWN
GUIDED WALKING TOURS
Visitor Center, 136 ½ E. German St., Shepherdstown, 304-876-2786

Take a walking tour of the historic sites in Shepherdstown. Most of the town is part of the Historic District on the National Register of Historic Places.
Visitor center: Daily 10 a.m.-4 p.m.

WHERE TO STAY

SHEPHERDSTOWN
★★★BAVARIAN INN & LODGE
164 Shepherd Grade Road, Shepherdstown, 304-876-2551; www.bavarianinnwv.com

This inn is decorated with Federal period reproductions and provides European-style hospitality. Four-poster mahogany beds, brass chandeliers and bathrooms with imported marble grace each room.
72 rooms. Restaurant, bar. Business center. Fitness center. Pool. Tennis. $151-250

WHERE TO EAT

SHEPHERDSTOWN
★★★BAVARIAN INN AND LODGE
164 Shepherd Grade Road, Shepherdstown, 304-876-2551; www.bavarianinnwv.com

Few places serve such authentic German fare. Seasonal dishes include pork tenderloin picatta on sautéed spatzle, wilted spinach and a Dijon mustard sauce. Stone fireplaces and dark woods create a rustic yet elegant ambience.

German. Breakfast, lunch (Monday-Saturday), dinner, Sunday brunch. Children's menu. Bar. $36-85

★★★YELLOW BRICK BANK RESTAURANT
201 E. German St., Shepherdstown, 304-876-2208; www.yellowbrickbank.com

Housed in a restored 19th-century bank building in a rural town near the upper Potomac, this surprisingly inventive restaurant serves creative cuisine in an airy, high-ceilinged dining room.

Contemporary American. Lunch (Tuesday-Saturday), dinner (Tuesday-Saturday), Sunday brunch. Closed Monday. Bar. $16-35

NORTHERN WEST VIRGINIA

Morgantown is both an educational and an industrial center. West Virginia University was founded here in 1867. After the Revolutionary War, Blennerhassett Island, in the Ohio River west of Parkersburg, was the scene of the alleged Burr-Blennerhassett plot. Harman Blennerhassett, a wealthy Irishman, built a lavish mansion on this island. After killing Alexander Hamilton in a duel, Aaron Burr came to the island, allegedly to seize the Southwest and set up an empire; Blennerhassett may have agreed to join him. On December 10, 1806, the plot was uncovered. Both men were acquitted of treason but ruined financially in the process. The Blennerhassett mansion burned in 1811 but was later rebuilt. Wheeling stands on the site of Fort Henry, built in 1774 by Colonel Ebenezer Zane and his two brothers, who named the fort for Virginia's Governor Patrick Henry.

WHAT TO SEE

MORGANTOWN
COOPERS ROCK STATE FOREST
Route 1, Morgantown, 304-594-1561; www.coopersrockstateforest.com

Just 13 miles east of Morgantown, Coopers Rock State Forest covers more than 12,700 acres. Offered here is everything from trout fishing to hunting and hiking trails to historical sites, including the Henry Clay Iron Furnace trail which takes you by a large stone structure. There are also cross-country ski trails, picnicking, a playground, concessions and tent and trailer camping.

Campgrounds: April-November.

PERSONAL RAPID TRANSIT SYSTEM
88 Beechhurst Ave., Morgantown, 304-293-5011; www.wvu.edu

A pioneering transit system, the PRT is the world's first totally automated

HIGHLIGHT

WHAT ARE THE TOP THINGS TO DO IN NORTHERN WEST VIRGINIA?

STEP INTO MOUNTAINEER TERRITORY

West Virginia University is home to nearly 30,000 students. The school spirit thrives throughout campus.

CLIMB ABOARD THE RIVERBOAT

Embark on a riverboat tour for a unique experience. Sightseeing on these stern-wheeler boats is worth the trip.

system. Operating without conductors or ticket takers, computer-directed cars travel between university campuses and downtown Morgantown.

Admission: $.50. Monday-Saturday; may not operate holidays and university breaks.

WEST VIRGINIA UNIVERSITY

Visitors Resource Center, 1 Waterfront Place, Morgantown, 304-293-0111; www.wvu.edu

The university, which was founded in 1867, has more than 28,000 students attending its 15 college and 185 degree programs. The Visitors Center in the Communications Building on Patterson Drive has touch-screen monitors and video presentations about the university. Of special interest on the downtown campus are Stewart Hall and the university's original buildings, located on Woodburn Circle. In the Evansdale area of Morgantown, visitors will find the Creative Arts Center, the 75-acre Core Arboretum and the 63,500-seat Coliseum.

Tours: Monday-Saturday. For reservations, call 304-293-3489.

PARKERSBURG

BLENNERHASSETT ISLAND HISTORICAL STATE PARK

137 Juliana St., Parkersburg, 304-420-4800, 800-225-5982; www.blennerhassettstatepark.com

This 500-acre island is only accessible by taking a sternwheeler over. There are self-guided walking tours of the island, horse-drawn wagon rides and tours of the Blennerhassett mansion. Tickets are available for the boat ride at the Blennerhassett Museum in Parkersburg.

Sternwheeler: adults $8, children 3-12 $7. Tour: adults $4, children $2. Island: May-October; see website for hours.

BLENNERHASSETT MUSEUM

Second and Juliana streets, Parkersburg, 304-420-4840; www.blennerhassettislandpark.com

This museum features archaeological and other exhibits relating to the history of Blennerhassett Island and the Parkersburg area, including artifacts dating back 12,000 years. You can purchase tickets here for the sternwheeler, which will take you to Blennerhassett Island Historical State Park.

Admission: adults $4, children 3-12 $2. Hours vary.

NORTH BEND STATE PARK

Route 1, Parkersburg, 304-643-2931, 800-225-5982; www.northbendsp.com

With approximately 1,400 acres, North Bend State Park is located in the wide valley of the North Fork of the Hughes River with scenic overlooks of famous horseshoe bend. There is a large swimming pool, miniature golf course, tennis courts and other game courts here. The 72-mile North Bend Rail Trail is great for hiking, biking and walking; there are 13 tunnels to pass through. A large lake allows for fishing, canoeing, kayaking and more. A picnic area, a playground, concessions and restaurants are also within the park.

Pool: June-August, Tuesday-Thursday noon-6 p.m., Friday-Saturday noon-7 p.m., Sunday 1-6 p.m.

RUBLE'S STERNWHEELERS RIVERBOAT CRUISES

Second and Ann streets, Parkersburg, 740-423-7268; www.rublessternwheelers.com

Ruble's offers public and private riverboat cruises, from weekend sightseeing tours to Friday night dances and Sunday night Bluegrass jam sessions.

May-October, daily.

WHEELING

ARTISAN CENTER

1400 Main St., Wheeling, 304-232-1810; www.artisancenter.com

This restored 1860s Victorian warehouse houses River City Restaurant, plenty of shopping and a market. You'll also find "Made in Wheeling" crafts and exhibits and artisan demonstrations here.

Monday-Thursday 11 a.m.-5 p.m., Friday-Saturday 11 a.m.-6 p.m.

WEST VIRGINIA INDEPENDENCE HALL

1528 Market St., Wheeling, 304-238-1300; www.wvculture.org

This is the site of the 1859 meeting at which Virginia's secession from the Union was declared unlawful, and the independent state of West Virginia was created. The building, used as a post office, custom office and federal court until 1912, has been restored. It now houses exhibits relating to the state's cultural heritage, including an interpretive film and rooms with period furniture.

Admission: Free. Monday-Saturday 10 a.m.-4 p.m.

WHEELING PARK

1801 National Road, Wheeling, 304-243-4085; www.wheeling-park.com

Opened in 1925 and covering more than 400 acres, Wheeling Park is a popular spot to visit and has both recreational activities and historic points of interest. There is an Olympic-sized swimming pool with a waterslide, boating on Good Lake, golf, tennis, ice skating rink and more.

WHERE TO STAY

MORGANTOWN

★★★LAKEVIEW GOLF RESORT & SPA

1 Lakeview Drive, Morgantown, 304-594-1111, 800-624-8300; www.lakeviewresort.com

The Lakeview Golf Resort & Spa offers more than just driving ranges and putting greens. Located in the foothills of the Allegheny Mountains, this resort offers comfortable and well-sized guest rooms, conference and meeting space, a fitness center, pool, and several dining and recreation options. There's also a spa on the premises.

187 rooms. Restaurant, bar. Fitness center. Pool. Spa. Golf. $61-150

PARKERSBURG
★★★THE BLENNERHASSETT HOTEL

320 Market St., Parkersburg, 304-422-3131, 800-262-2536;
www.theblennerhassett.com

This landmark hotel was built before the turn of the century in the gaslight era and was fully restored in 1986. The hotel's Victorian style is evident in the rich crown molding, authentic English doors, brass and leaded-glass chandeliers and antiques.

94 rooms. Restaurant, bar. Business center. Fitness center. Pool. Pets accepted. $61-150

WHERE TO EAT

PARKERSBURG
★★★SPATS AT THE BLENNERHASSETT

320 Market St., Parkersburg, 304-422-3131, 800-262-2536; www.theblennerhassett.com

Its downtown location makes Blennerhassett a great place to stop for a lunch break, and its continental menu makes it easy for everyone to find something to eat. The restaurant features dark wood ceilings, crown molding, wainscoting and leather armchairs. A charming garden patio area includes a bar, a dining area, a music stage and a large screen for sporting events. The restaurant also features a martini night, wine tastings and live music.

Continental. Breakfast, lunch, dinner, Sunday brunch. Reservations recommended. Outdoor seating. Bar. $36-85

WHEELING
★★★ERNIE'S ESQUIRE

1015 E. Bethlehem Blvd., Wheeling, 304-242-2800

A local landmark for nearly 50 years, this fine-dining restaurant serves a wide variety of options to suit any palate. Diners can enjoy the likes of tableside cooking and steaks cut to order.

American. Lunch, dinner, late night, Sunday brunch. Children's menu. Bar. $36-85

SOUTHERN WEST VIRGINIA

Charleston, the state capital, is the trading hub for the Great Kanawha Valley. Daniel Boone lived around Charleston until 1795. In the 18th century, White Sulphur Springs became a fashionable destination for rich and famous colonists who came for the "curative" powers of the mineral waters. It has, for the most part, remained a popular resort ever since. President John Tyler and his wife spent their honeymoon at the famous "Old White" Hotel. In 1913, the Old White Hotel gave way to the Greenbrier Hotel, where President Wilson honeymooned with the second Mrs. Wilson.

WHAT TO SEE

CHARLESTON

ELK RIVER SCENIC DRIVE
Charleston

Along the Elk River, you can take a beautiful drive from Charleston northeast to Sutton (approximately 60 miles). The drive begins just north of town; take Highway 119 northeast to Clendenin, then Highway 4 northeast to Highway 19 in Sutton.

PEARL S. BUCK BIRTHPLACE MUSEUM
Route 219, Hillsboro, 304-653-4430; www.pearlsbuckbirthplace.com

The Stulting House is the birthplace of the Pulitzer and Nobel Prize-winning novelist, restored to its 1892 appearance with original and period furniture and memorabilia displayed inside. Sydenstricker House, the birthplace and home of Buck's father and his ancestors, was moved 40 miles from its original site and restored here and now serves as a cultural center.

Admission: adults $6, seniors $5. May-November, Monday-Saturday 9 a.m.-4 p.m.

STATE CAPITOL
1900 E. Kanawha Blvd., Charleston, 304-558-4839, 800-225-5982

One of America's most beautiful state capitols, the building was designed by Cass Gilbert in Italian Renaissance style and built in 1932. Within the gold-leaf dome, which rises nearly 300 feet above the street, hangs a 10,080-piece, hand-cut imported chandelier weighing more than two tons. Nearby is the Governor's Mansion.

WHITEWATER RAFTING
90 MacCorkle Ave. S.W., Charleston, 304-558-2200, 800-225-5982; www.wvriversports.com

Many outfitters offer guided whitewater rafting, canoeing and fishing trips on the New and Gauley rivers. You can choose between an intense adventure or a more tame trip. For a listing of rafting companies and other information, visit the website.

WHERE TO STAY

CHARLESTON

★★★MARRIOTT CHARLESTON TOWN CENTER
200 Lee St. East, Charleston, 304-345-6500, 800-228-9290; www.charlestonmarriott.com

This hotel, which is conveniently located just off the Interstate 77 and Interstate 64 interchange, sits adjacent to the Charleston Town Center and Civic Center in the heart of downtown. Many services and amenities are offered here, and there are plenty of recreational activities, restaurants and shops in the immediate area. Guest rooms are attractively decorated in hues of green and terra cotta.

352 rooms. Restaurant, bar. Business center. Fitness center. Pool. $61-150

HIGHLIGHT

WHAT ARE THE TOP THINGS TO DO IN SOUTHERN WEST VIRGINIA?

TAKE A SCENIC DRIVE
Drive along the Elk River from Charleston to Sutton.

HAVE A SPA DAY
White Sulphur Springs has long drawn visitors to its waters for its purported healing powers. Modern-day wellness seekers visit the Greenbrier for its state-of-the-art spa facility.

WHITE SULPHUR SPRINGS
★★★★THE GREENBRIER
300 W. Main St., White Sulphur Springs, 304-536-1110, 800-453-4858; www.greenbrier.com

Resting on a 6,500-acre estate in the picturesque Allegheny Mountains, The Greenbrier is one of America's oldest and finest resorts. The resort offers more than 50 recreational activities on its sprawling grounds. In addition to the three championship golf courses, the highly acclaimed Golf Academy, tennis courts and fitness and spa facilities, guests are invited to partake in unique adventures like falconry, sporting clays and trap and skeet shooting. Consisting of rooms, suites, guest and estate houses, the accommodations reflect the resort's renowned tradition. Enjoy a delicious meal at the Main Dining Room where classic American cuisine is served.

635 rooms. Restaurant, bar. Fitness center. Pool. Spa. Golf. Tennis. $251-350

WHERE TO EAT

CHARLESTON
★★★LAURY'S
350 MacCorkle Ave. Southeast, Charleston, 304-343-0055

Located downtown near the Kanawha River in the old C&O Railroad Depot, this French-American Continental restaurant has welcomed diners since 1979. The dining room is an elegant space with dramatic high ceilings, floor-to-ceiling windows, oil paintings, crystal chandeliers and fresh flowers.

American, French. Dinner. Closed Sunday. Reservations recommended. Bar. $16-35

WHITE SULPHUR SPRINGS
★★★THE GREENBRIER MAIN DINING ROOM
The Greenbrier, 300 W. Main St., White Sulphur Springs, 24986, 304-536-1110; 800-453-4858; www.greenbrier.com

The breakfast menu changes with the seasons and the dinner menu changes daily at this elegant yet family-friendly resort, where diners can expect contemporary riffs on classic American dishes along with a Southern-influenced continental style. The dinner menu offers lighter meals for those watching their intake, as well as a tempting dessert menu for those who are not.

American. Breakfast, dinner. Children's menu. Reservations recommended. Bar. $36-85

SPA

WHITE SULPHUR SPRINGS
★★★★THE GREENBRIER SPA
The Greenbrier, 300 W. Main St., White Sulphur Springs, 800-453-4858; www.greenbrier.com

White Sulphur Springs has long drawn visitors to its waters for its purported healing powers. Modern-day wellness seekers visit the Greenbrier for its state-of-the-art spa facility. The spa's treatment menu draws on the history of the mineral springs, and guests are encouraged to enjoy one of the spa's famous hydrotherapy treatments, from mountain rain showers and sulphur soaks to detoxifying marine baths and mineral mountain baths. Mud, rose petal, mineral and marine wraps release toxins and revitalize skin, whereas black walnut and aromatherapy salt glows exfoliate and polish skin. Treatments designed for men, pregnant women and teenagers round out this spa's comprehensive approach to well being.

INDEX

M

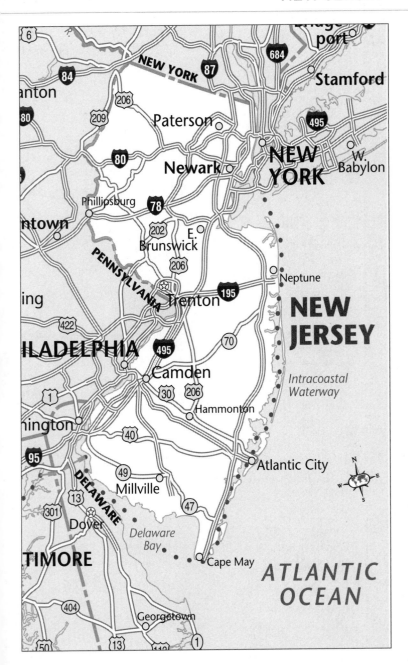

DELAWARE, MARYLAND AND WASHINGTON, D.C

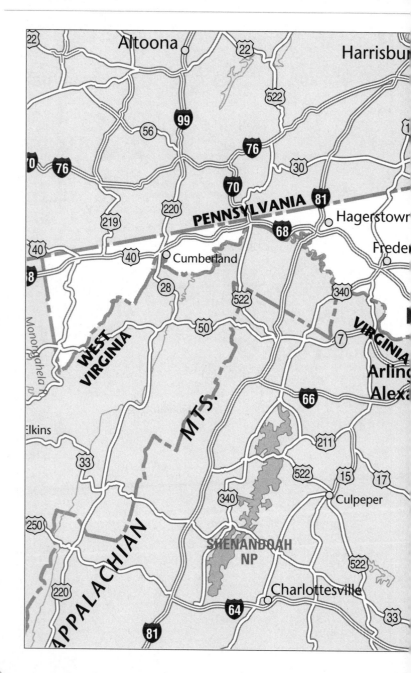

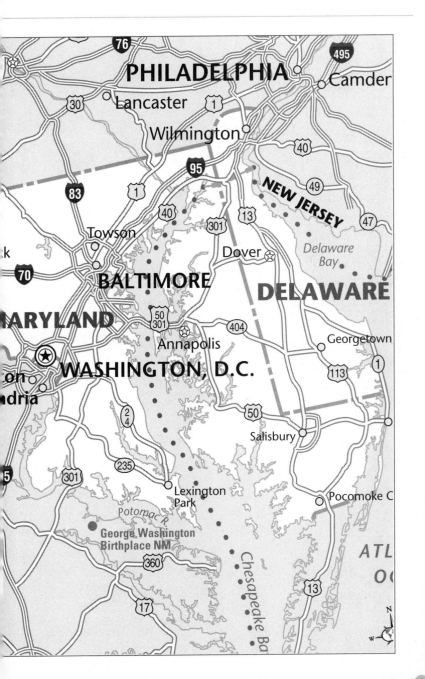

WEST VIRGINIA AND VIRGINIA

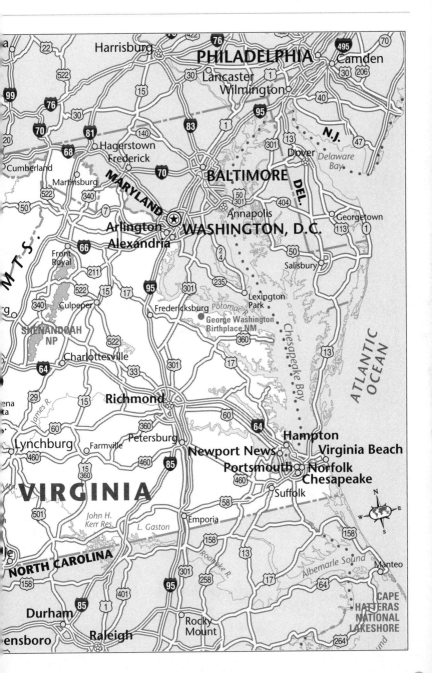

PENNSYLVANIA

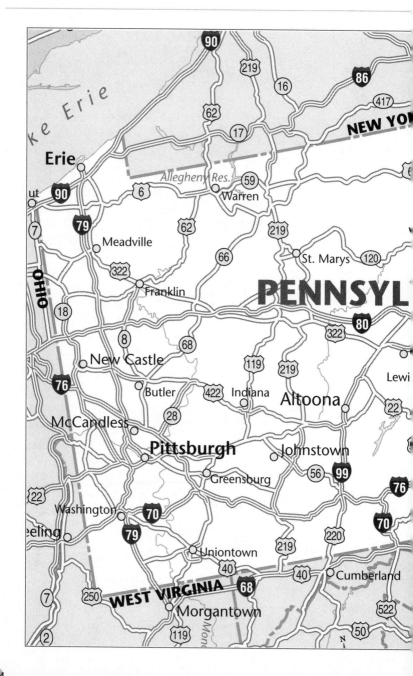

NOTES

NOTES

NOTES